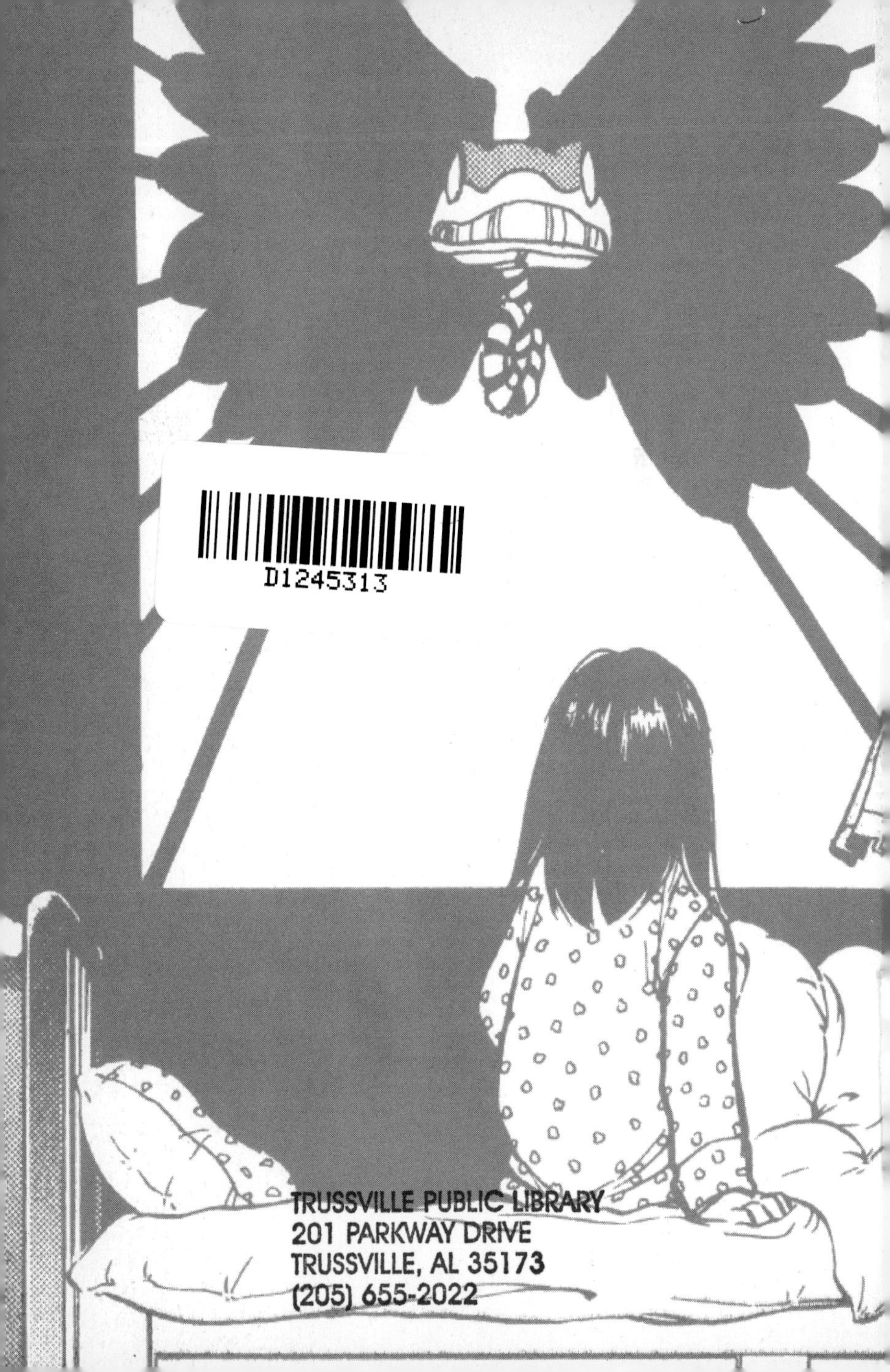

**Laura Jackson
& Yoko Kobayashi**
Translators

Mark McMurray
Retouching & Lettering

Veronica Casson
Designer

Frank Pannone
Project Manager

Mike Lackey
Print Production Manager

Stephanie Shalofsky
Vice President, Production

John O'Donnell
Publisher

World Peace Through Shared Popular Culture™
centralparkmedia.com
cpmmanga.com

Alien Nine – Book Three. Published by CPM Manga, a division of Central
Park Media Corporation. Office of Publication – 250 West 57th Street, Suite
317, New York, NY 10107. Original Japanese version "Alien 9" ©1999
Hitoshi TOMIZAWA (Akita Publishing Co., Ltd.). Originally published in
Japan in 1999 by Akita Publishing Co., Ltd. English version ©2003 Central
Park Media Corporation. CPM Manga and logos are registered trademarks
of Central Park Media Corporation. Original Manga and logo are trade-
marks of Central Park Media Corporation. All rights reserved. Price per
copy $15.95, price in Canada may vary. ISBN 1-58664-893-4.
Catalog: CMX 64203G. UPC: 7-19987-00642-3-00311. Printed in Canada.

ALIEN NINE

Hitoshi Tomizawa

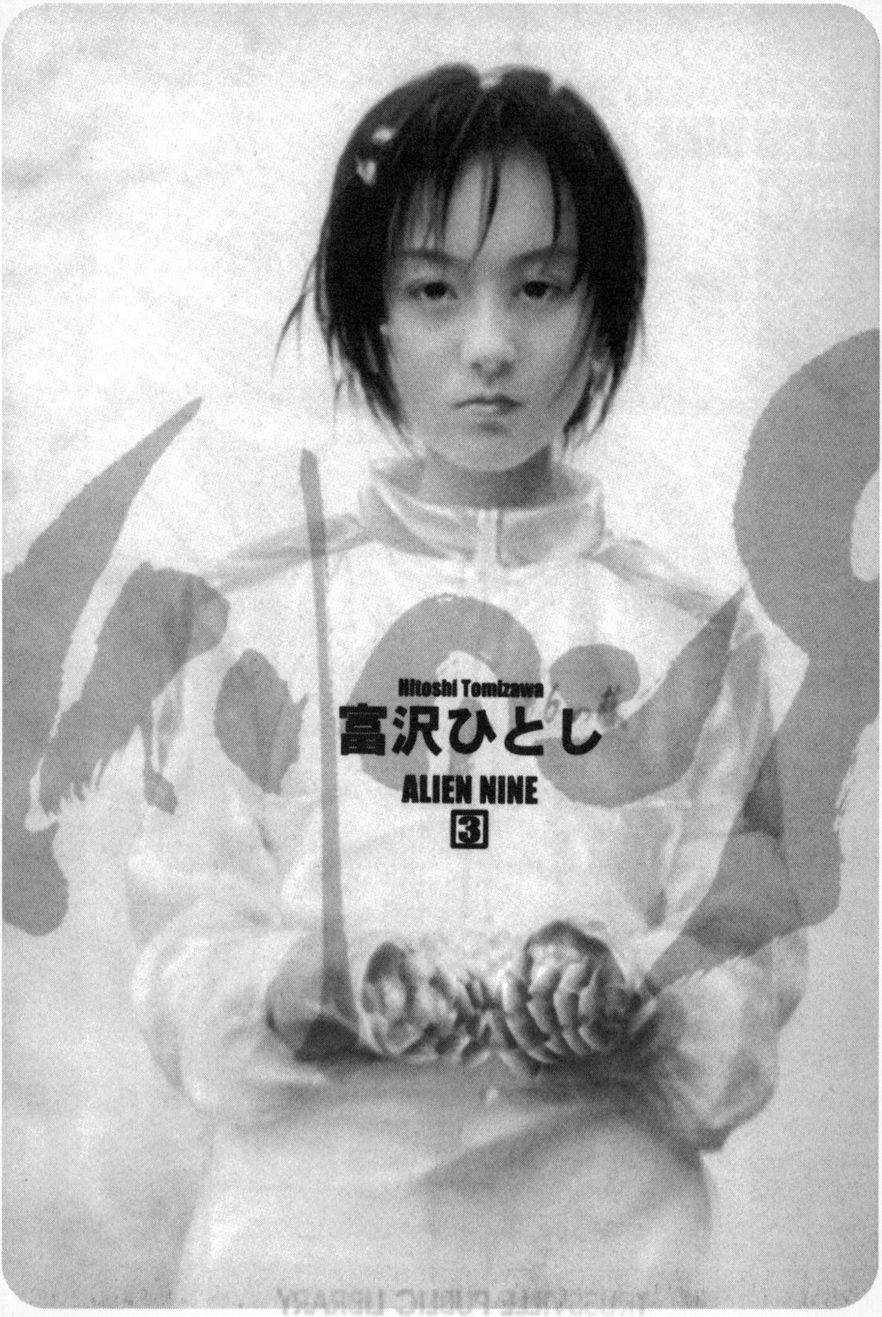

Hitoshi Tomizawa

富沢ひとし

ALIEN NINE

3

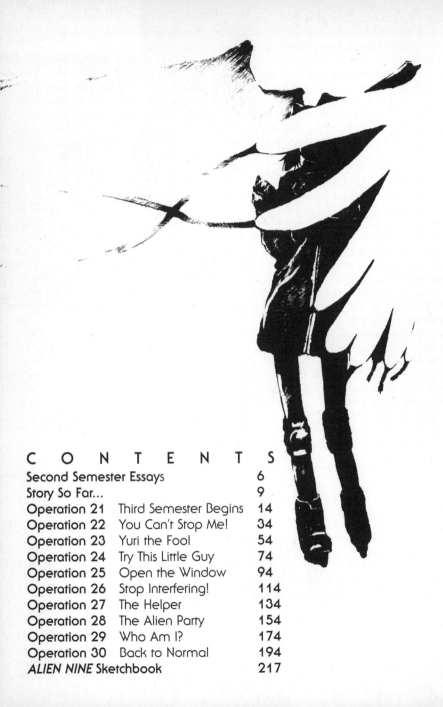

C O N T E N T S

Kasumi's Essay

Kasumi Tomine
Grade 6 Momo Class (Peach Class)
Born: July 1, 2002
Blood type: AB

The second semester was a time of great changes for me. When I started out, I had a deep feeling of loneliness. I missed my brother because he was overseas studying, but since my encounter with Yellow Knife, I am no longer alone. Whatever I do and wherever I go, I know that there is always someone to support me and help me be my best.

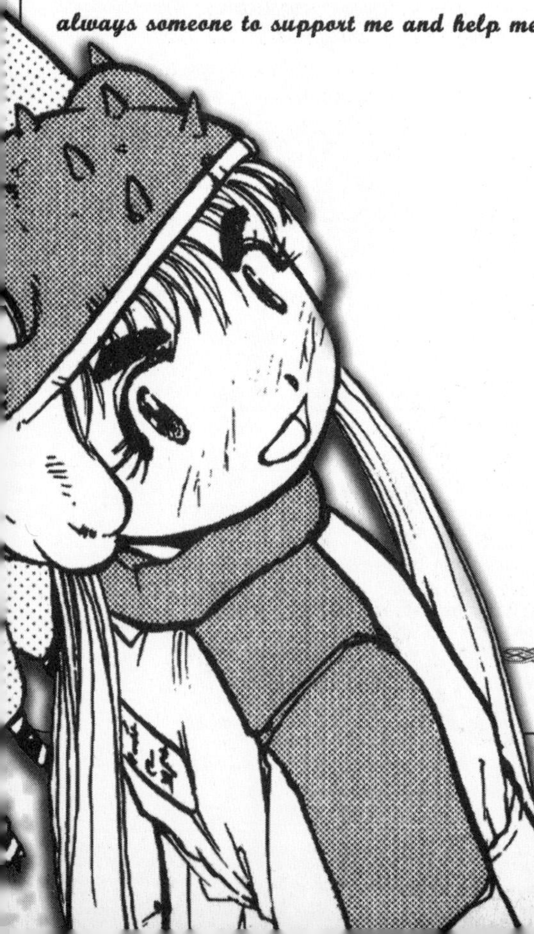

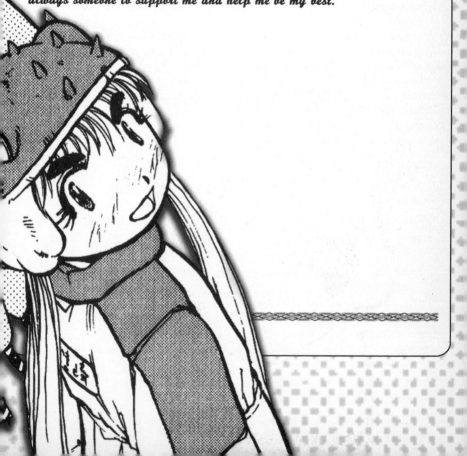

Kumi's Essay

KUMI KAWAMURA
Grade 6   Fuji Class   (Wisteria Class)
Born: September 11, 2002
Blood type: AB

When I first started in the Alien Party, I thought it would be a great way to get away from my former responsibilities of class president and student council. Everyone depended on me and it was a lot of pressure. I had no idea what real pressure was.

As a member of the Alien Party, I find myself responsible for the lives and well-being of everyone in the school, especially Yuri, who I have grown close to over the months working together.

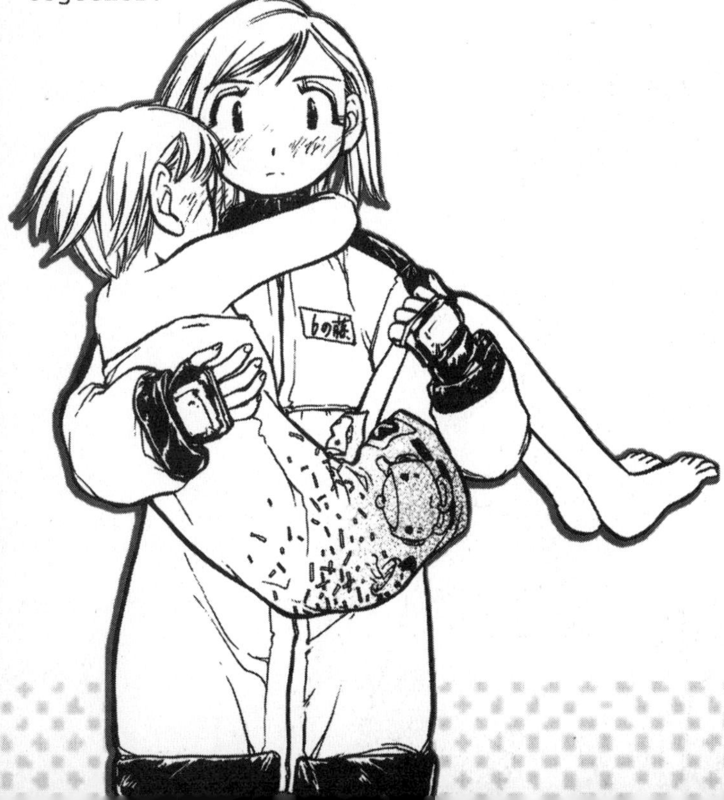
6の藤

Yuri's Essay

YURI OTANI
Grade 6 Tsubaki Class (Camellia Class)
Born: June 8, 2002
Blood type: AB

I never wanted to be in the Alien Party. Aliens are gross and slimy and they show up at the worst times. There is a big positive to being in the Alien Party though. I have made some really good friends, most especially Kumi. I hope that we can all stay friends even if I have to leave the Alien Party, even if they aren't the same people that they used to be.

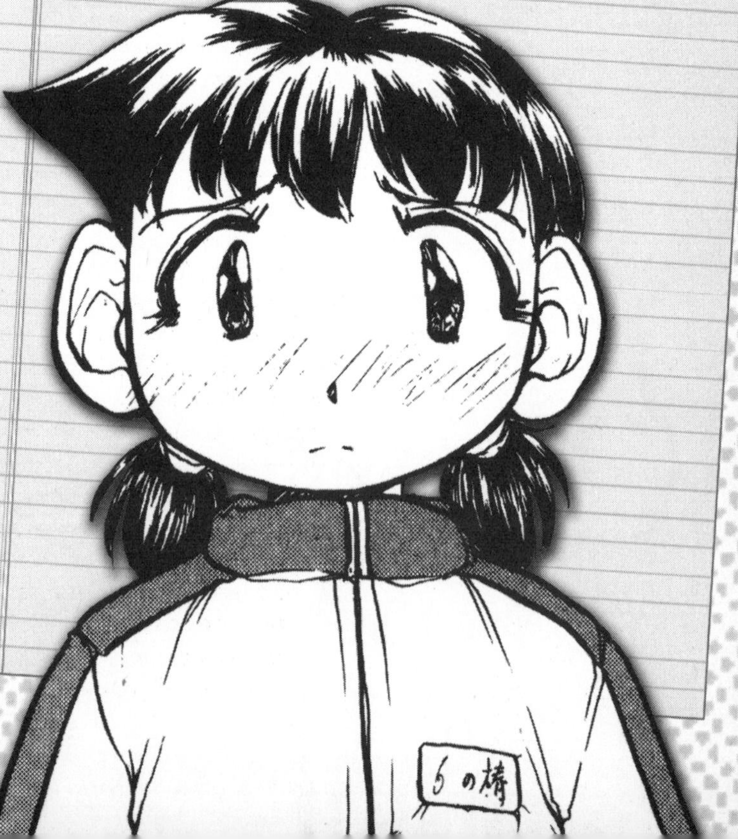
6の椿

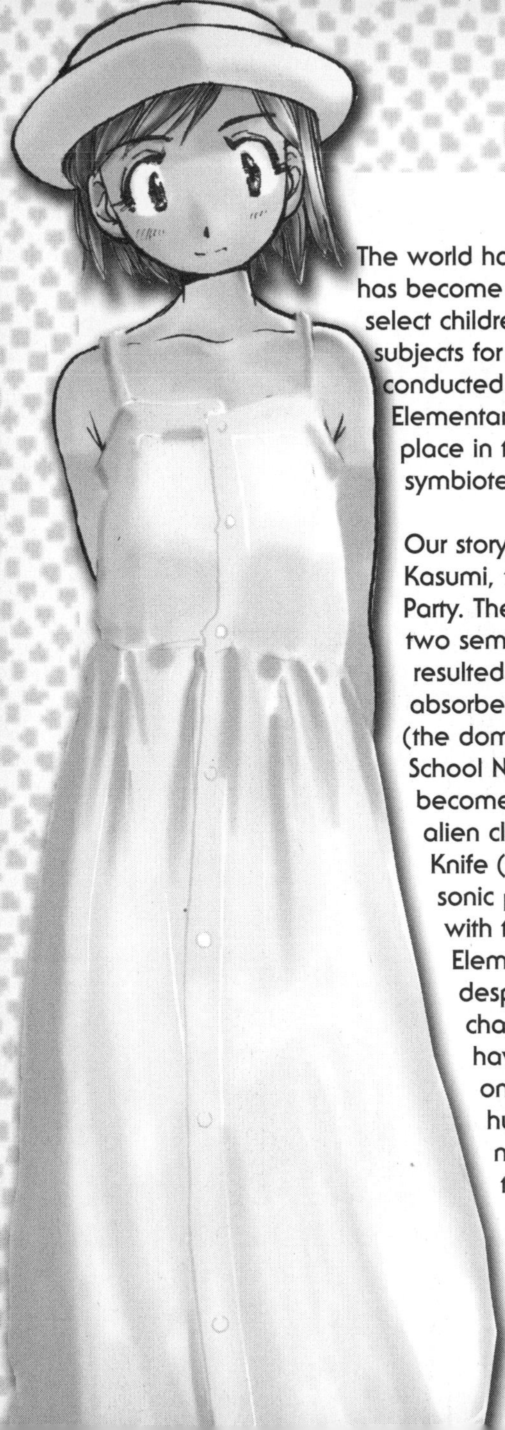

Story so far…

The world has changed. Alien invasion has become a part of everyday life and select children have become the test subjects for clandestine experiments conducted by clans of alien symbiotes. Elementary School Nine is just one place in the world where the symbiotes are in control.

Our story focuses on Yuri, Kumi, and Kasumi, the members of the Alien Party. These girls have been through two semesters of hell, which have resulted in Kumi becoming absorbed into the 'Borg's Drill Clan (the dominant clan in Elementary School Nine). Also, Kasumi has become a member of another alien clan known as the Yellow Knife (this granted her disorienting sonic powers and put her at odds with those in power at Elementary School Nine). But, despite all of these drastic changes to the two girls, they have managed to hold onto one last vestige of their humanity. Both have vowed never to let what happened to them ever happen to Yuri, the last member of the group that is still completely human.

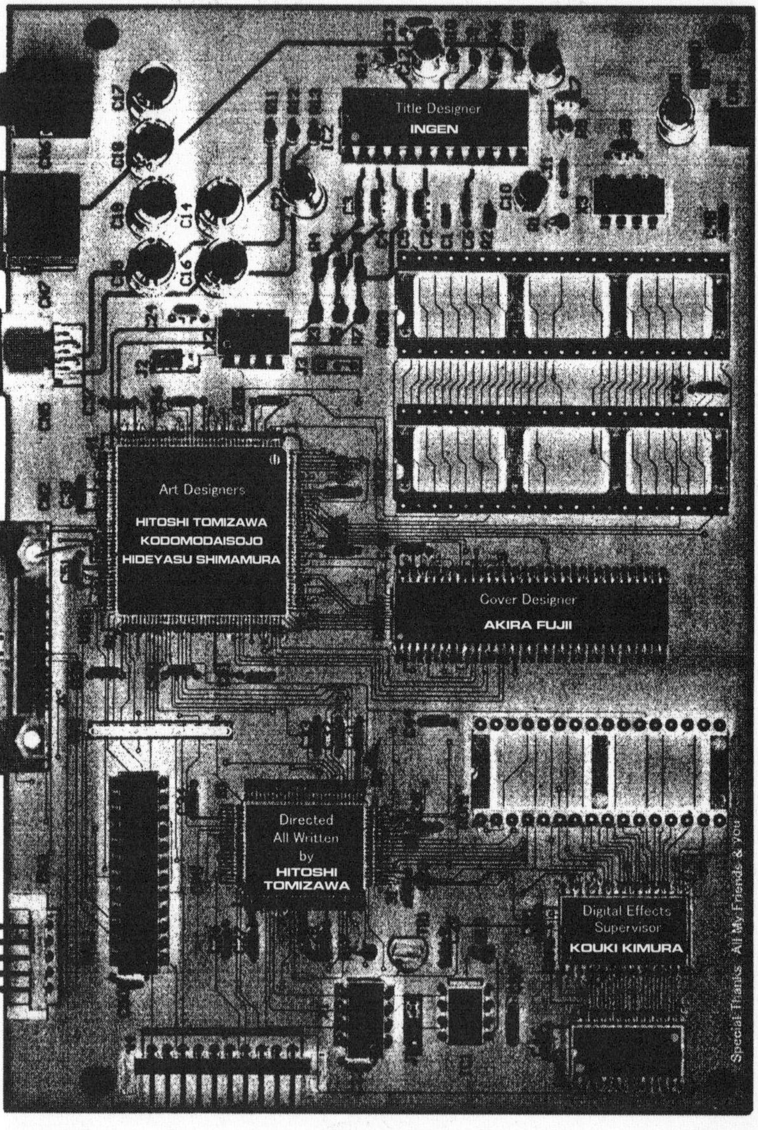

Title Designer
INGEN
Art Designers
HITOSHI TOMIZAWA
KODOMODAISOJO
HIDEYASU SHIMAMURA
Cover Designer
AKIRA FUJII
Directed
All Written
by
HITOSHI
TOMIZAWA
Digital Effects
Supervisor
KOUKI KIMURA
Special Thanks All My Friends & you

エイリアン9

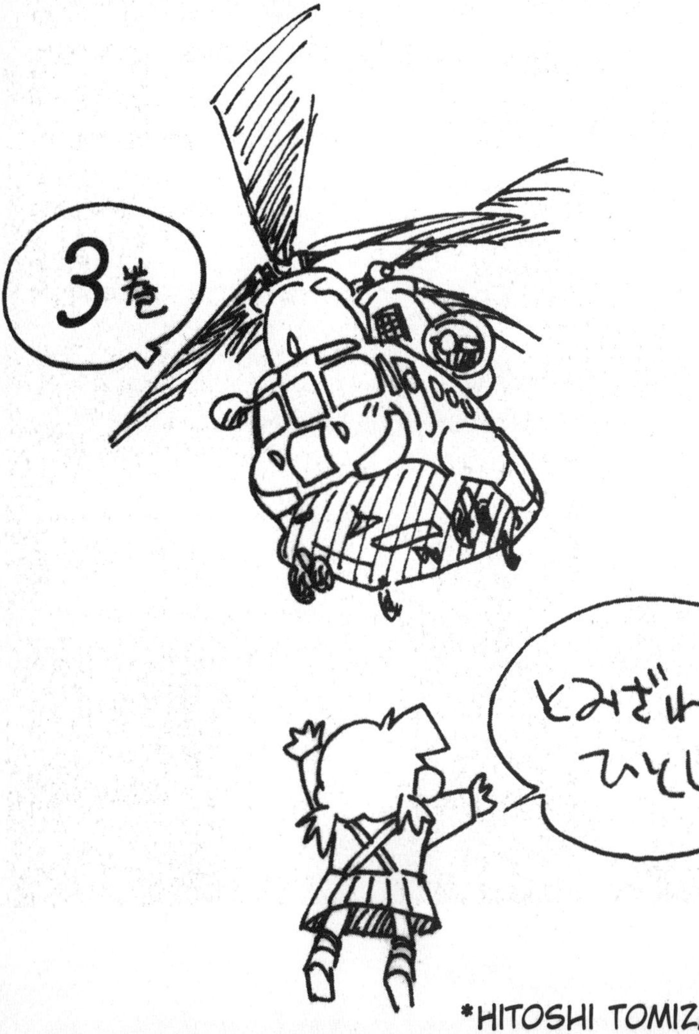
3巻
とみざわ*
ひとし♡

*HITOSHI TOMIZAWA

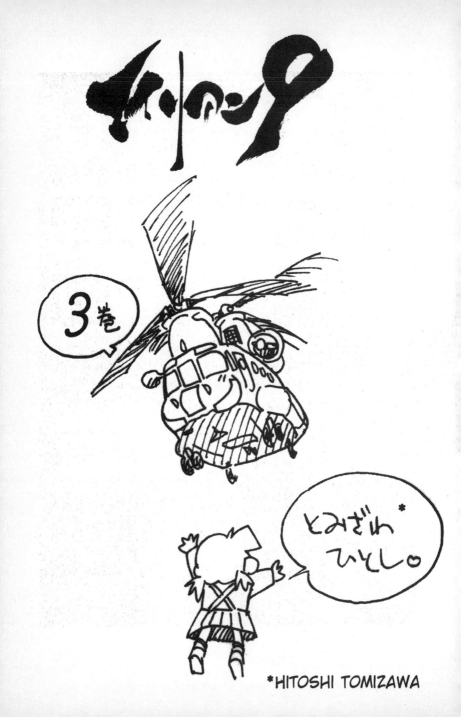

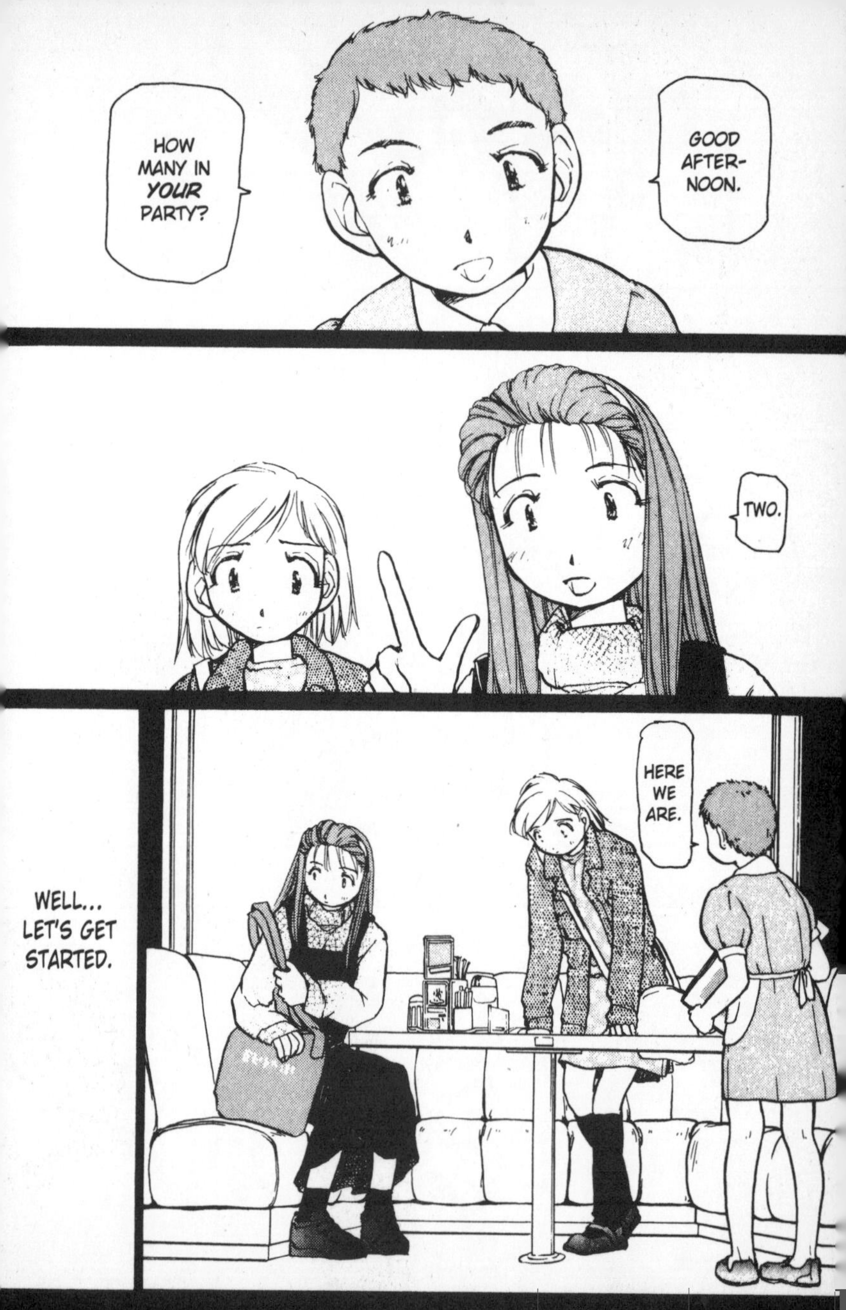
GOOD AFTER-NOON.
HOW MANY IN *YOUR* PARTY?
TWO.
HERE WE ARE.
WELL... LET'S GET STARTED.

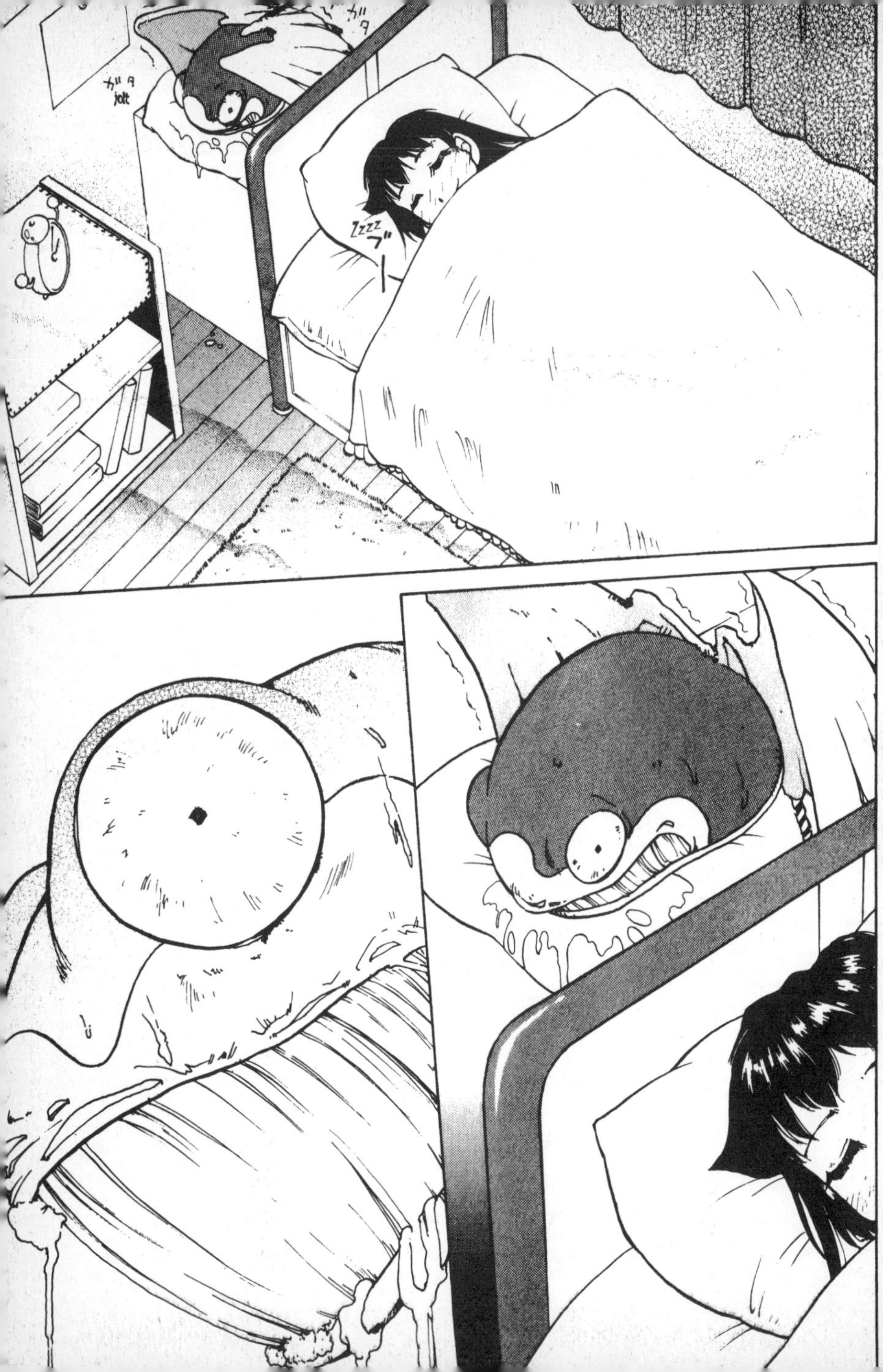
ガタ
ガタ
jolt
Zzzz
ブー

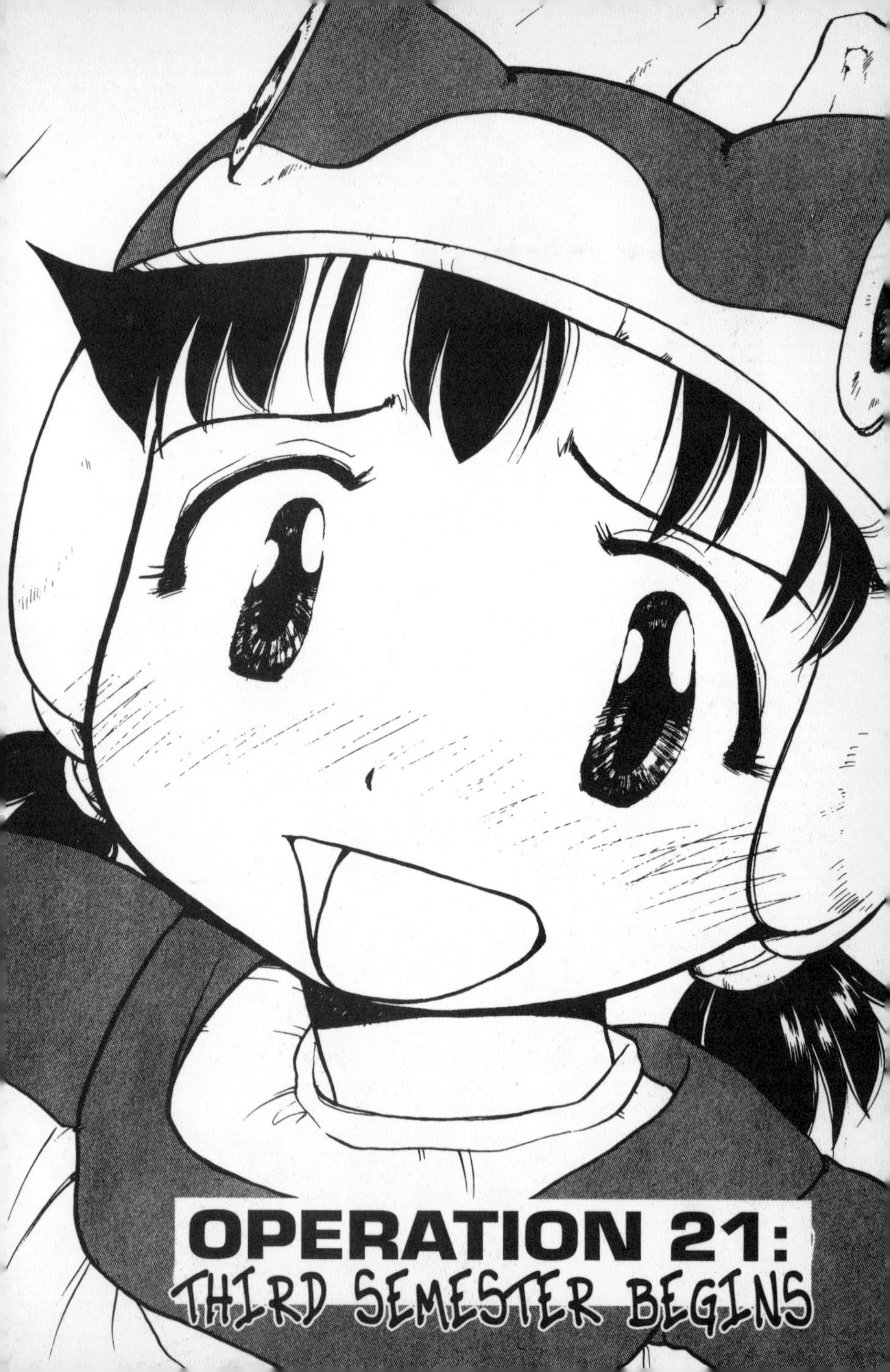

OPERATION 21: THIRD SEMESTER BEGINS

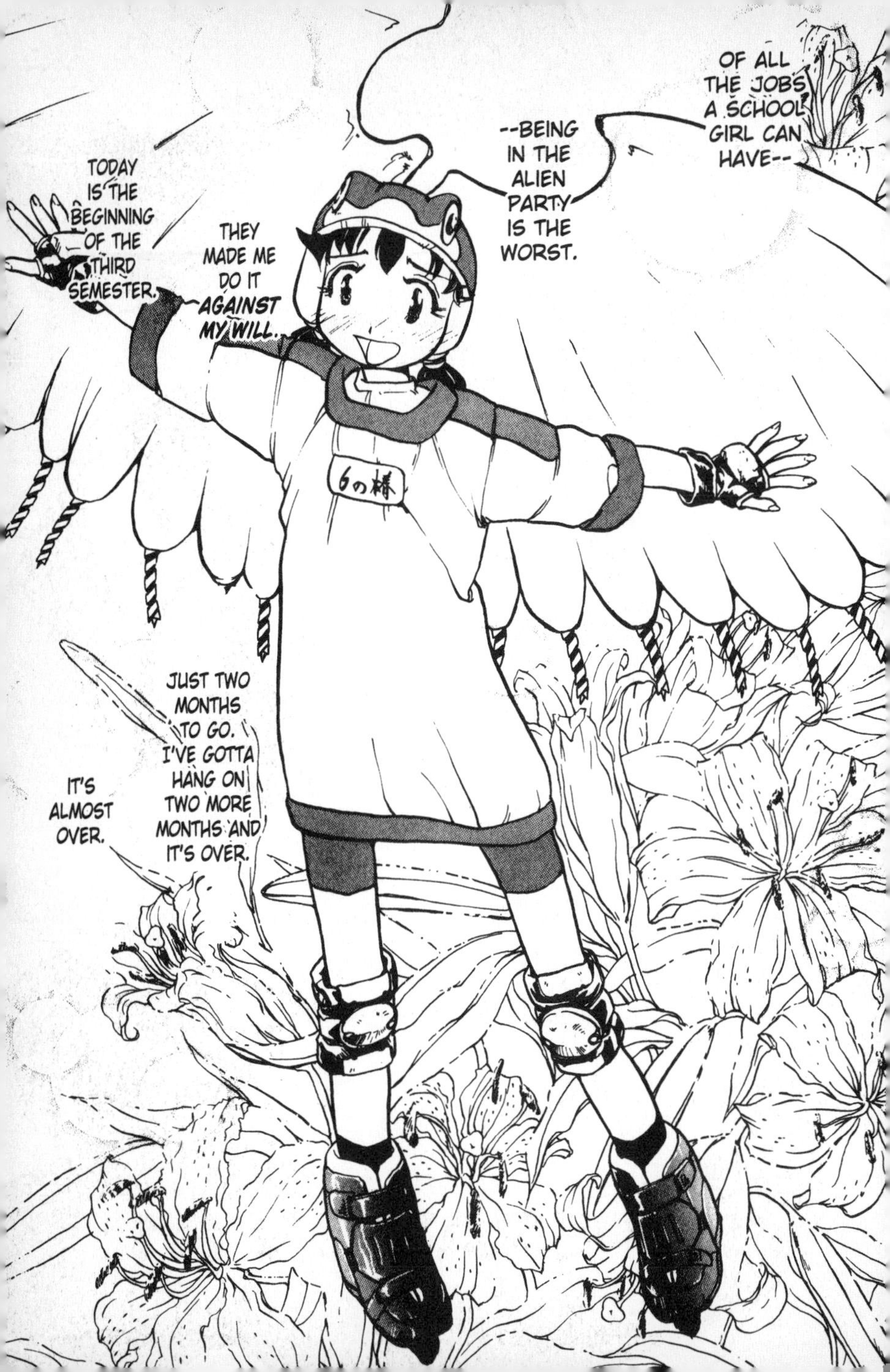
OF ALL THE JOBS A SCHOOL GIRL CAN HAVE--
--BEING IN THE ALIEN PARTY IS THE WORST.
THEY MADE ME DO IT **AGAINST MY WILL.**
TODAY IS THE BEGINNING OF THE THIRD SEMESTER.
JUST TWO MONTHS TO GO. I'VE GOTTA HANG ON TWO MORE MONTHS AND IT'S OVER.
IT'S ALMOST OVER.

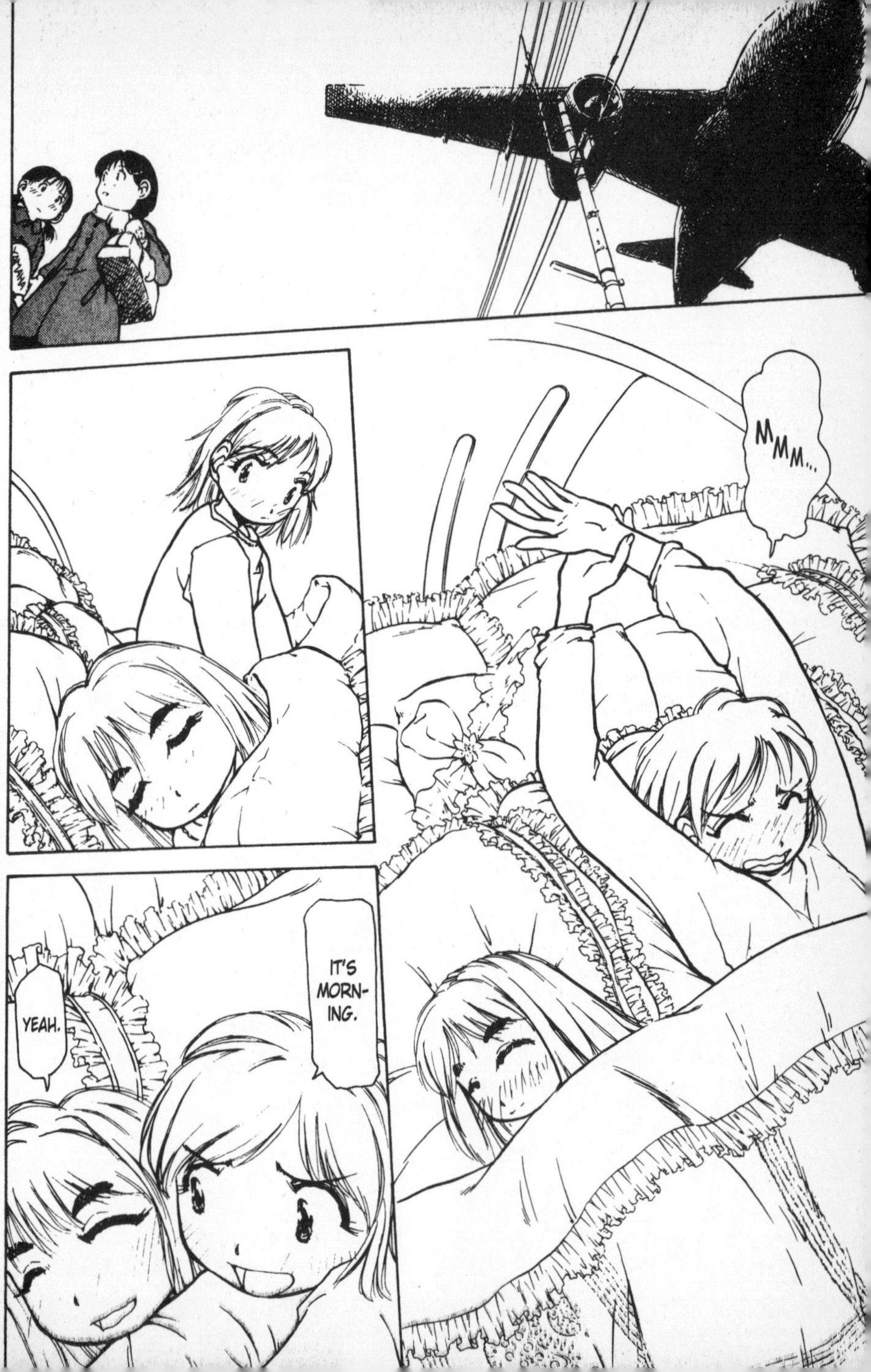
MMM..
IT'S MORNING.
YEAH.

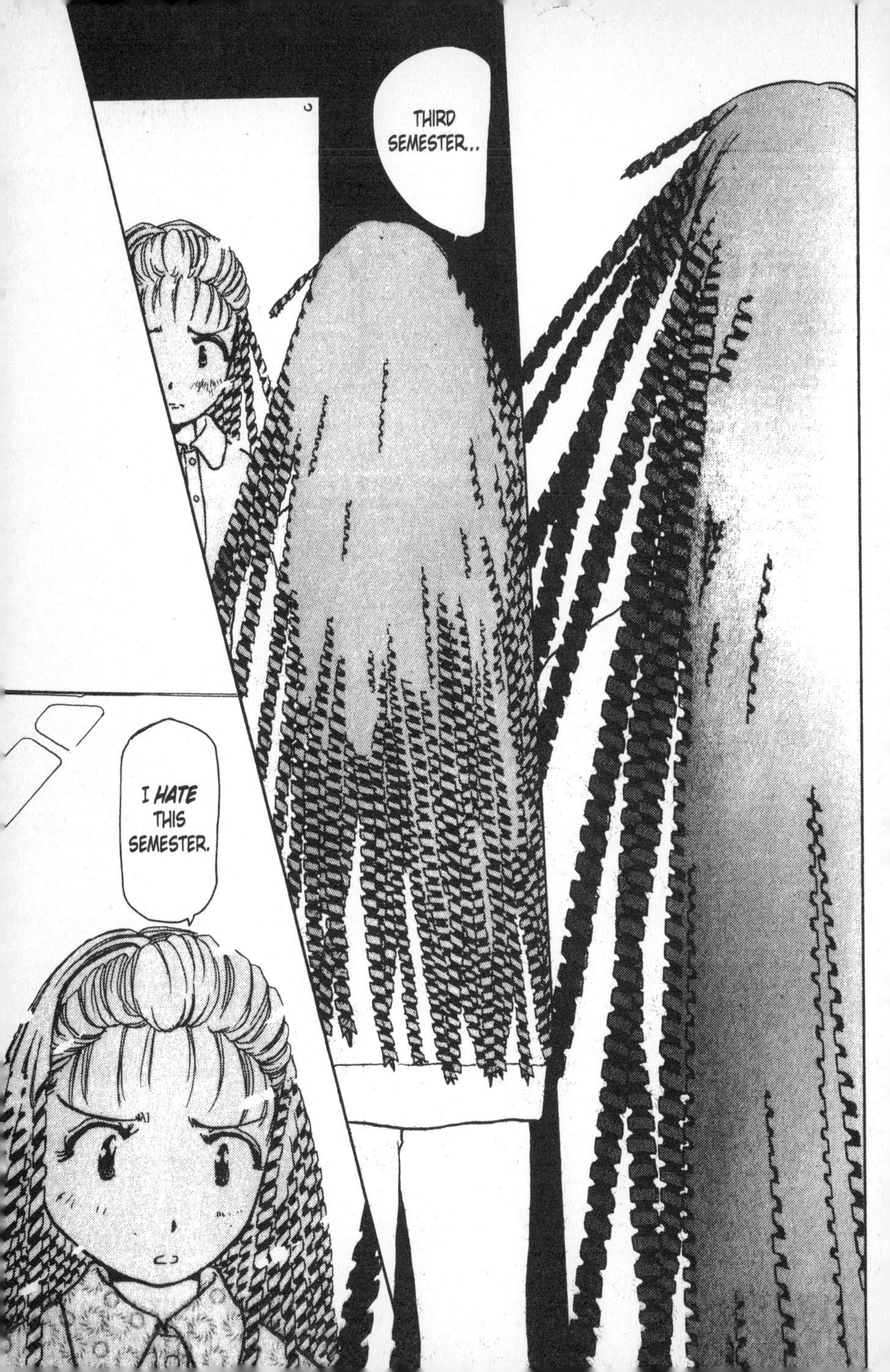
THIRD SEMESTER...
I *HATE* THIS SEMESTER.

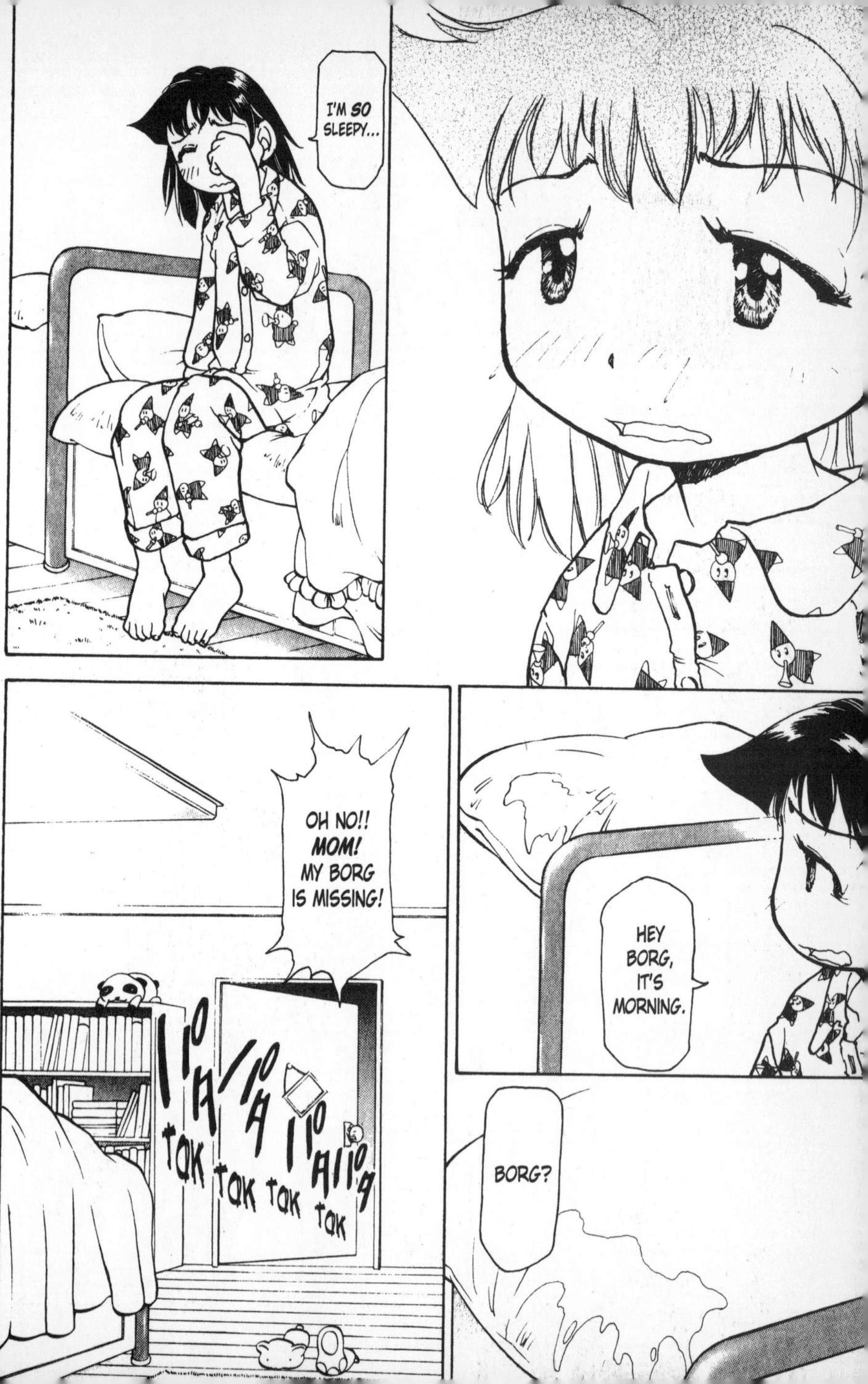
I'M SO SLEEPY...
HEY BORG, IT'S MORNING.
BORG?
OH NO!! MOM! MY BORG IS MISSING!
TAK TAK TAK TAK

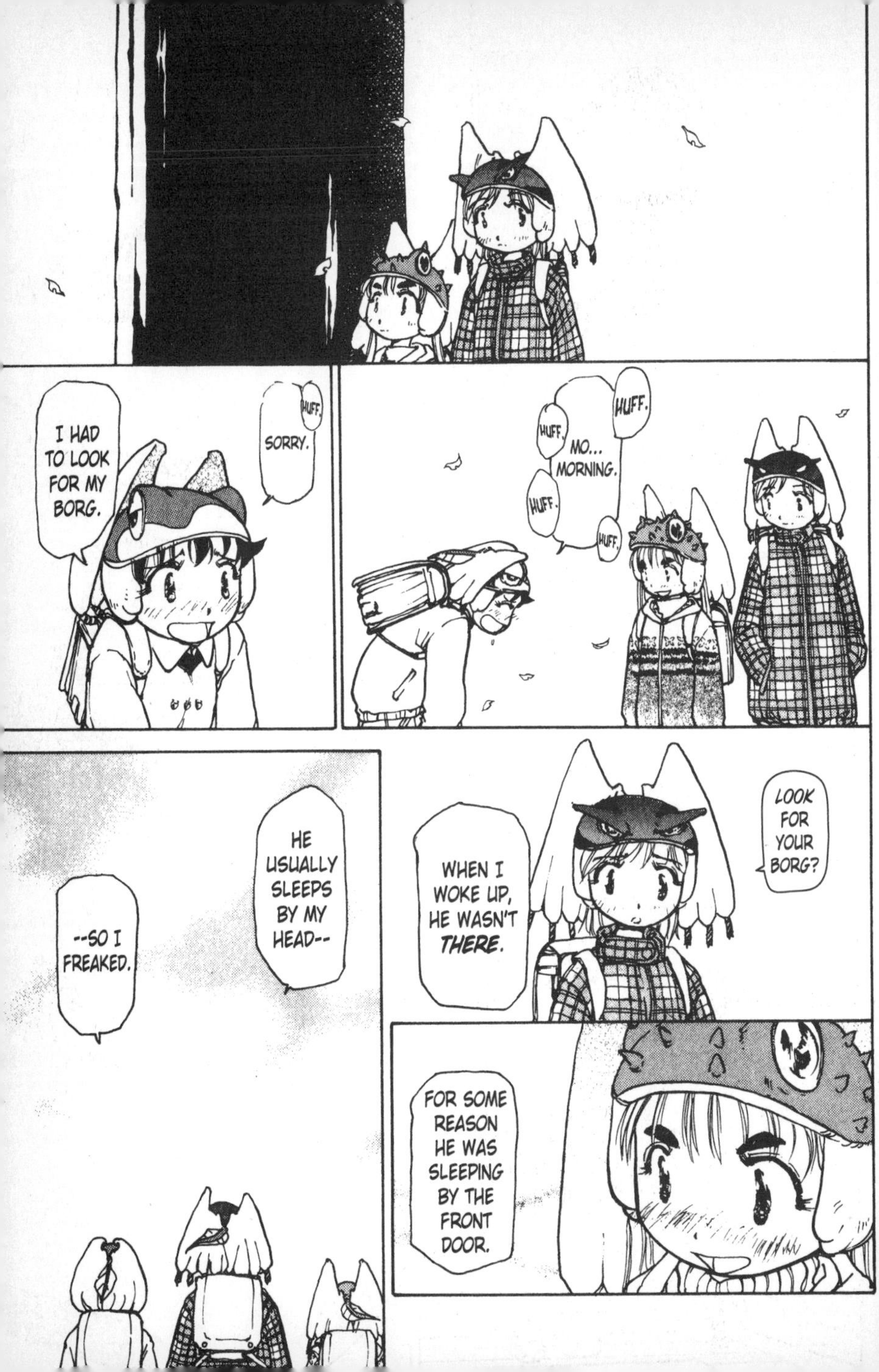
HUFF.
HUFF.
MO... MORNING.
HUFF.
HUFF.
HUFF.
SORRY.
I HAD TO LOOK FOR MY BORG.
LOOK FOR YOUR BORG?
WHEN I WOKE UP, HE WASN'T *THERE*.
FOR SOME REASON HE WAS SLEEPING BY THE FRONT DOOR.
HE USUALLY SLEEPS BY MY HEAD--
--SO I FREAKED.

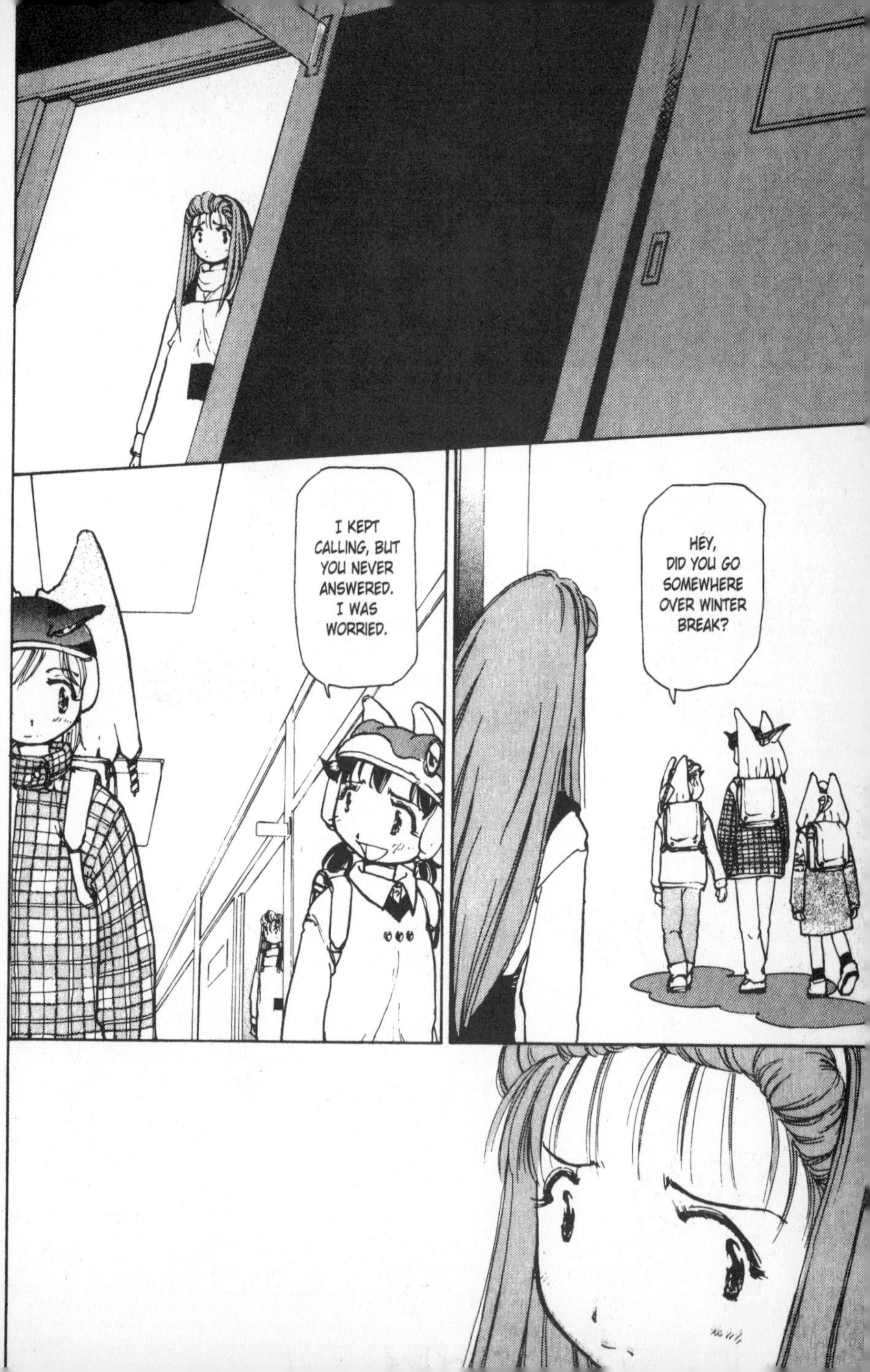
HEY, DID YOU GO SOMEWHERE OVER WINTER BREAK?
I KEPT CALLING, BUT YOU NEVER ANSWERED. I WAS WORRIED.

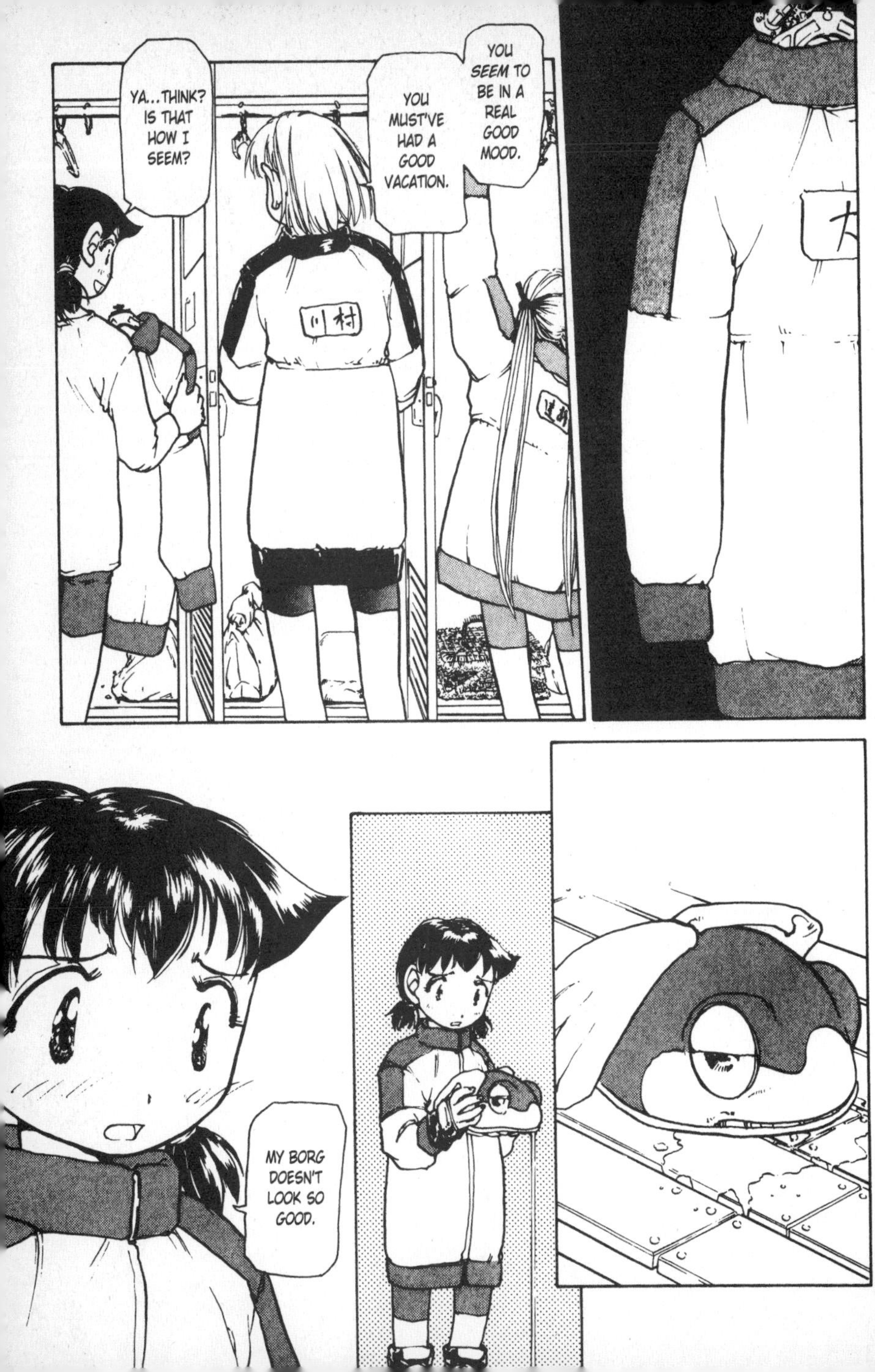
YOU SEEM TO BE IN A REAL GOOD MOOD.
YOU MUST'VE HAD A GOOD VACATION.
YA...THINK? IS THAT HOW I SEEM?
MY BORG DOESN'T LOOK SO GOOD.

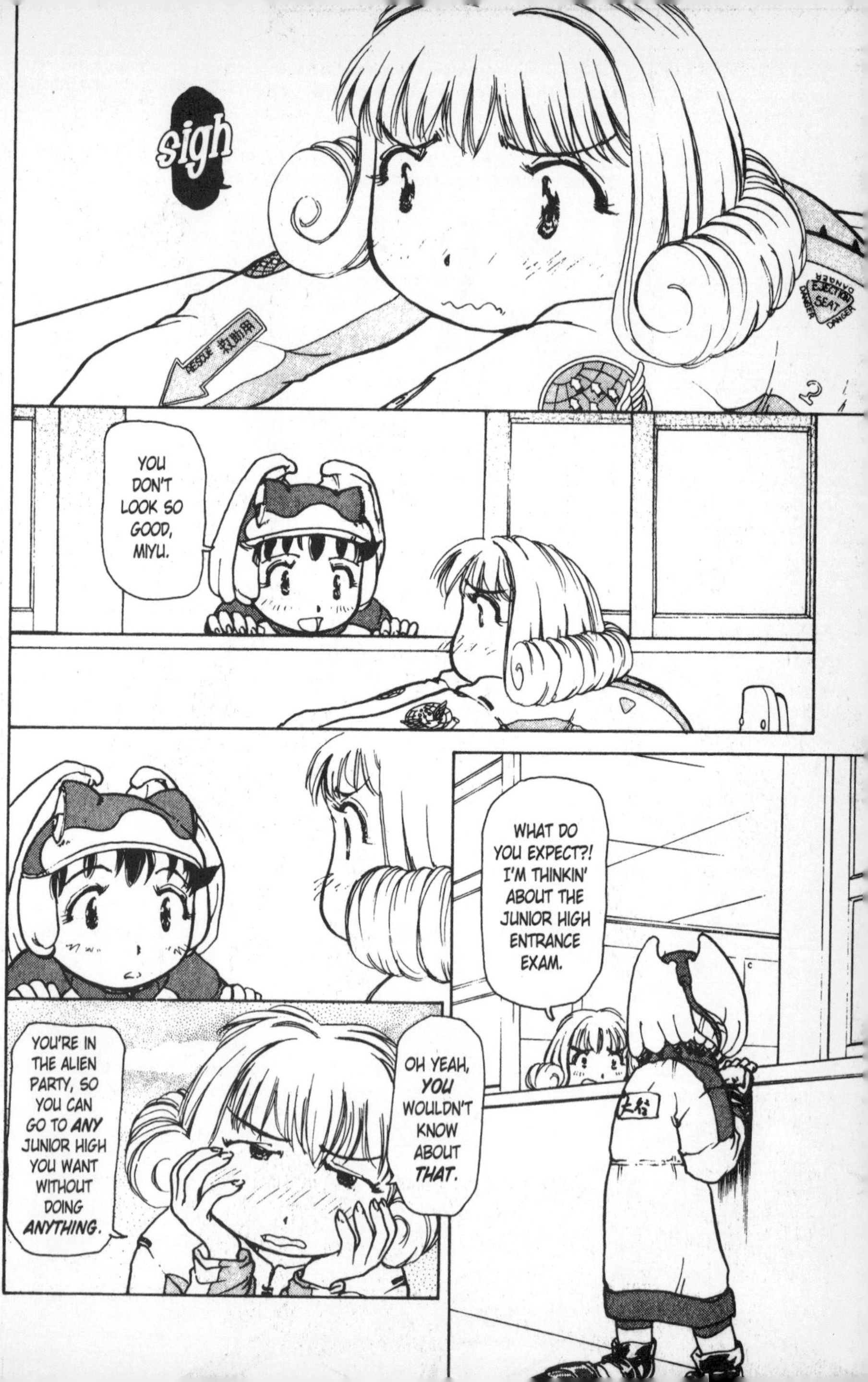
sigh
RESCUE 救助用
EJECTION SEAT
DANGER
DANGER
YOU DON'T LOOK SO GOOD, MIYU.
WHAT DO YOU EXPECT?! I'M THINKIN' ABOUT THE JUNIOR HIGH ENTRANCE EXAM.
OH YEAH, *YOU* WOULDN'T KNOW ABOUT *THAT*.
YOU'RE IN THE ALIEN PARTY, SO YOU CAN GO TO *ANY* JUNIOR HIGH YOU WANT WITHOUT DOING *ANYTHING*.

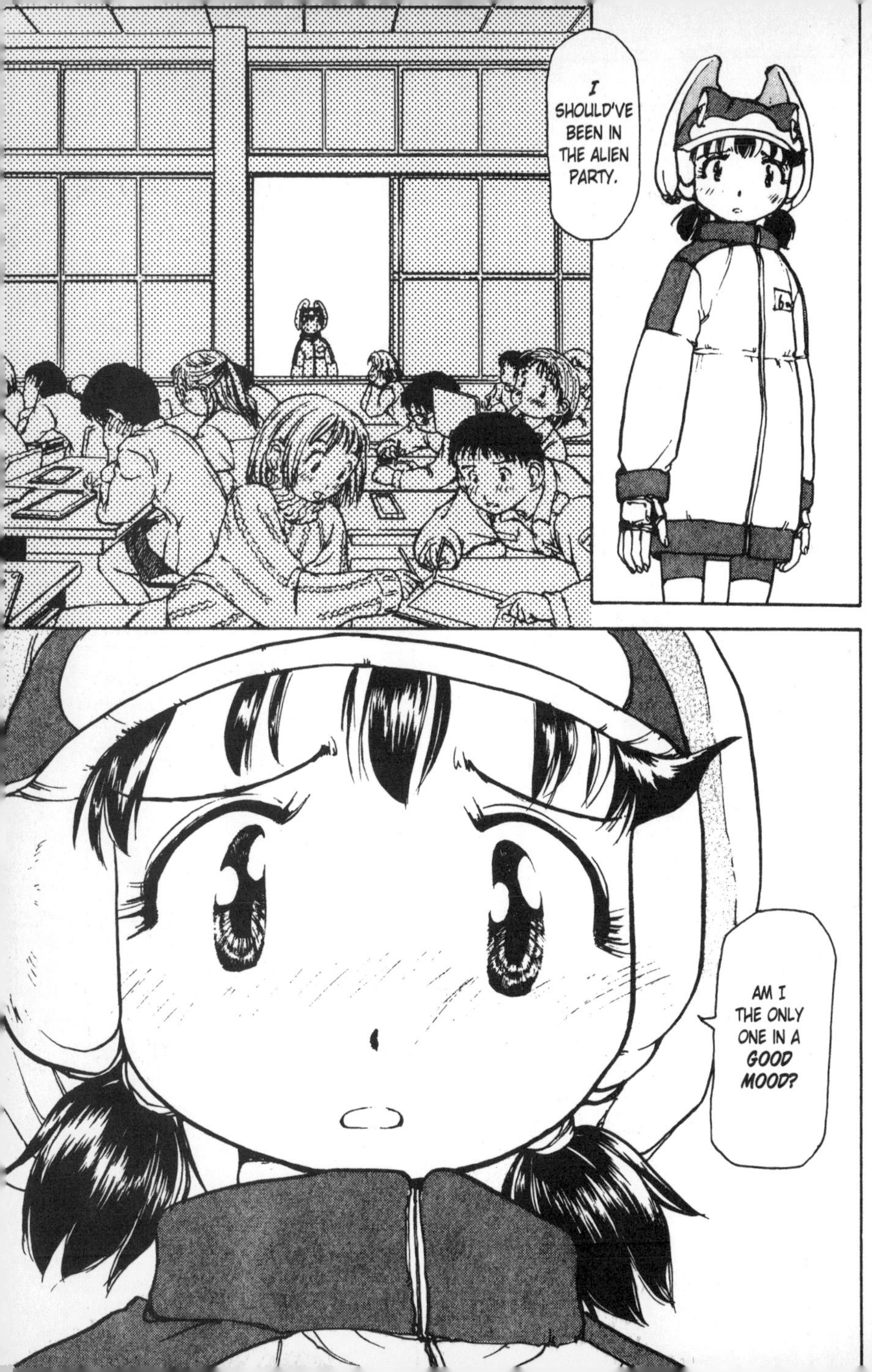
I SHOULD'VE BEEN IN THE ALIEN PARTY.
AM I THE ONLY ONE IN A *GOOD MOOD*?

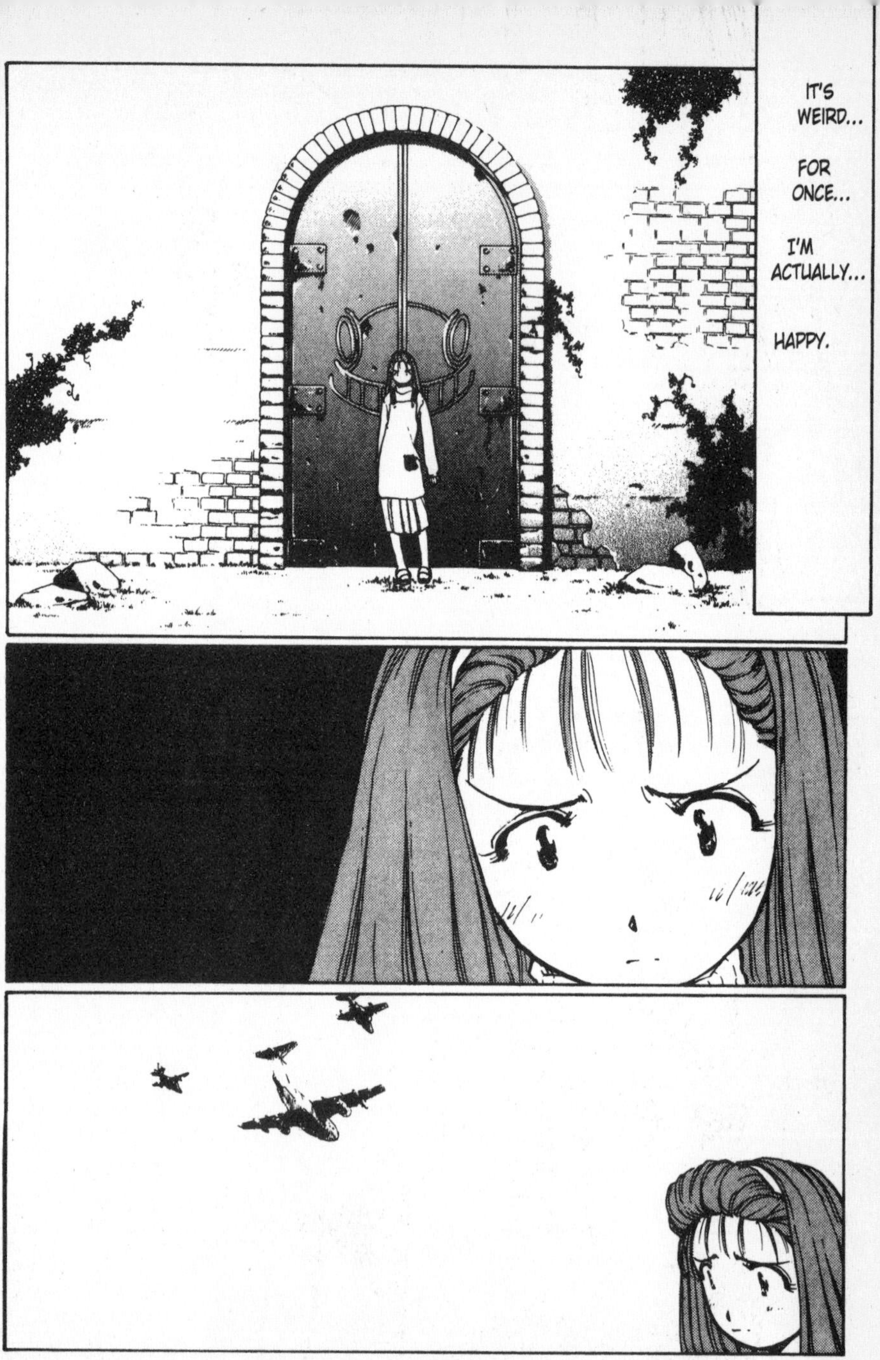
IT'S WEIRD...
FOR ONCE...
I'M ACTUALLY...
HAPPY.

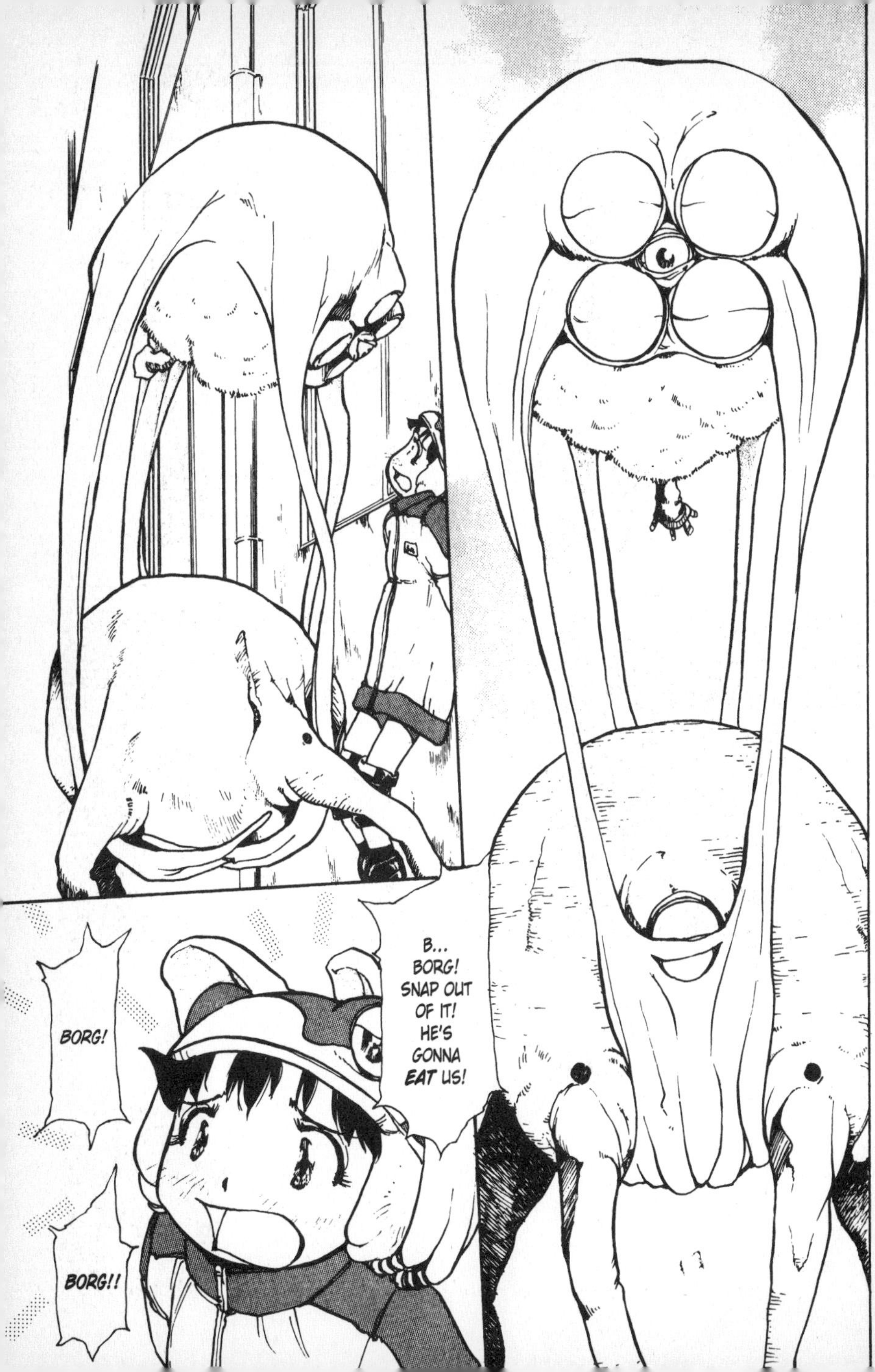
B... BORG! SNAP OUT OF IT! HE'S GONNA EAT US!
BORG!
BORG!!

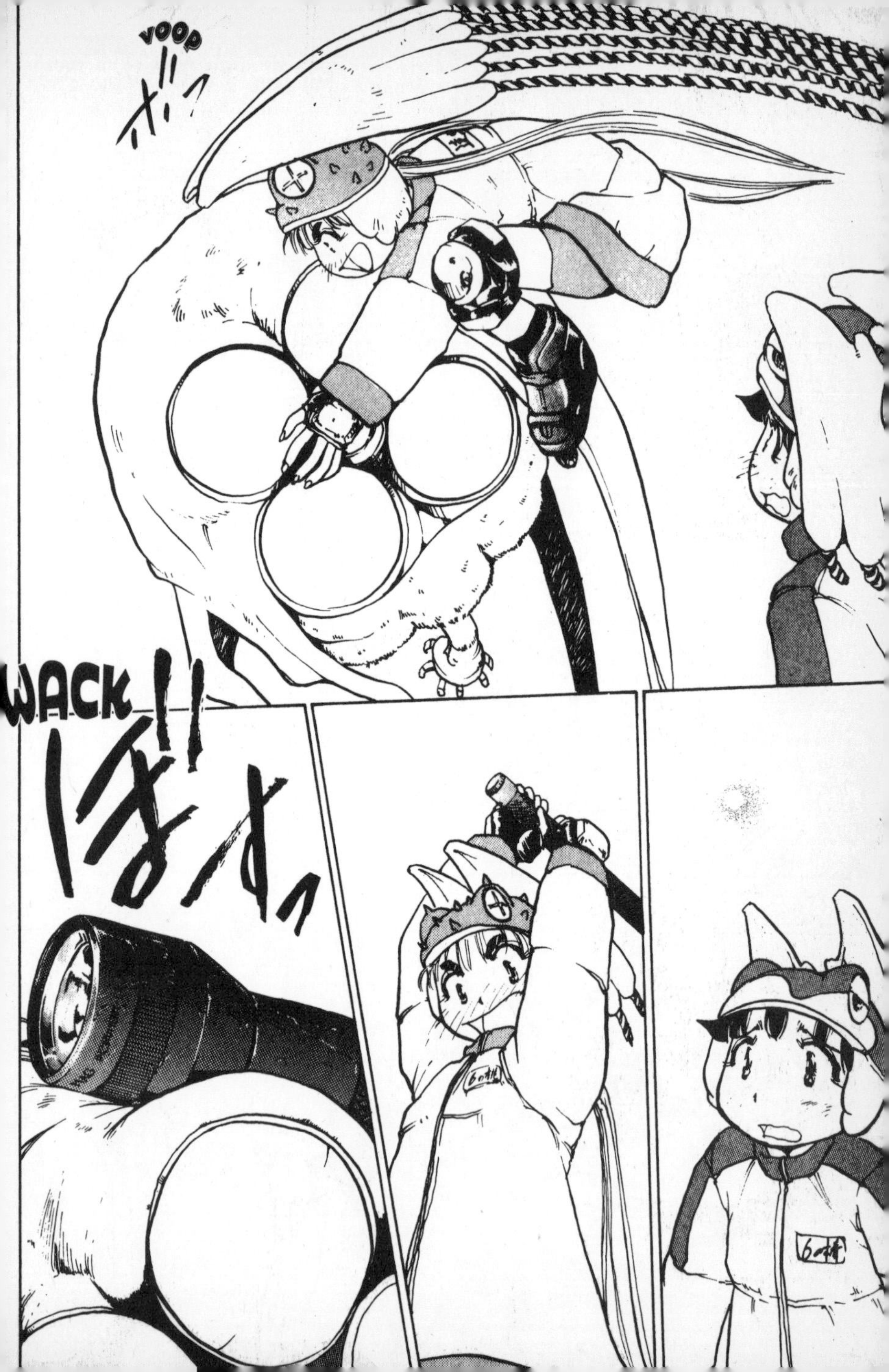
VOOP
WACK!!
ぼすっ

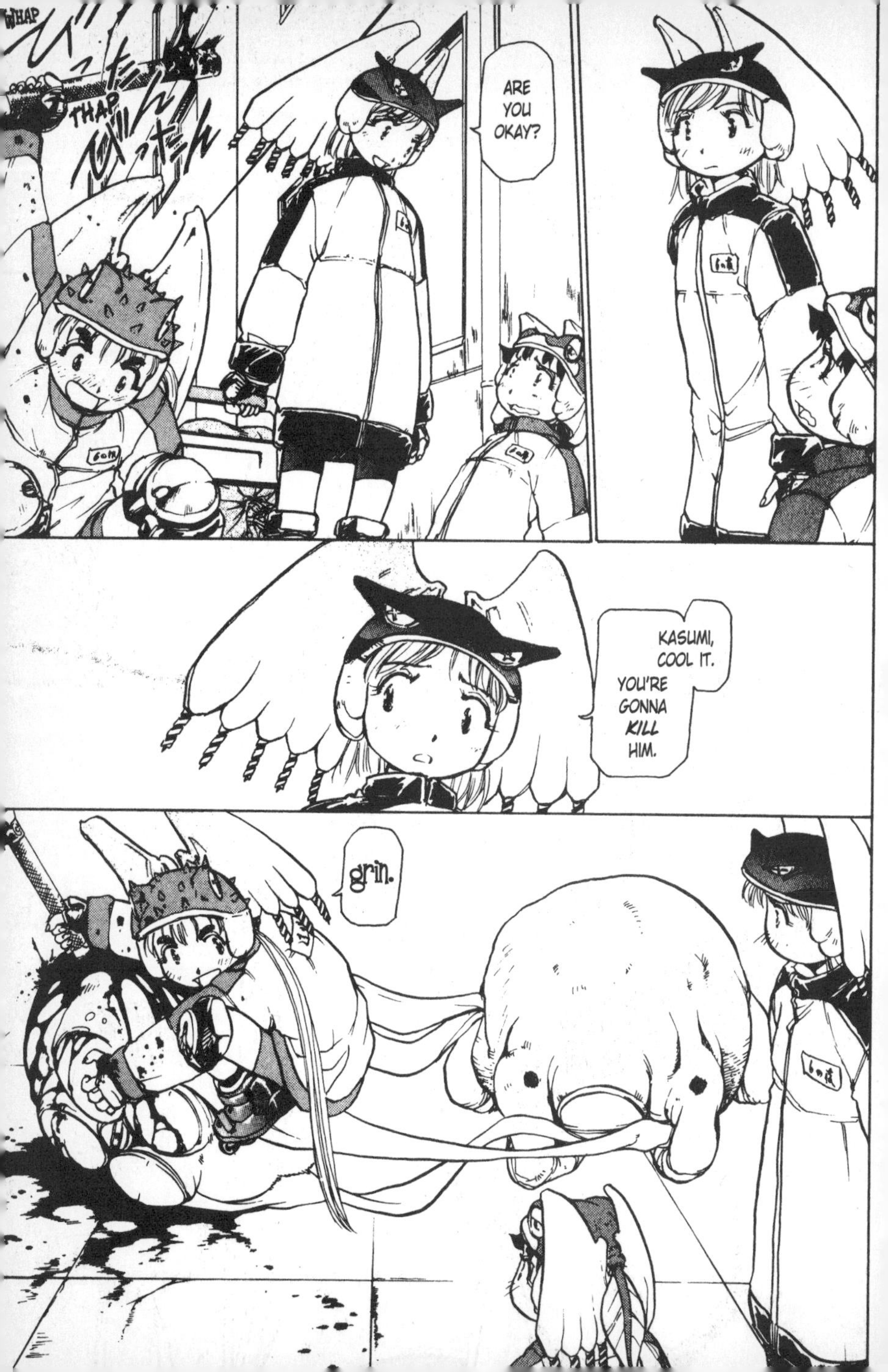
ARE YOU OKAY?
WHAP
THAP
KASUMI, COOL IT. YOU'RE GONNA **KILL** HIM.
grin.

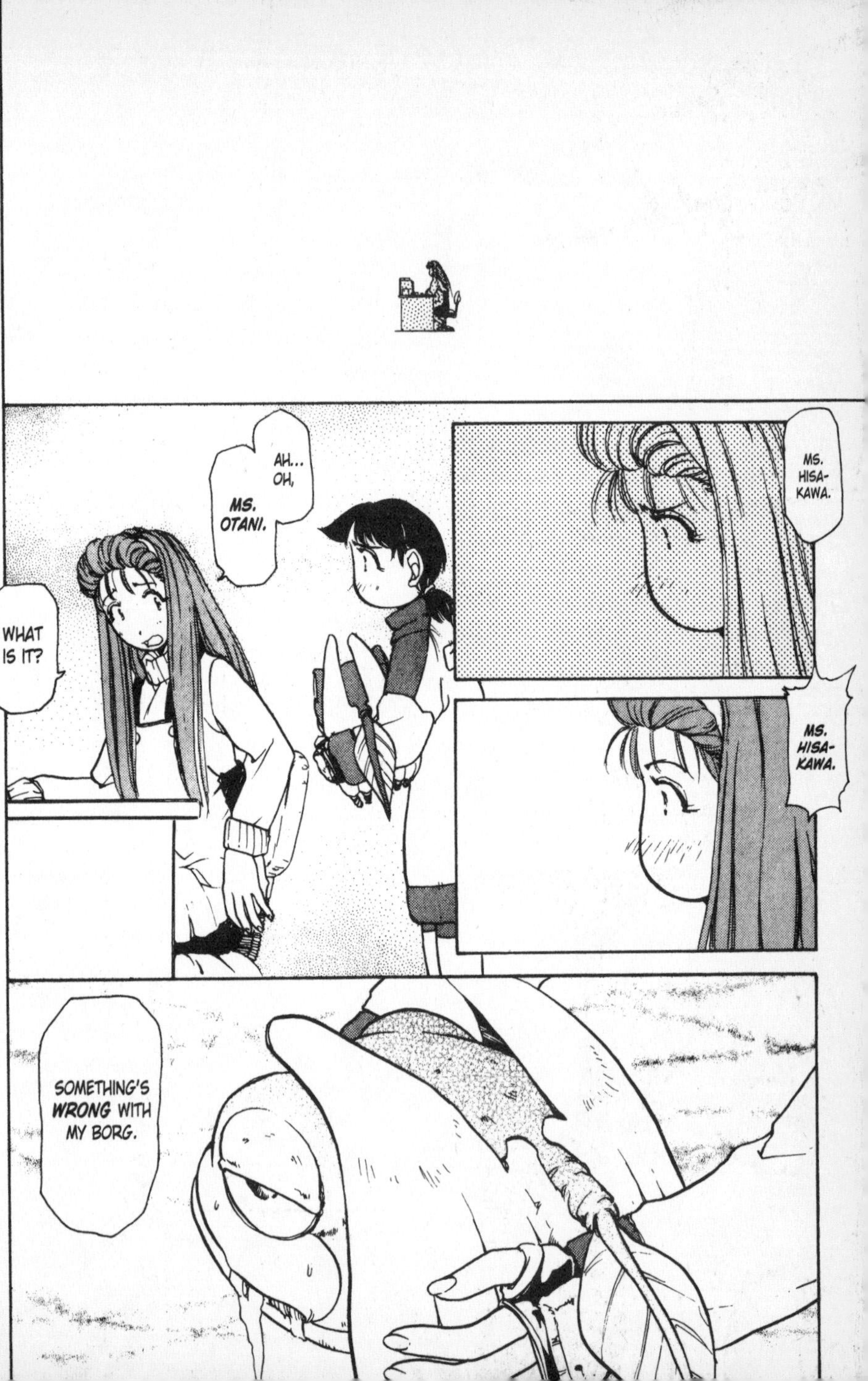
MS. HISA-KAWA.
MS. HISA-KAWA.
AH... OH, MS. OTANI.
WHAT IS IT?
SOMETHING'S WRONG WITH MY BORG.

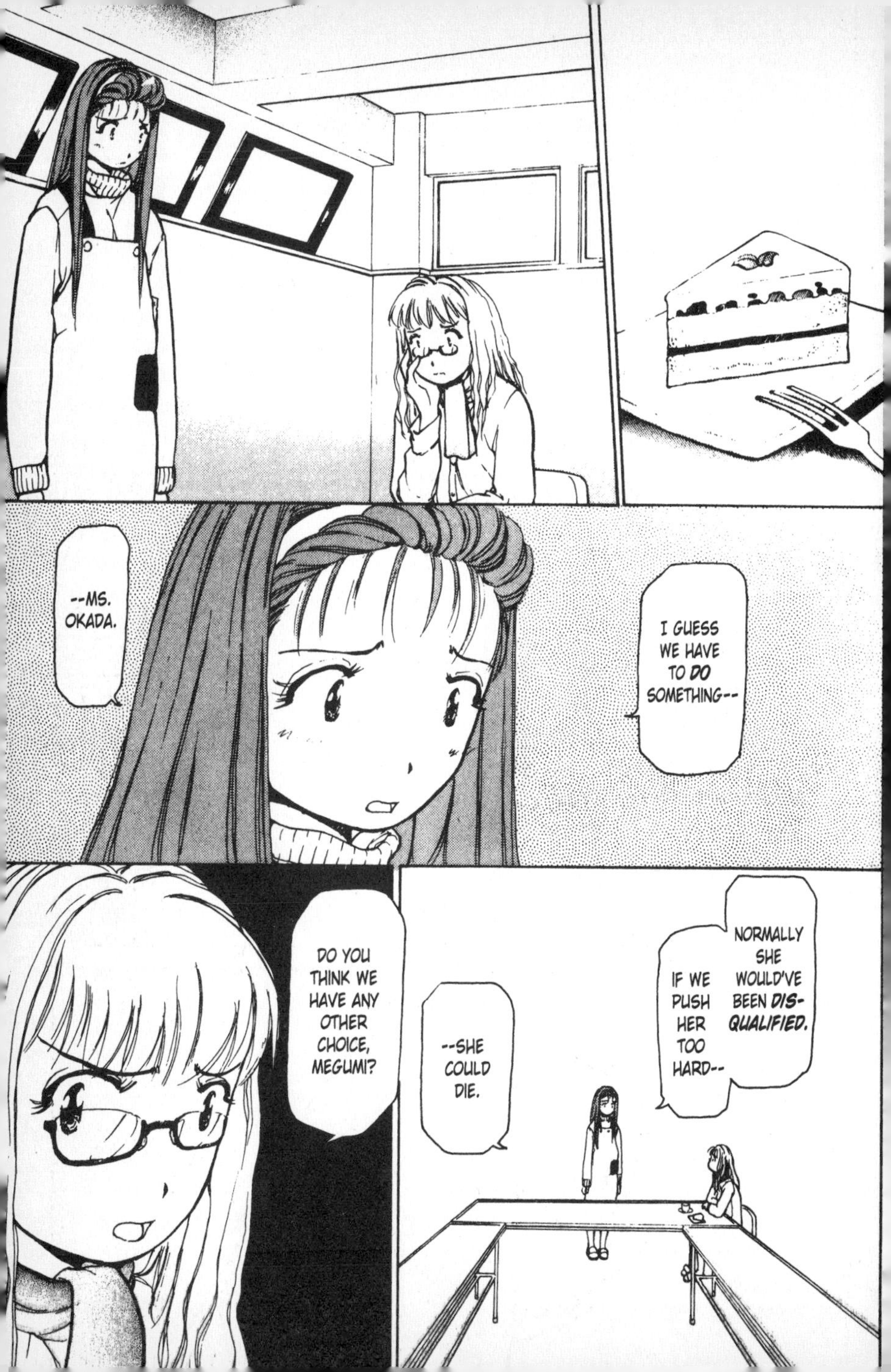

I GUESS WE HAVE TO **DO** SOMETHING--
--MS. OKADA.
NORMALLY SHE WOULD'VE BEEN ***DIS-QUALIFIED.***
IF WE PUSH HER TOO HARD--
--SHE COULD DIE.
DO YOU THINK WE HAVE ANY OTHER CHOICE, MEGUMI?

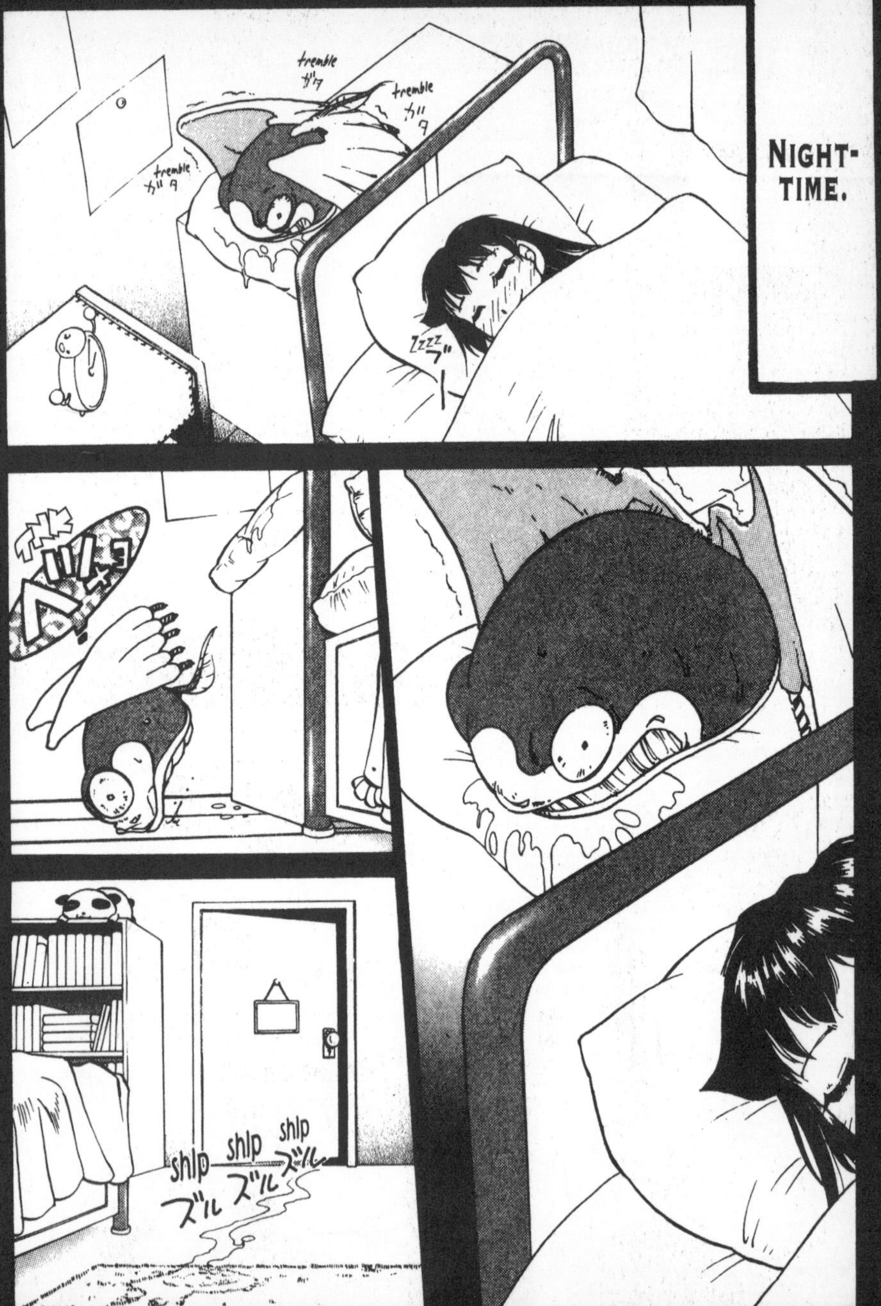
NIGHT-TIME.
tremble
tremble
tremble
Zzzz
shlp
shlp
shlp

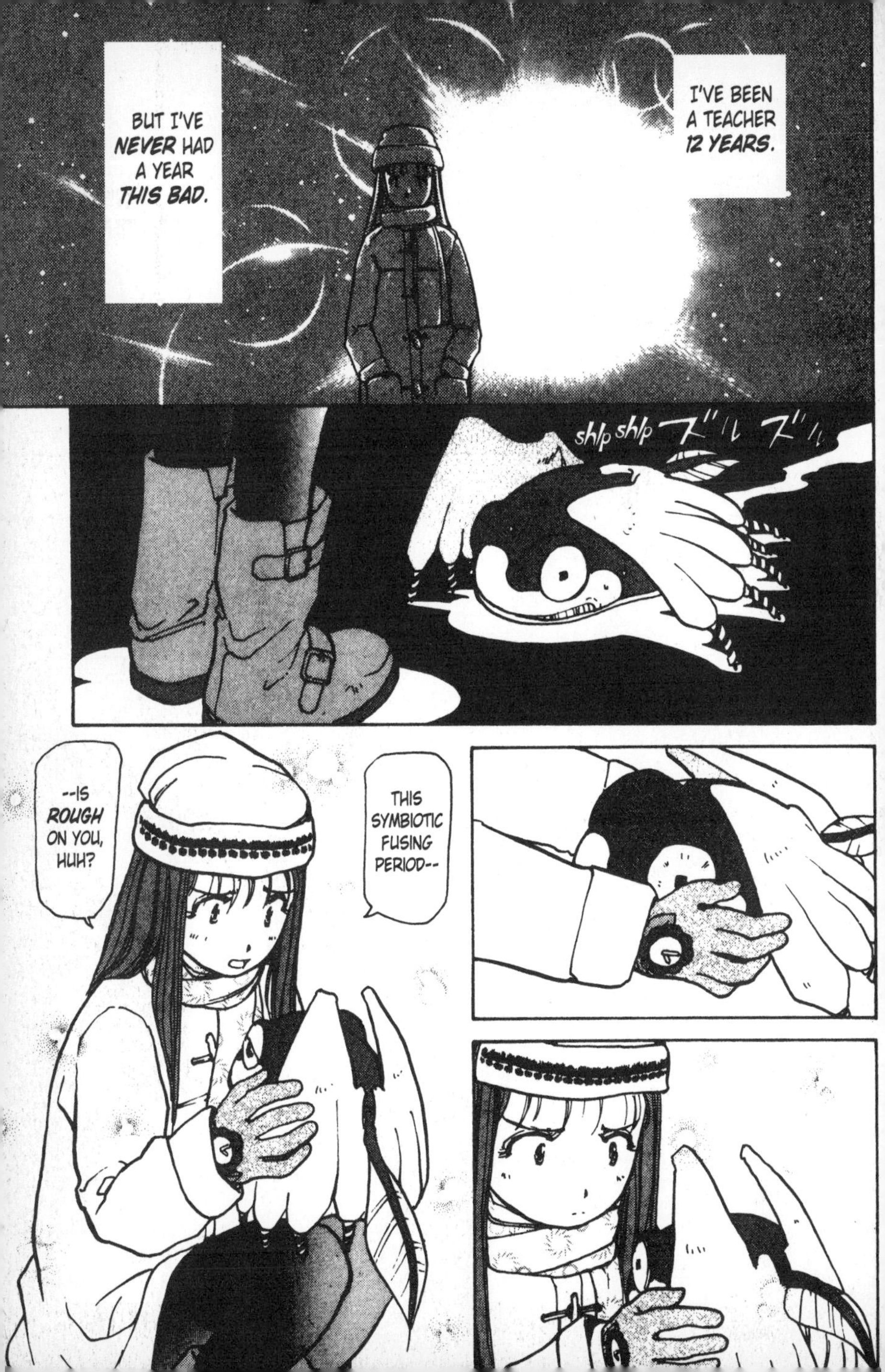
I'VE BEEN A TEACHER 12 YEARS.
BUT I'VE NEVER HAD A YEAR THIS BAD.
shlp shlp ズルズル
THIS SYMBIOTIC FUSING PERIOD--
--IS ROUGH ON YOU, HUH?

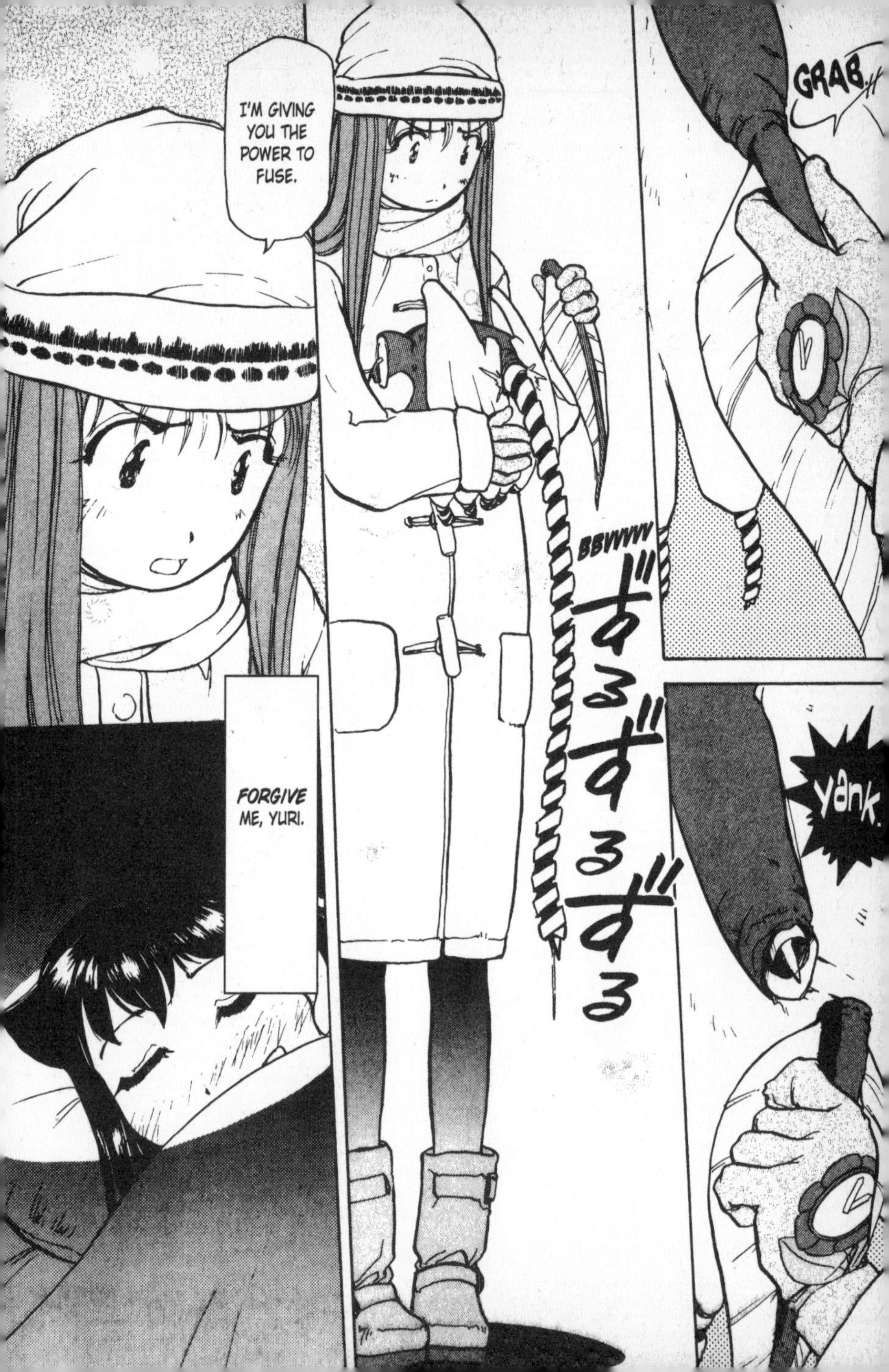
GRAB
yank
BBVVVVV
ずるずるずるずる
I'M GIVING YOU THE POWER TO FUSE.
FORGIVE ME, YURI.

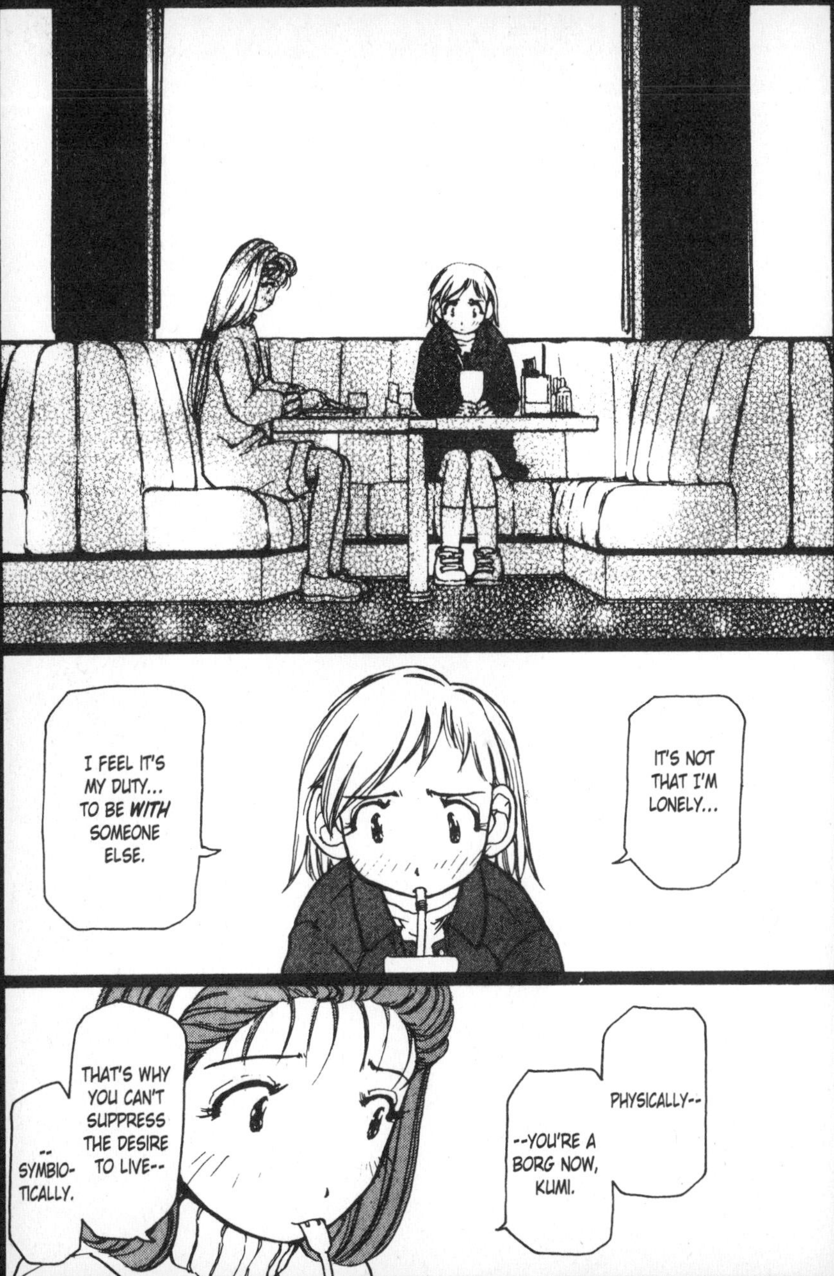
IT'S NOT THAT I'M LONELY...
I FEEL IT'S MY DUTY... TO BE *WITH* SOMEONE ELSE.
PHYSICALLY--
--YOU'RE A BORG NOW, KUMI.
THAT'S WHY YOU CAN'T SUPPRESS THE DESIRE TO LIVE--
--SYMBIO-TICALLY.

OPERATION 22: YOU CAN'T STOP ME!

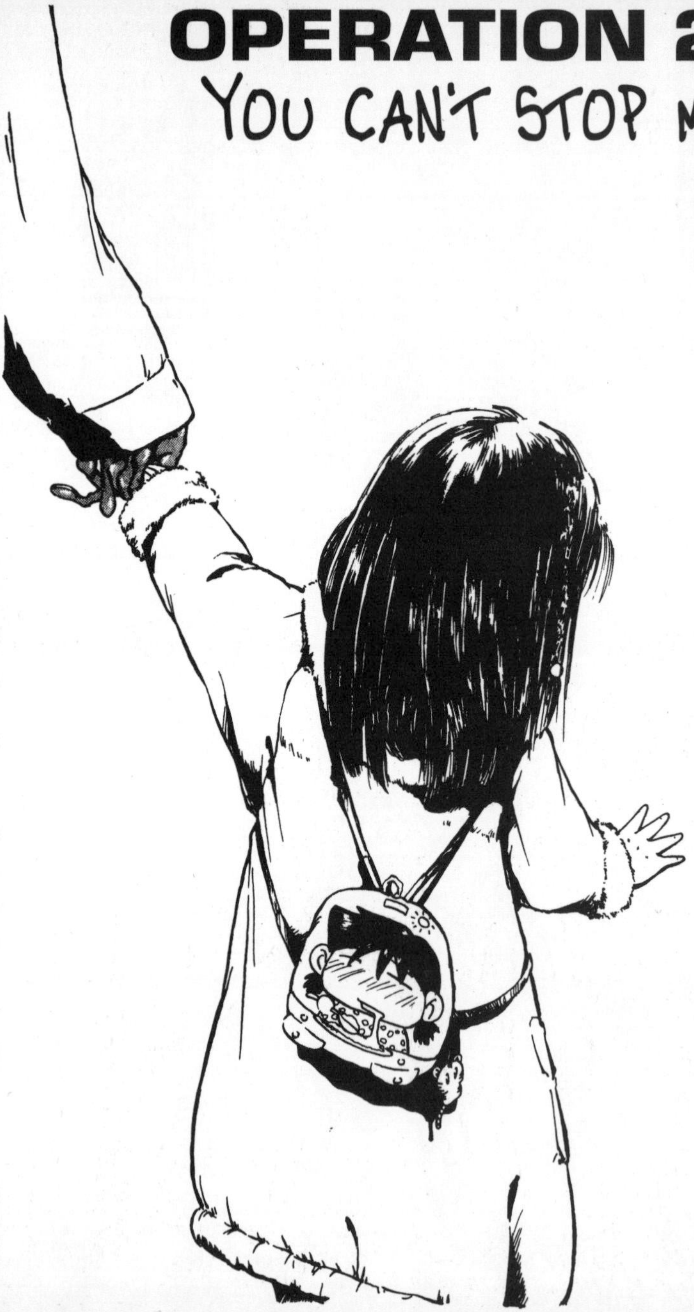

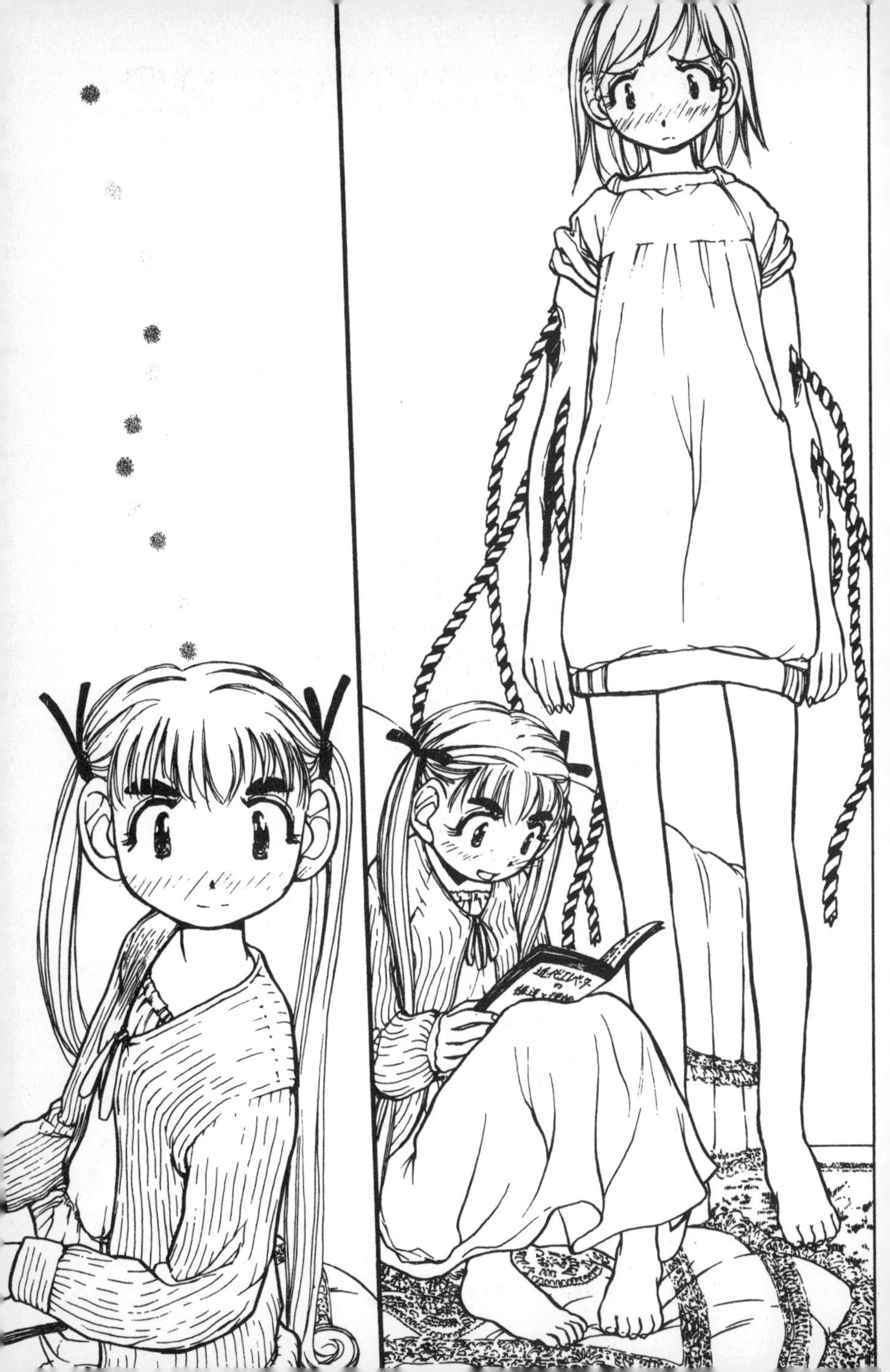
近代エレベータ
の

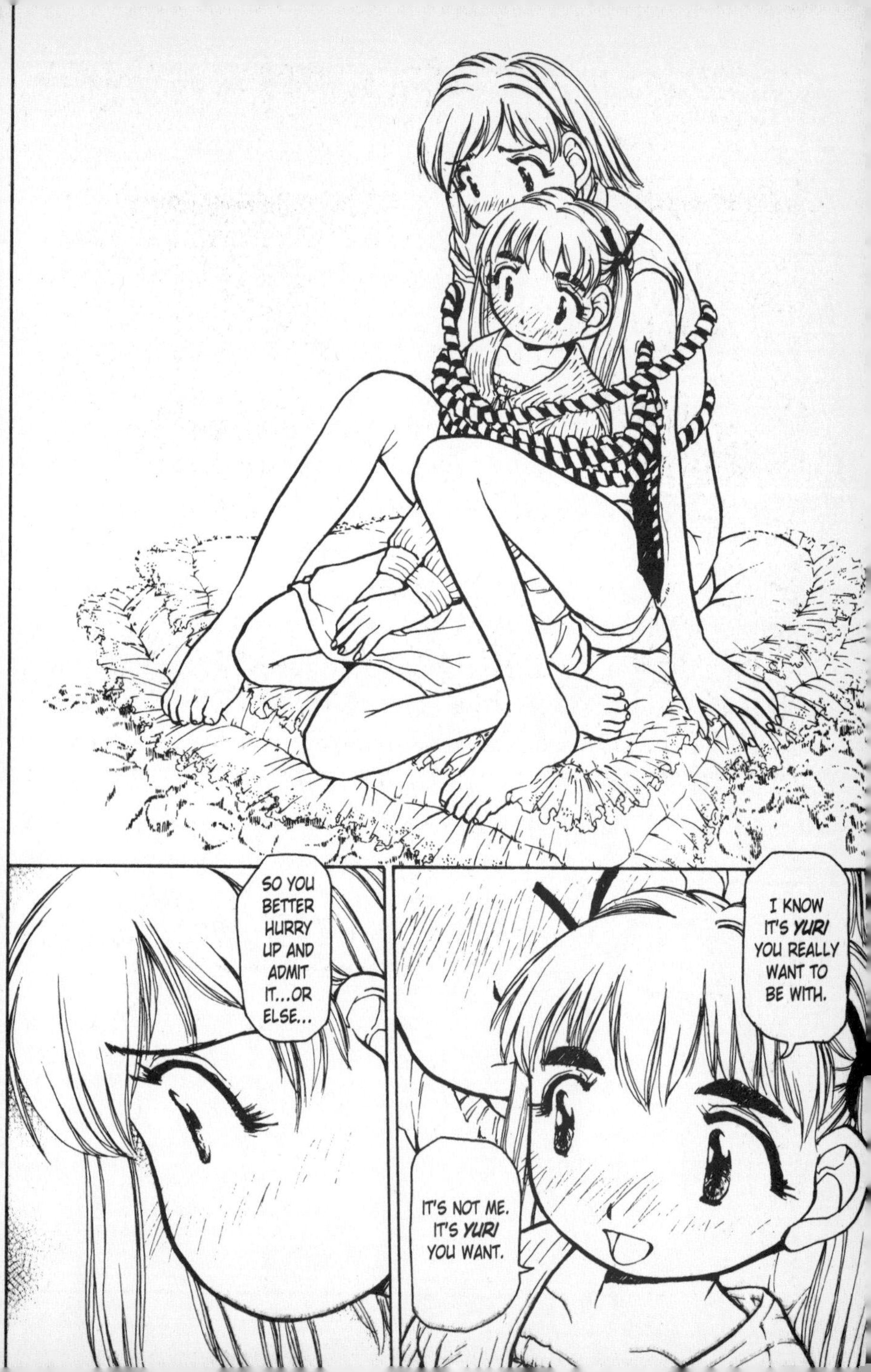
I KNOW IT'S YURI YOU REALLY WANT TO BE WITH.
IT'S NOT ME. IT'S YURI YOU WANT.
SO YOU BETTER HURRY UP AND ADMIT IT...OR ELSE...

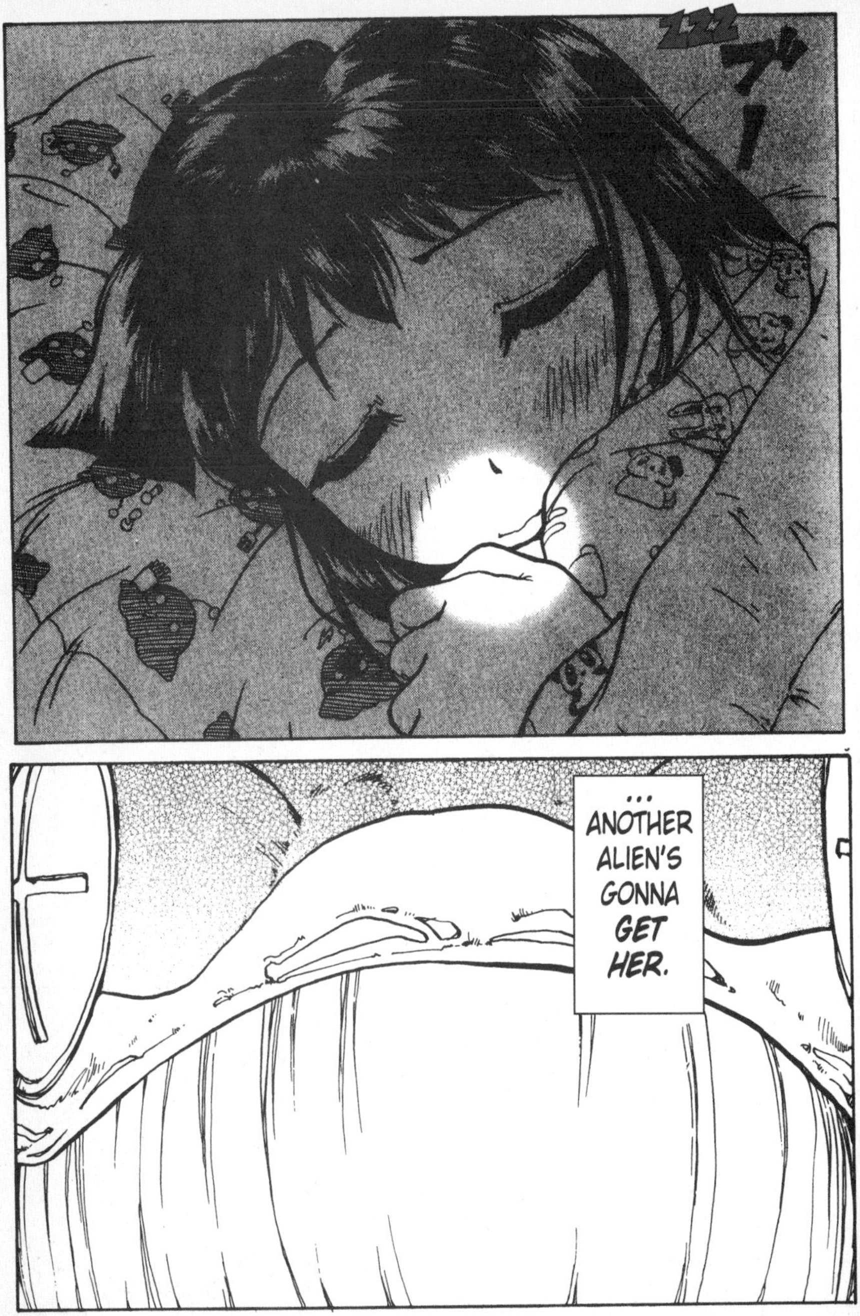
ZZZ
ブー
... ANOTHER ALIEN'S GONNA GET HER.

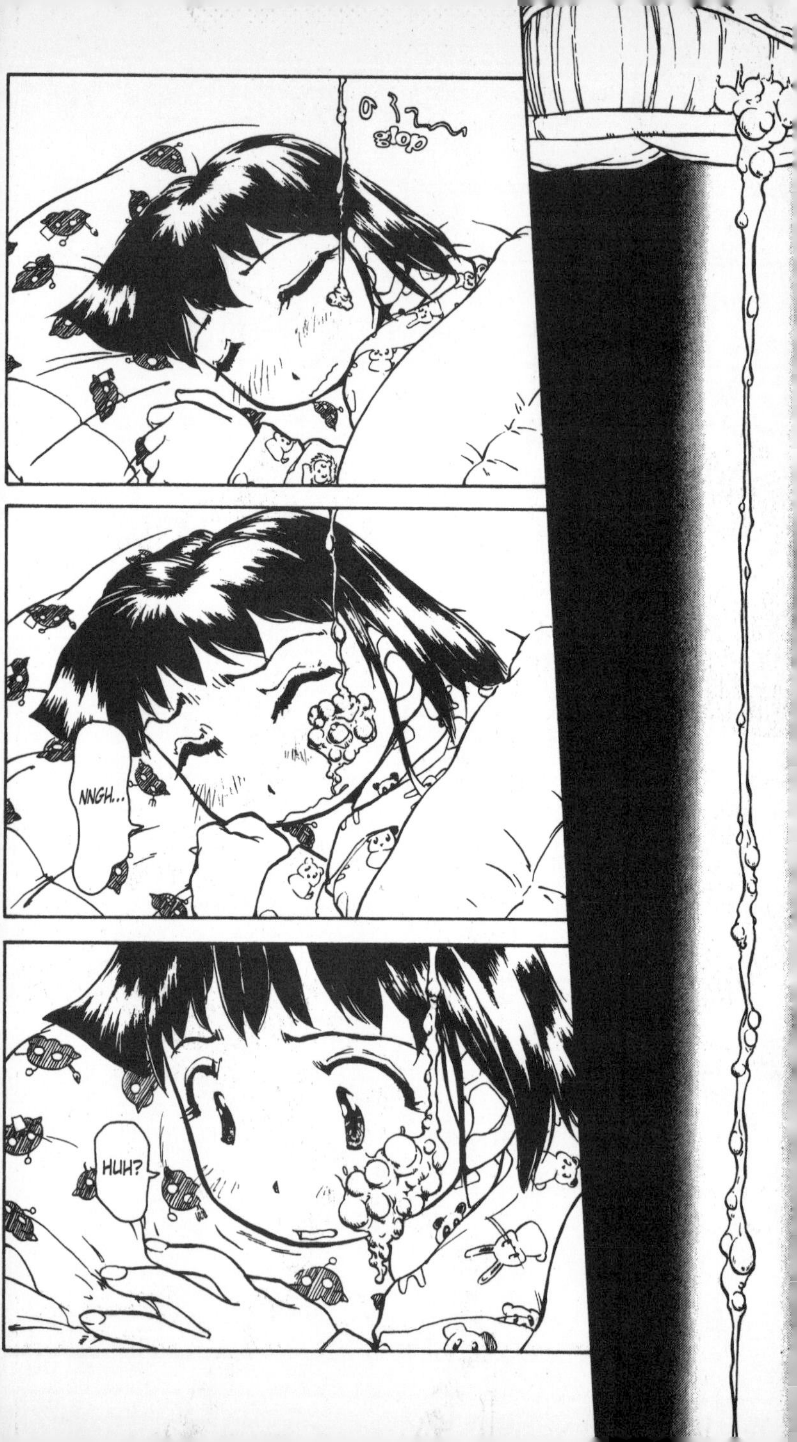
glop
NNGH...
HUH?

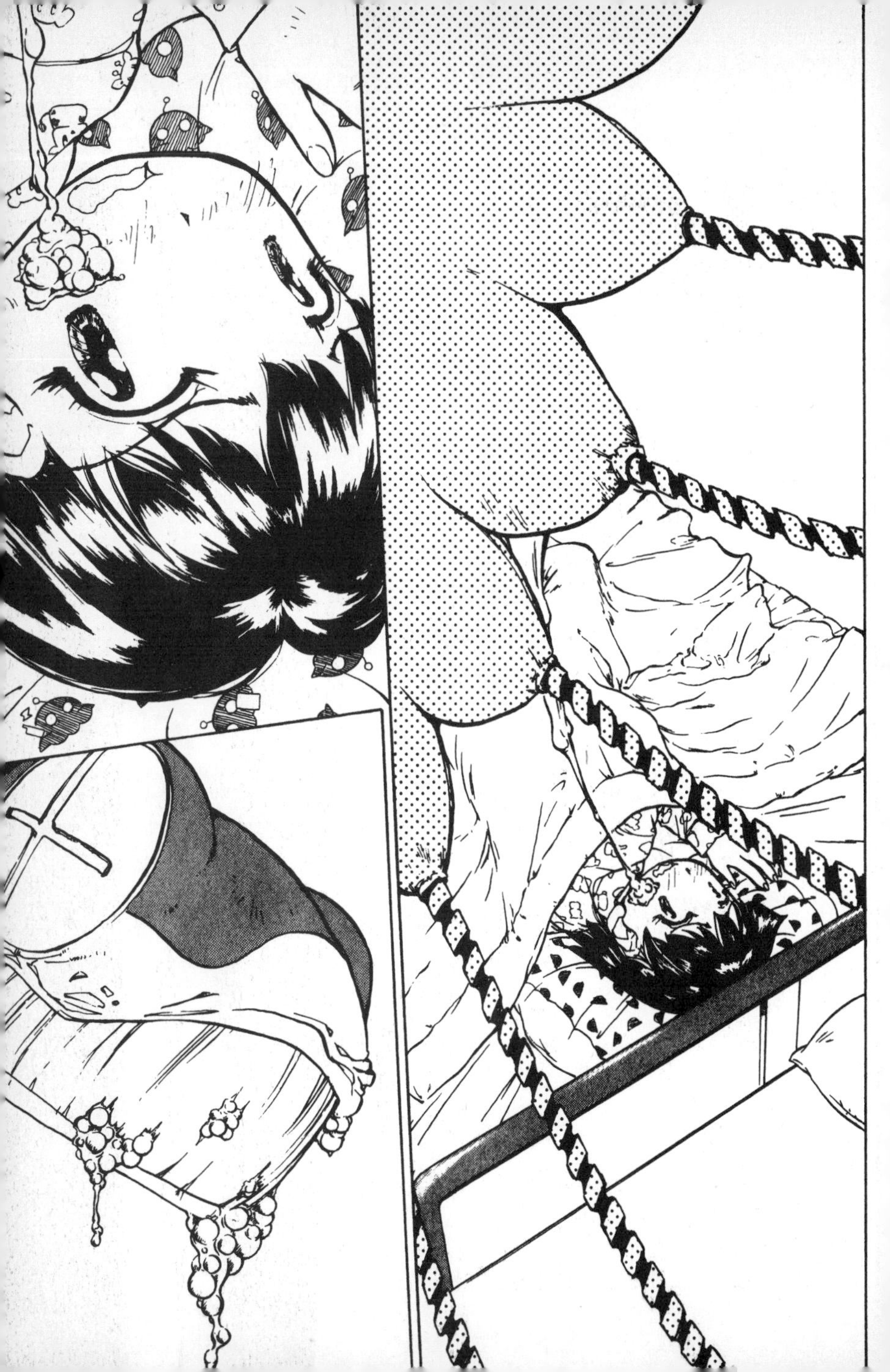

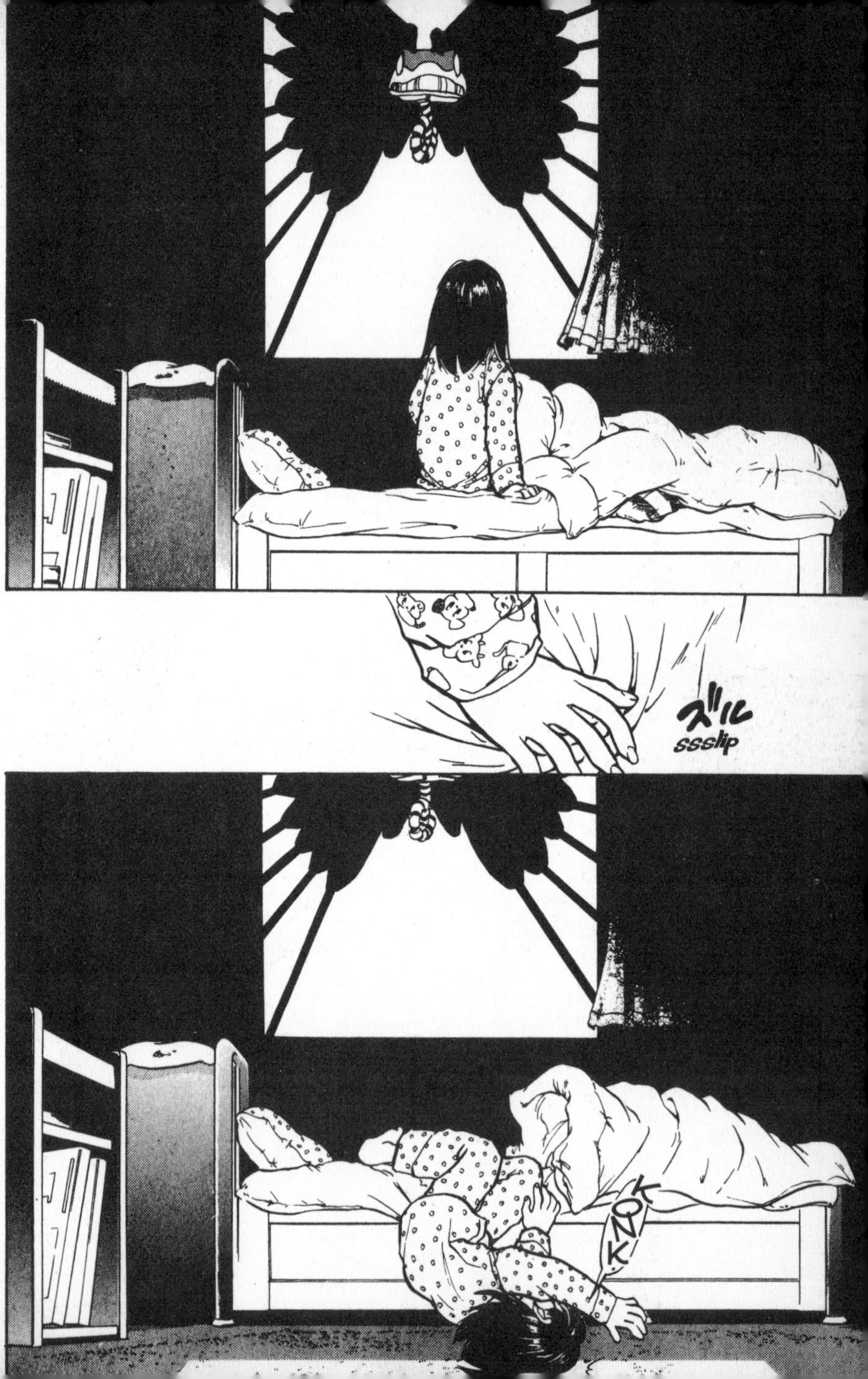
ズル
ssslip
KONK

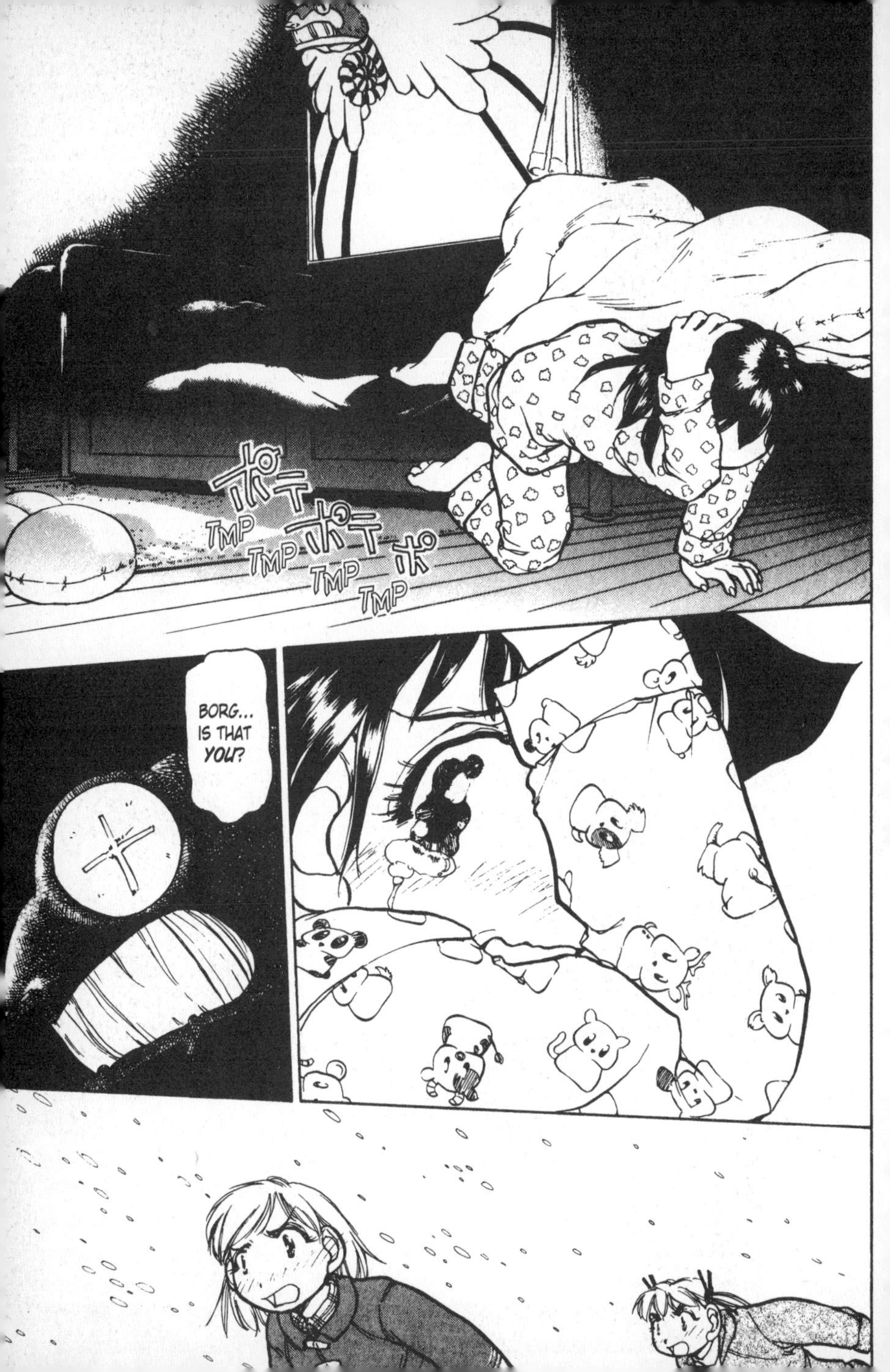
ポテ
TMP
ポテ
TMP
ポテ
TMP
ポ
TMP
BORG... IS THAT *YOU?*

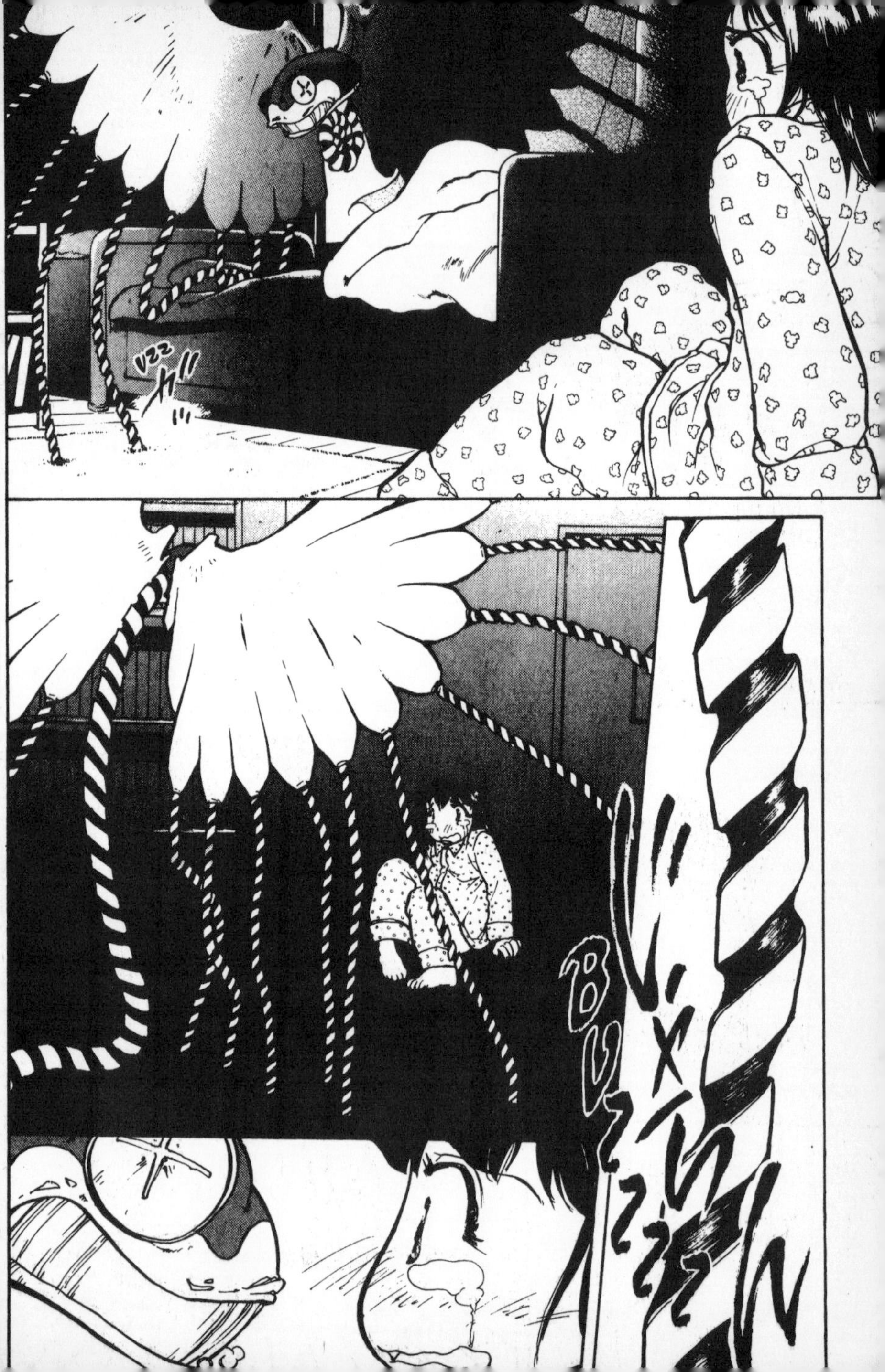
VZZ
BUZZ

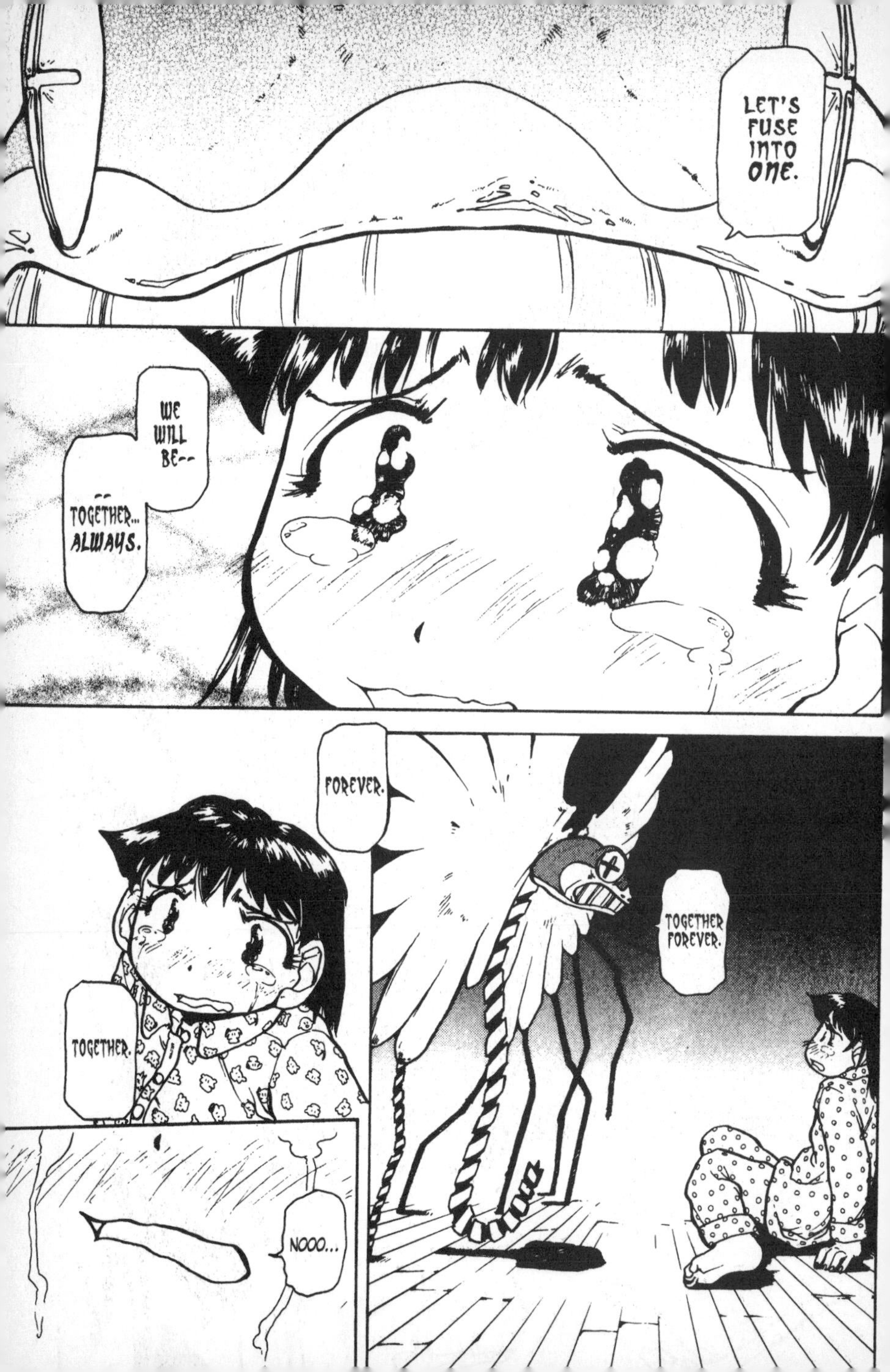

LET'S FUSE INTO ONE.
WE WILL BE--
--TOGETHER... ALWAYS.
FOREVER.
TOGETHER FOREVER.
TOGETHER.
NOOO...

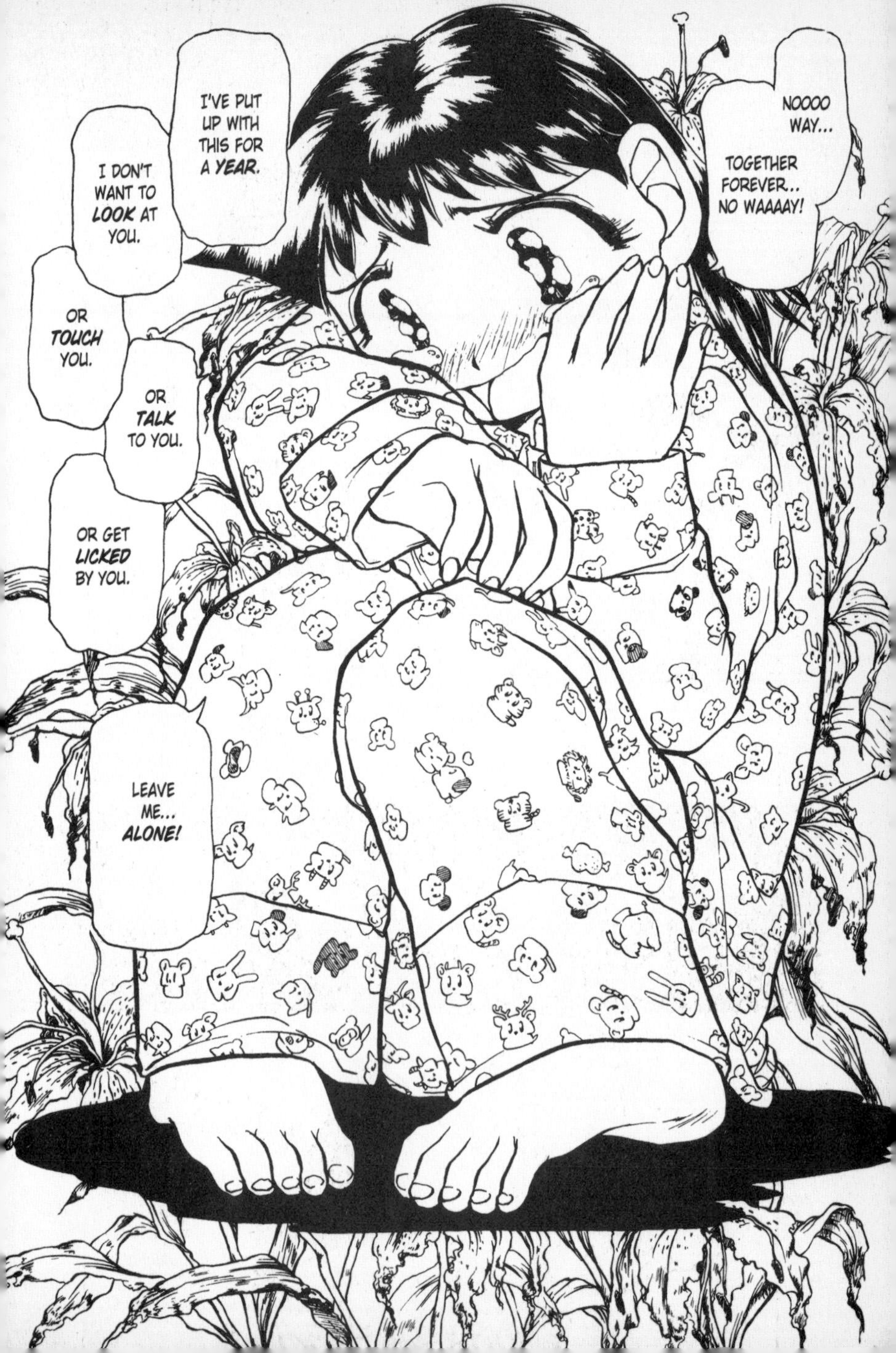
NOOOO WAY... TOGETHER FOREVER.. NO WAAAAY!
I'VE PUT UP WITH THIS FOR A YEAR.
I DON'T WANT TO LOOK AT YOU.
OR TOUCH YOU.
OR TALK TO YOU.
OR GET LICKED BY YOU.
LEAVE ME... ALONE!

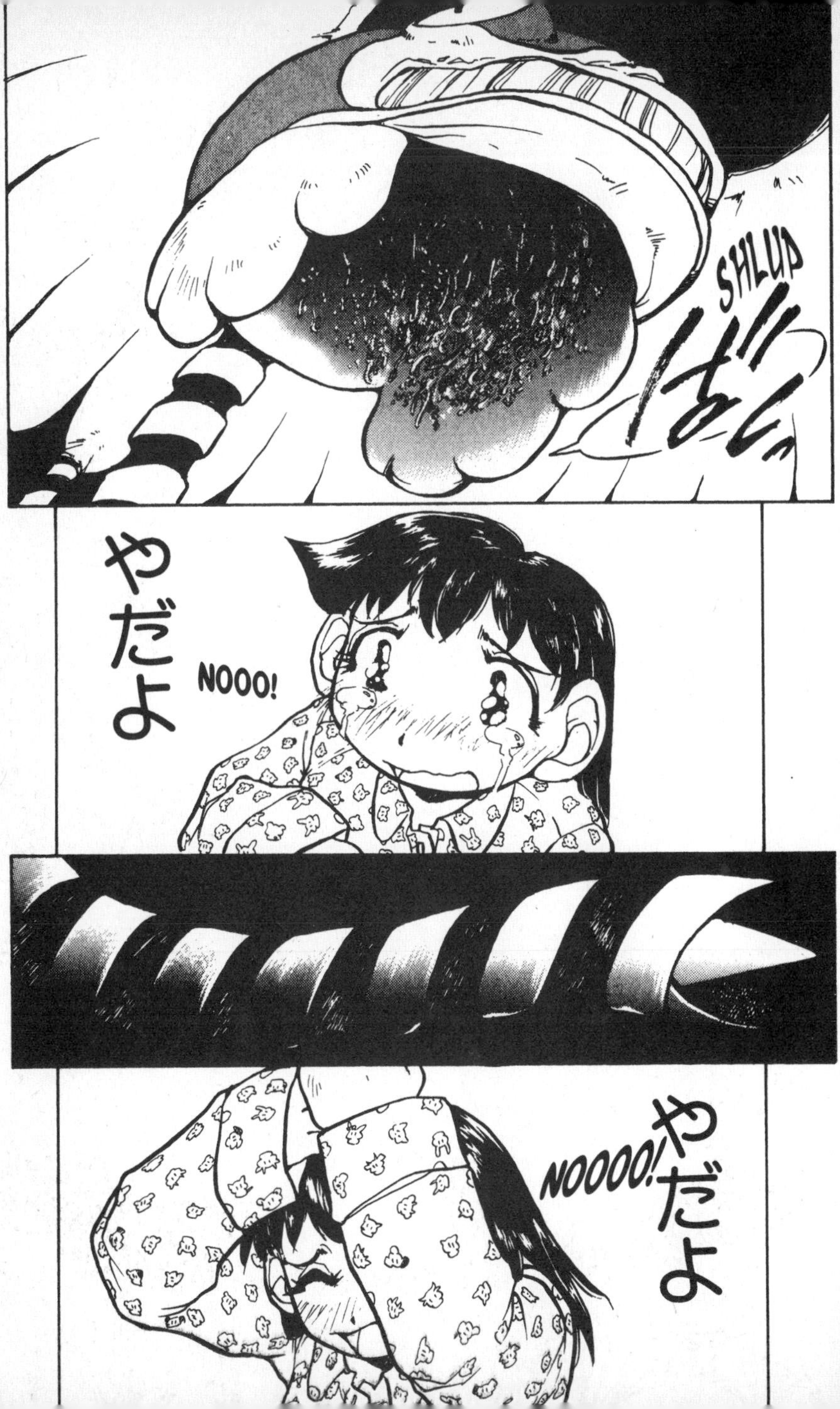
SHLUP
ばくっ
やだよ
NOOO!
やだよ
NOOOO!

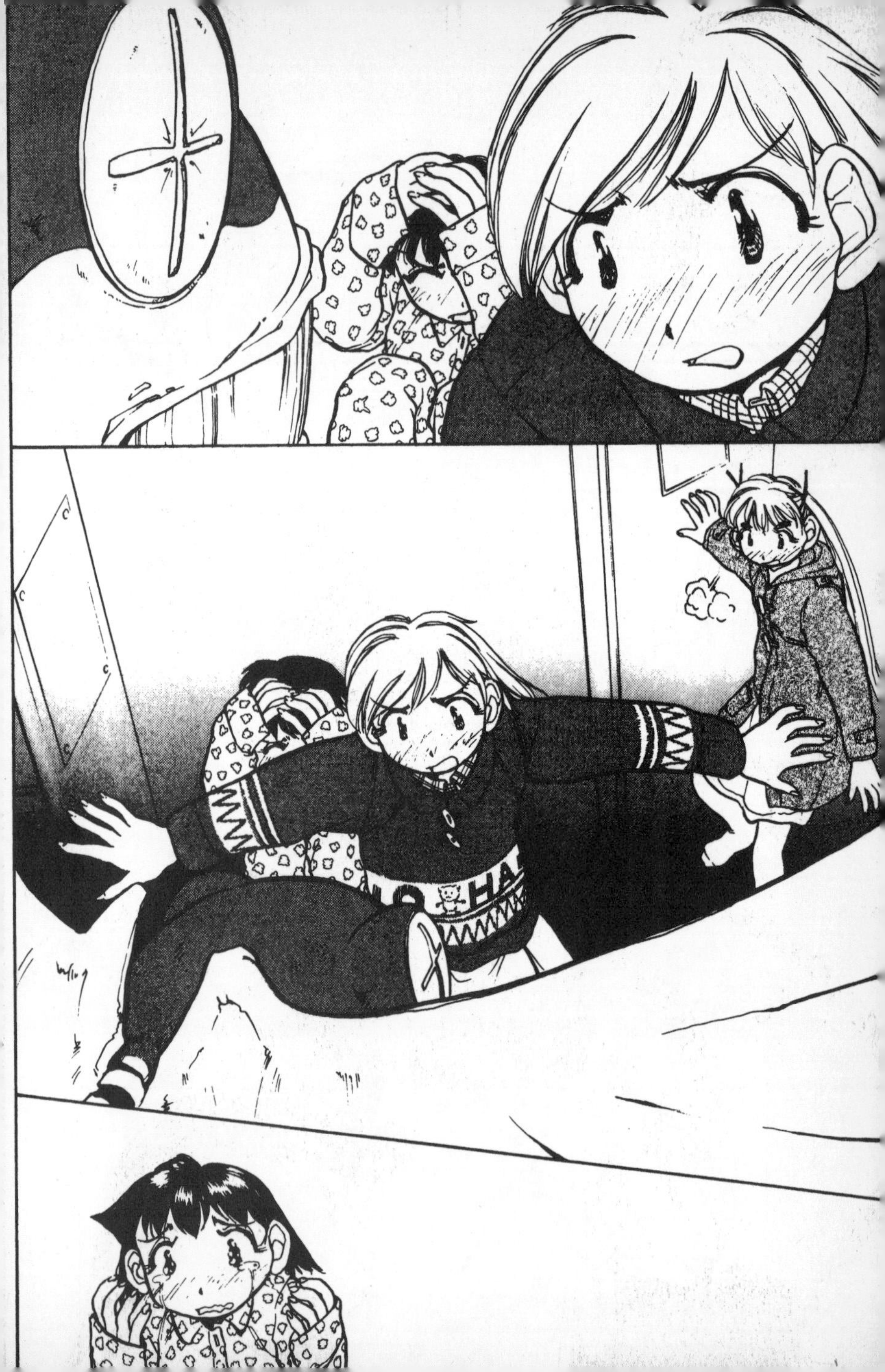

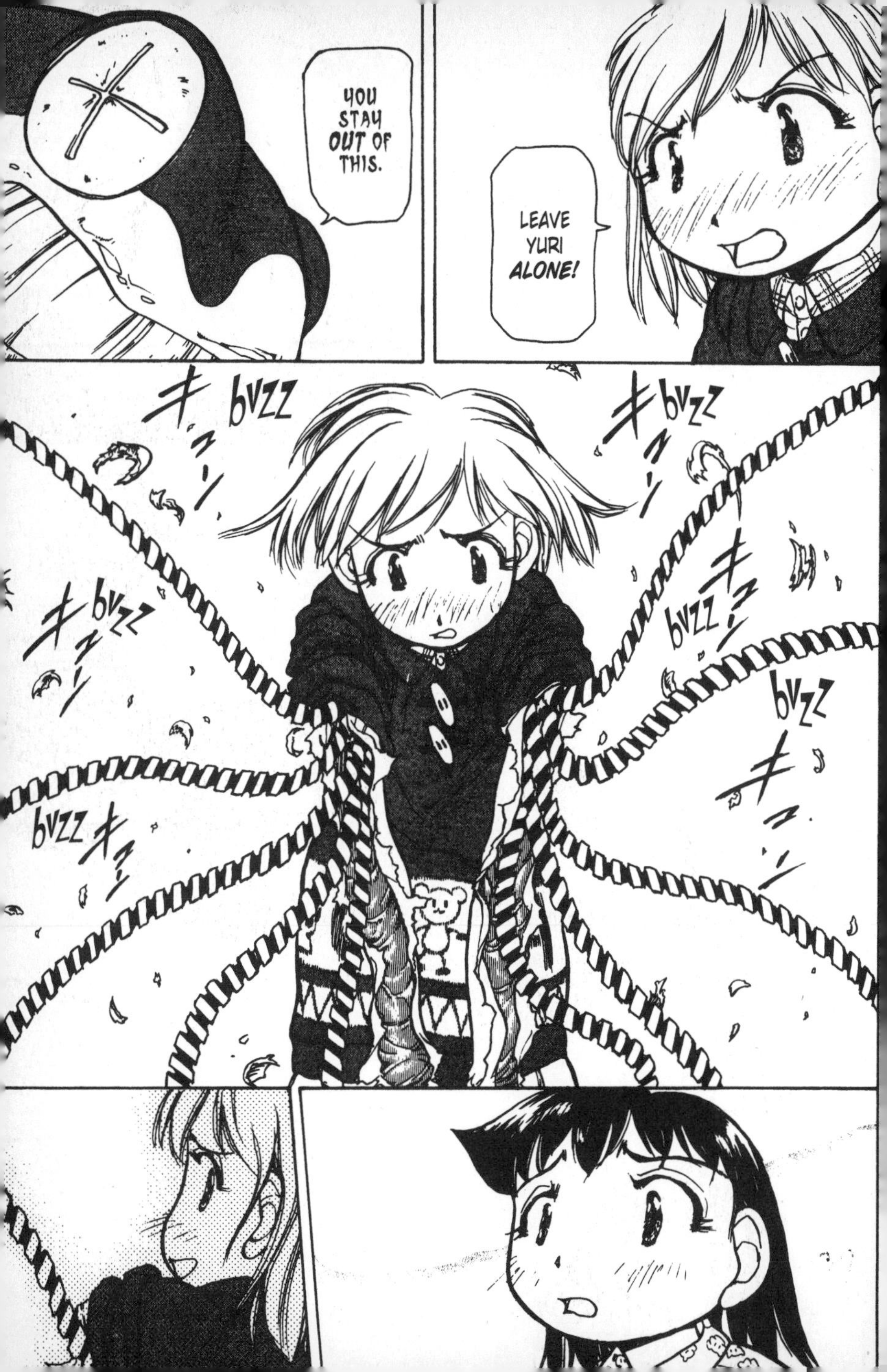
LEAVE YURI ALONE!
YOU STAY OUT OF THIS.
bvzz
bvzz
bvzz
bvzz
bvzz
bvzz

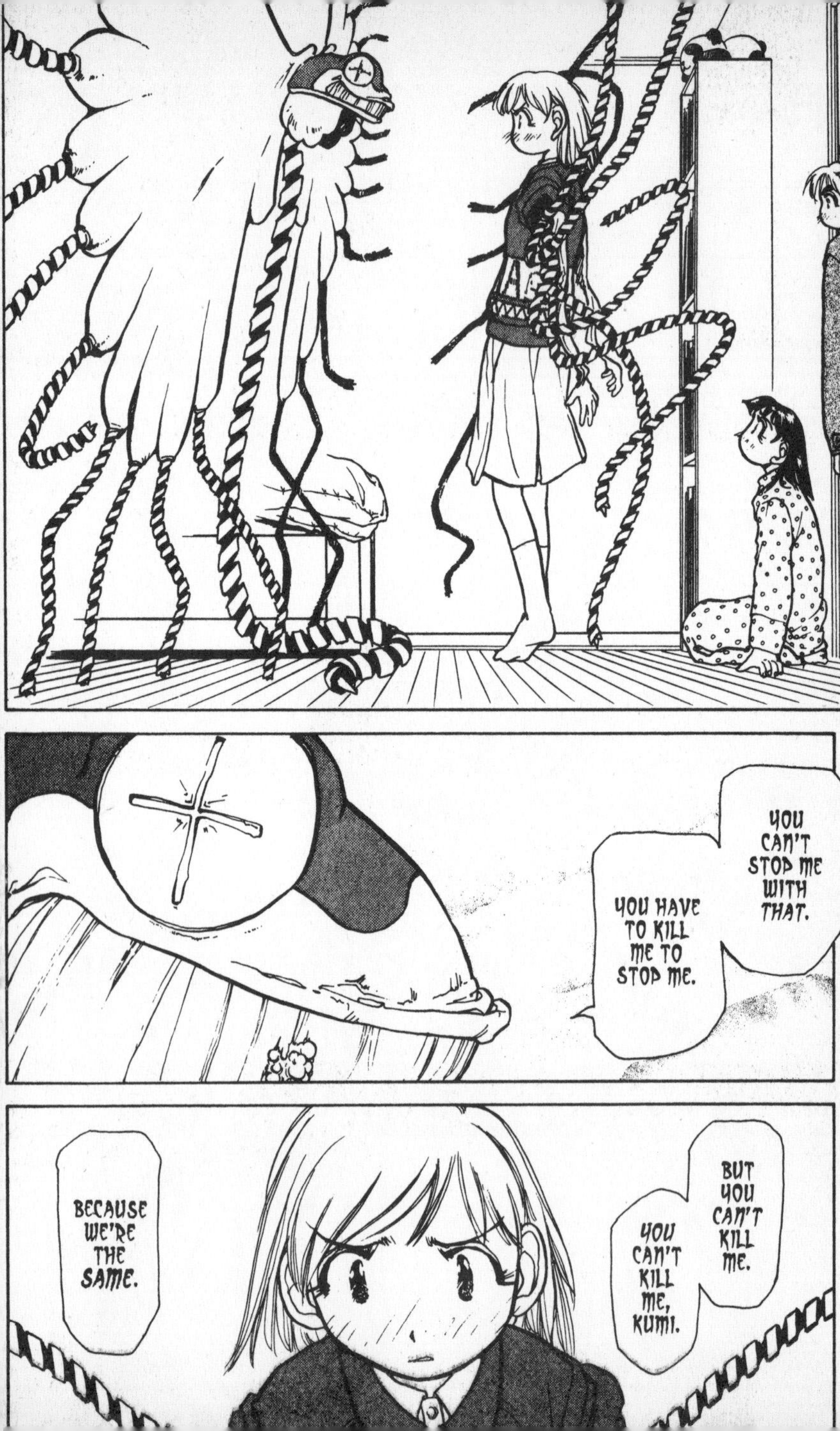
YOU CAN'T STOP ME WITH THAT.
YOU HAVE TO KILL ME TO STOP ME.
BUT YOU CAN'T KILL ME.
YOU CAN'T KILL ME, KUMI.
BECAUSE WE'RE THE SAME.

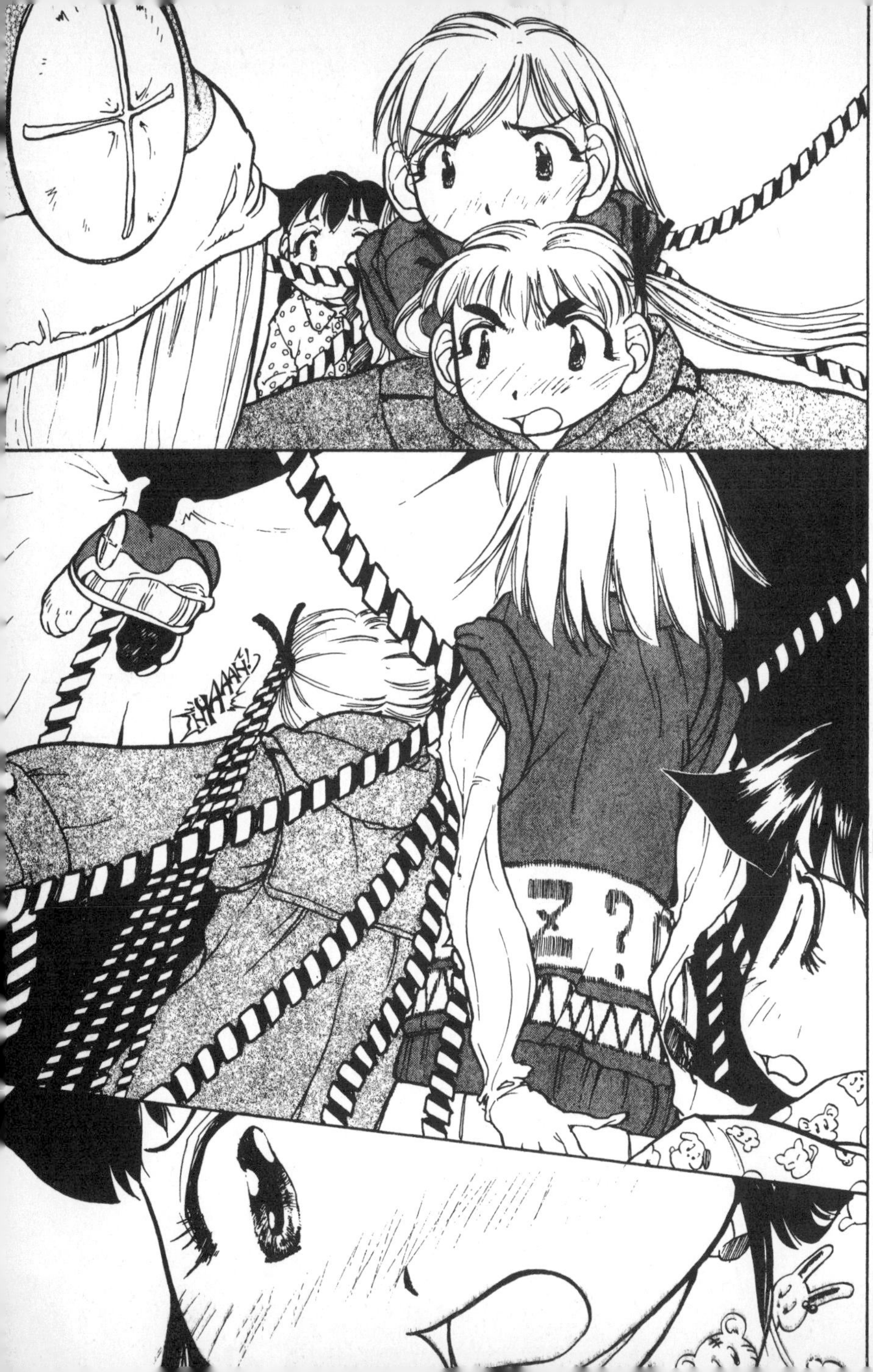
CHAAAK!

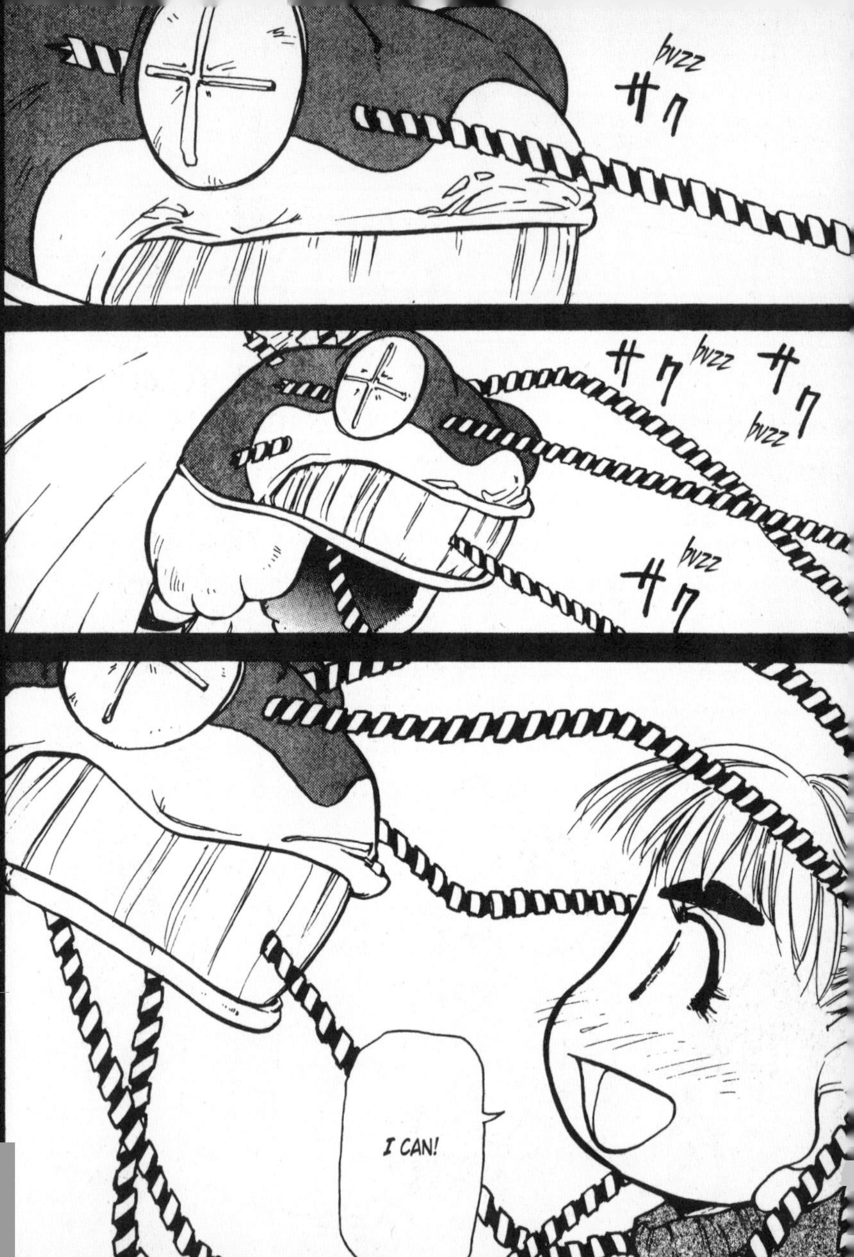
buzz
サク
buzz
サク
buzz
サク
buzz
サク
I CAN!

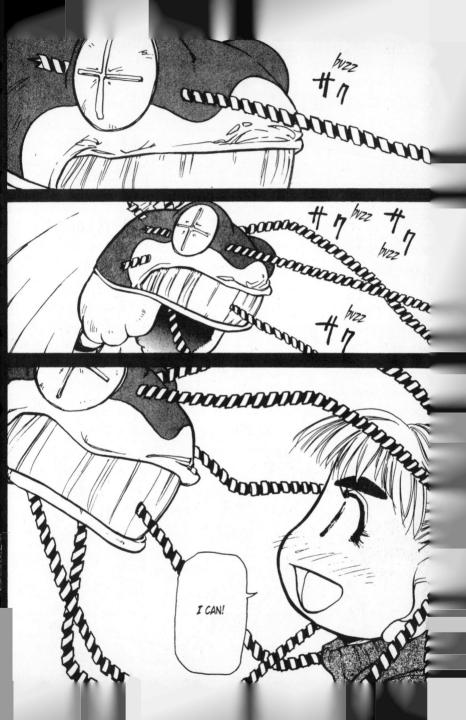

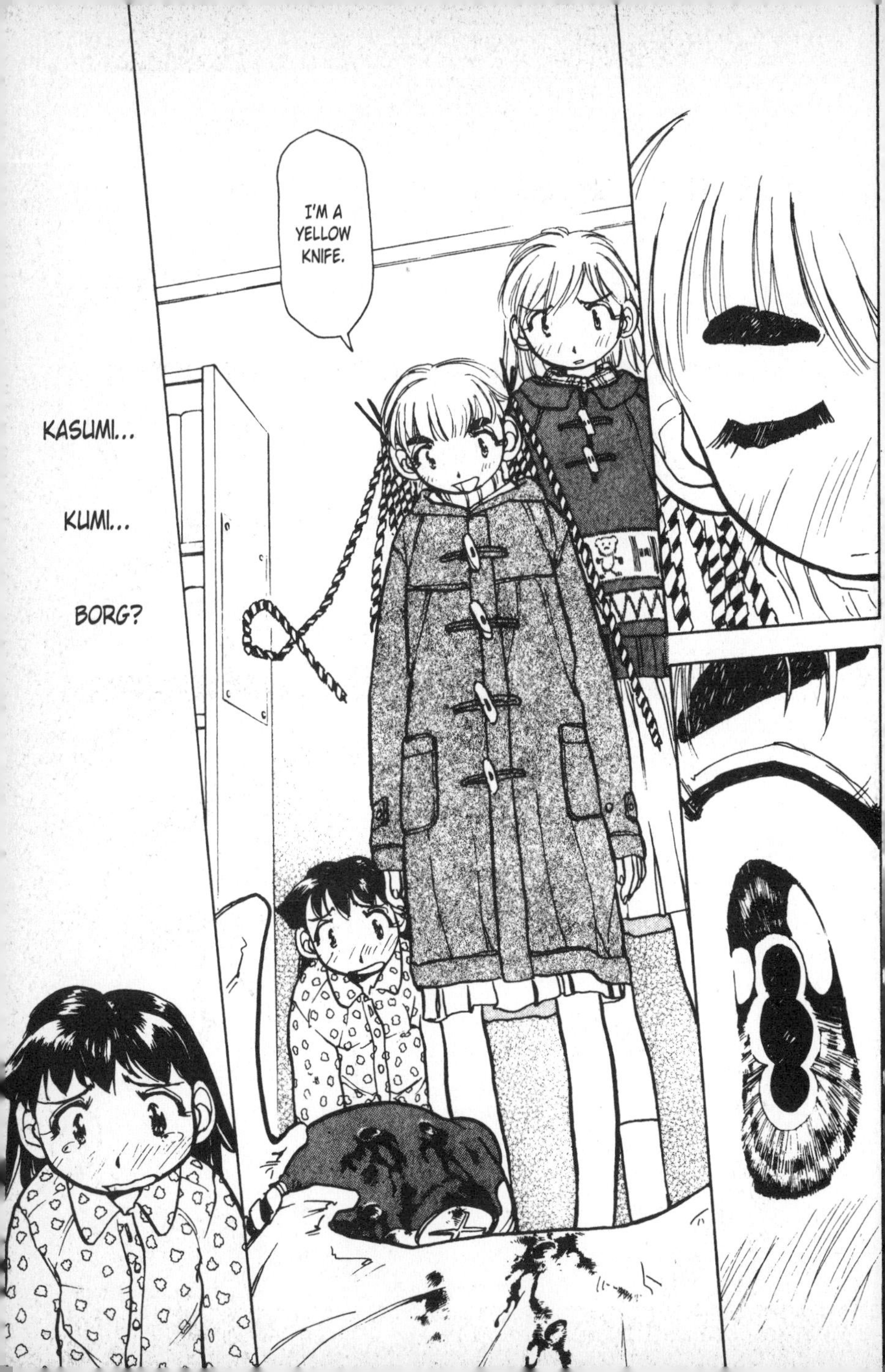
I'M A YELLOW KNIFE.
KASUMI...
KUMI...
BORG?

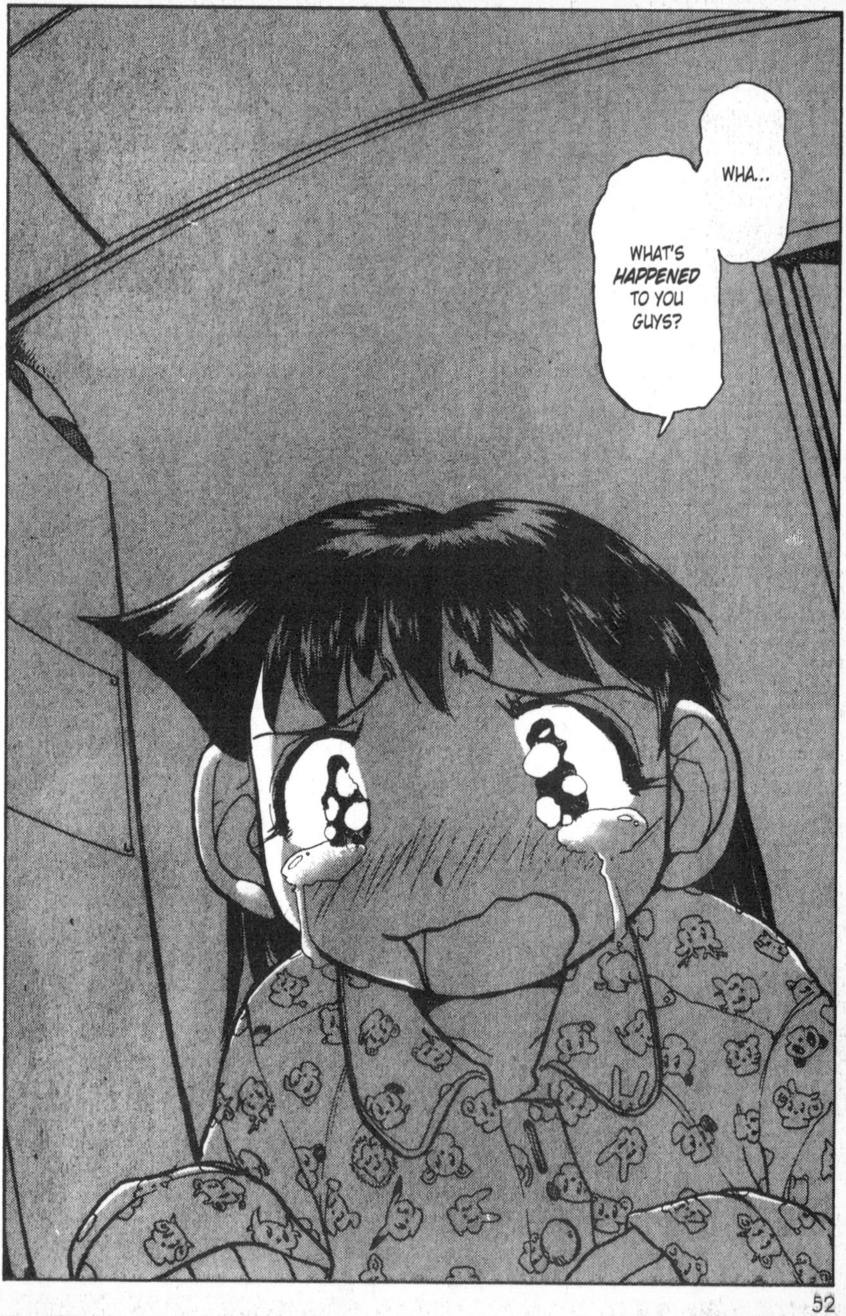
WHA...
WHAT'S *HAPPENED* TO YOU GUYS?

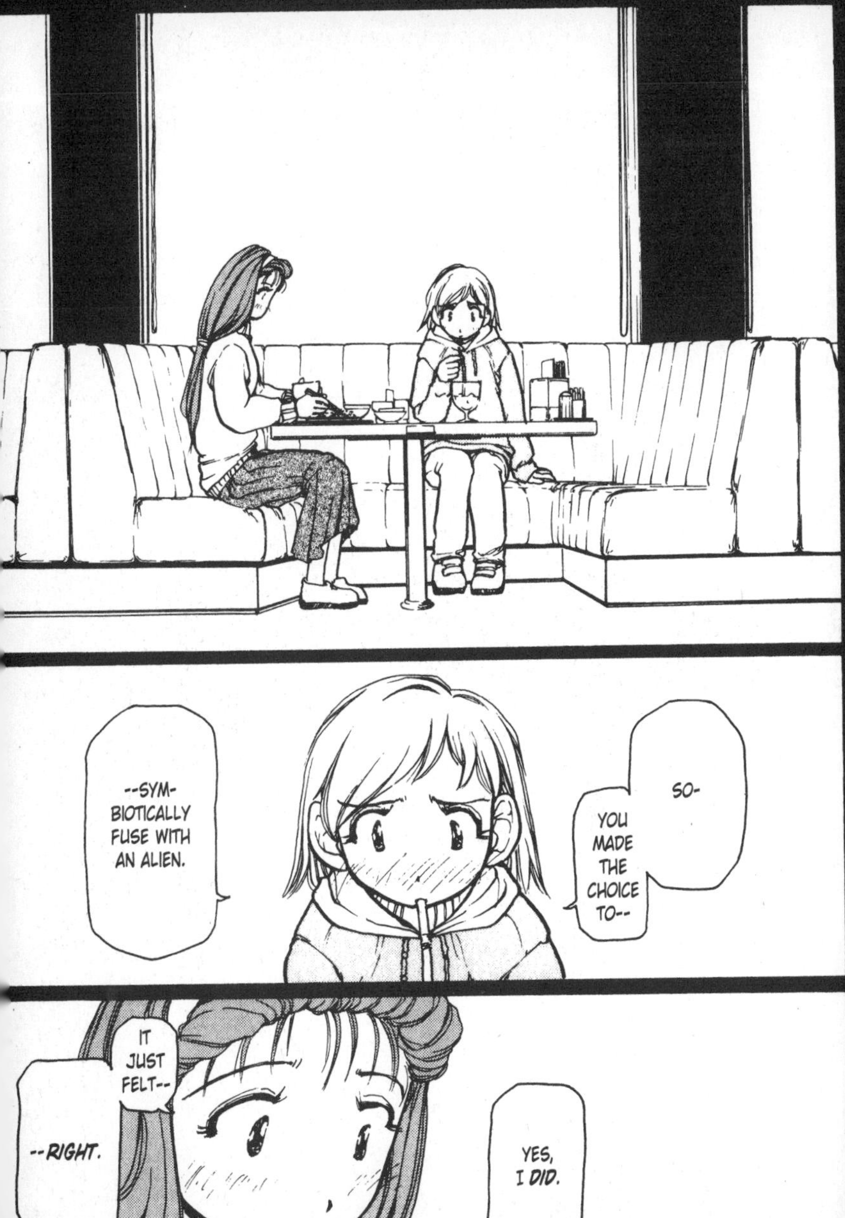
SO-
YOU MADE THE CHOICE TO--
--SYM-BIOTICALLY FUSE WITH AN ALIEN.
YES, I *DID*.
IT JUST FELT--
--*RIGHT*.

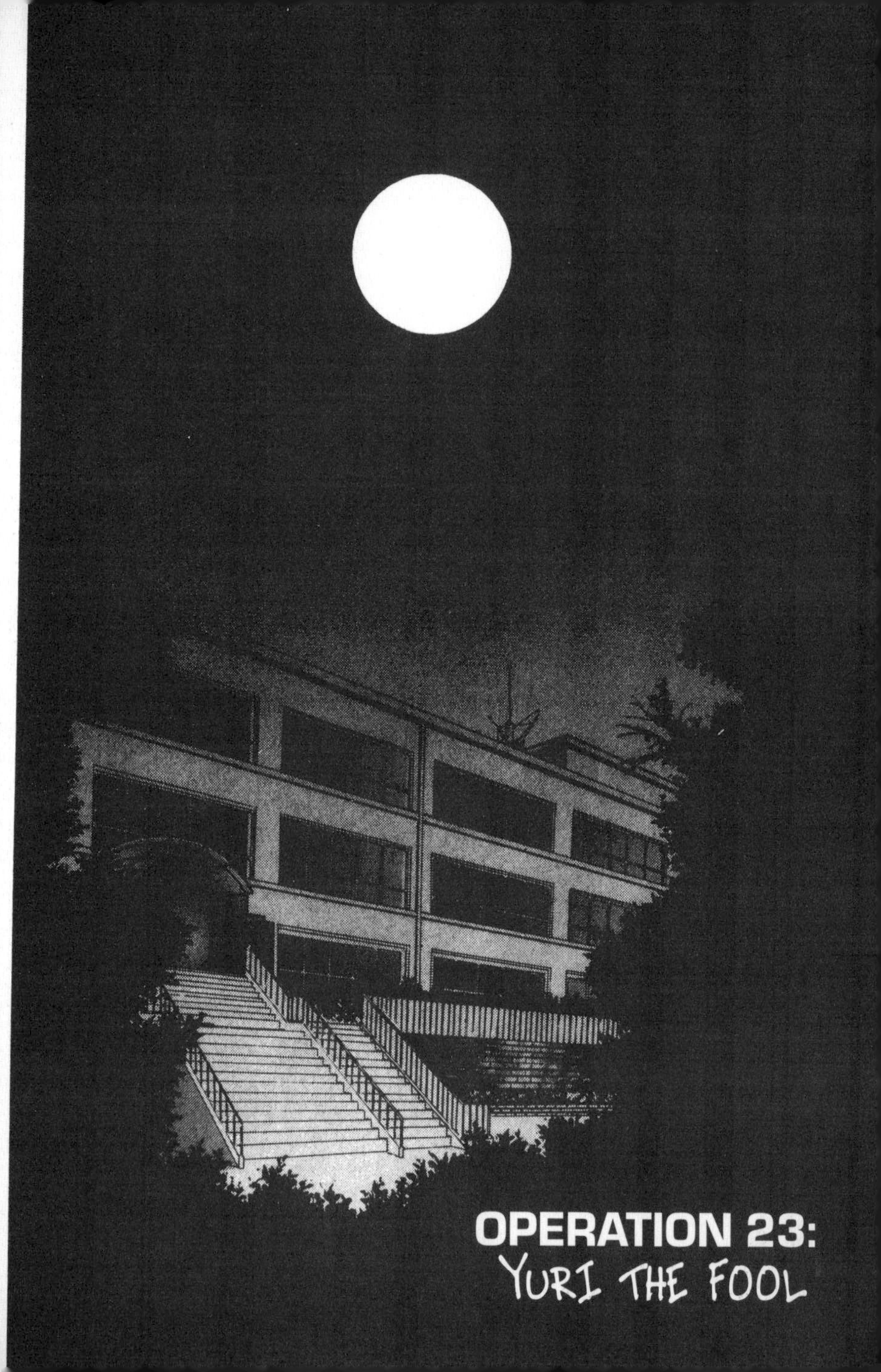
OPERATION 23:
YURI THE FOOL

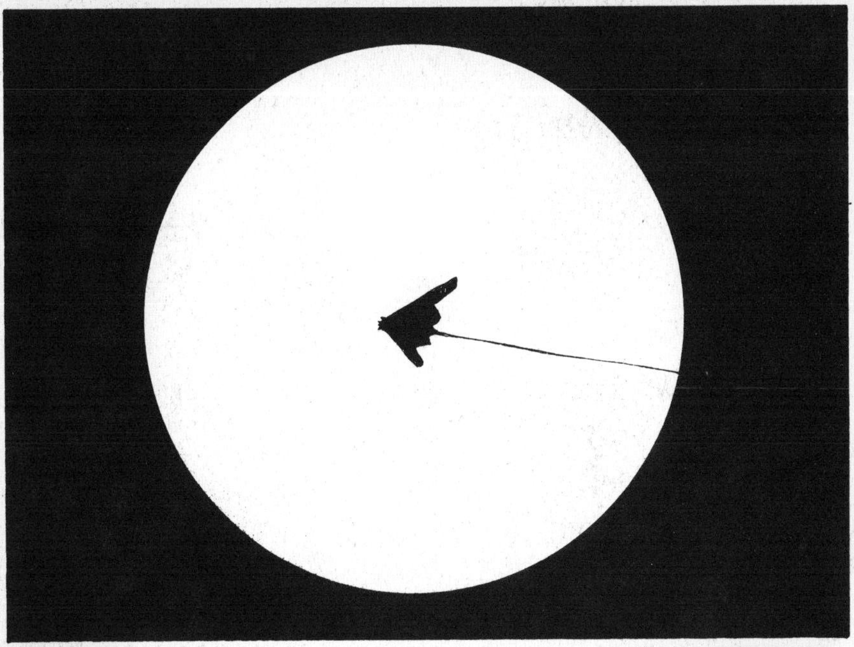

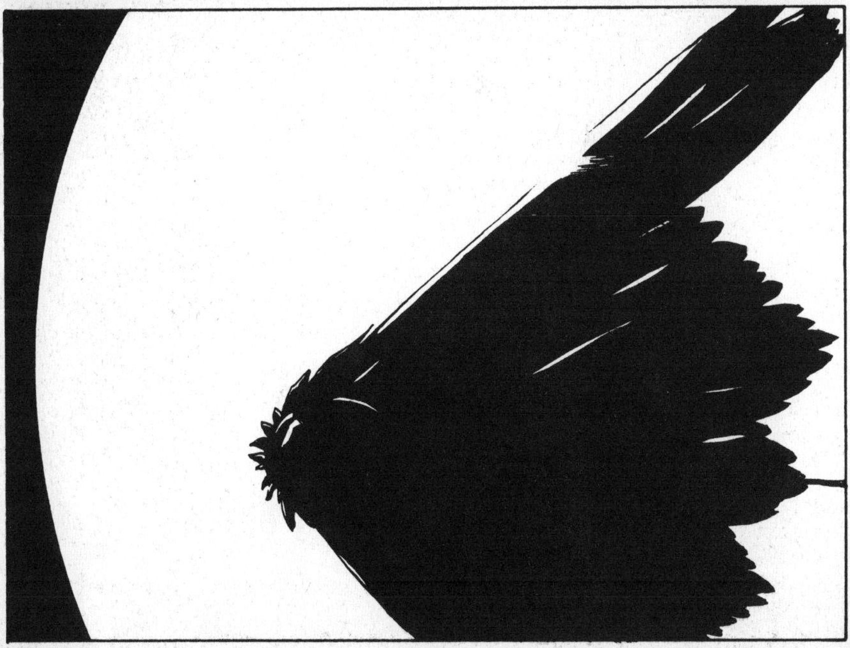

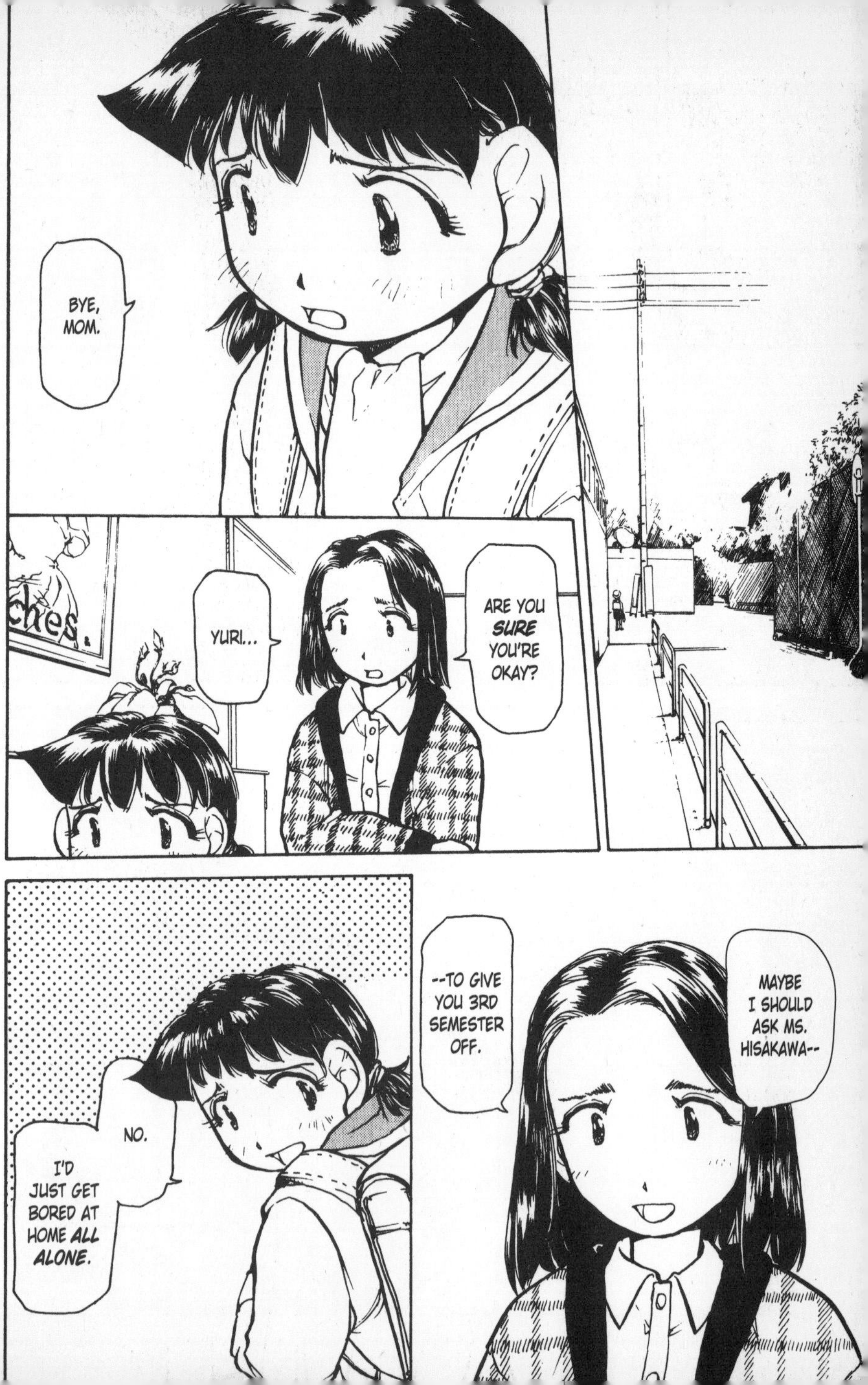
BYE, MOM.
ARE YOU SURE YOU'RE OKAY?
YURI...
MAYBE I SHOULD ASK MS. HISAKAWA--
--TO GIVE YOU 3RD SEMESTER OFF.
NO.
I'D JUST GET BORED AT HOME ALL ALONE.

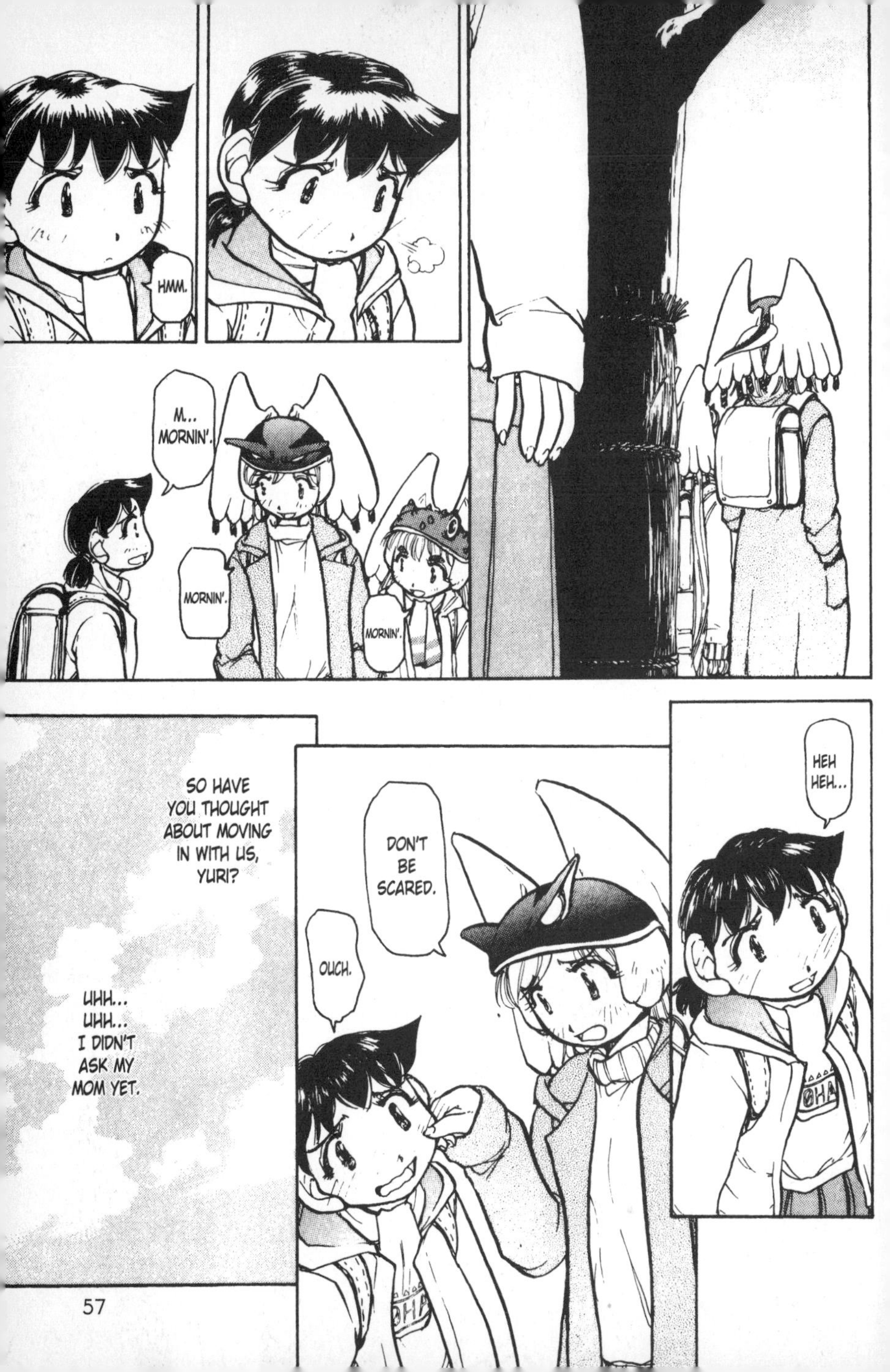
HMM.
M... MORNIN'.
MORNIN'.
MORNIN'.
HEH HEH...
DON'T BE SCARED.
OUCH.
SO HAVE YOU THOUGHT ABOUT MOVING IN WITH US, YURI?
UHH... UHH... I DIDN'T ASK MY MOM YET.

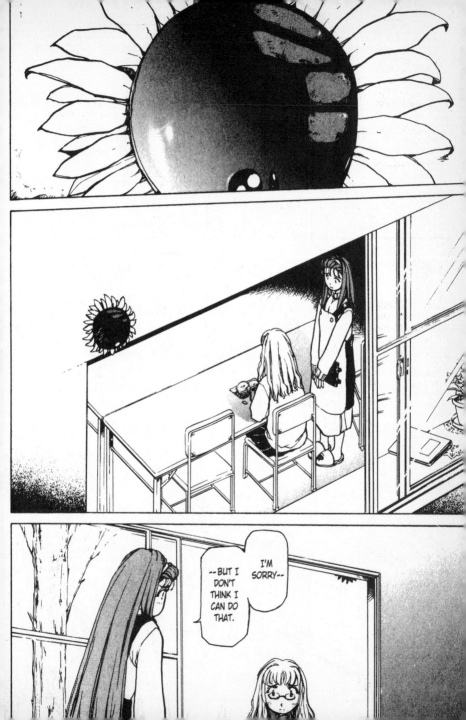

--BUT I DON'T THINK I CAN DO THAT.

I'M SORRY--

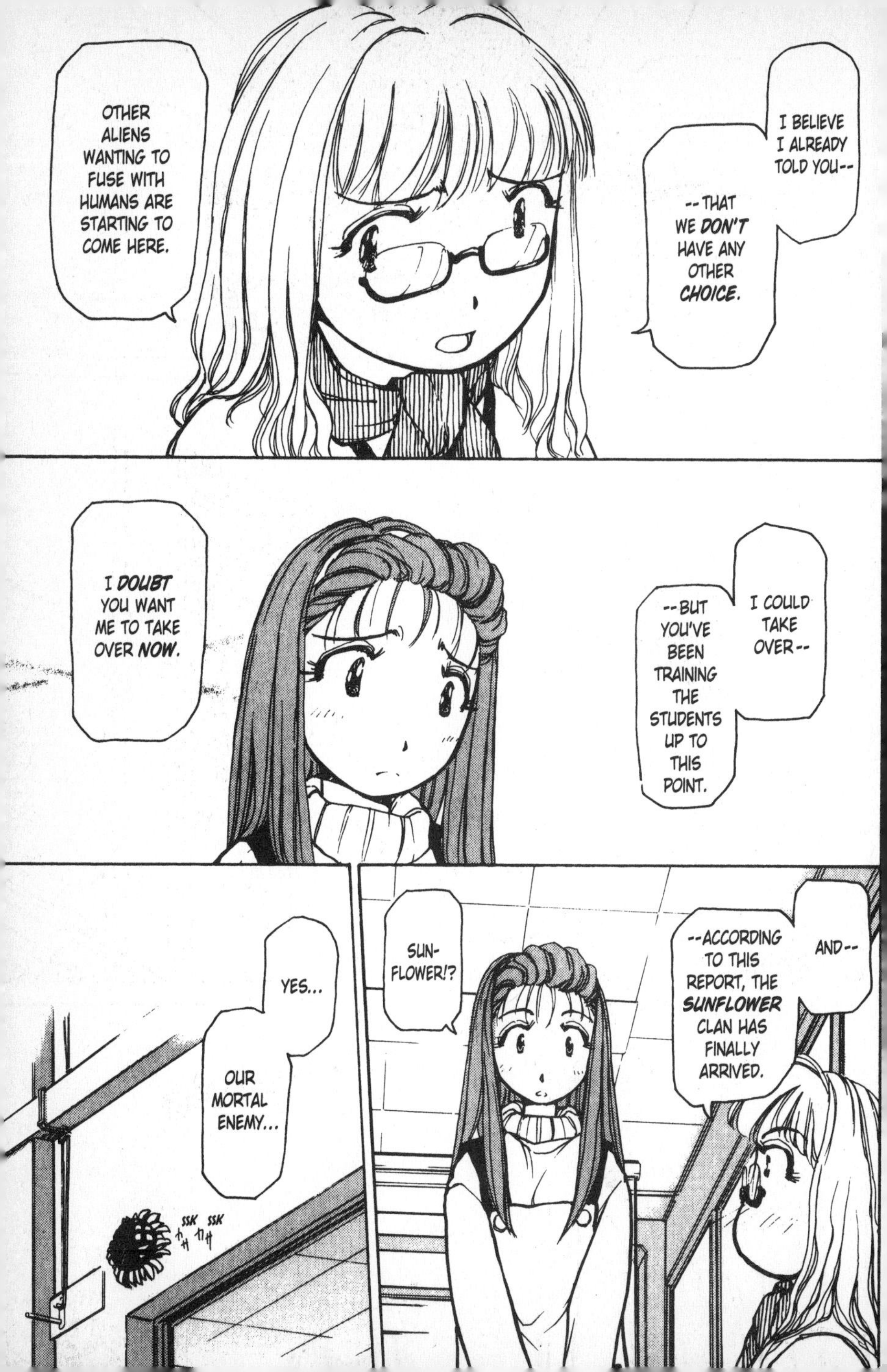

I BELIEVE I ALREADY TOLD YOU--
--THAT WE **DON'T** HAVE ANY OTHER **CHOICE**.
OTHER ALIENS WANTING TO FUSE WITH HUMANS ARE STARTING TO COME HERE.
I COULD TAKE OVER--
--BUT YOU'VE BEEN TRAINING THE STUDENTS UP TO THIS POINT.
I **DOUBT** YOU WANT ME TO TAKE OVER **NOW**.
AND--
--ACCORDING TO THIS REPORT, THE **SUNFLOWER** CLAN HAS FINALLY ARRIVED.
SUN-FLOWER!?
YES...
OUR MORTAL ENEMY...
SSK SSK

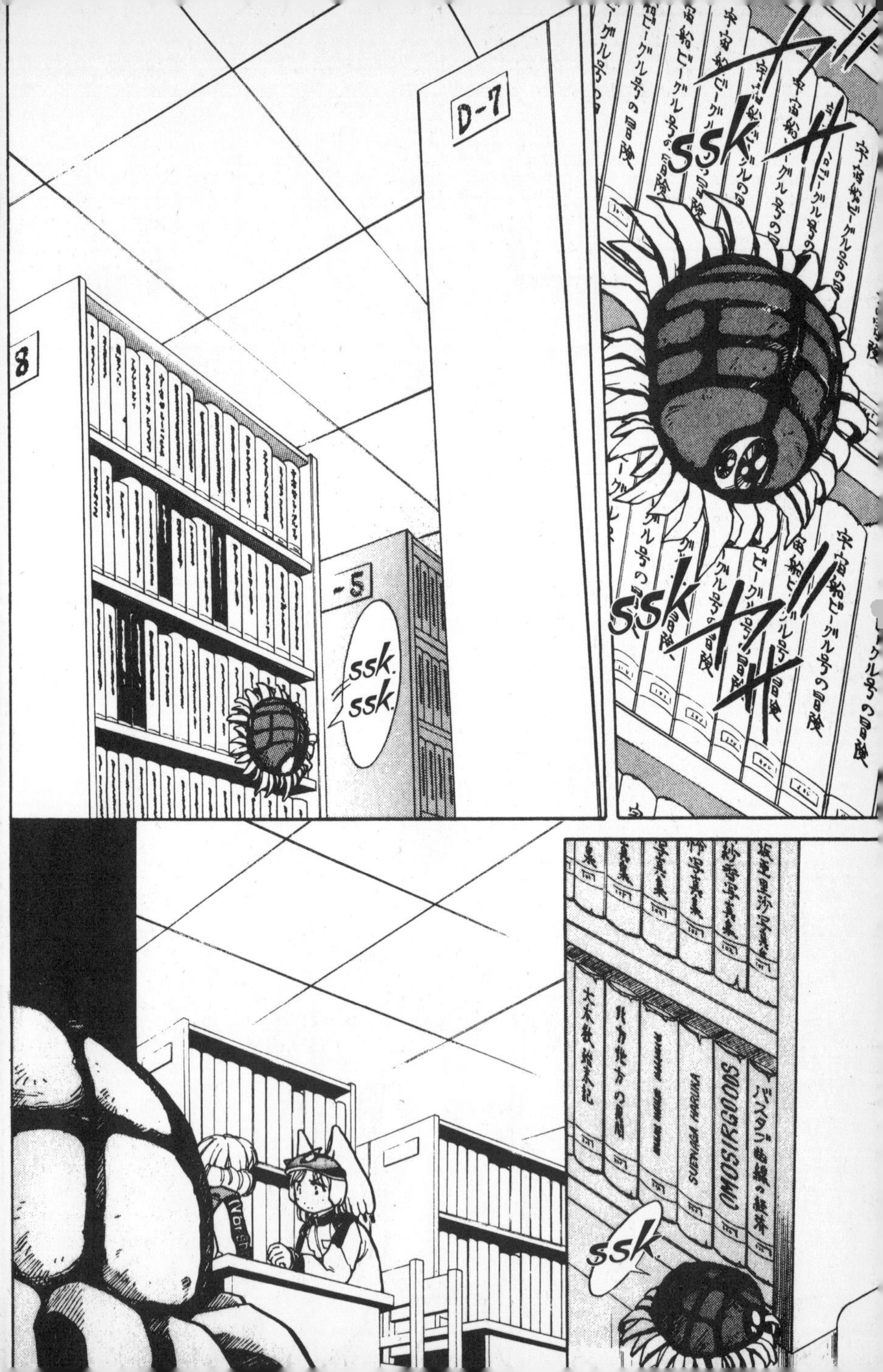
SSK
SSK
D-7
ssk. ssk.
-5
8
ssk.

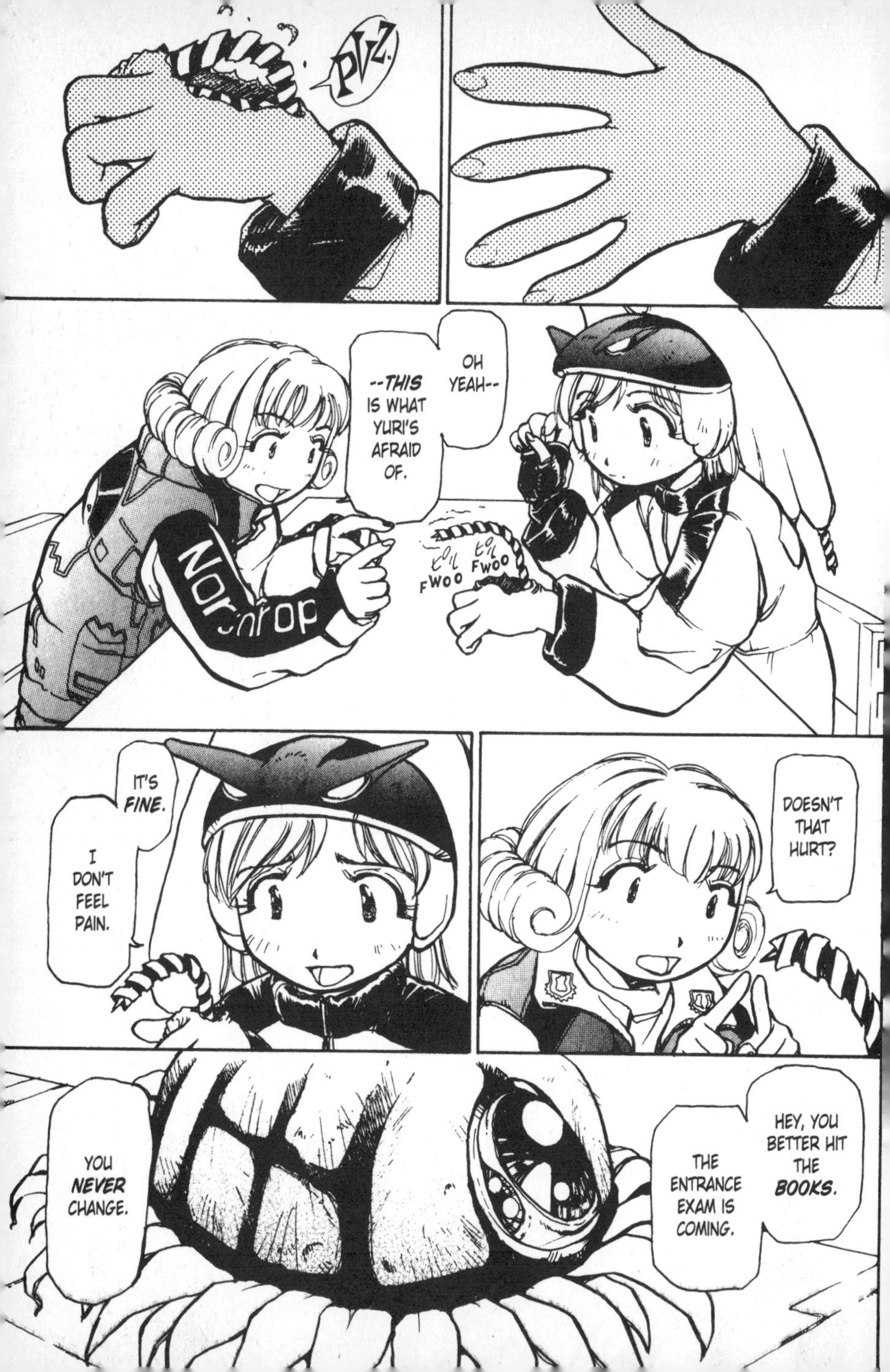
PVZ.
OH YEAH--
--THIS IS WHAT YURI'S AFRAID OF.
ピル FWOO ピル FWOO
DOESN'T THAT HURT?
IT'S FINE.
I DON'T FEEL PAIN.
HEY, YOU BETTER HIT THE BOOKS.
THE ENTRANCE EXAM IS COMING.
YOU NEVER CHANGE.

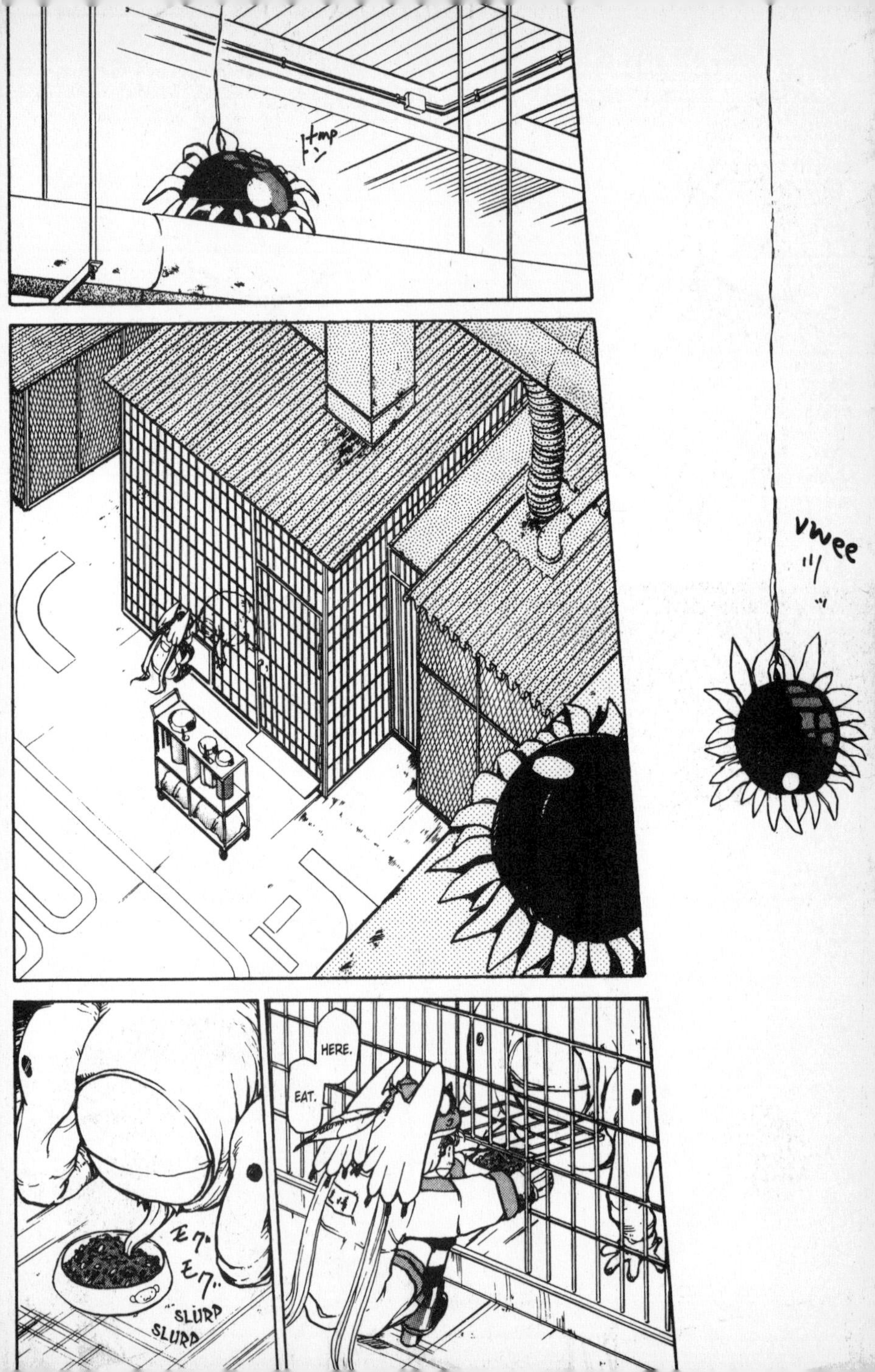
tmp
vwee
HERE.
EAT.
SLURP
SLURP

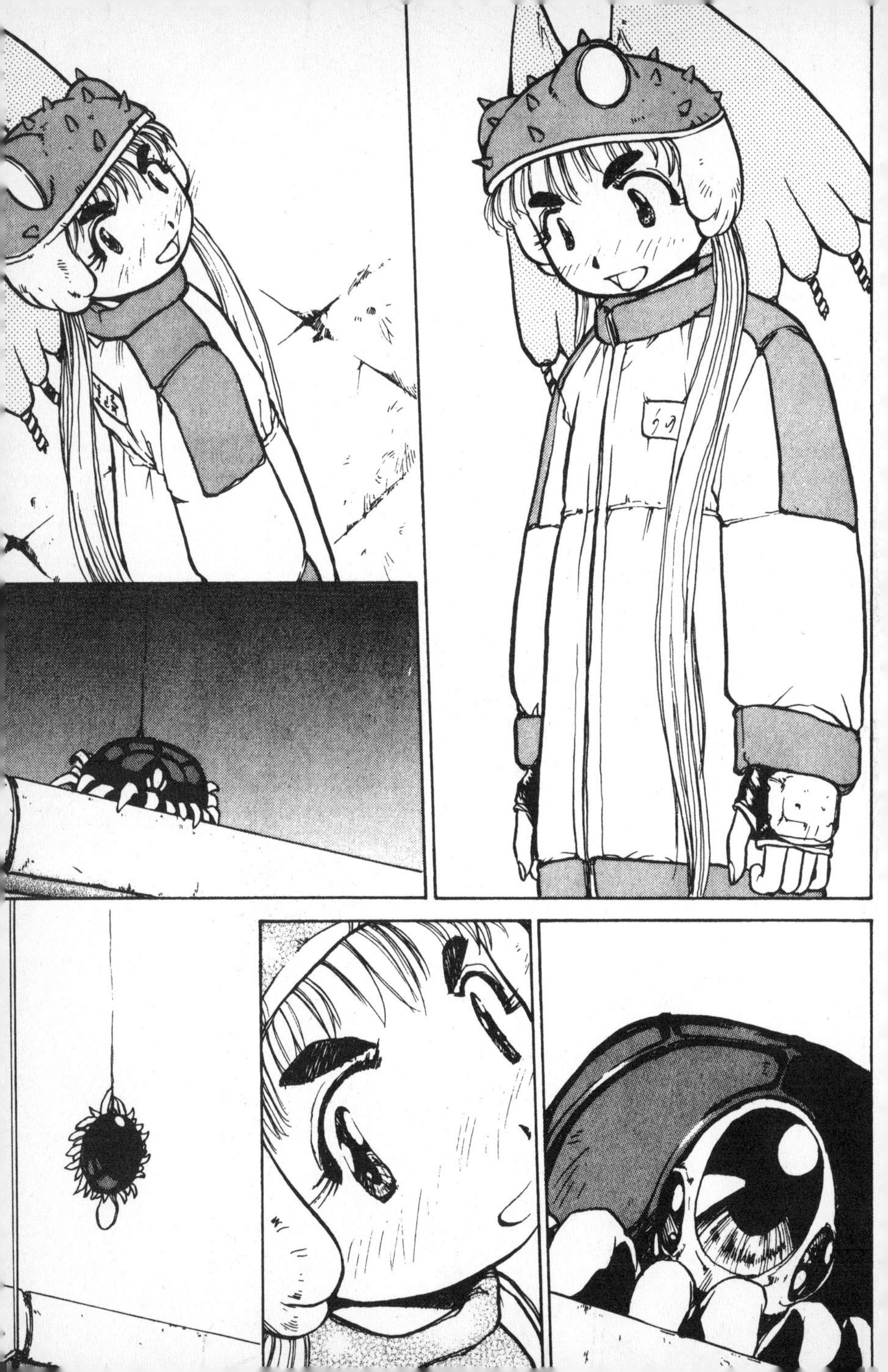

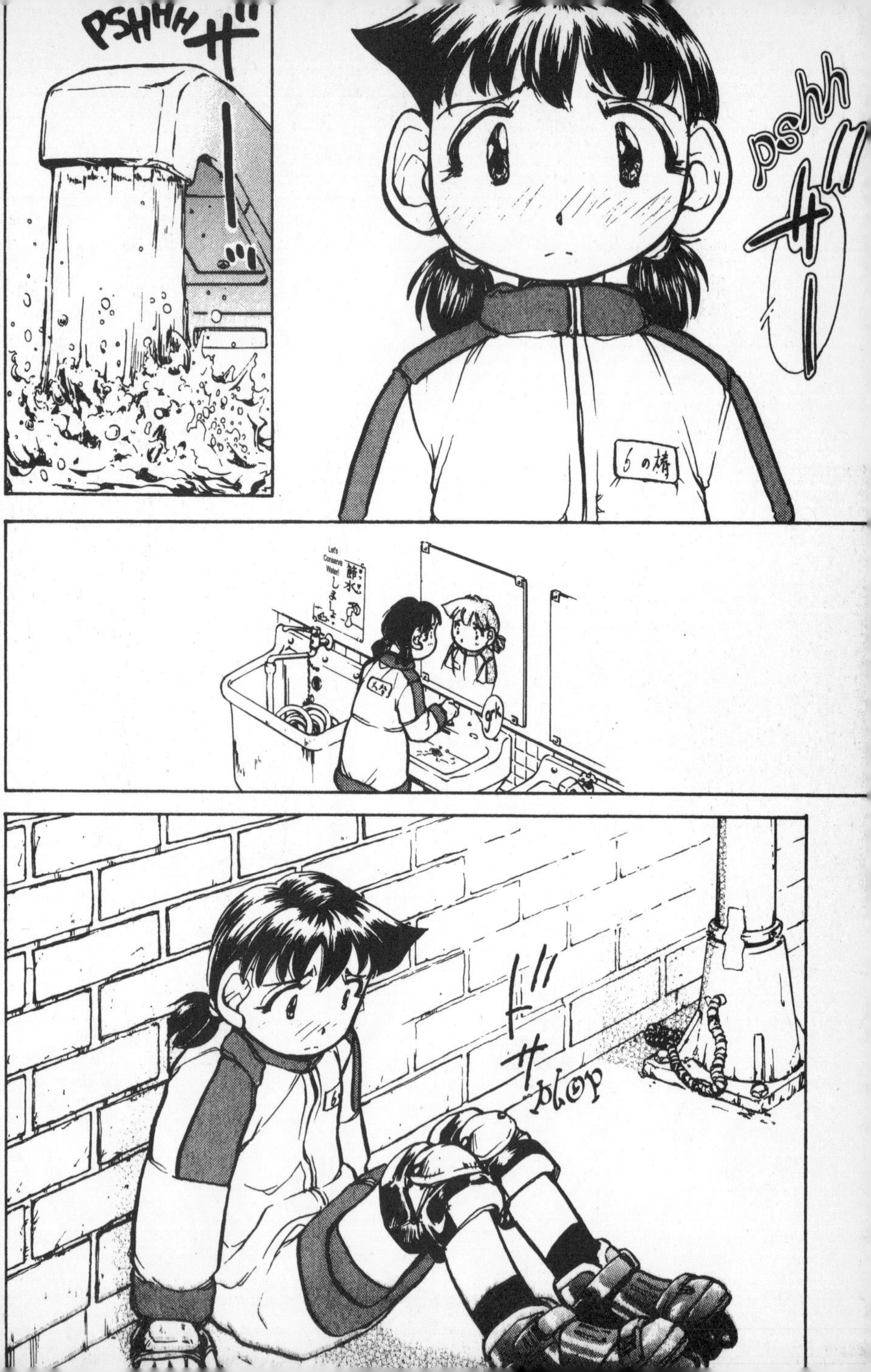
pshh
サー
PSHHH ザ
Let's Conserve Water!
節水しましょう
grk
ドサ
plop

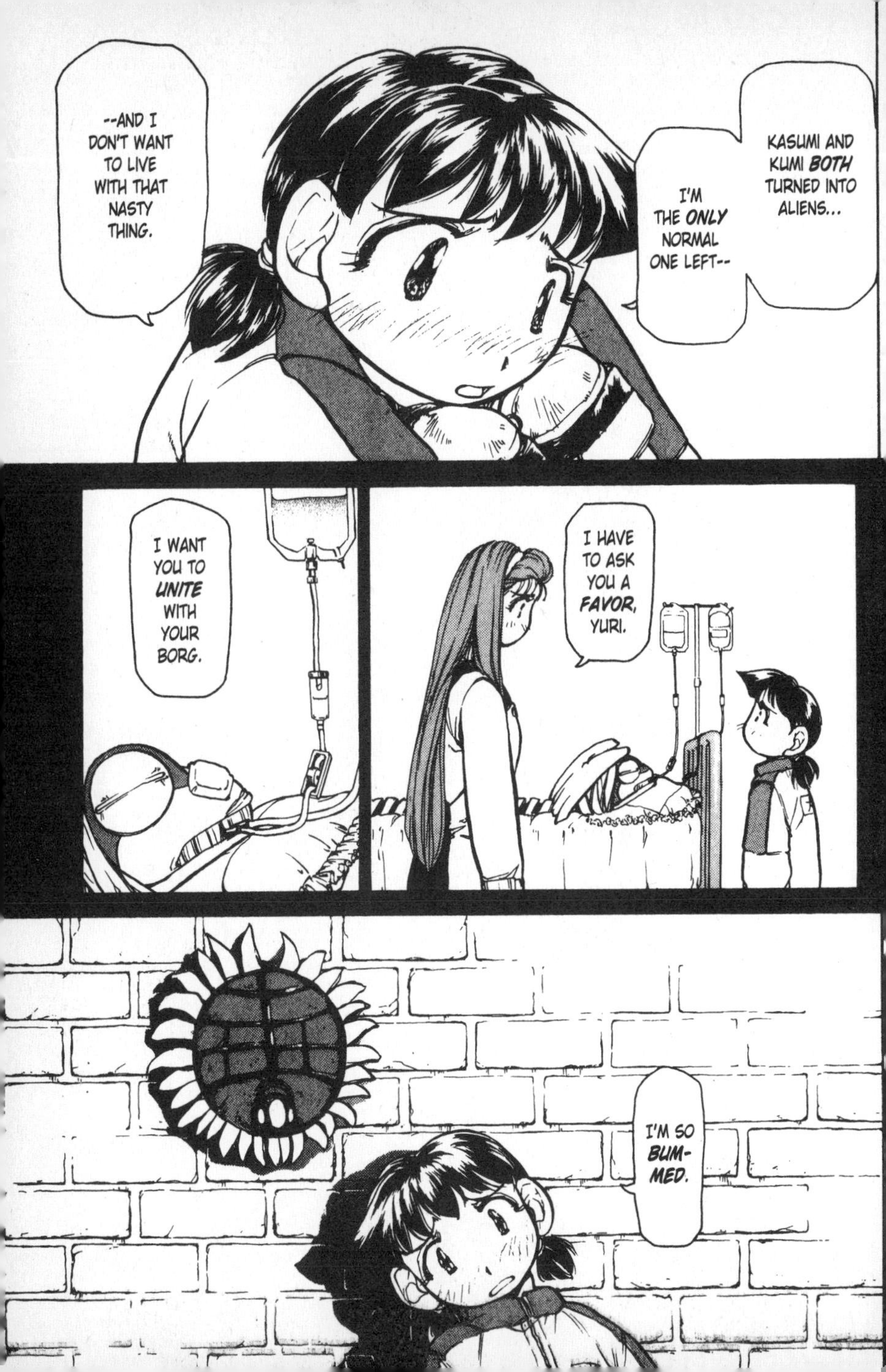
KASUMI AND KUMI BOTH TURNED INTO ALIENS...
I'M THE ONLY NORMAL ONE LEFT--
--AND I DON'T WANT TO LIVE WITH THAT NASTY THING.
I HAVE TO ASK YOU A FAVOR, YURI.
I WANT YOU TO UNITE WITH YOUR BORG.
I'M SO BUM-MED.

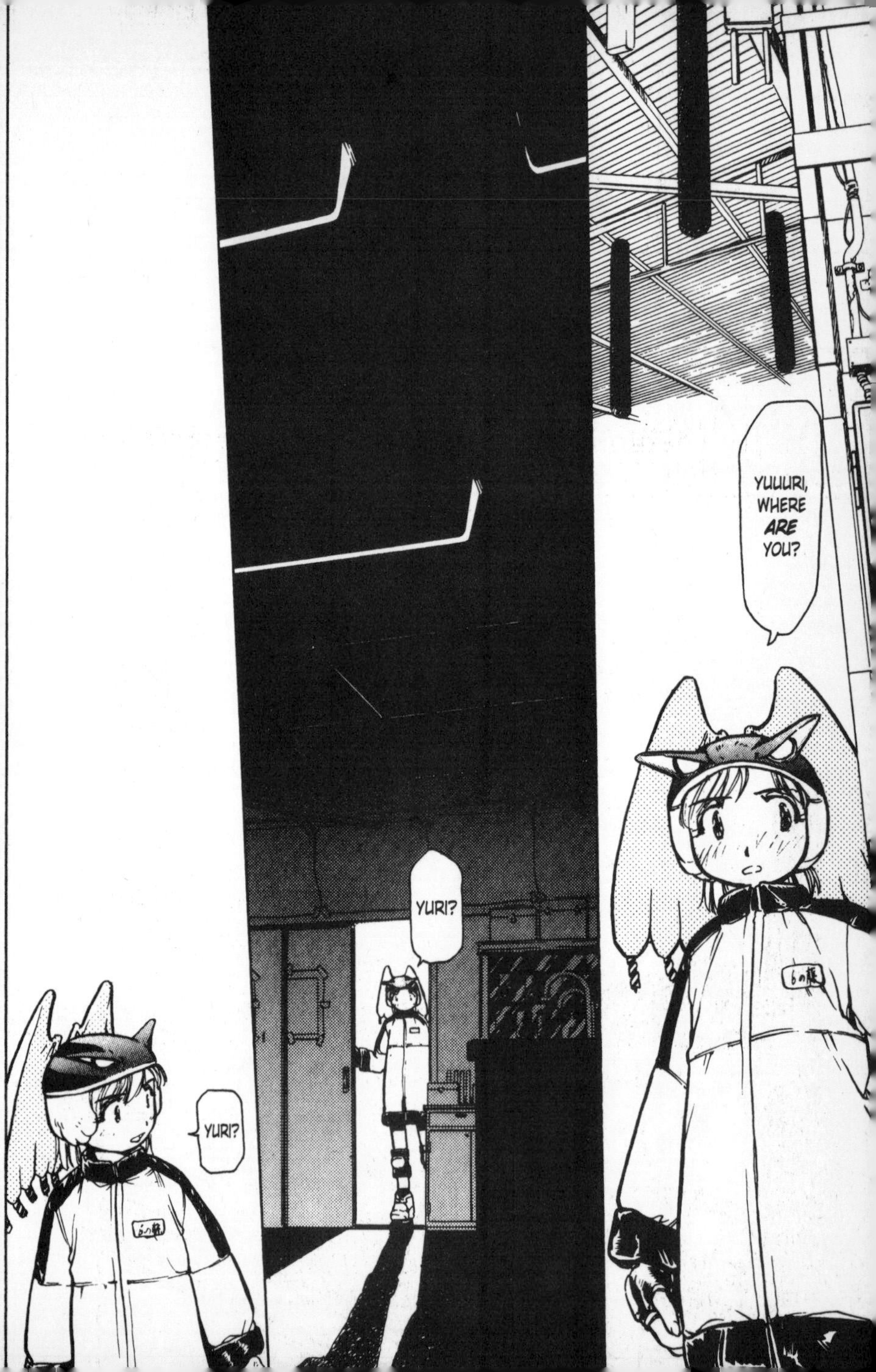
YUUURI, WHERE *ARE* YOU?
YURI?
YURI?

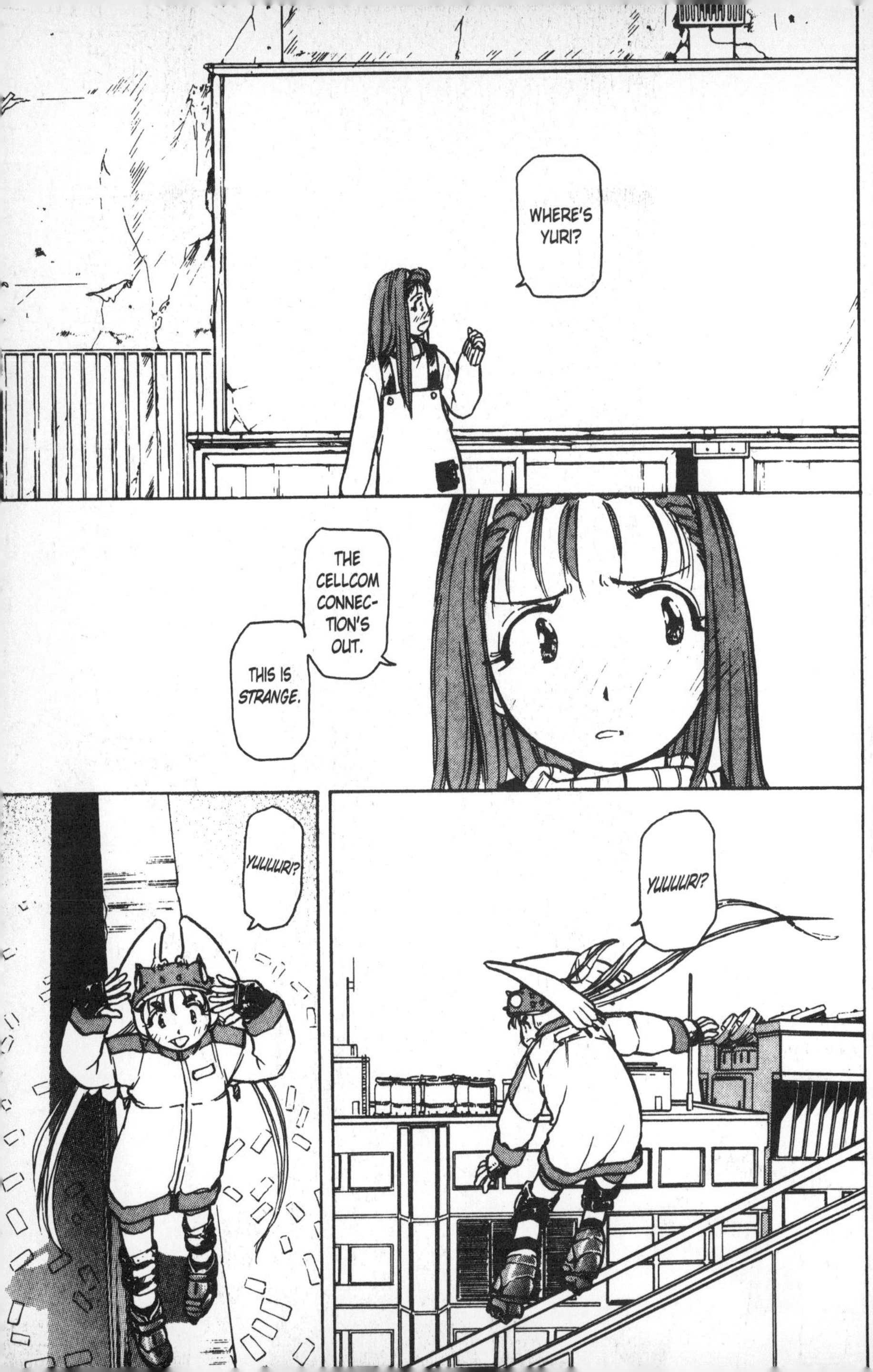
WHERE'S YURI?
THE CELLCOM CONNECTION'S OUT.
THIS IS STRANGE.
YUUUURI?
YUUUURI?

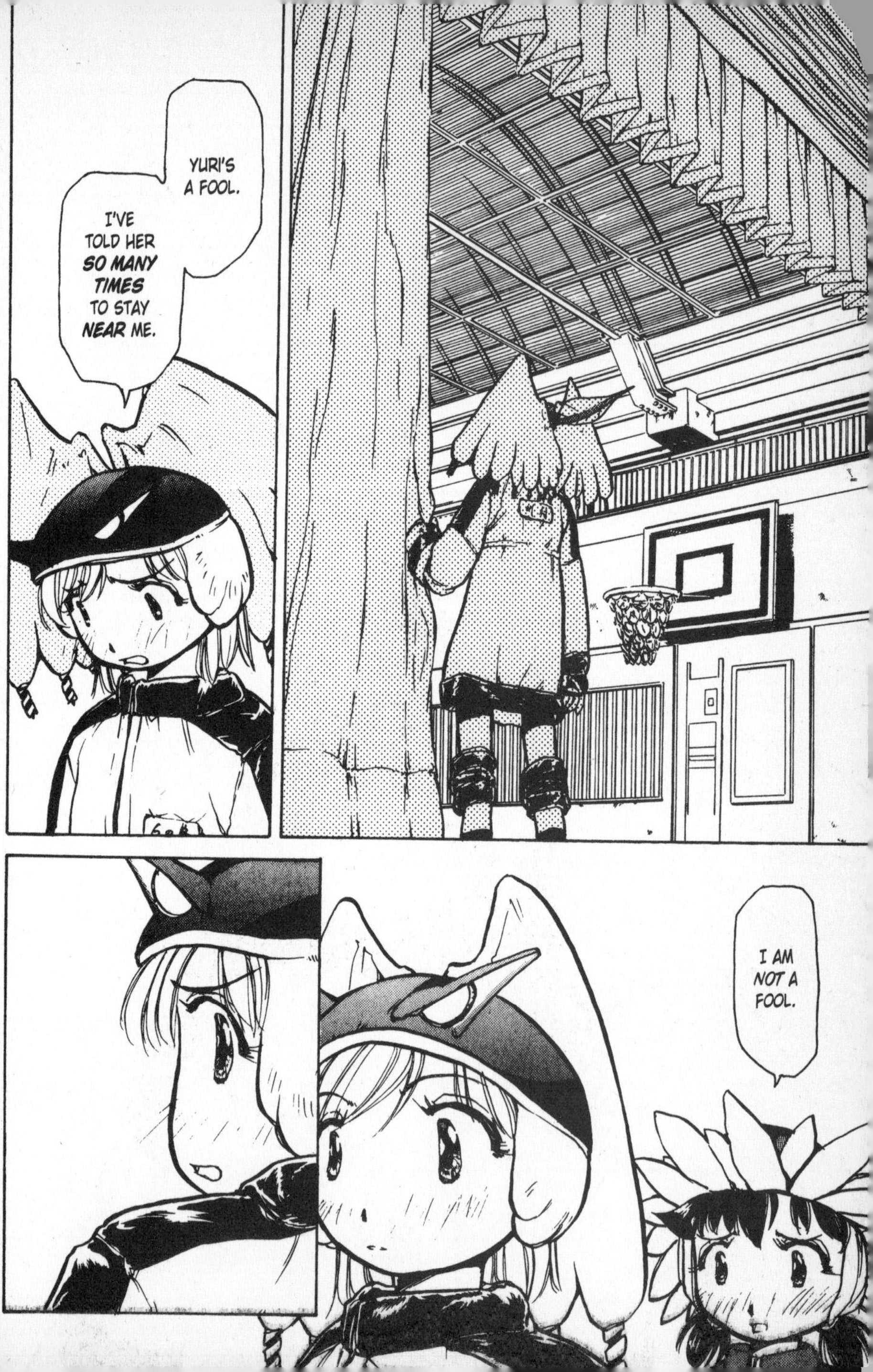
YURI'S A FOOL.
I'VE TOLD HER **SO MANY TIMES** TO STAY **NEAR** ME.
I AM **NOT** A FOOL.

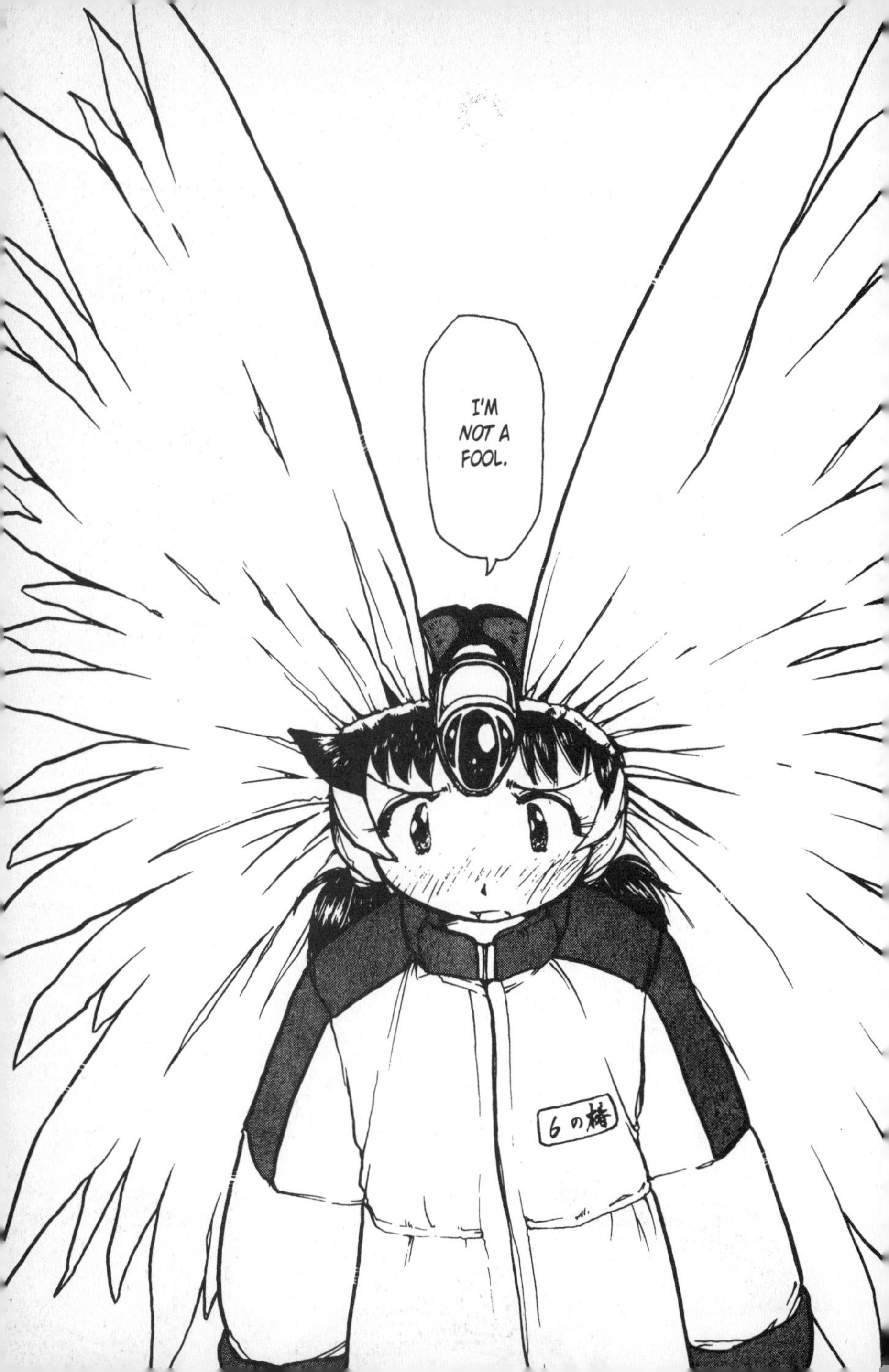
I'M NOT A FOOL.
6の椅

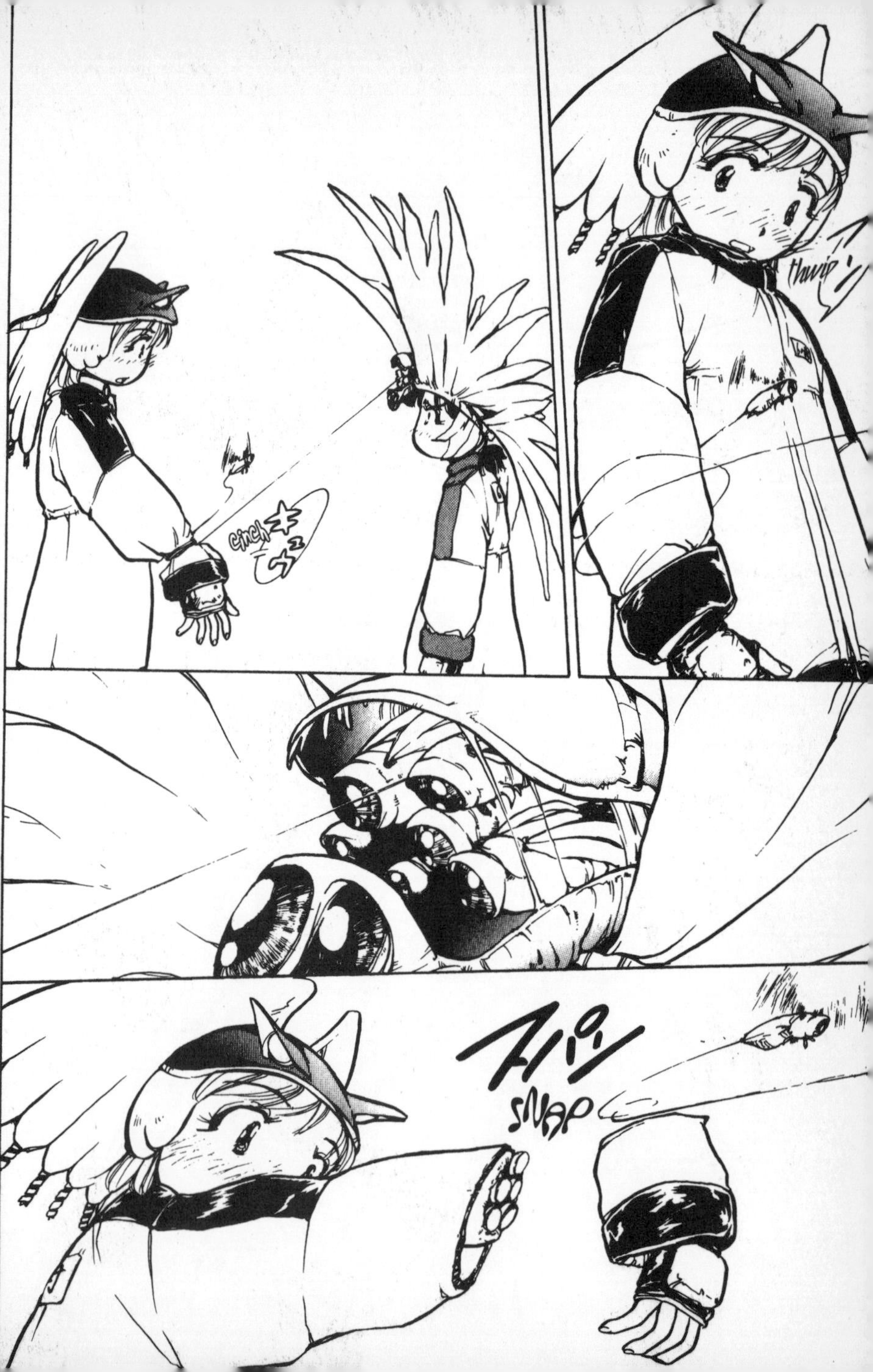

thwip
cinch キュッ
パシッ
SNAP

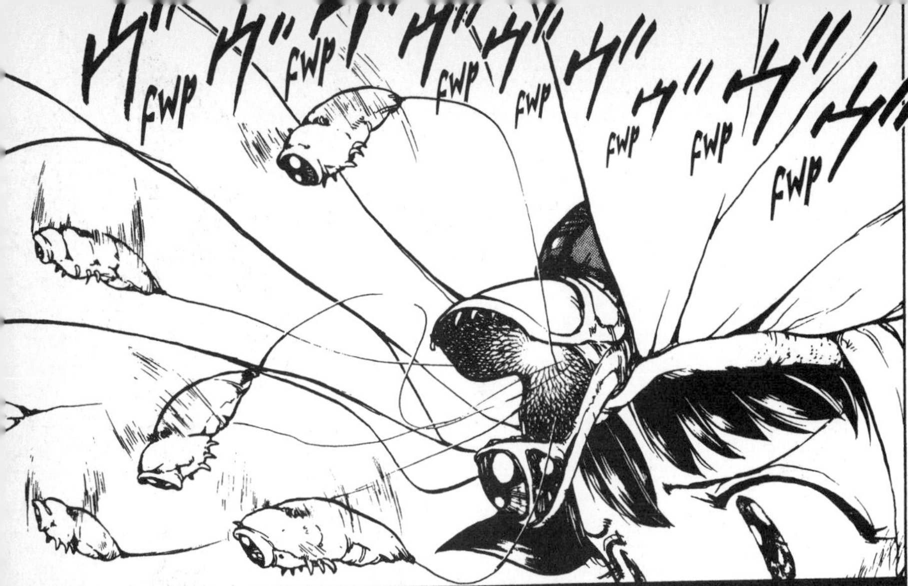
FWP
FWP
FWP
FWP
FWP
FWP
FWP
FWP
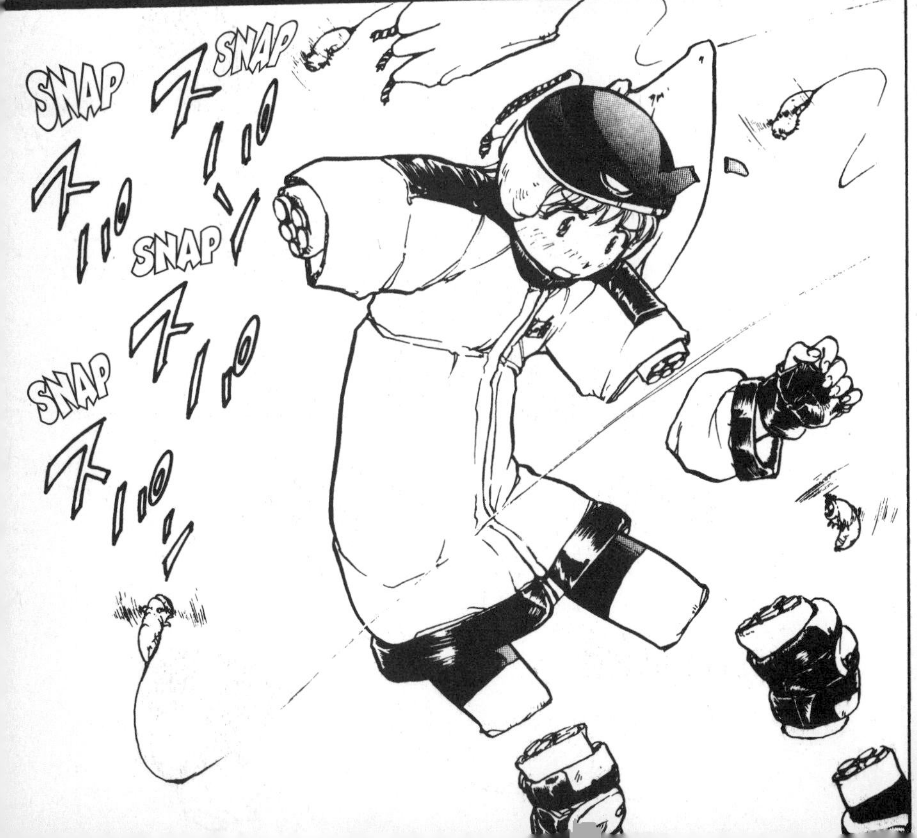
SNAP
SNAP
SNAP
SNAP

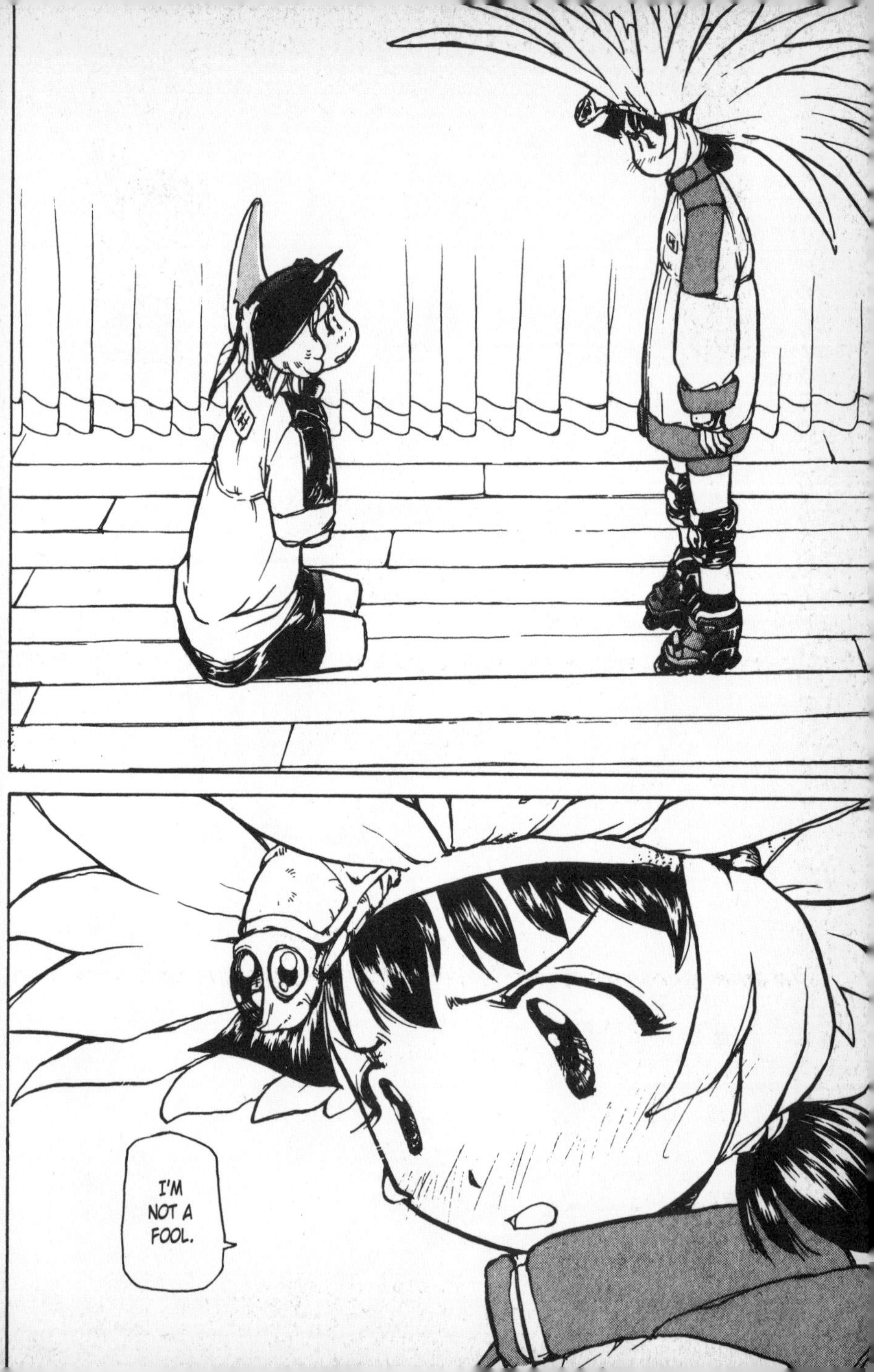
I'M NOT A FOOL.

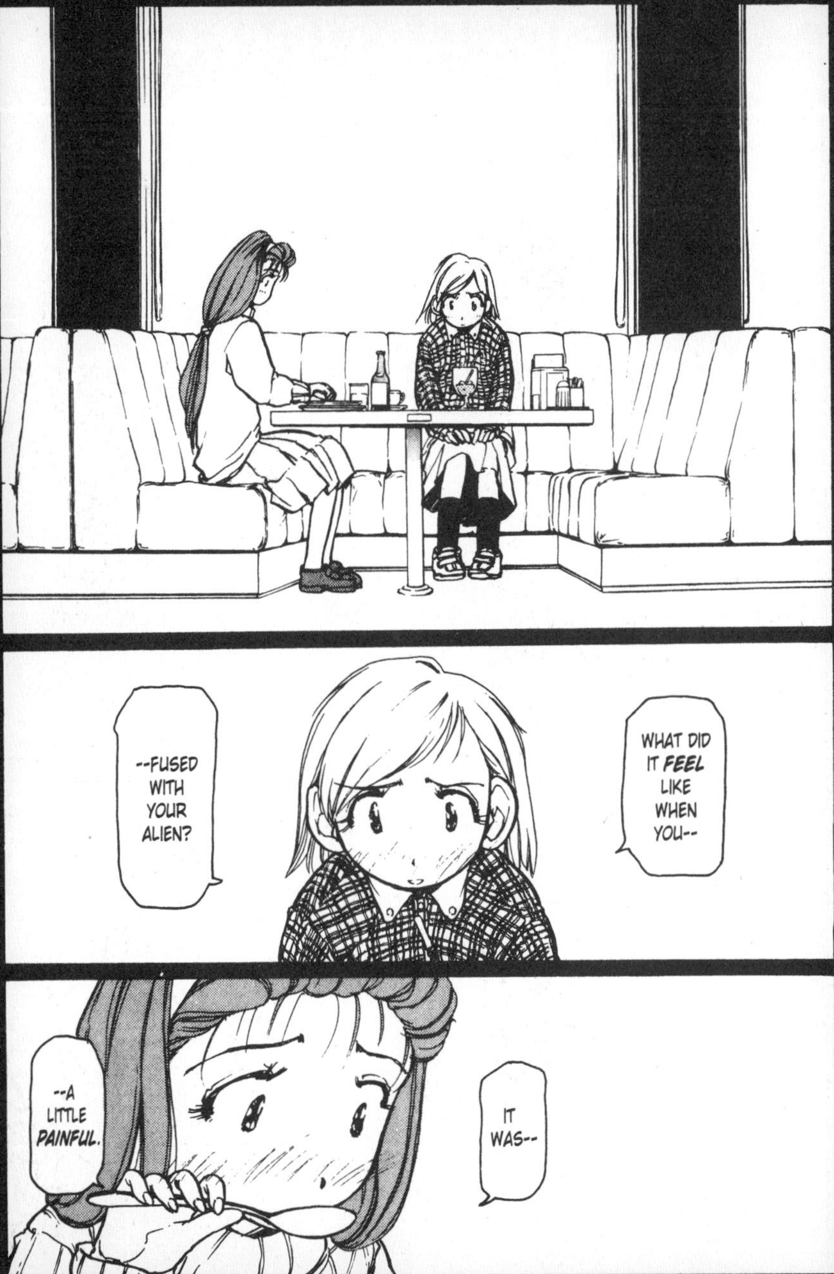
WHAT DID IT FEEL LIKE WHEN YOU--
--FUSED WITH YOUR ALIEN?
IT WAS--
--A LITTLE PAINFUL.

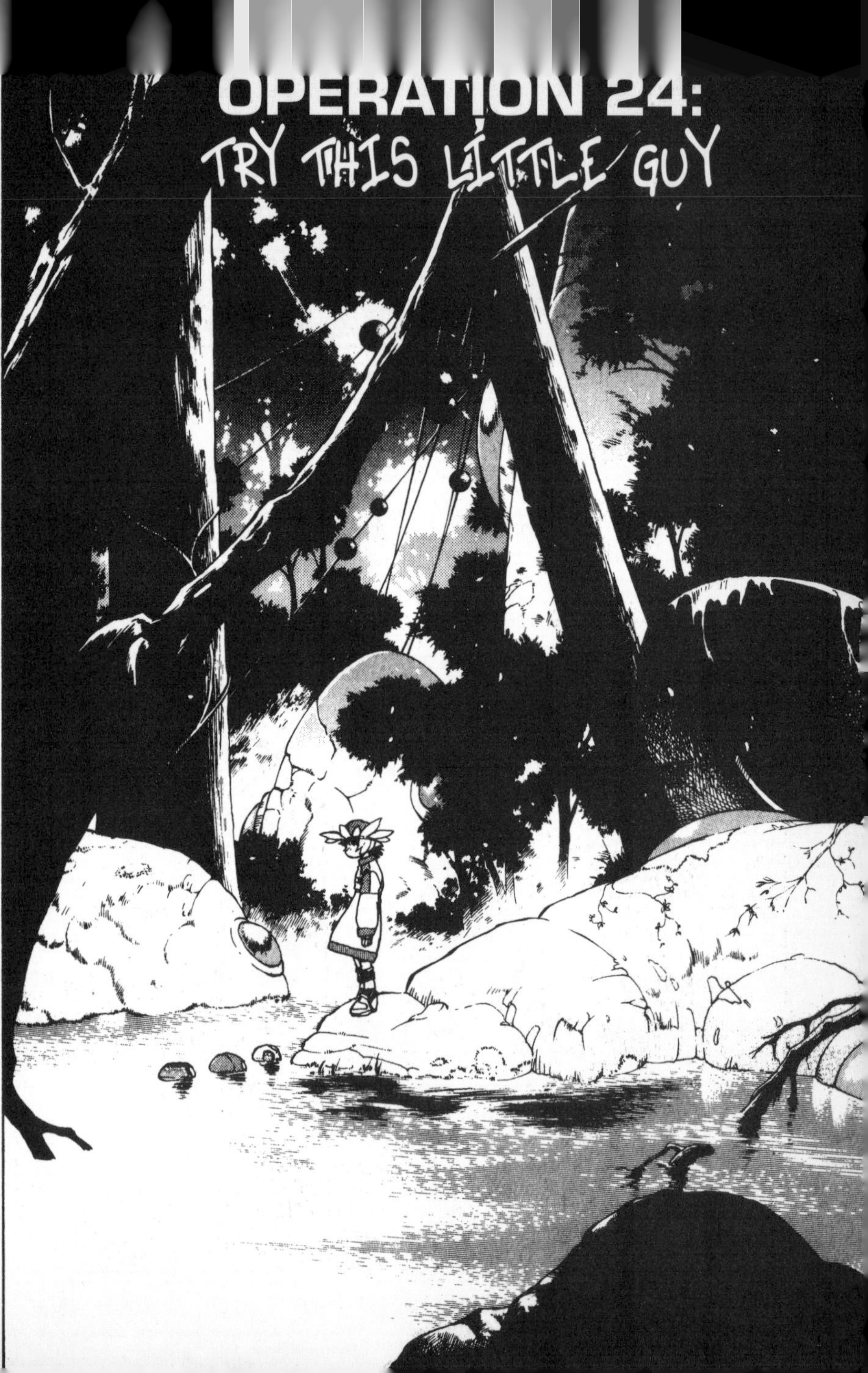
OPERATION 24:
TRY THIS LITTLE GUY

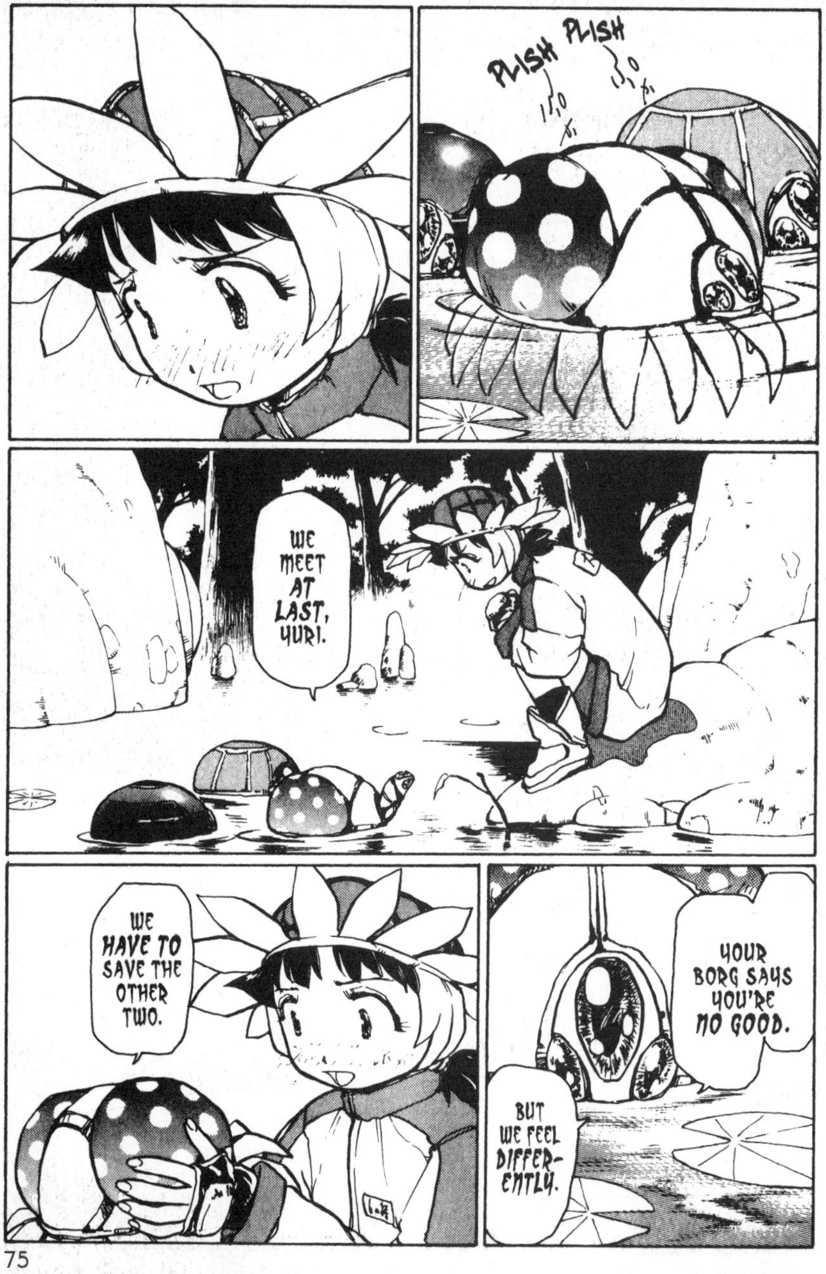
PLISH
PLISH
WE MEET AT LAST, YURI.
YOUR BORG SAYS YOU'RE NO GOOD.
BUT WE FEEL DIFFER-ENTLY.
WE HAVE TO SAVE THE OTHER TWO.

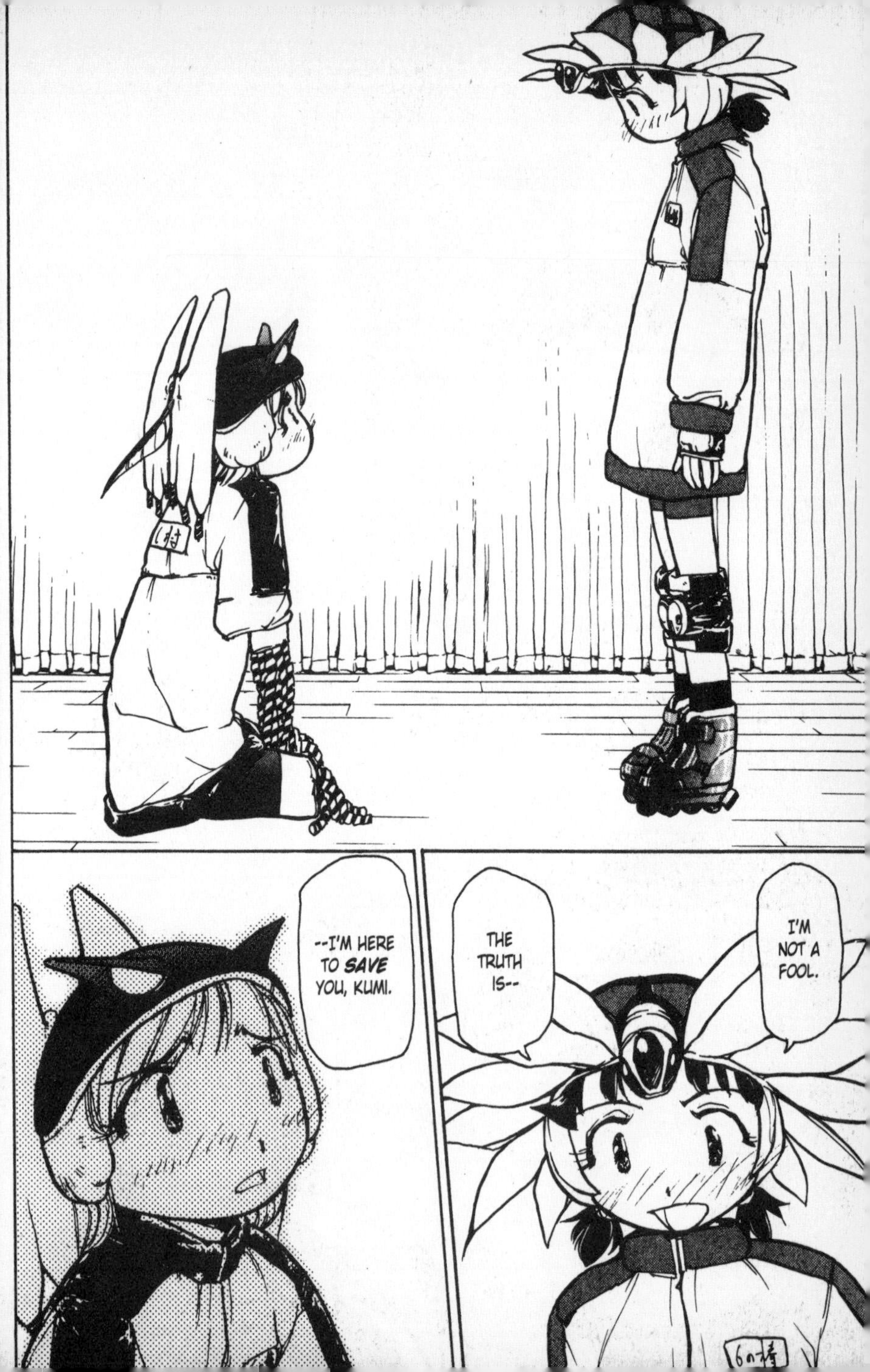
I'M NOT A FOOL.
THE TRUTH IS--
--I'M HERE TO SAVE YOU, KUMI.

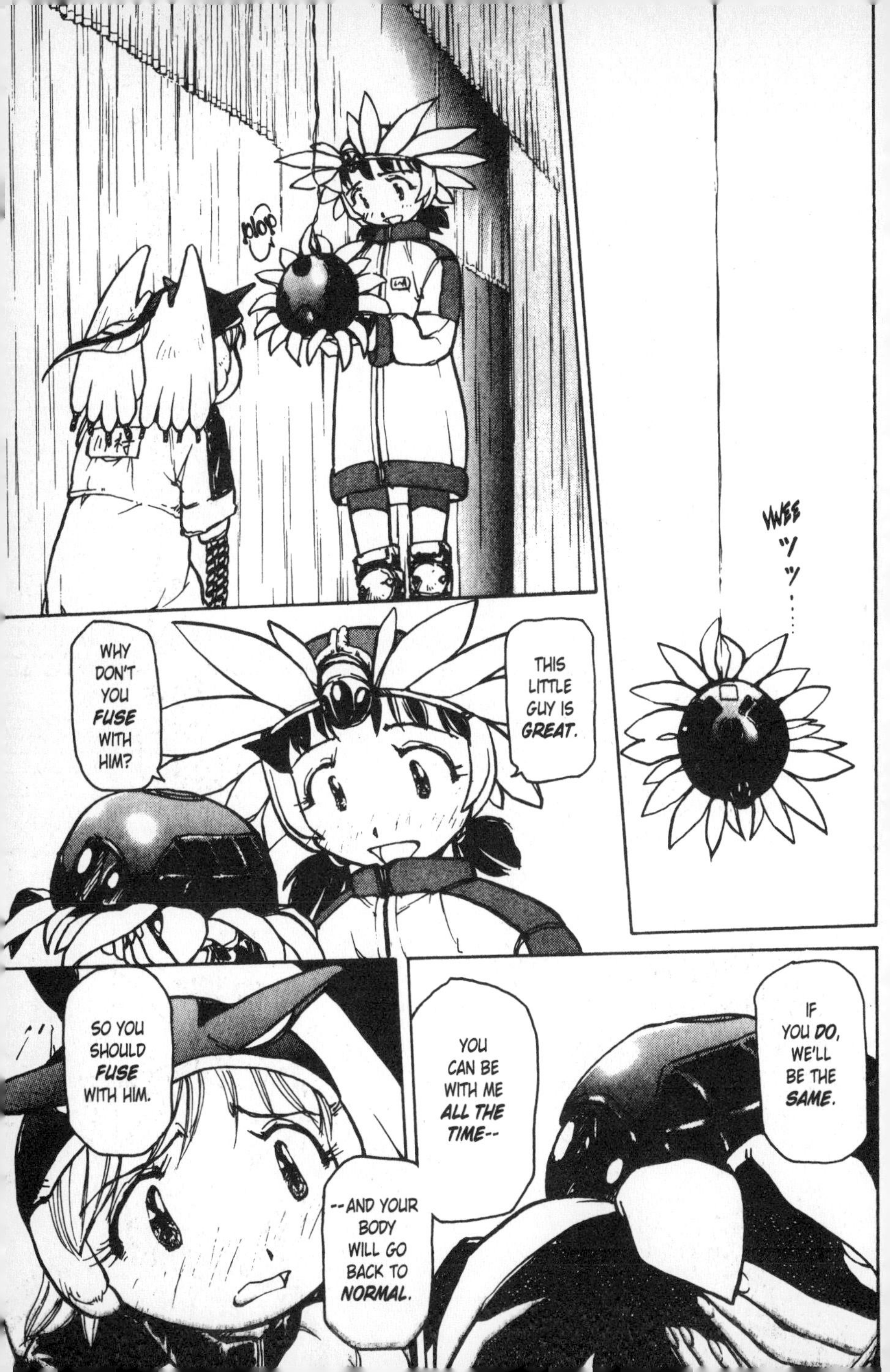
WEE
ツツ....
plop
THIS LITTLE GUY IS **GREAT**.
WHY DON'T YOU **FUSE** WITH HIM?
IF YOU **DO**, WE'LL BE THE **SAME**.
YOU CAN BE WITH ME **ALL THE TIME--**
--AND YOUR BODY WILL GO BACK TO **NORMAL**.
SO YOU SHOULD **FUSE** WITH HIM.

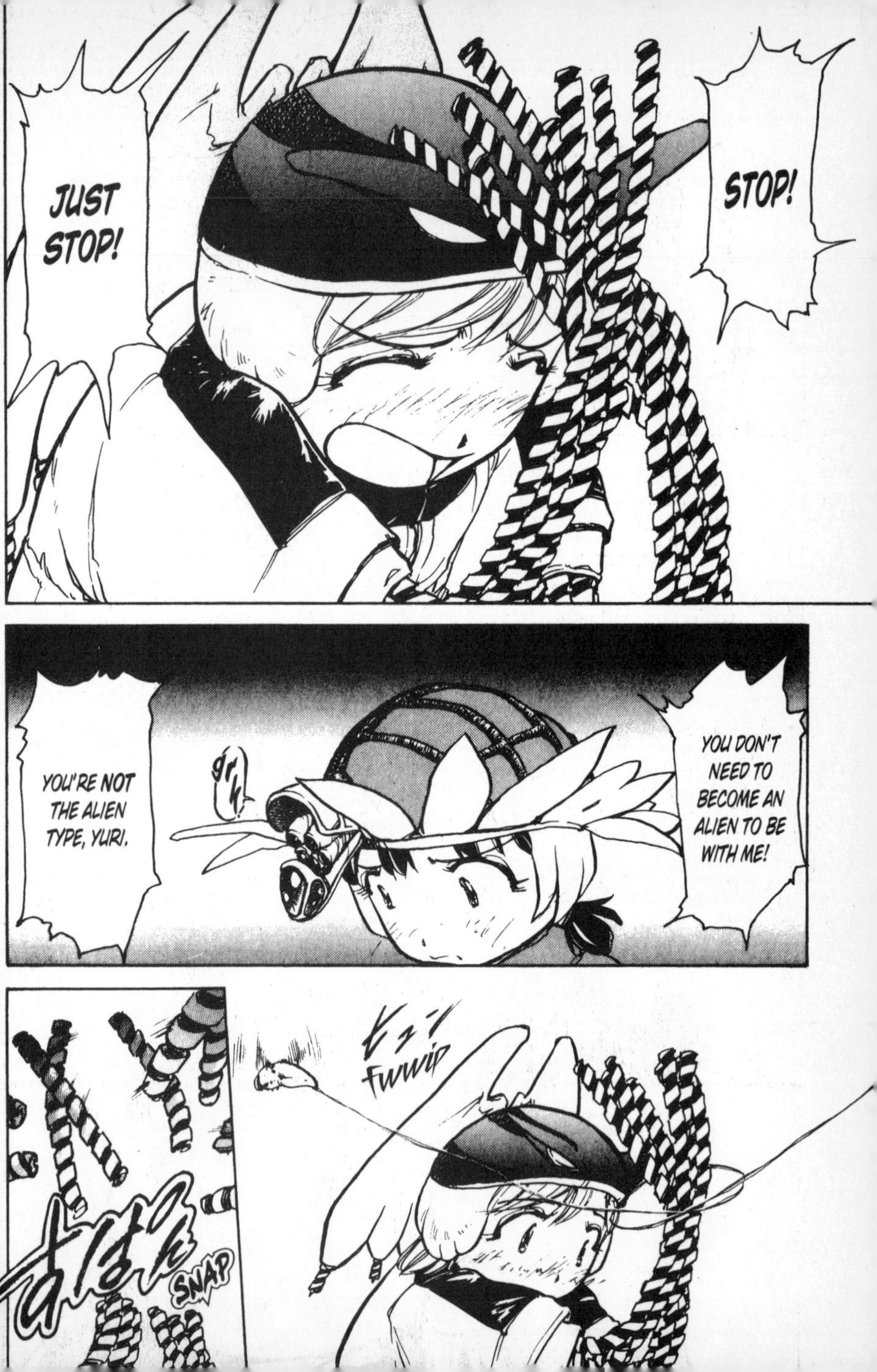
STOP!
JUST STOP!
YOU DON'T NEED TO BECOME AN ALIEN TO BE WITH ME!
grk!
YOU'RE NOT THE ALIEN TYPE, YURI.
FWWIP
SNAP

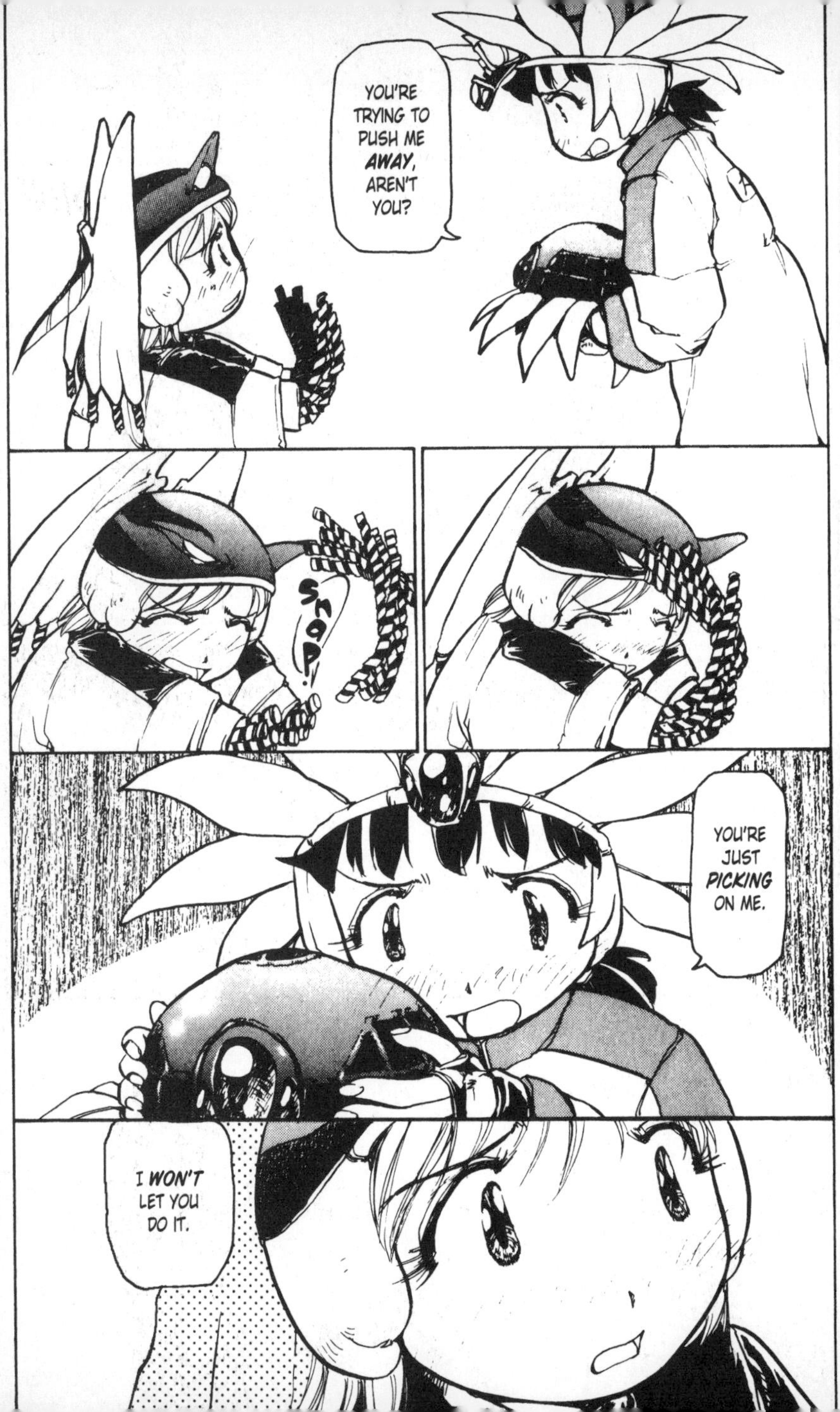
YOU'RE TRYING TO PUSH ME AWAY, AREN'T YOU?
SNAP!
YOU'RE JUST PICKING ON ME.
I WON'T LET YOU DO IT.

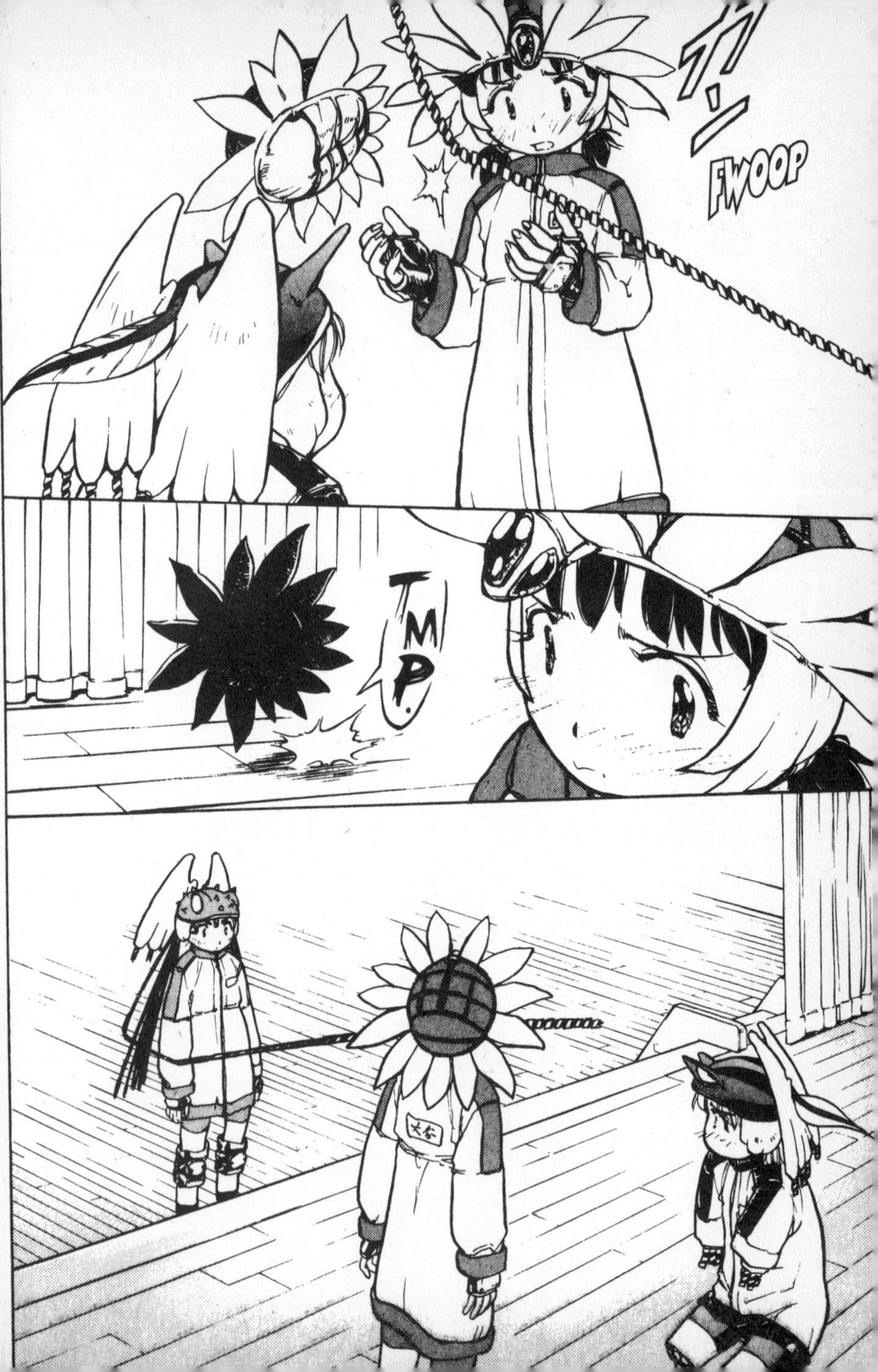
FWOOP
TMP.
大谷

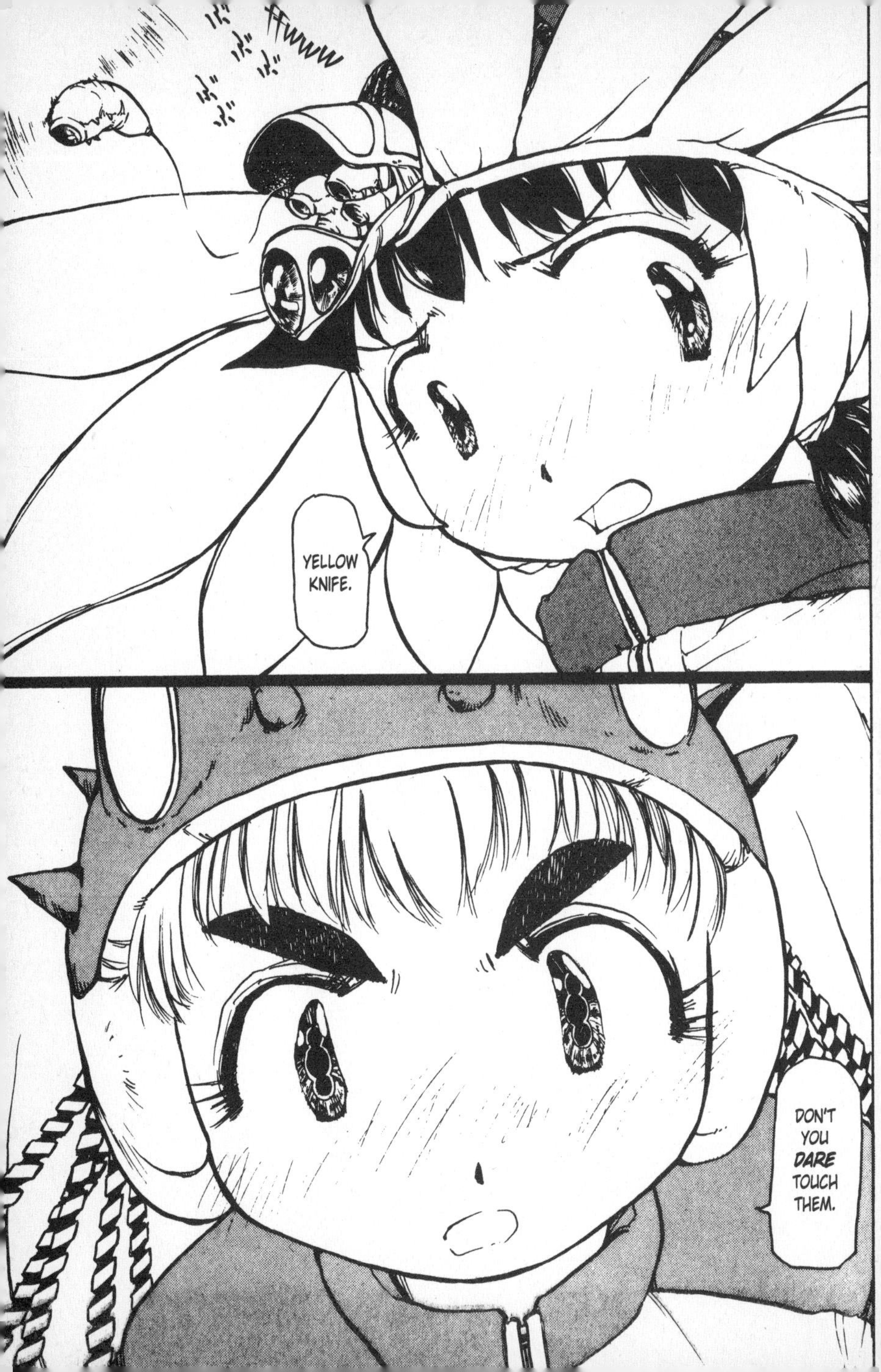
ffwww
ぶぶぶぶぶ
YELLOW KNIFE.
DON'T YOU **DARE** TOUCH THEM.

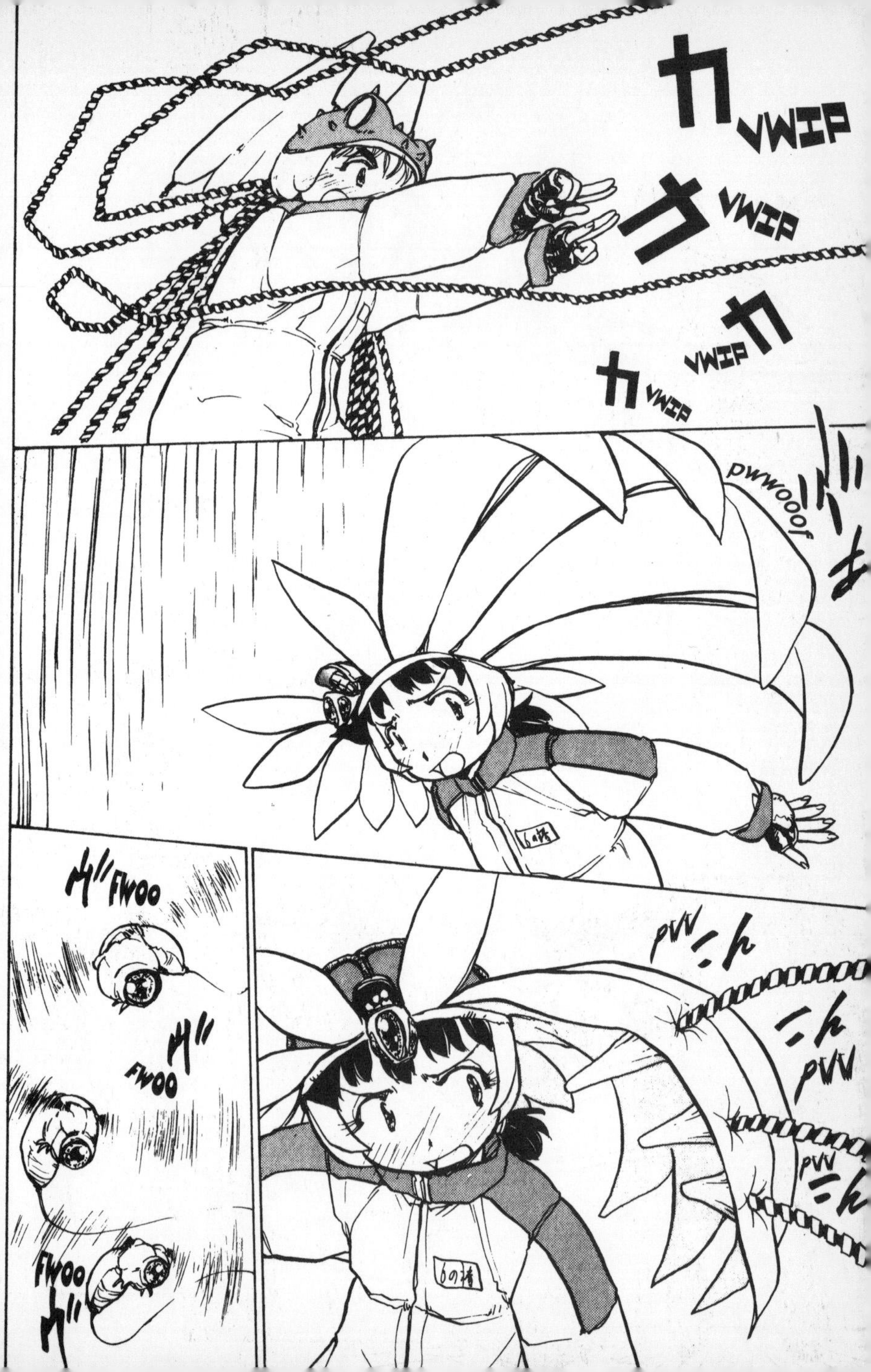
カ VWIP
カ VWIP
カ VWIP
カ VWIP
pwwooof
PVV
PVV
PVV
FWOO
FWOO
FWOO

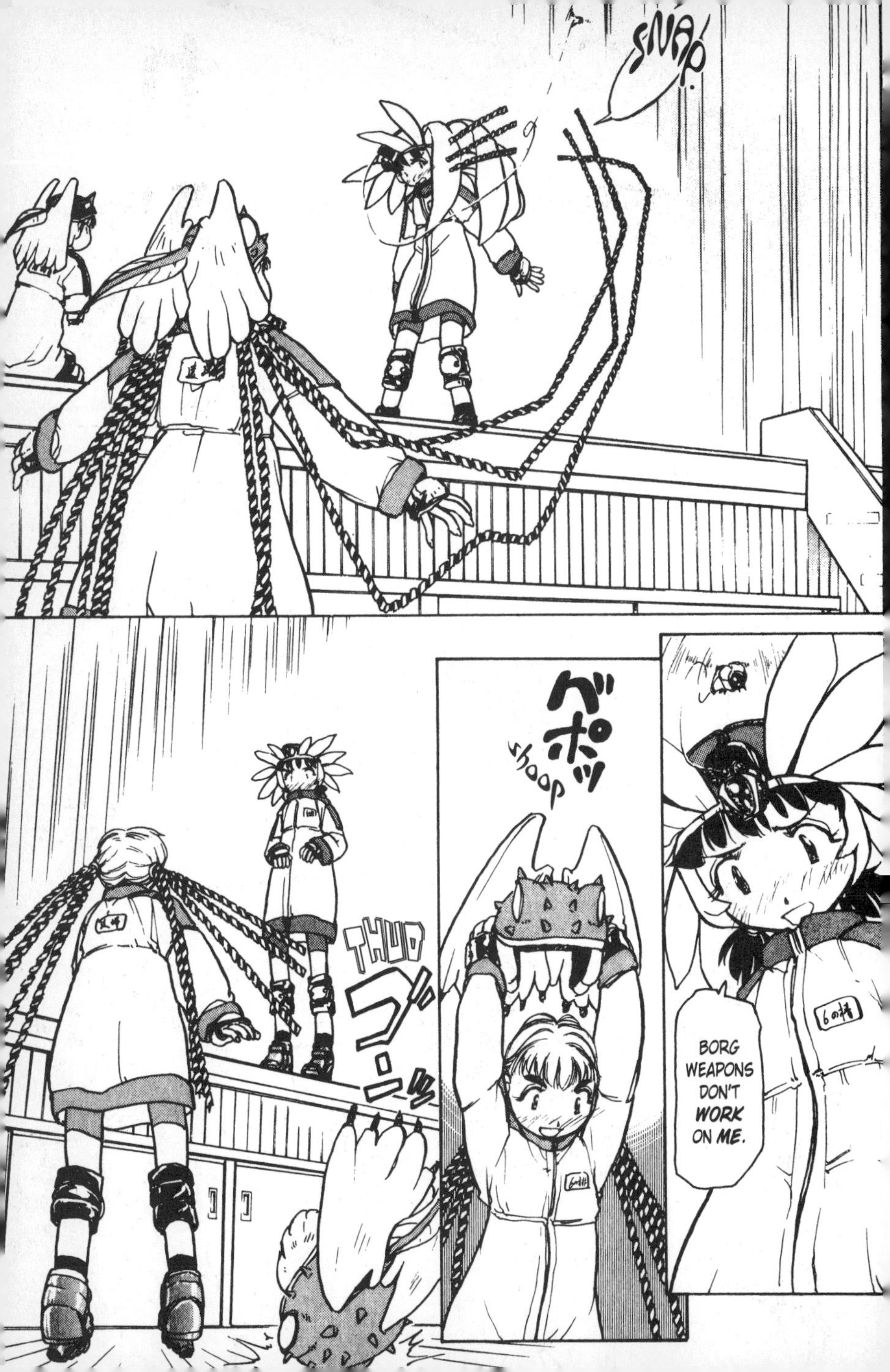
SNAP.
BORG WEAPONS DON'T WORK ON ME.
ベポッ
shoop
THUD

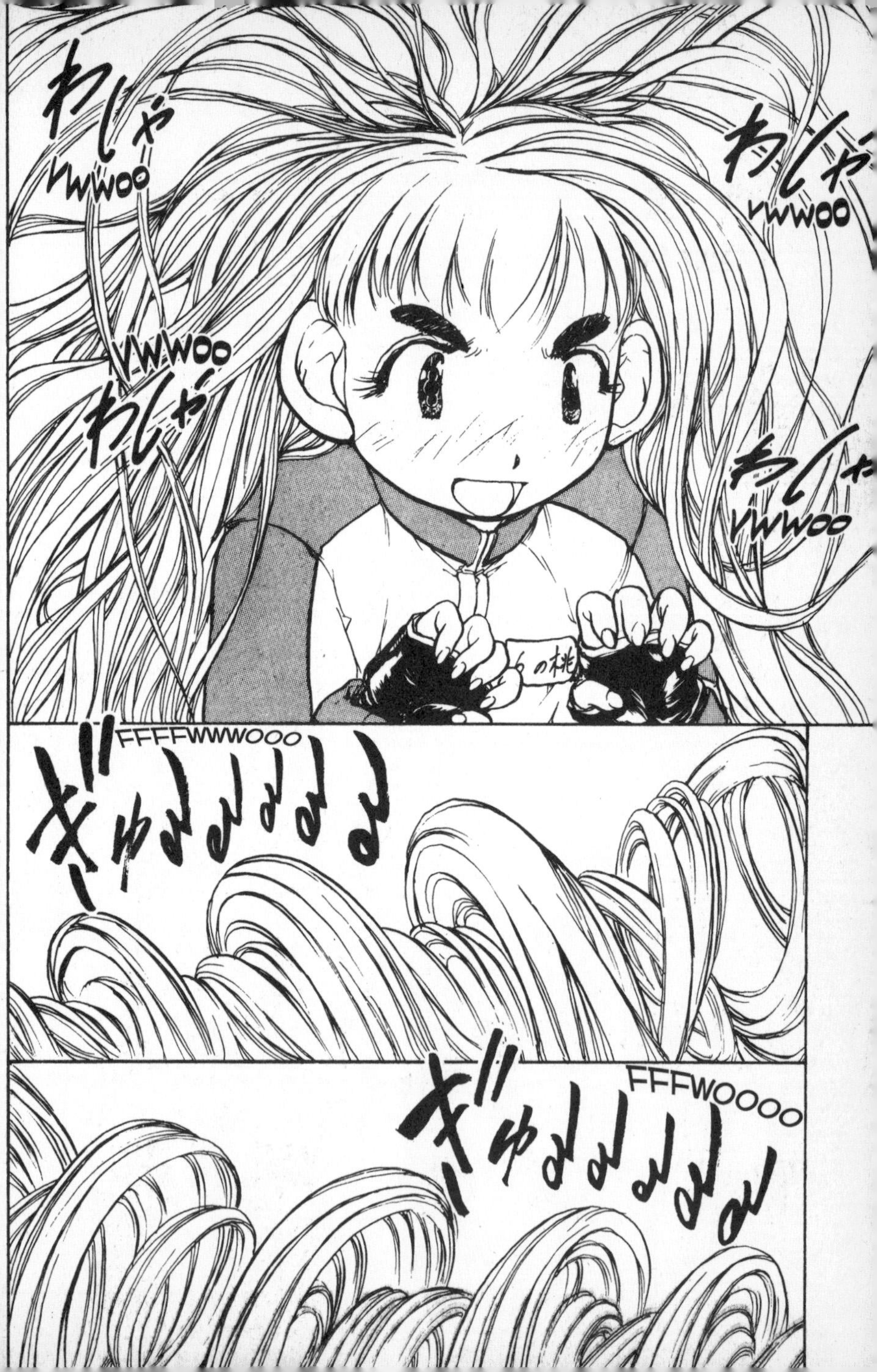

わしゃ
VWWOO
わしゃ
VWWOO
わしゃ
VWWOO
VWWOO
わしゃ
ぎゅるるるるる
FFFFWWWOOO
ぎゅるるるるるる
FFFWOOOO

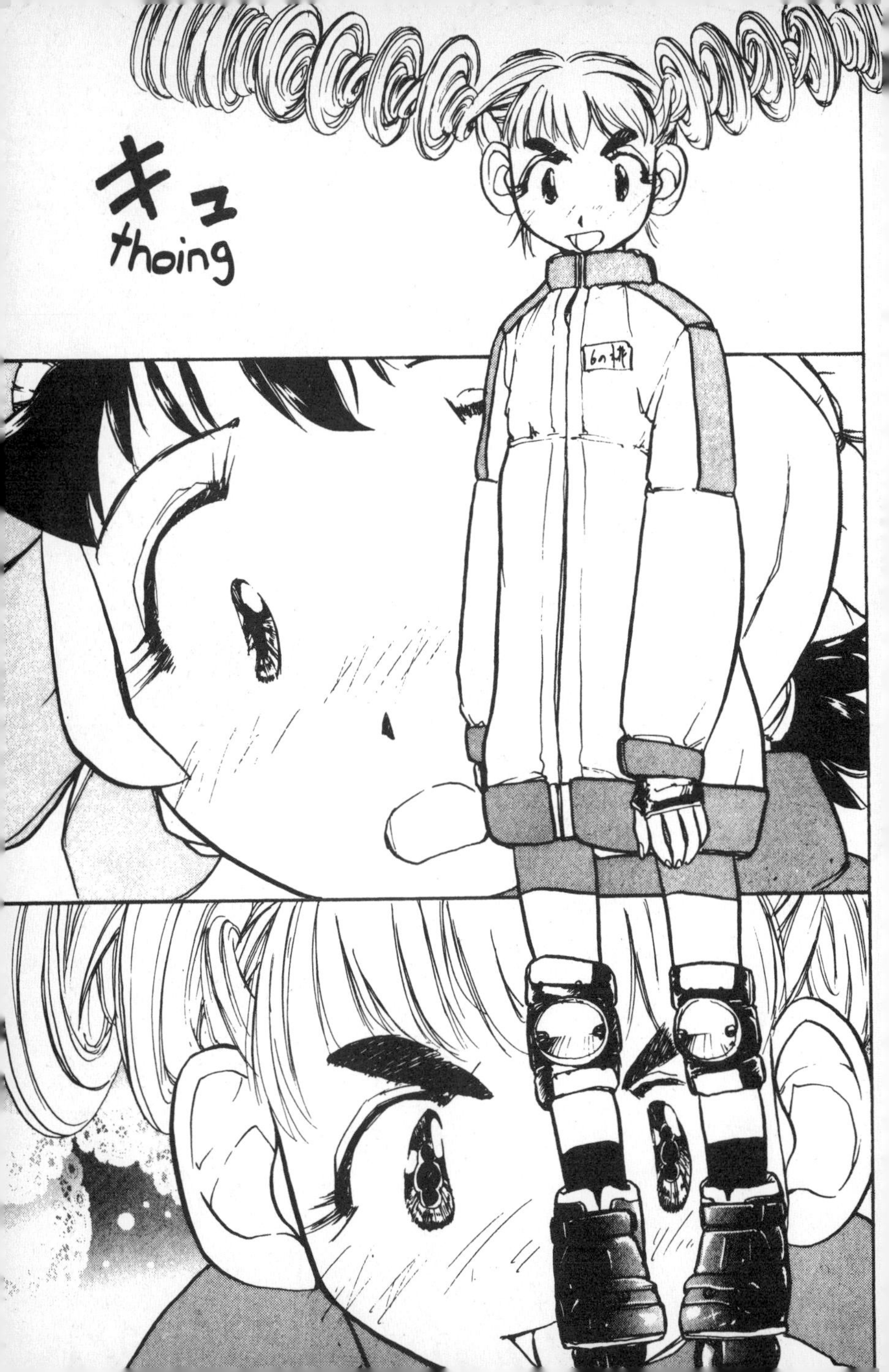
キュ
thoing

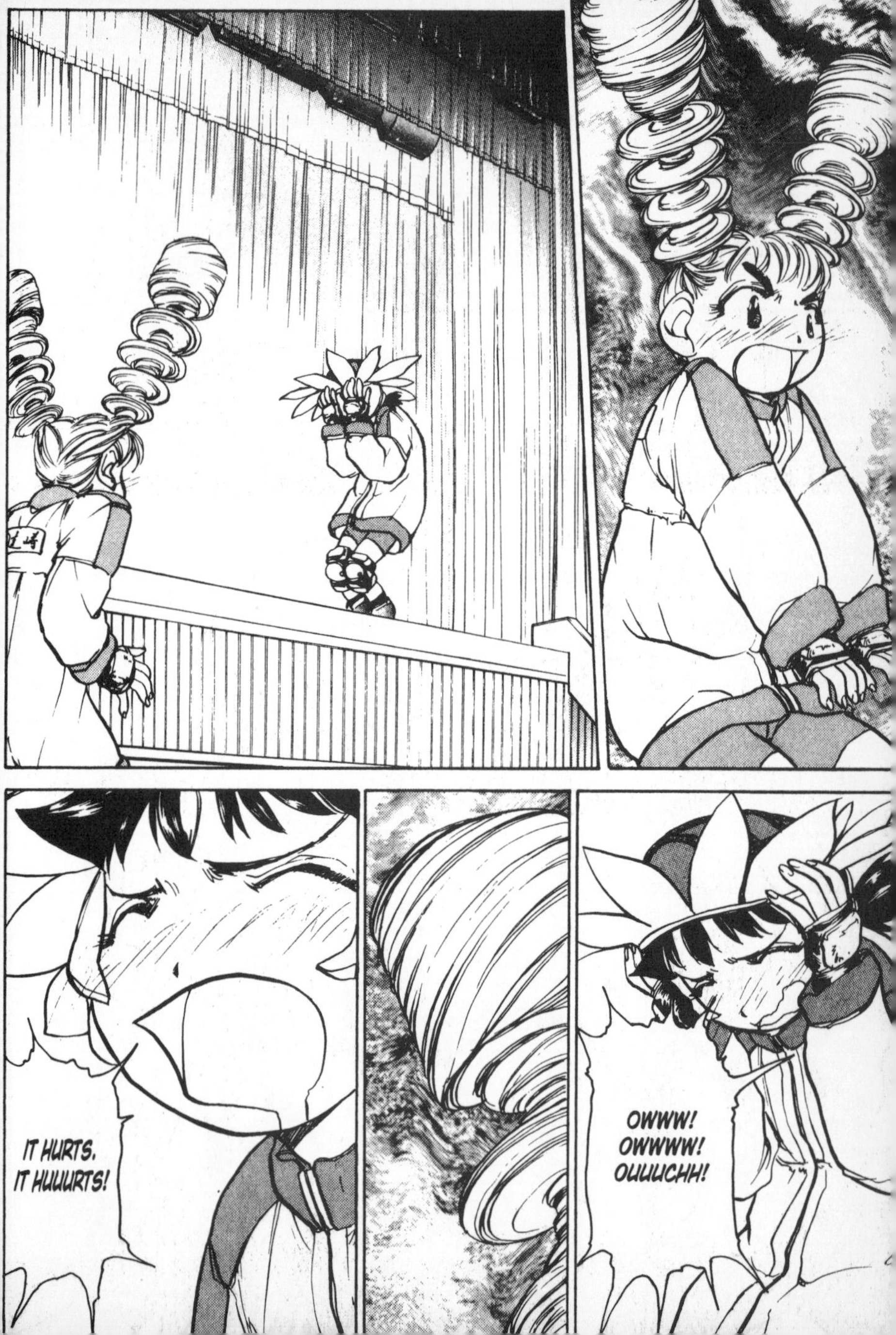
OWWW! OWWWW! OUUUCHH!
IT HURTS. IT HUUURTS!

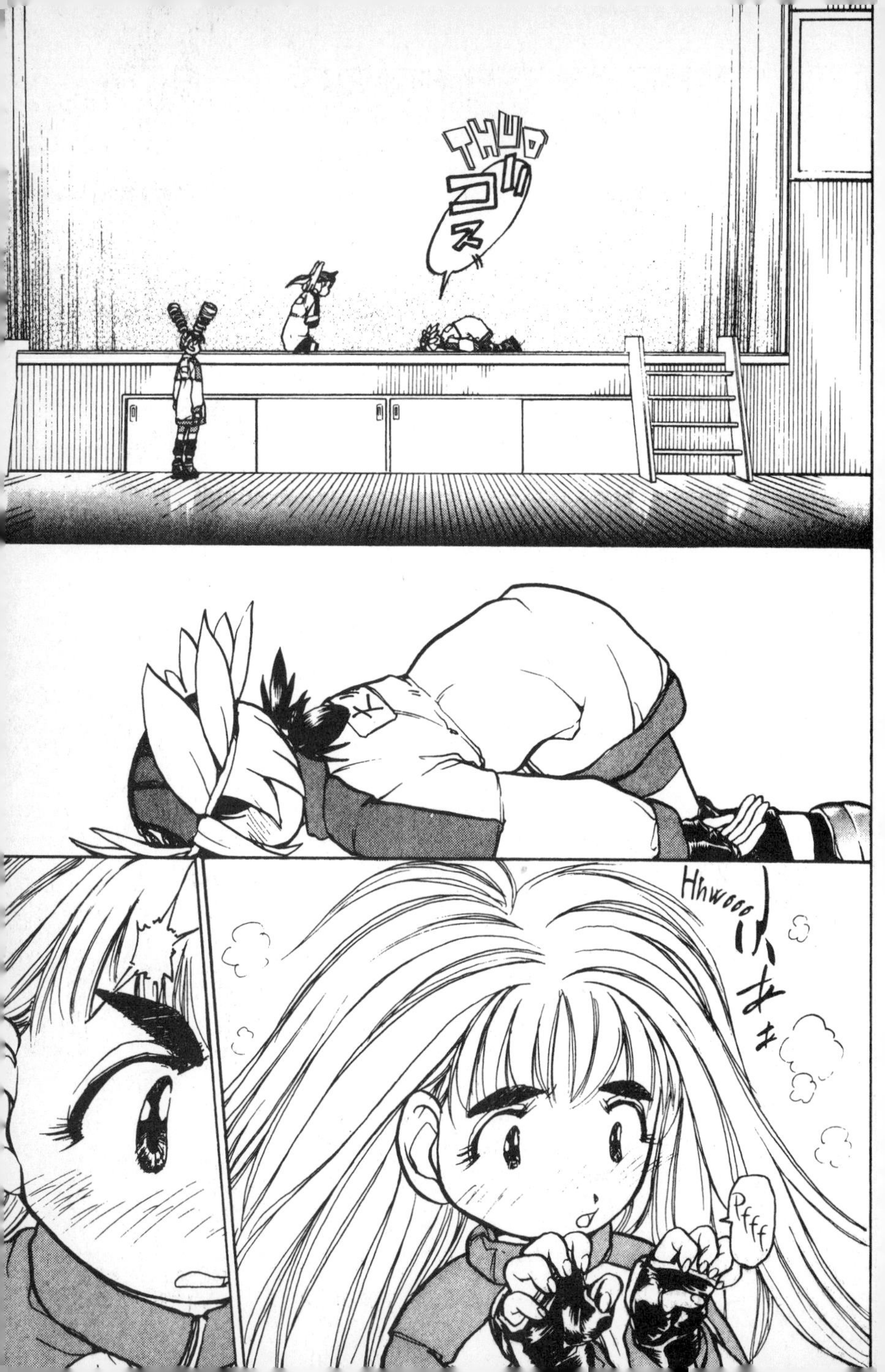
THUD
Hnwooo
Pfff.

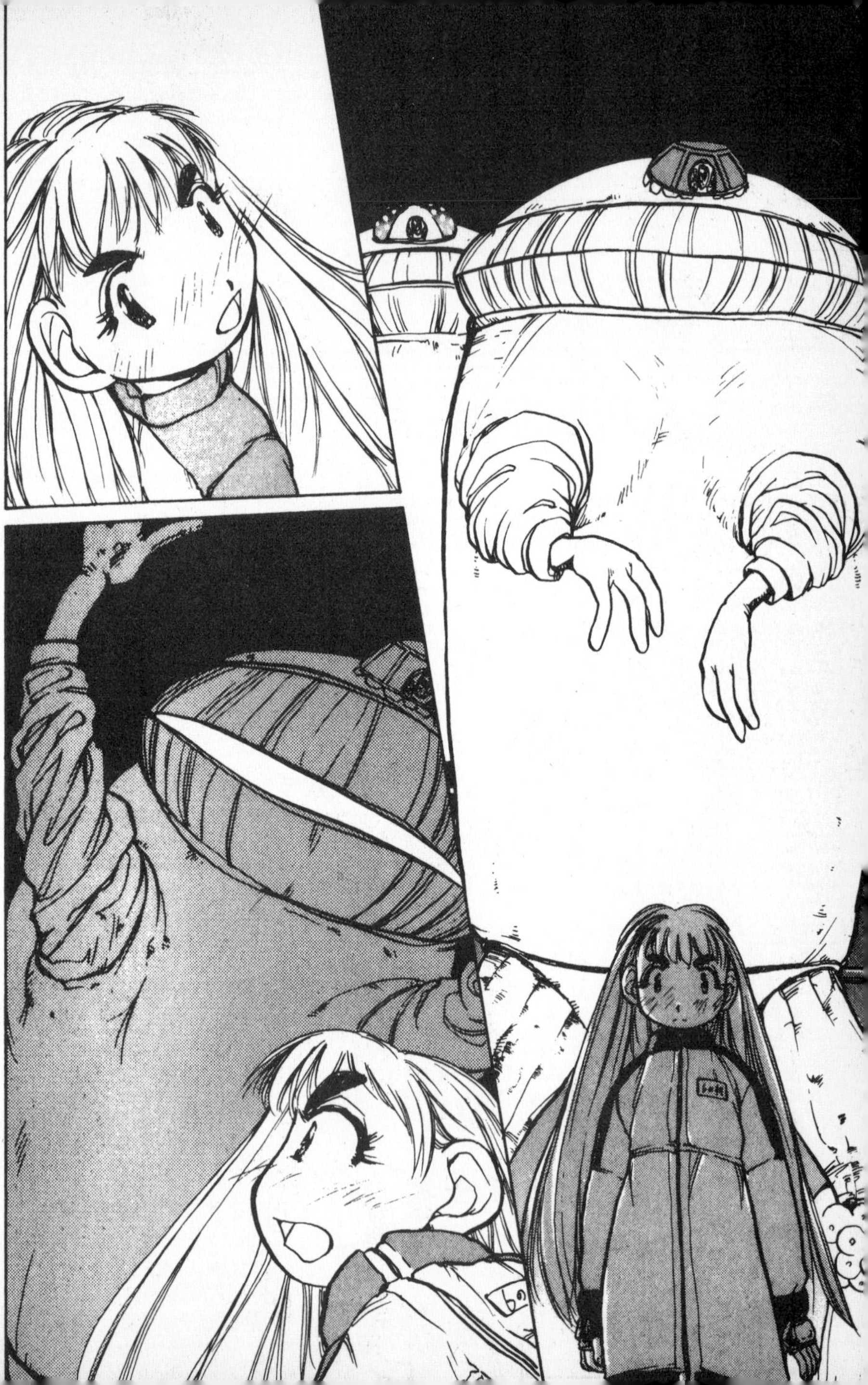

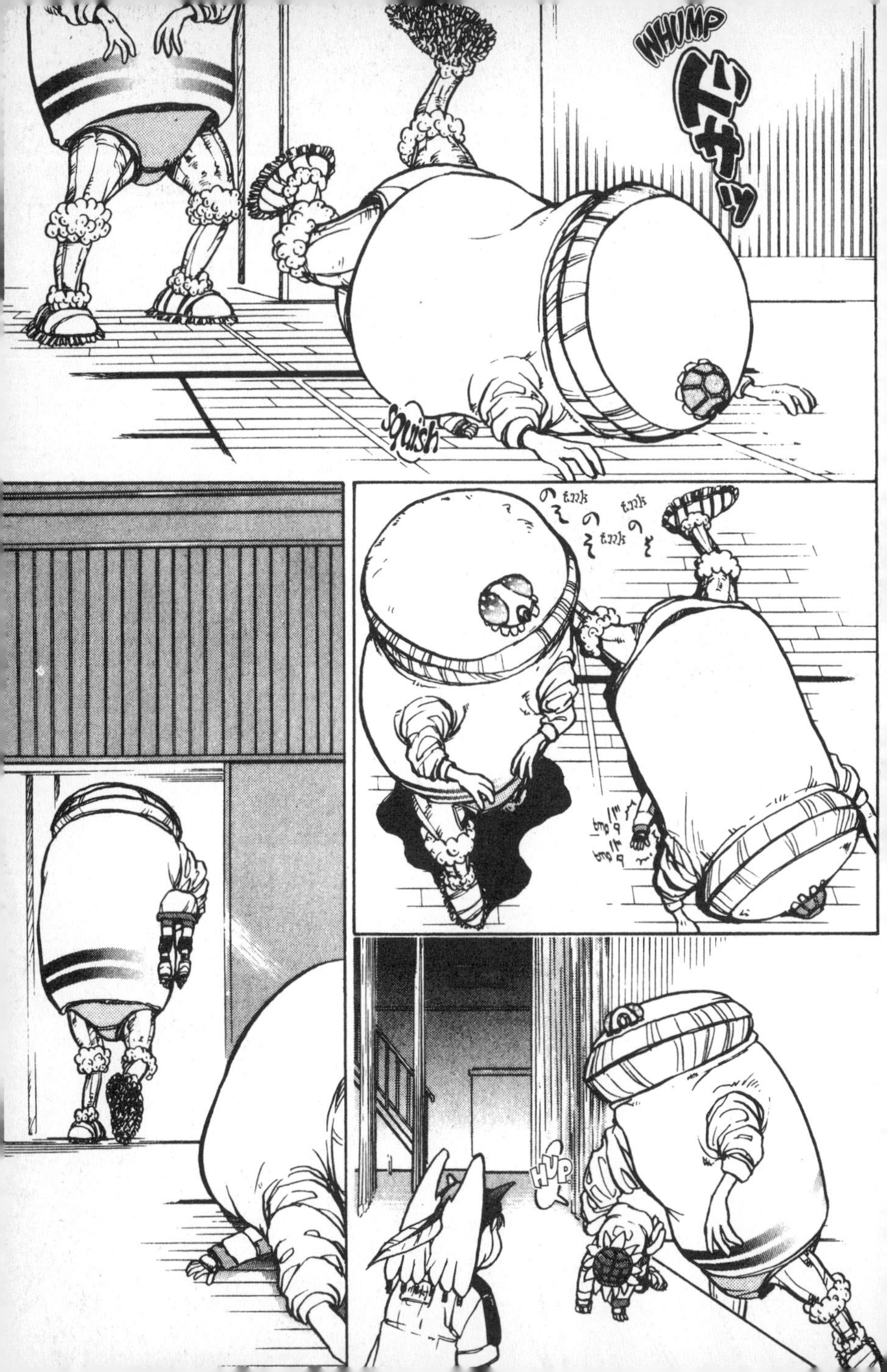
WHUMP
squish
tnk
tnk
tnk
HUP

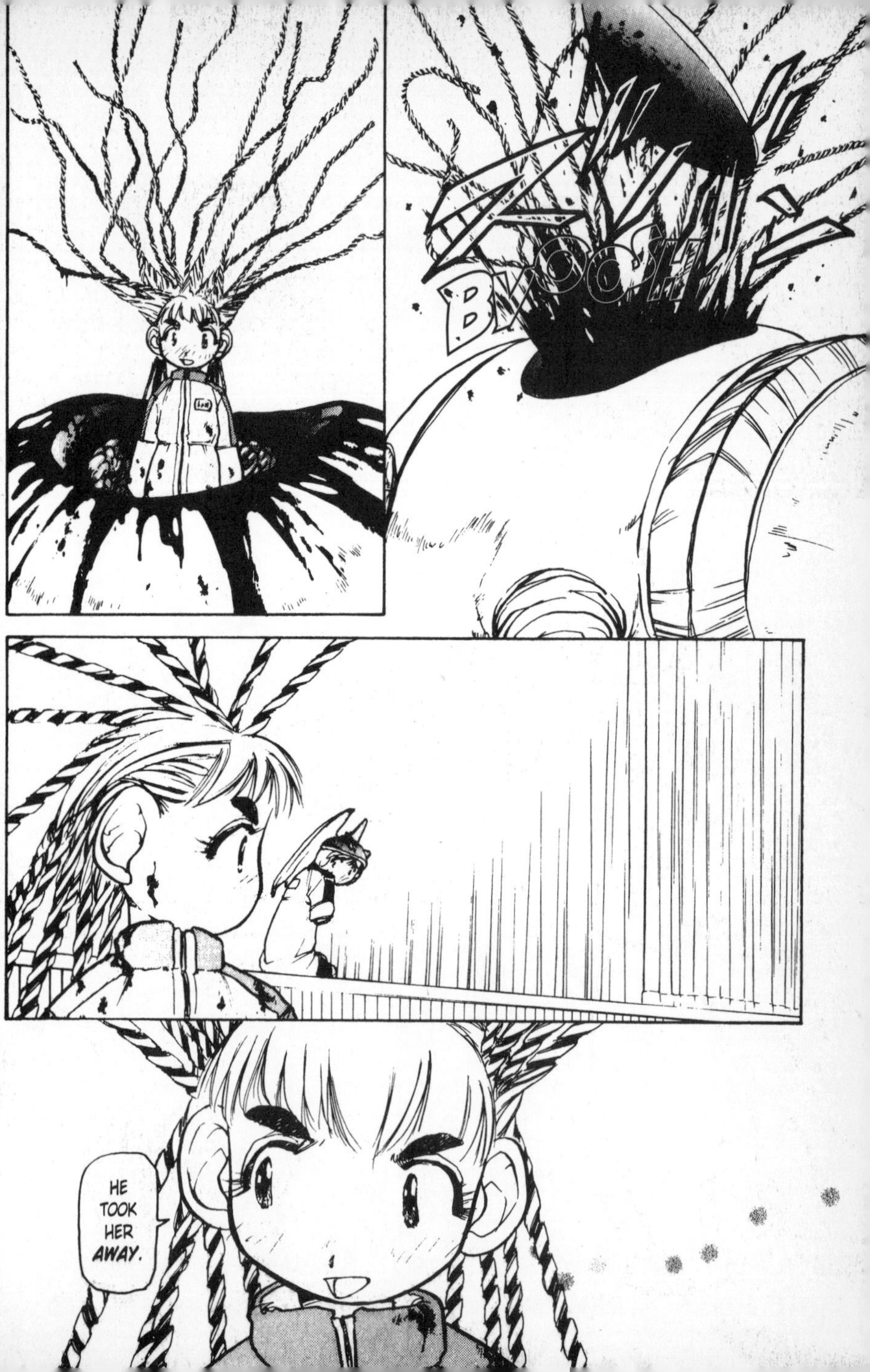
BYOOSH!!
HE TOOK HER AWAY.

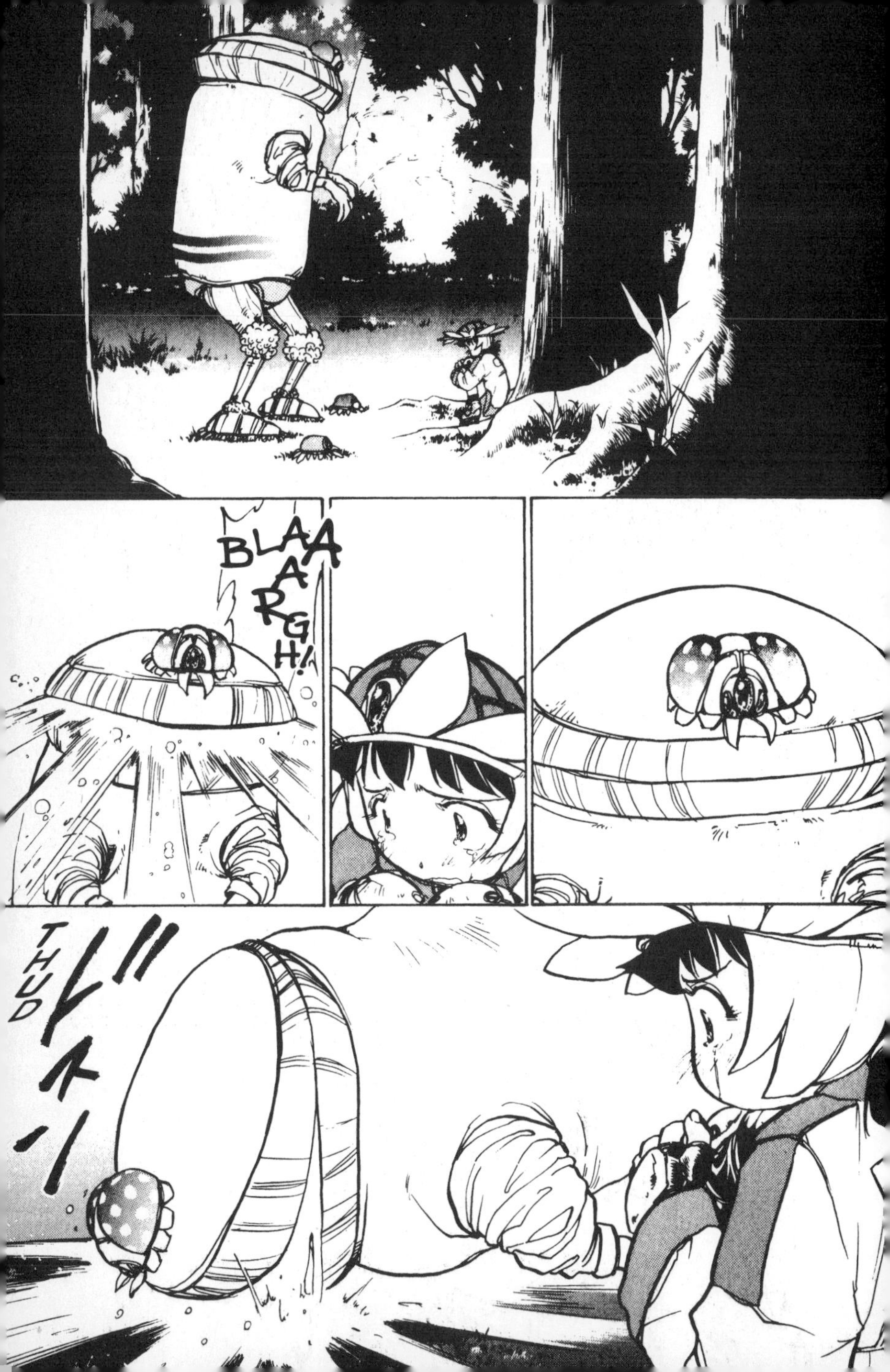
BLAAARGH!
THUD

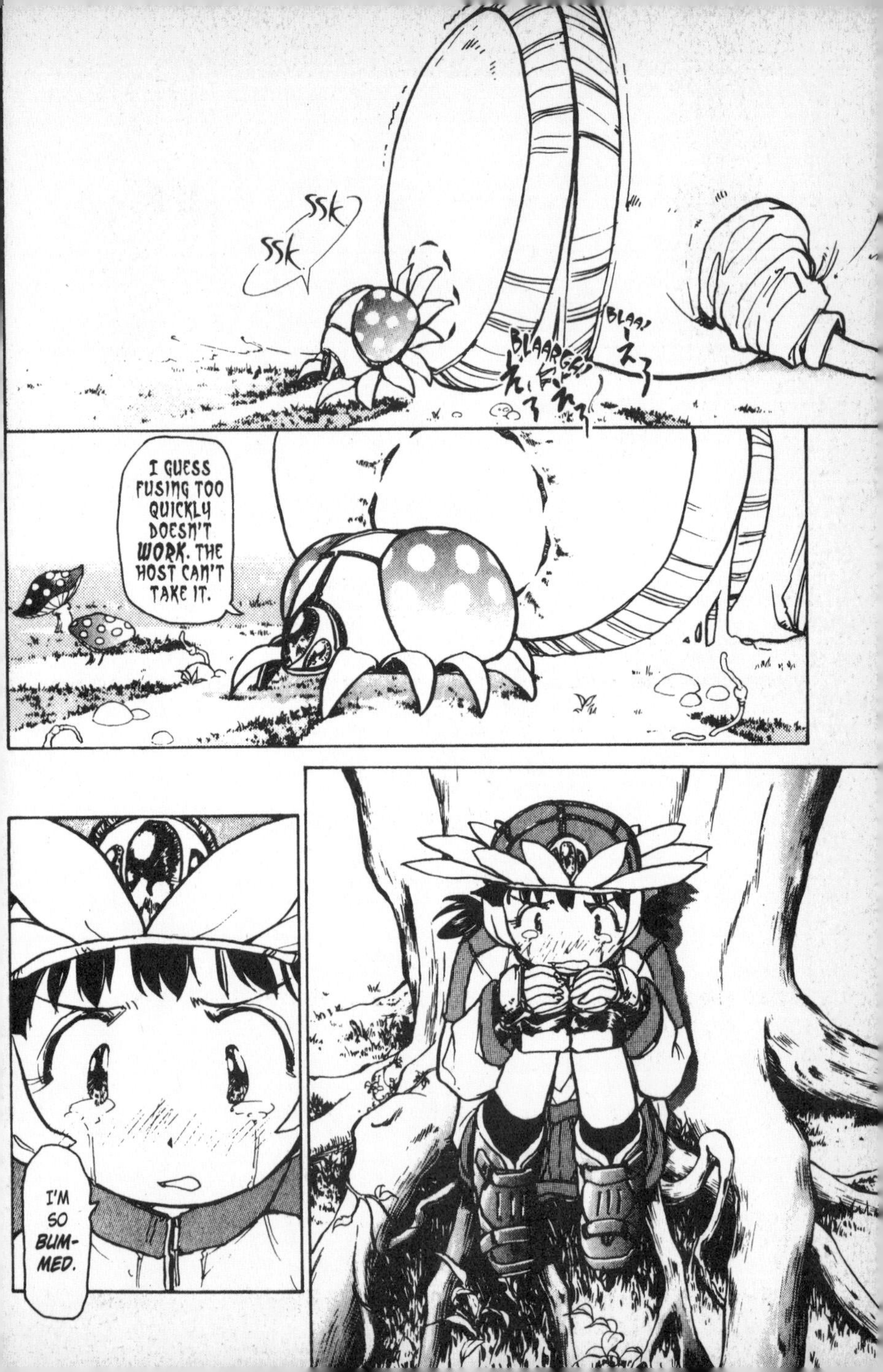
BLAA!
BLAARGH!
SSk
SSk
I GUESS FUSING TOO QUICKLY DOESN'T **WORK**. THE HOST CAN'T TAKE IT.
I'M SO **BUM-MED**.

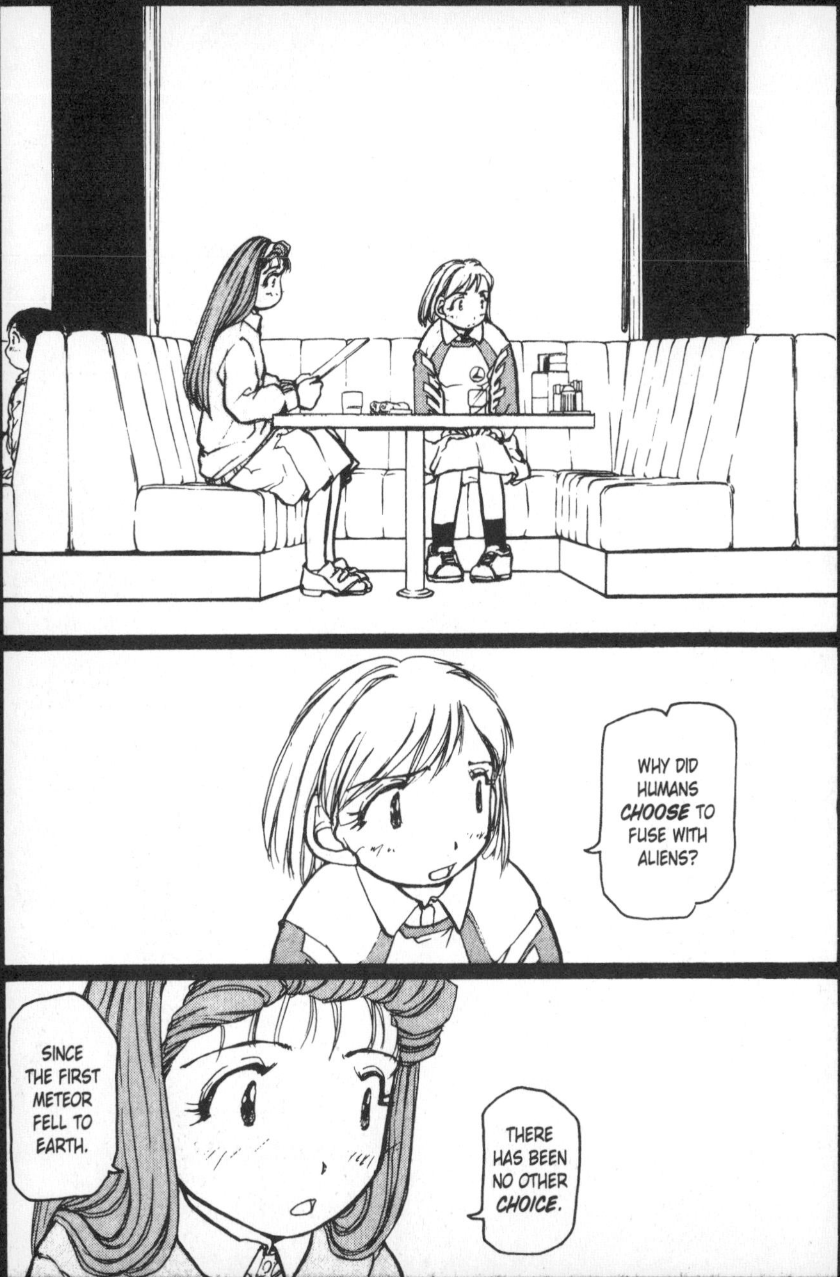
WHY DID HUMANS CHOOSE TO FUSE WITH ALIENS?
THERE HAS BEEN NO OTHER CHOICE.
SINCE THE FIRST METEOR FELL TO EARTH.

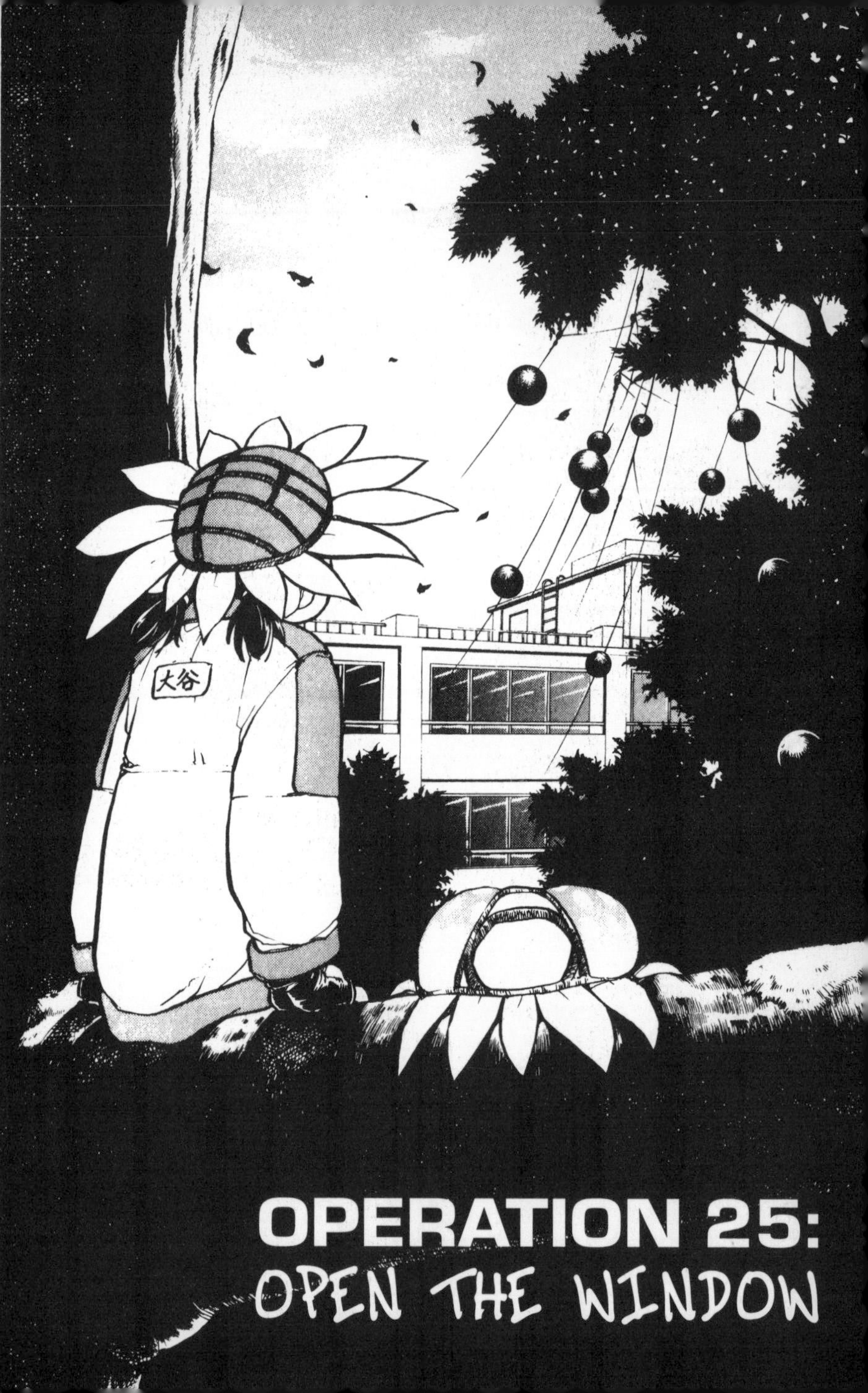
大谷

OPERATION 25:
OPEN THE WINDOW

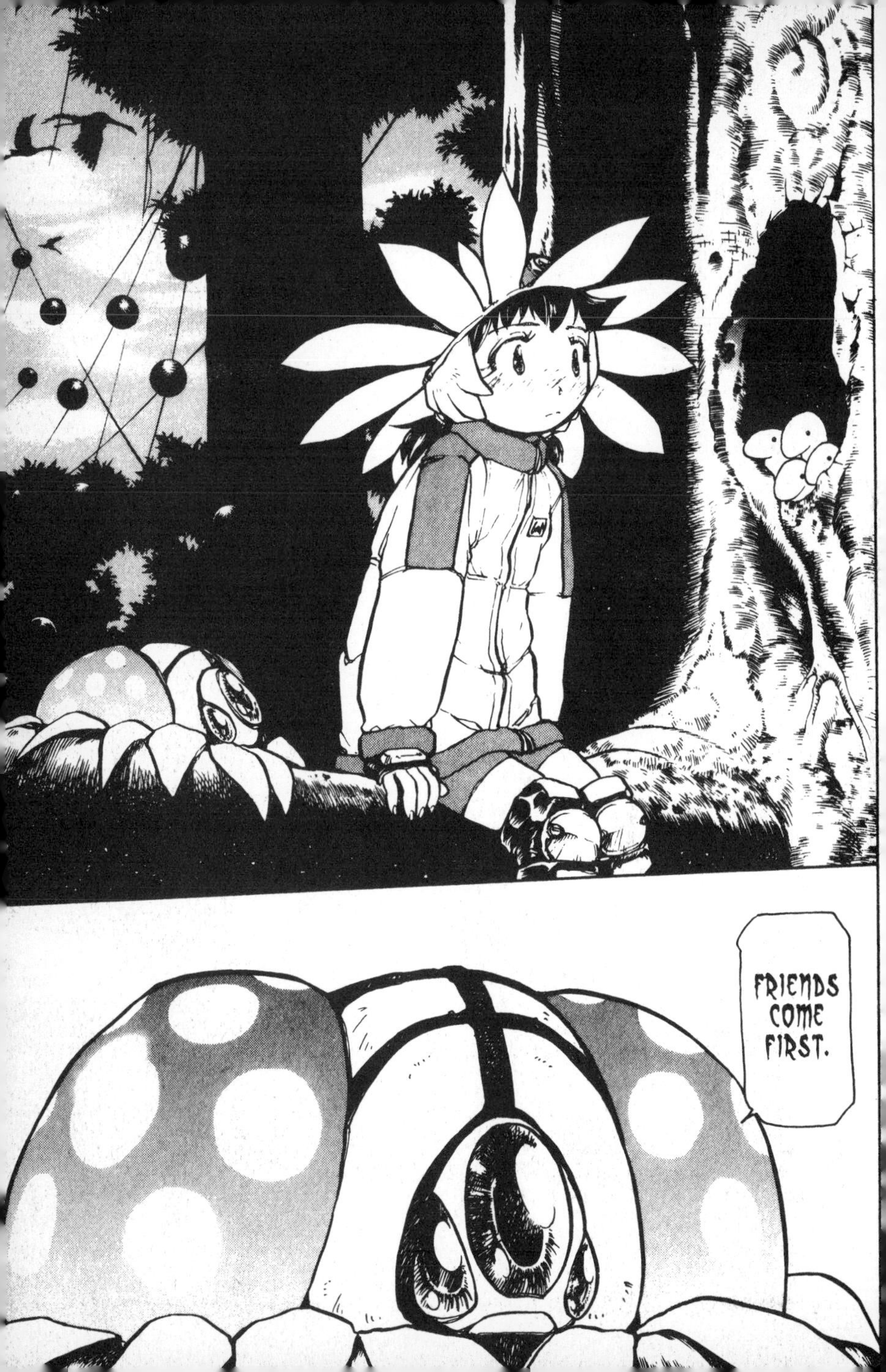
FRIENDS COME FIRST.

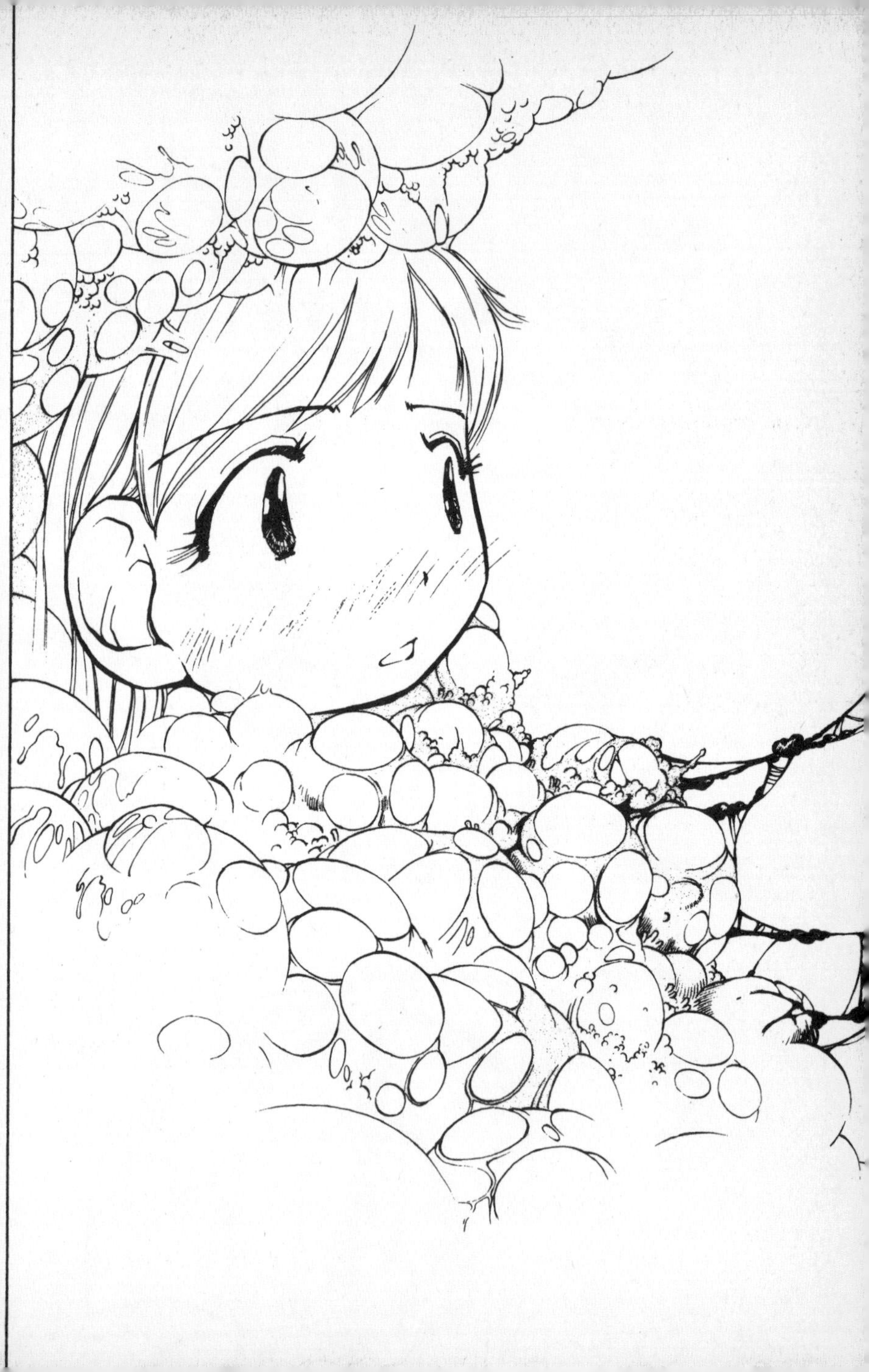

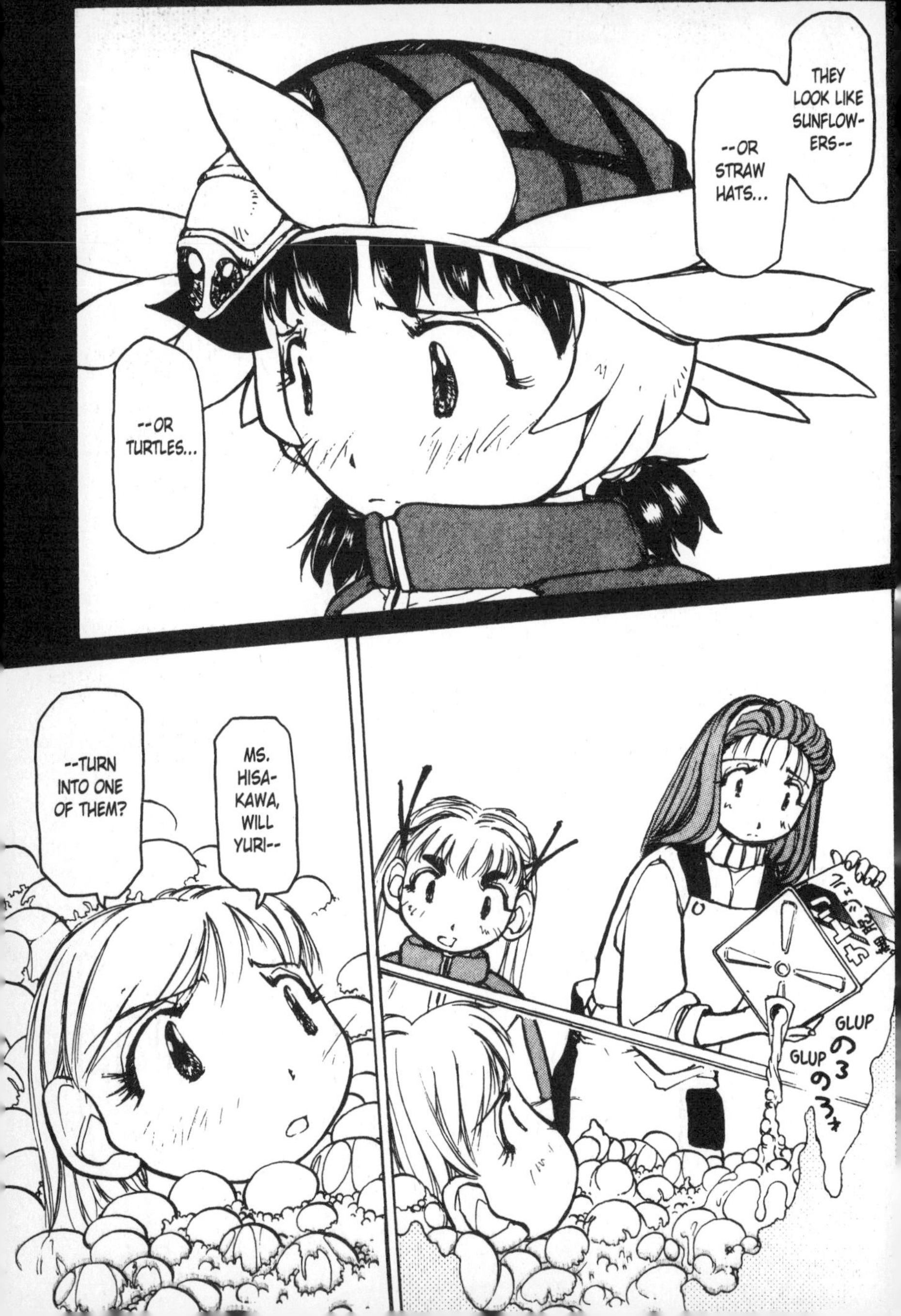
THEY LOOK LIKE SUNFLOWERS--
--OR STRAW HATS...
--OR TURTLES...
GLUP
GLUP
MS. HISAKAWA, WILL YURI--
--TURN INTO ONE OF THEM?

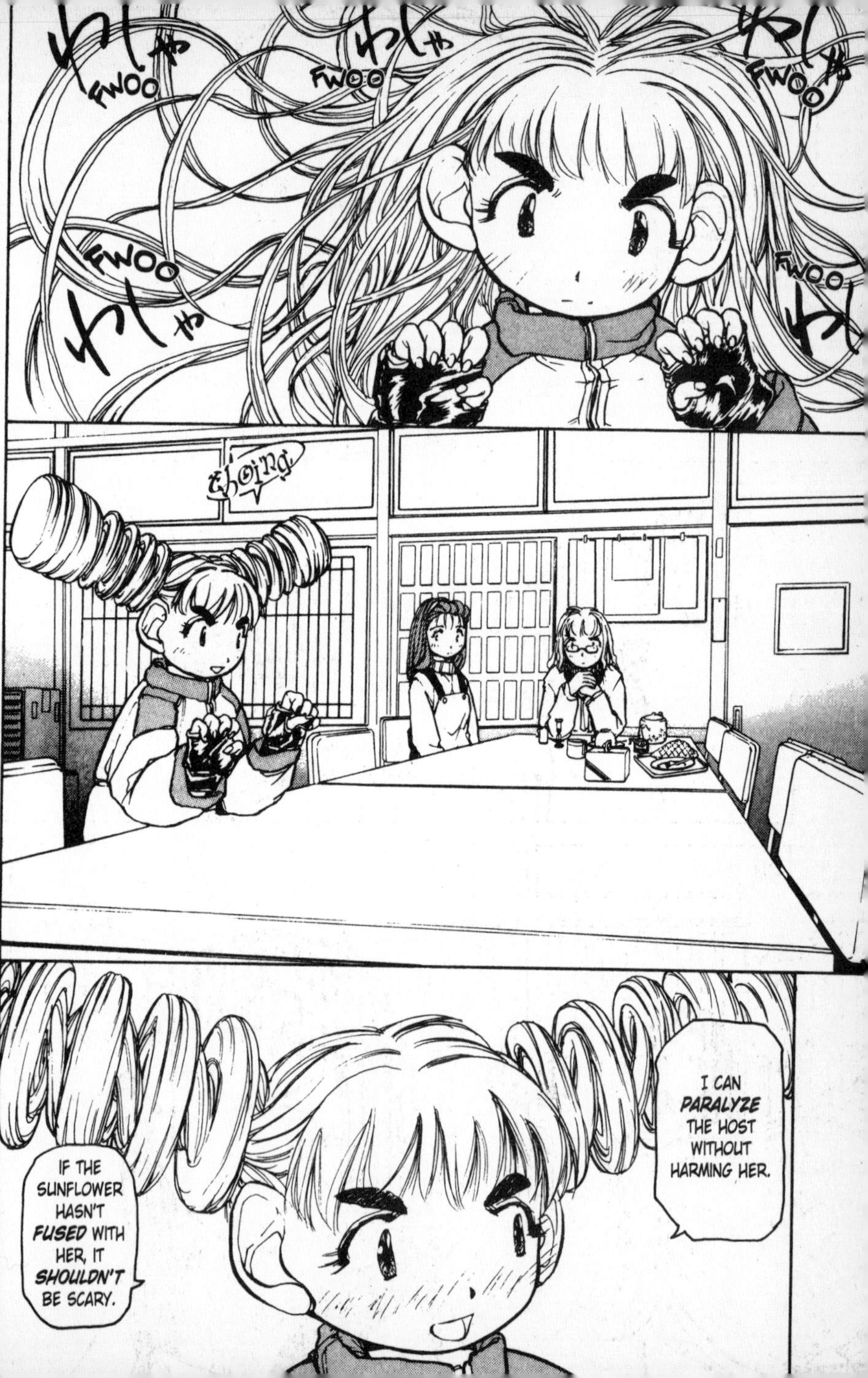

わしゃ
FWOO
わしゃ
FWOO
わしゃ
FWOO
FWOO
わしゃ
FWOO
わしゃ
thoing
I CAN *PARALYZE* THE HOST WITHOUT HARMING HER.
IF THE SUNFLOWER HASN'T *FUSED* WITH HER, IT *SHOULDN'T* BE SCARY.

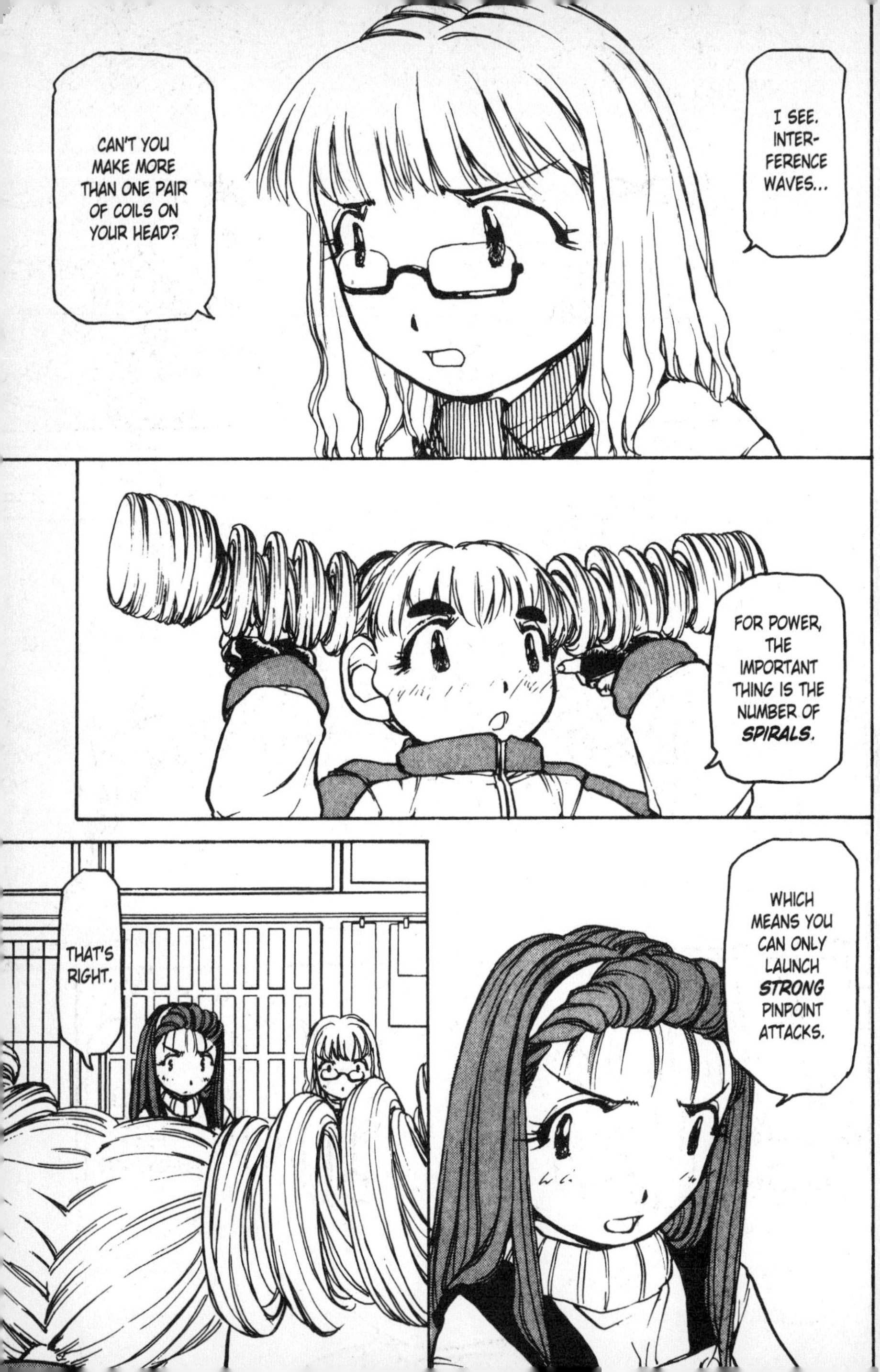
I SEE. INTERFERENCE WAVES...
CAN'T YOU MAKE MORE THAN ONE PAIR OF COILS ON YOUR HEAD?
FOR POWER, THE IMPORTANT THING IS THE NUMBER OF **SPIRALS**.
WHICH MEANS YOU CAN ONLY LAUNCH **STRONG** PINPOINT ATTACKS.
THAT'S RIGHT.

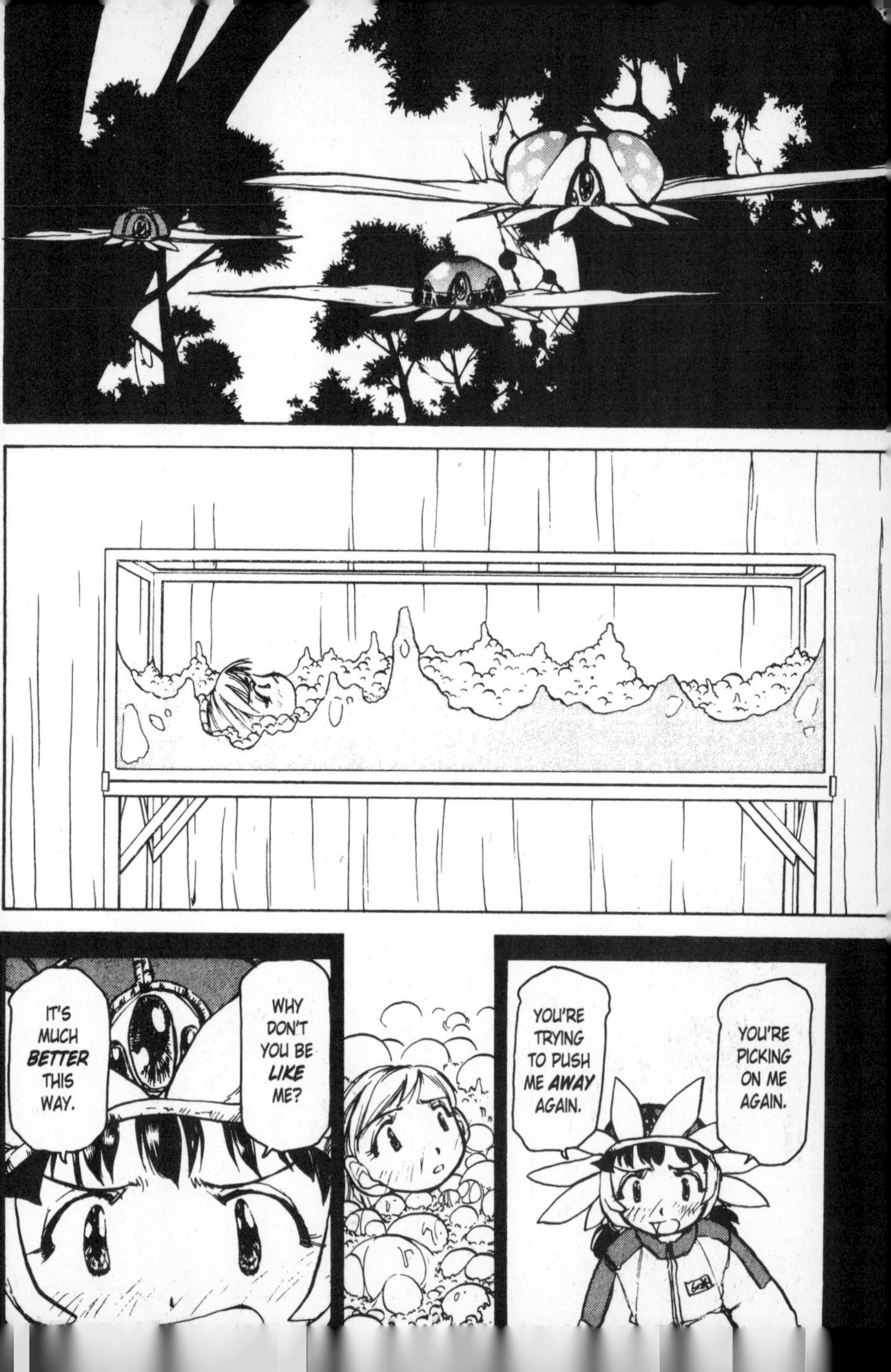
YOU'RE PICKING ON ME AGAIN.
YOU'RE TRYING TO PUSH ME AWAY AGAIN.
WHY DON'T YOU BE LIKE ME?
IT'S MUCH BETTER THIS WAY.

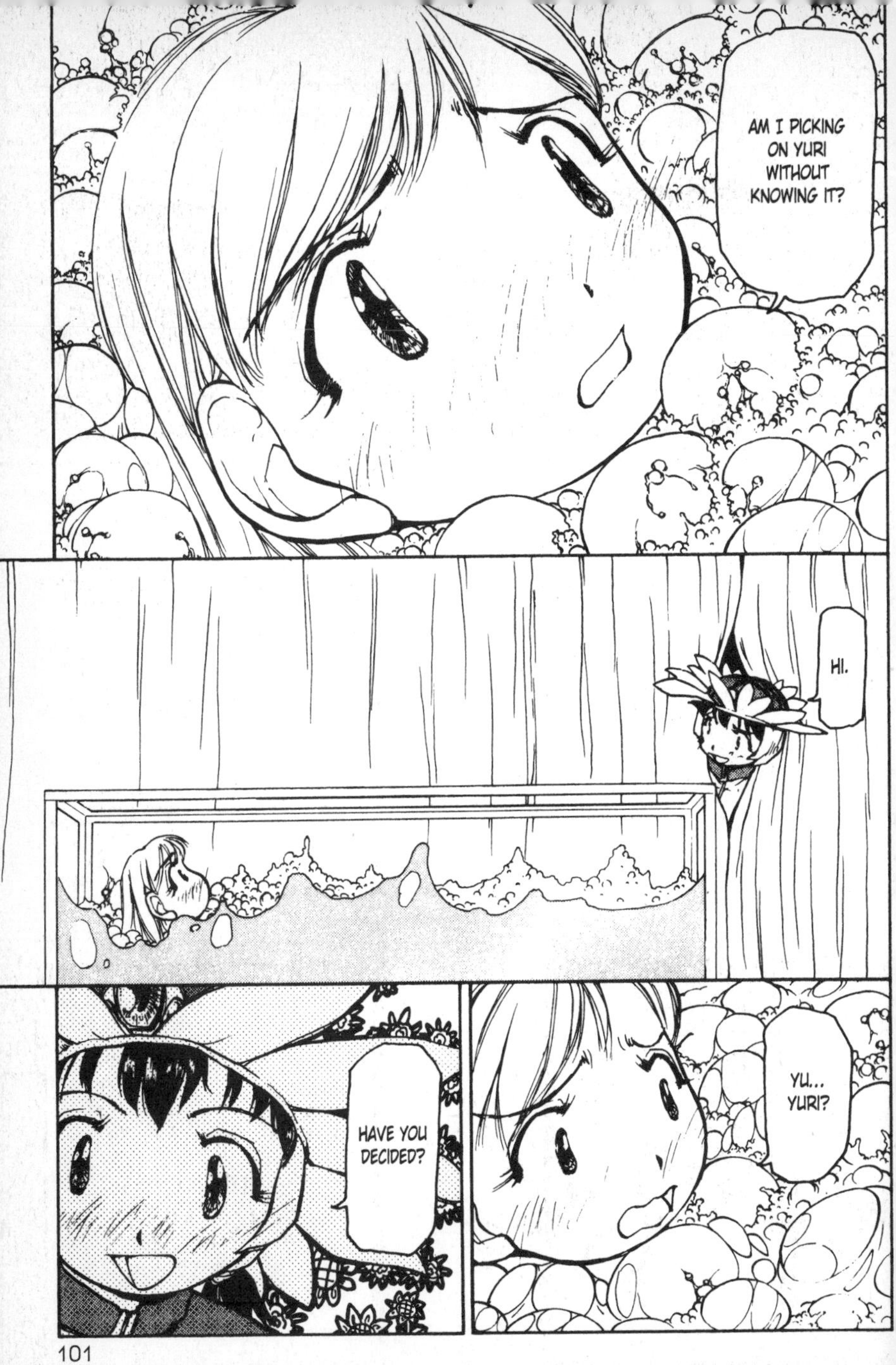
AM I PICKING ON YURI WITHOUT KNOWING IT?
HI.
YU... YURI?
HAVE YOU DECIDED?

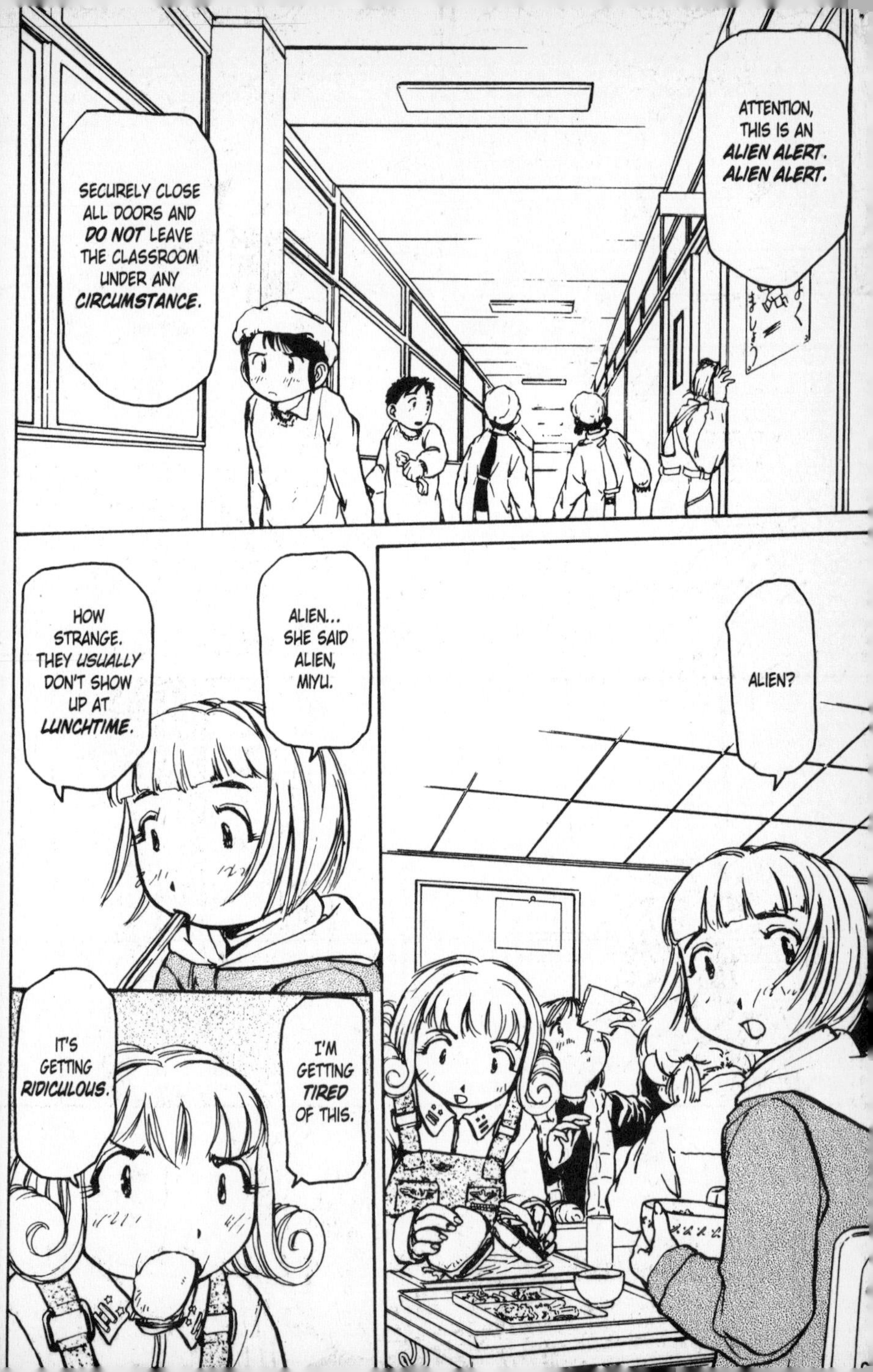
ATTENTION, THIS IS AN ALIEN ALERT. ALIEN ALERT.
SECURELY CLOSE ALL DOORS AND DO NOT LEAVE THE CLASSROOM UNDER ANY CIRCUMSTANCE.
ALIEN?
ALIEN... SHE SAID ALIEN, MIYU.
HOW STRANGE. THEY USUALLY DON'T SHOW UP AT LUNCHTIME.
I'M GETTING TIRED OF THIS.
IT'S GETTING RIDICULOUS.

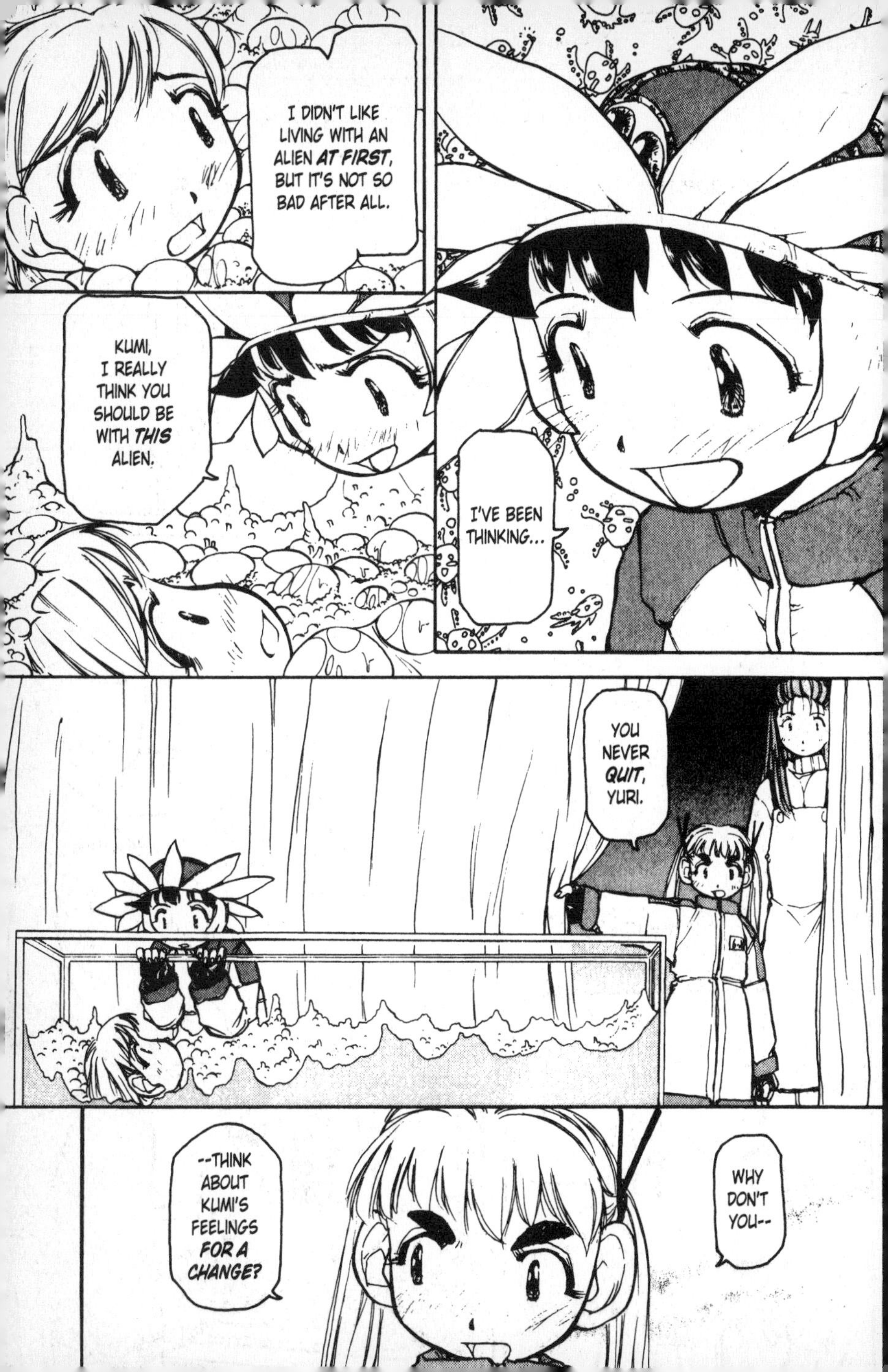
I'VE BEEN THINKING...
I DIDN'T LIKE LIVING WITH AN ALIEN AT FIRST, BUT IT'S NOT SO BAD AFTER ALL.
KUMI, I REALLY THINK YOU SHOULD BE WITH THIS ALIEN.
YOU NEVER QUIT, YURI.
WHY DON'T YOU--
--THINK ABOUT KUMI'S FEELINGS FOR A CHANGE?

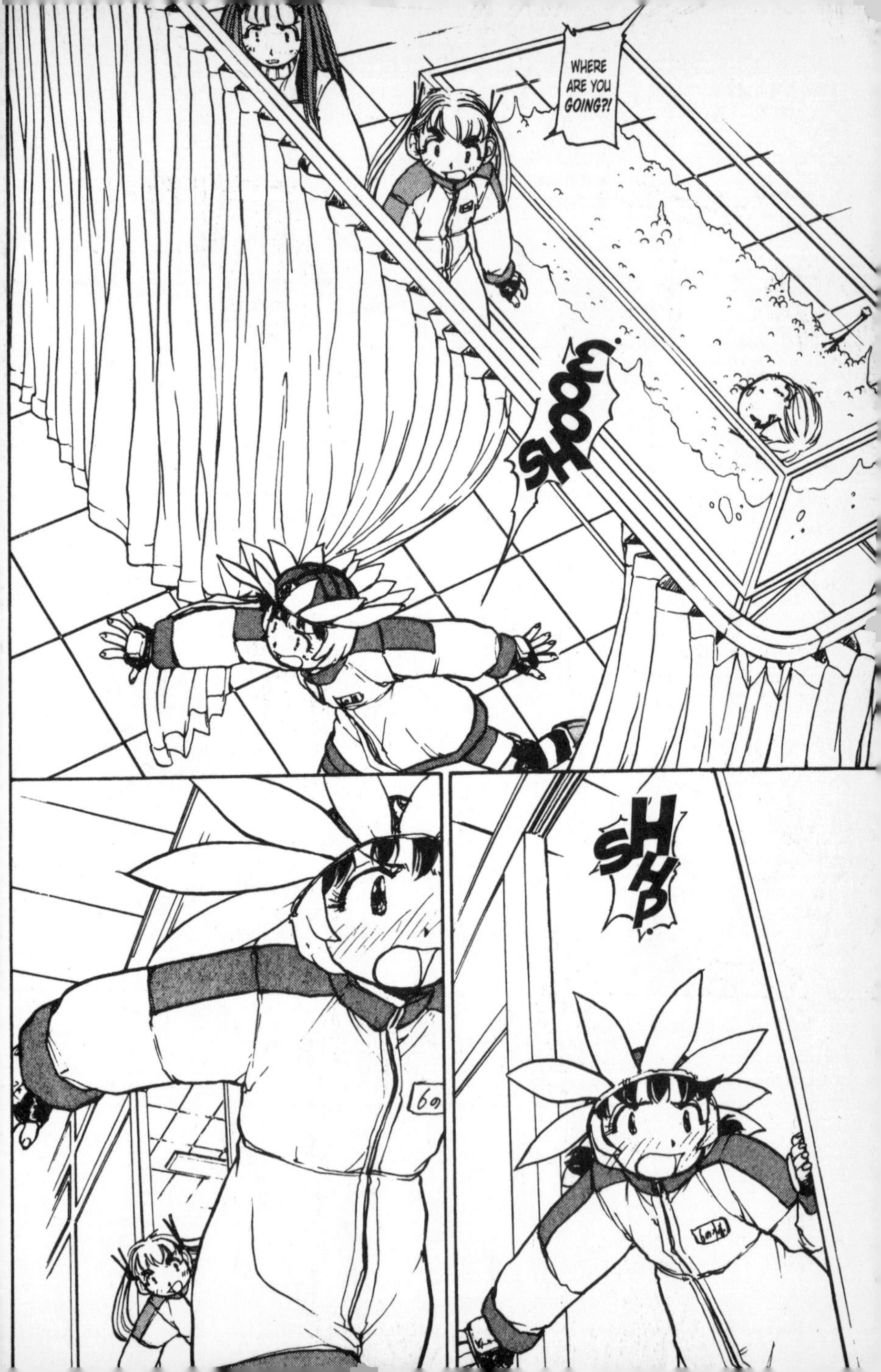
WHERE ARE YOU GOING?!
SHOOM
SHUP

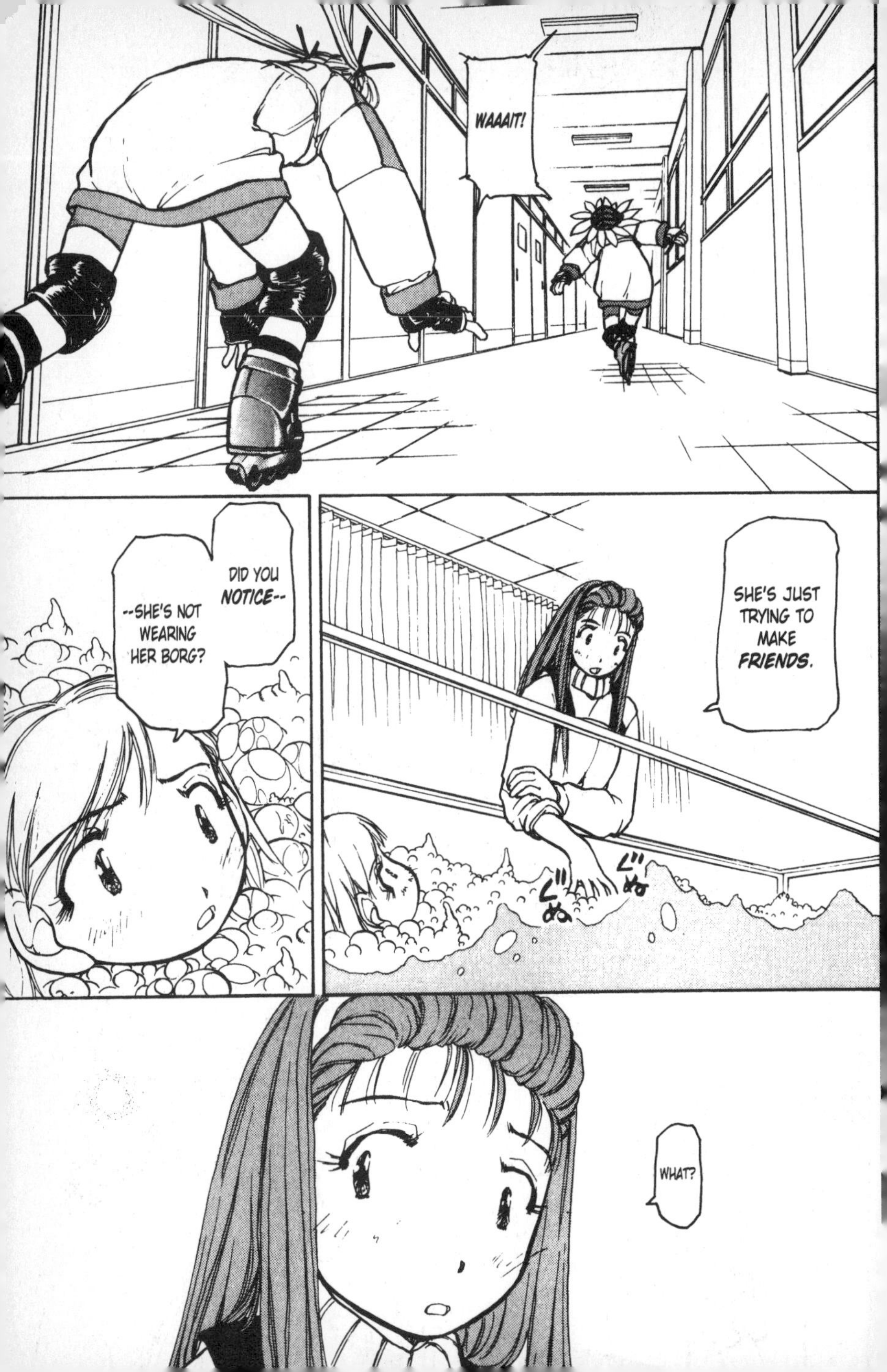
WAAAIT!
SHE'S JUST TRYING TO MAKE FRIENDS.
DID YOU NOTICE--
--SHE'S NOT WEARING HER BORG?
WHAT?

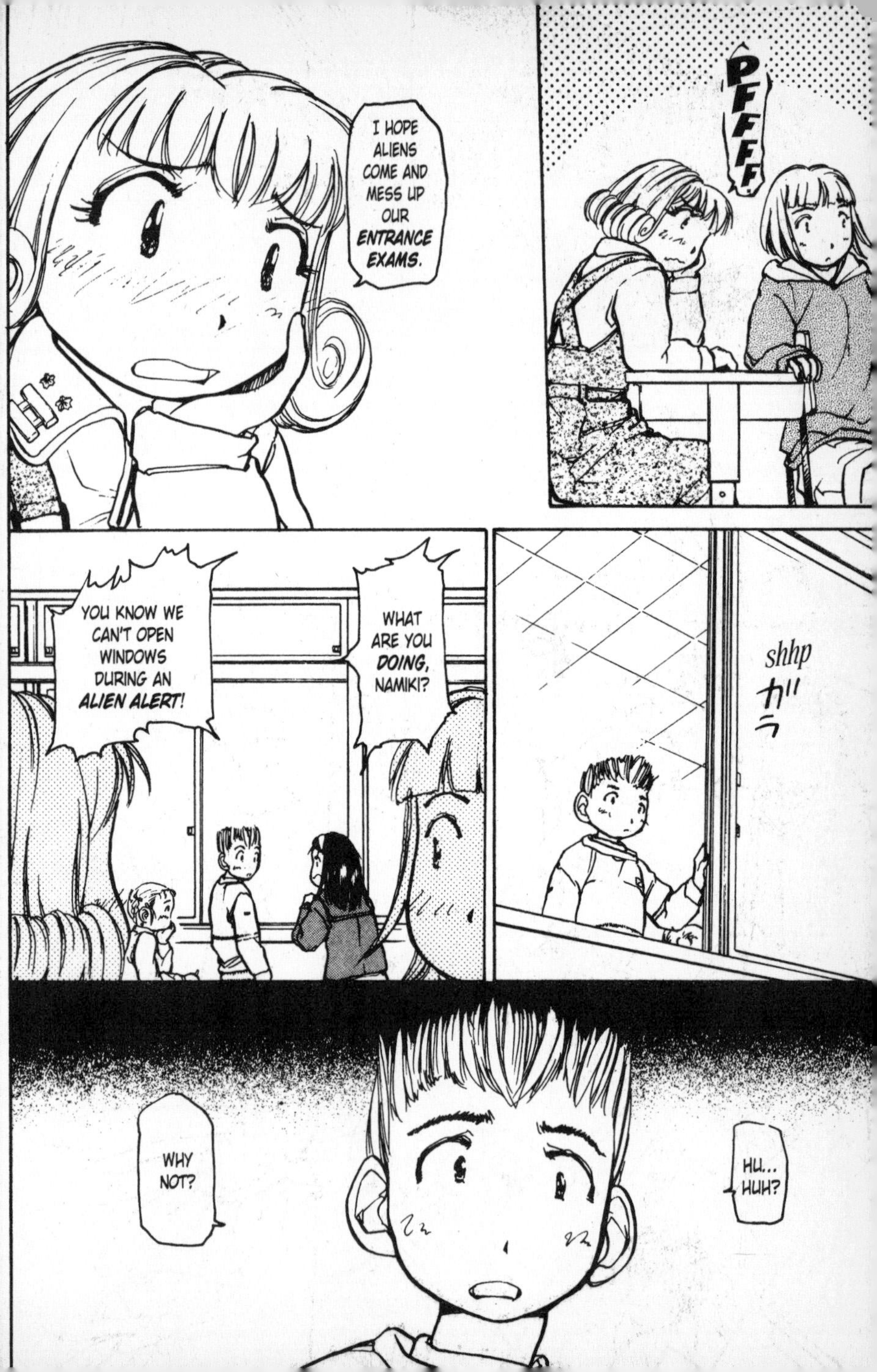
PFFFF
I HOPE ALIENS COME AND MESS UP OUR ENTRANCE EXAMS.
shhp
ガラ
WHAT ARE YOU DOING, NAMIKI?
YOU KNOW WE CAN'T OPEN WINDOWS DURING AN ALIEN ALERT!
HU... HUH?
WHY NOT?

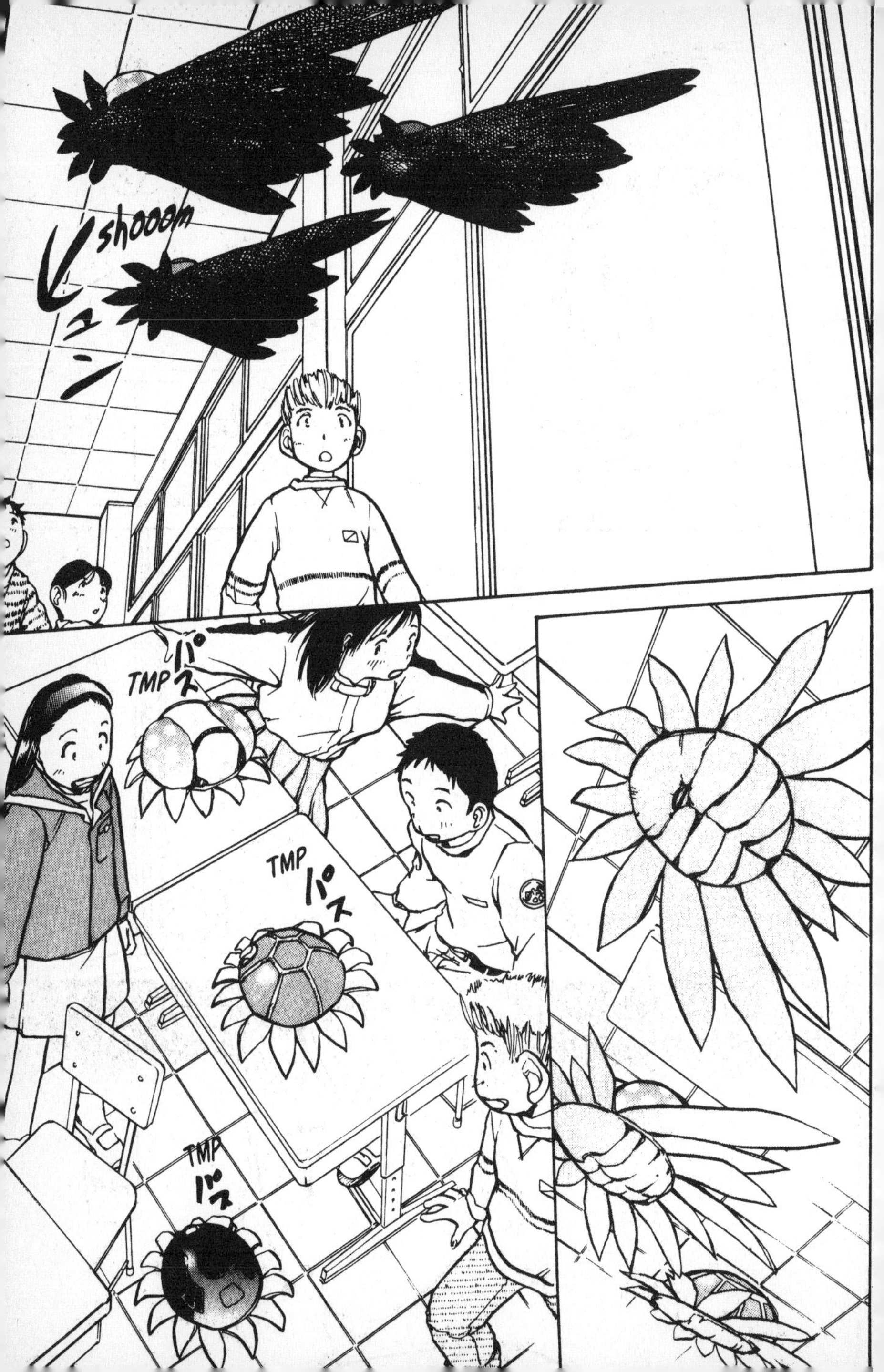
shoooom
ビュン
TMP
パス
TMP
パス
TMP
パス

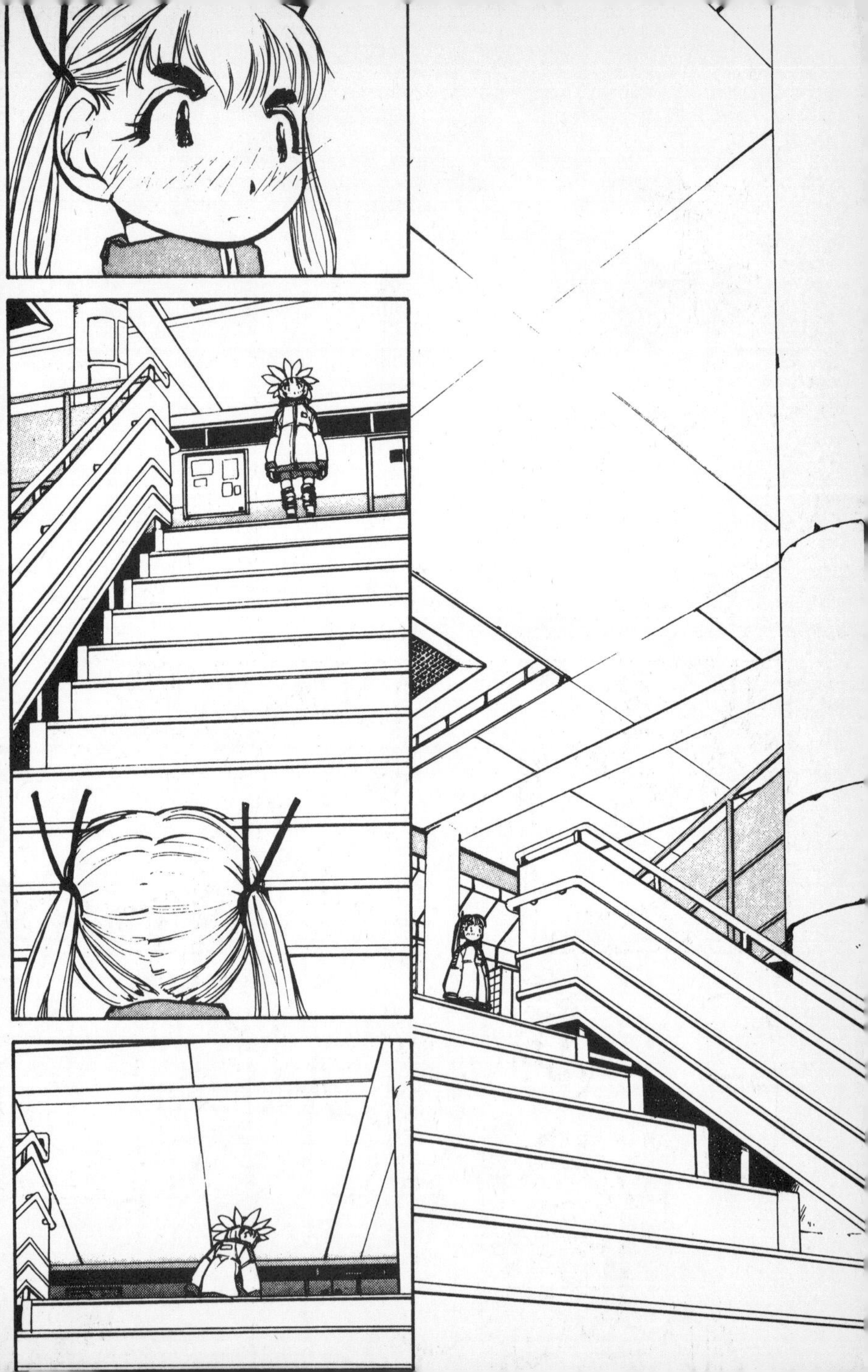

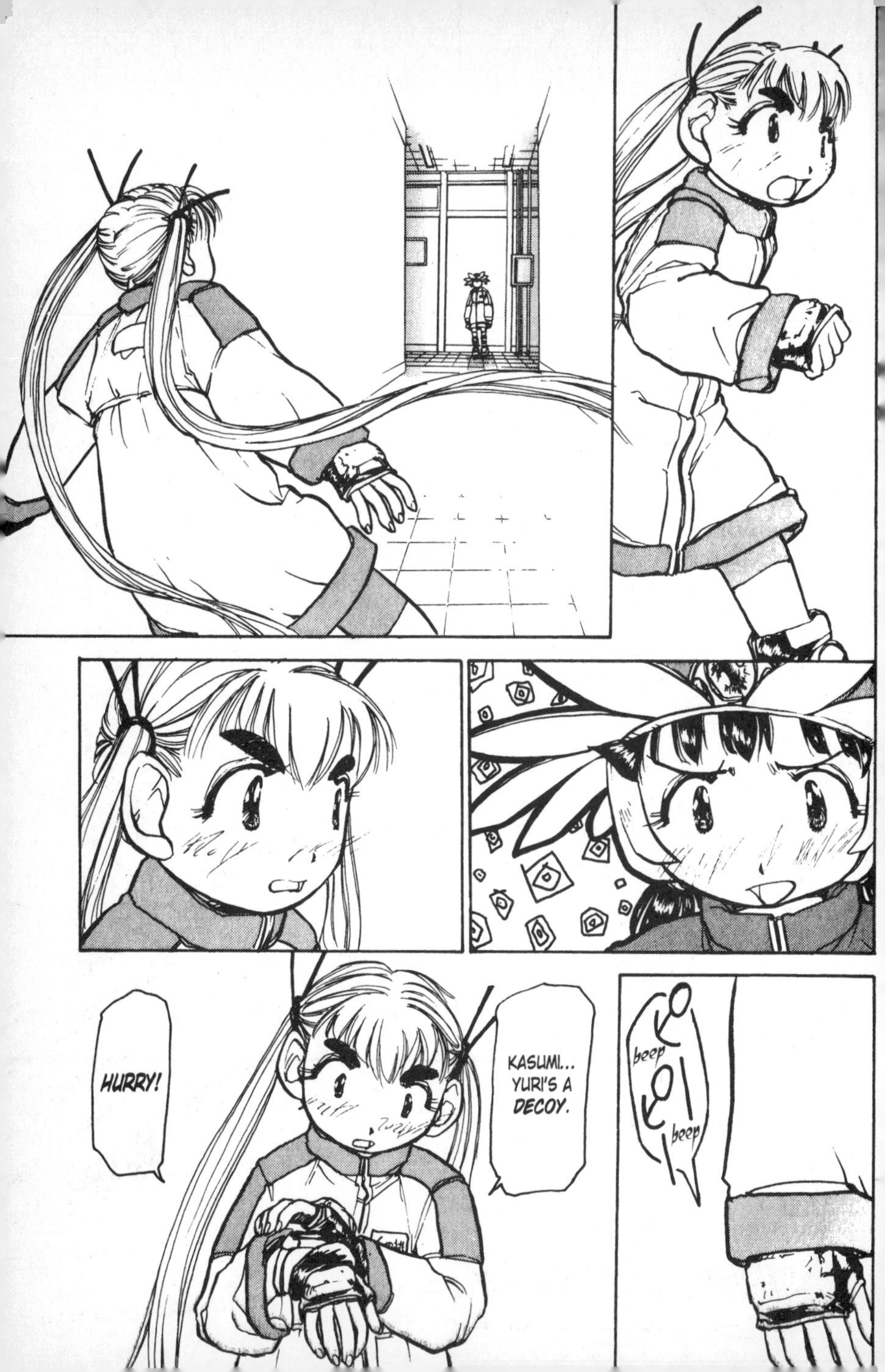
beep
beep
KASUMI... YURI'S A DECOY.
HURRY!

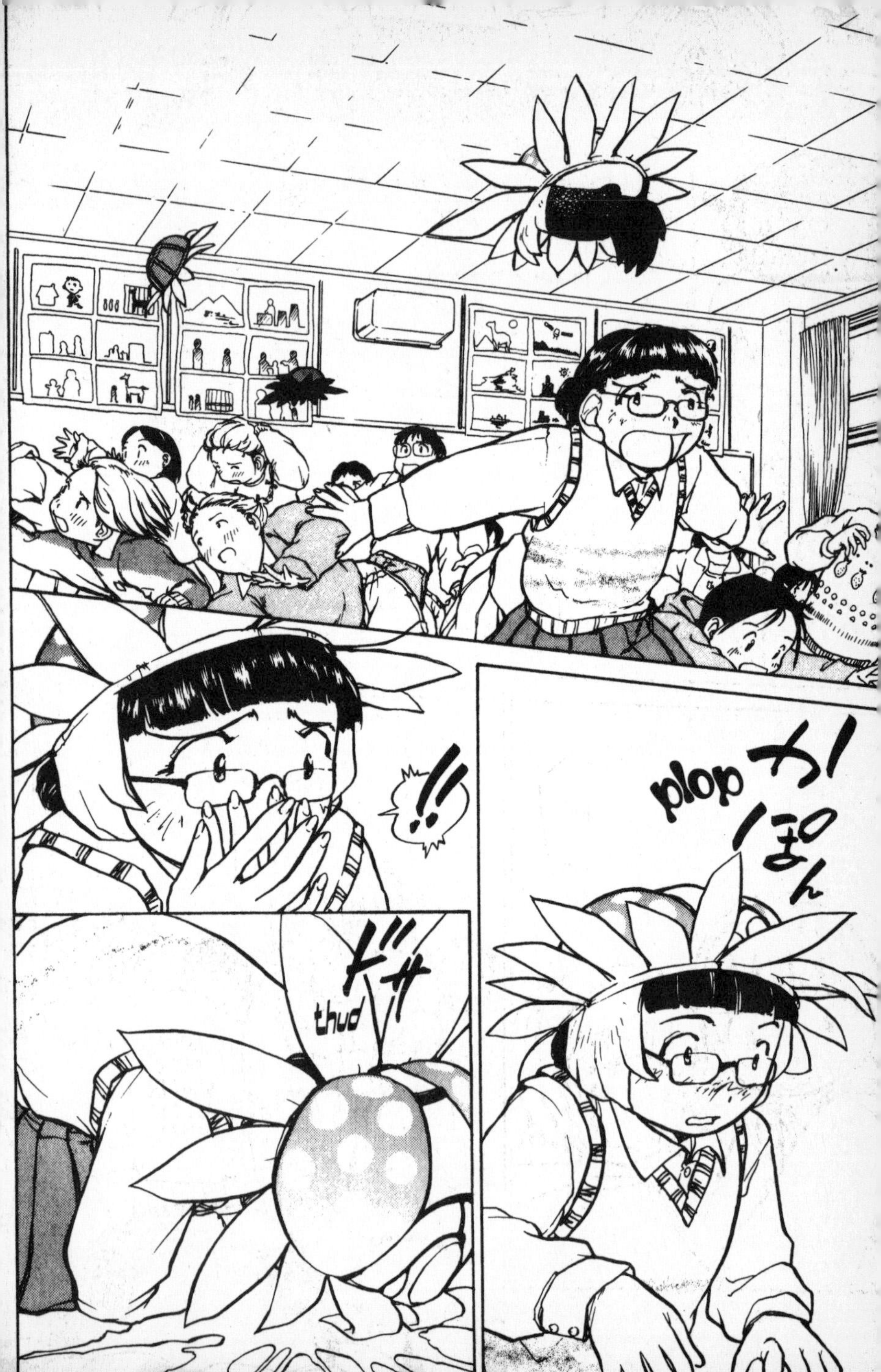

かぽん
plop
!!
ドサ
thud

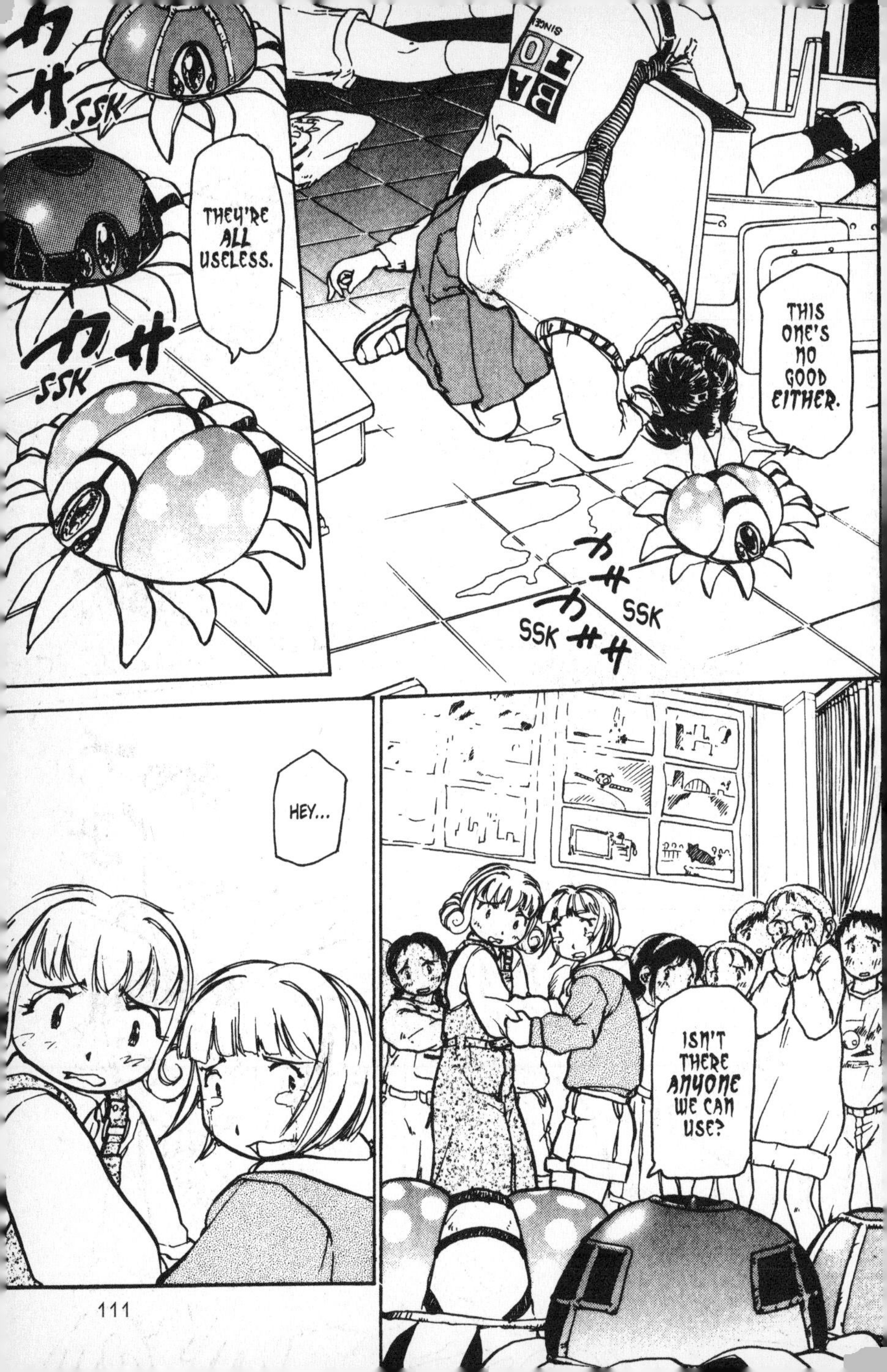
THIS ONE'S NO GOOD EITHER.
カサ SSK
カサ SSK
カサ SSK
THEY'RE ALL USELESS.
カサ SSK
ISN'T THERE ANYONE WE CAN USE?
HEY...

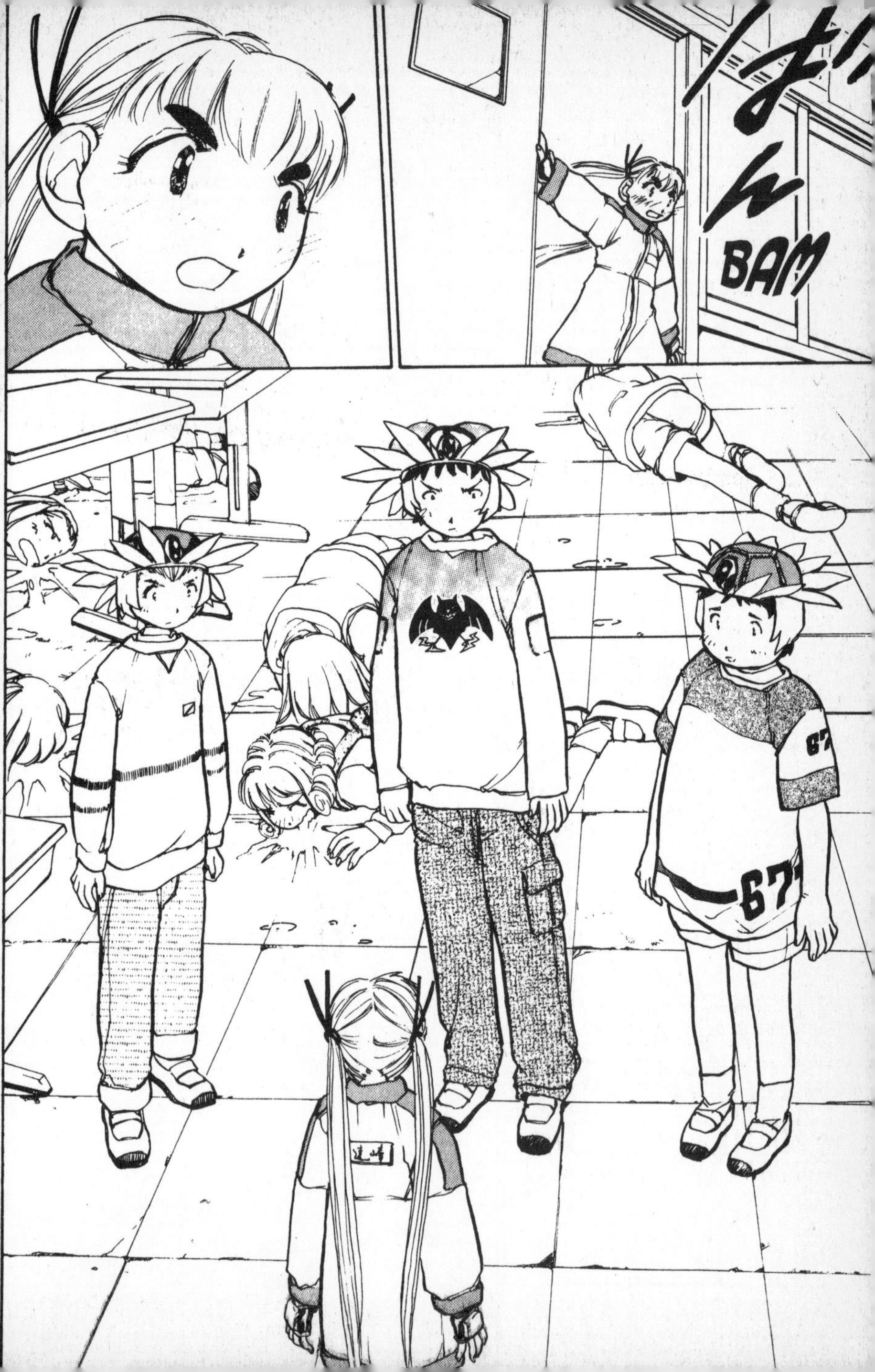
ばん
BAM

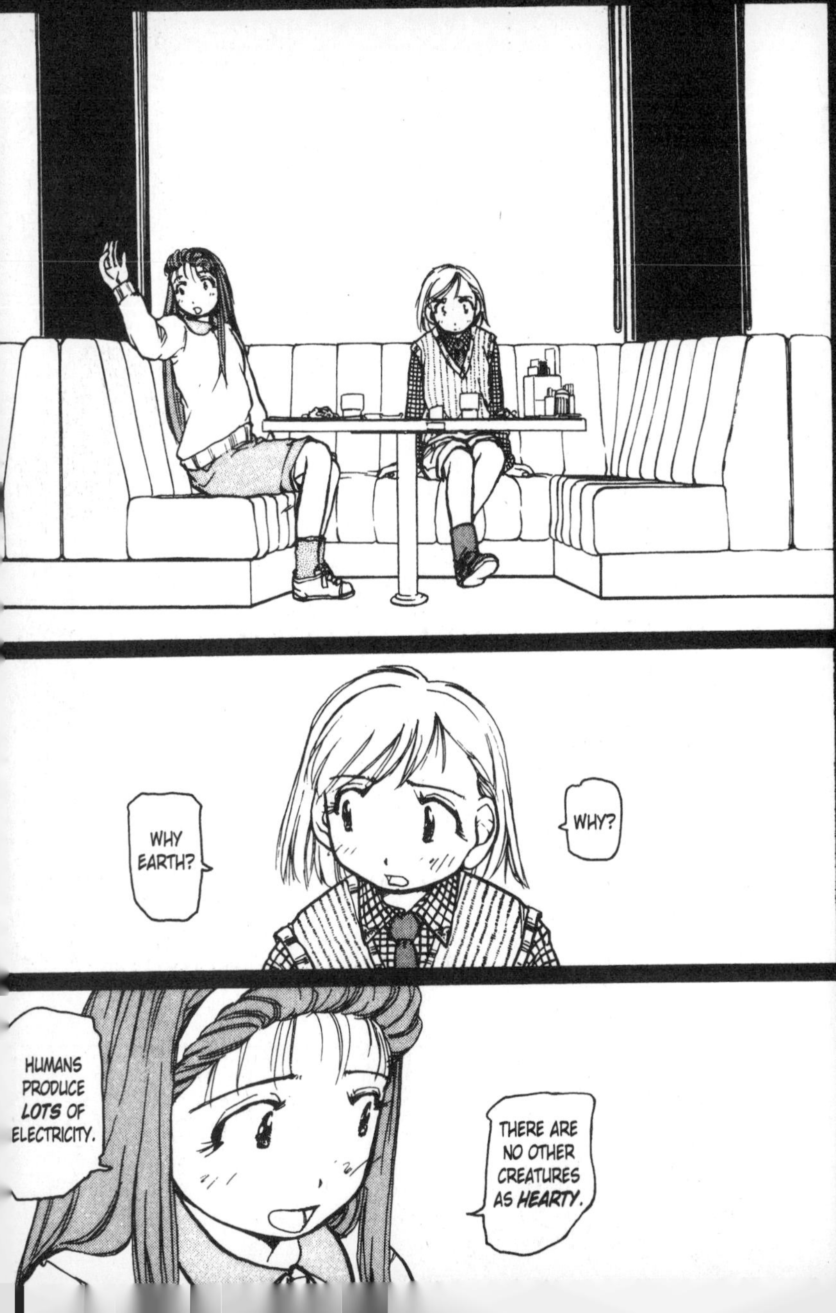
WHY?
WHY EARTH?
THERE ARE NO OTHER CREATURES AS HEARTY.
HUMANS PRODUCE LOTS OF ELECTRICITY.

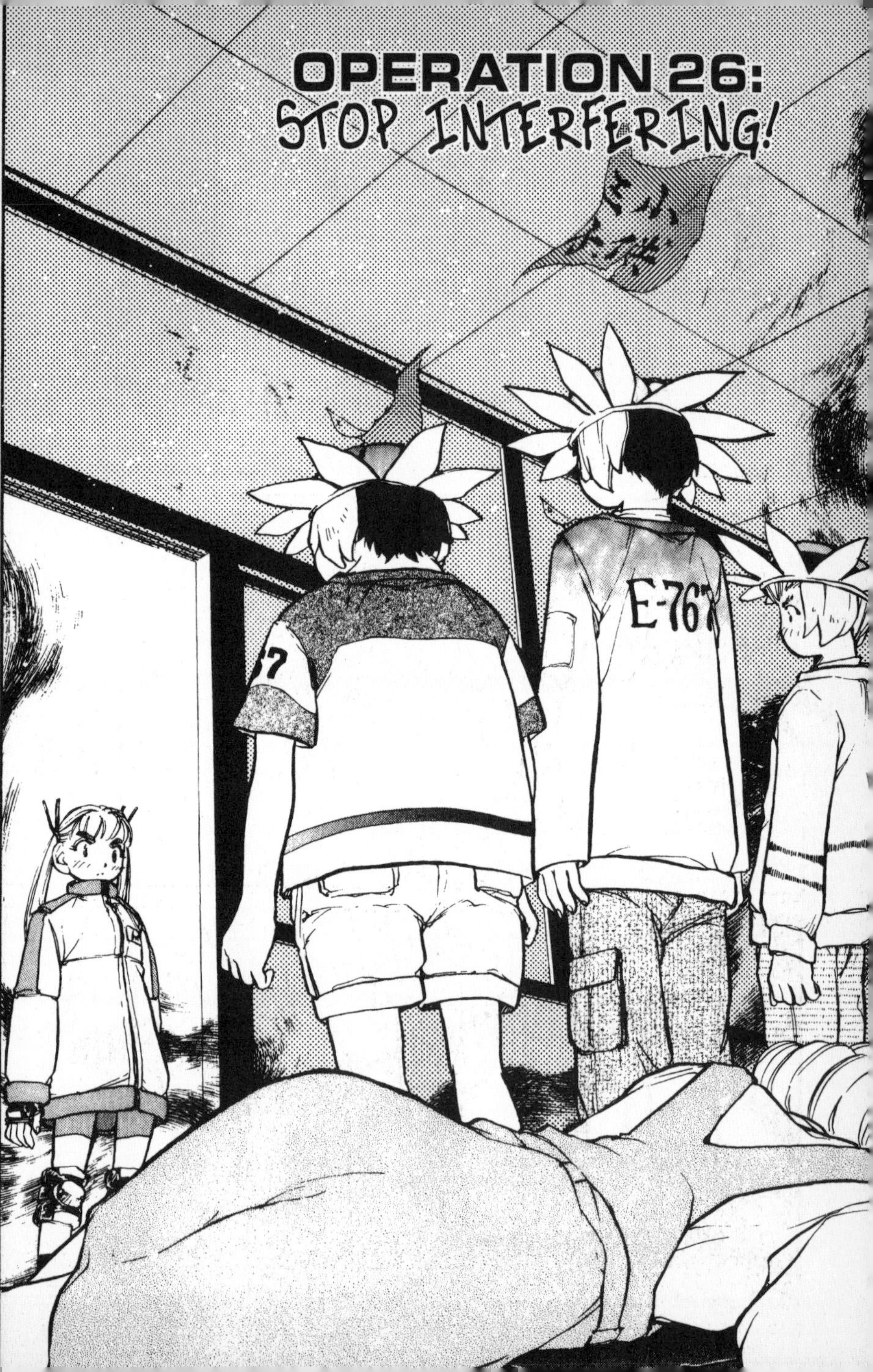
OPERATION 26:
STOP INTERFERING!
E-767
67

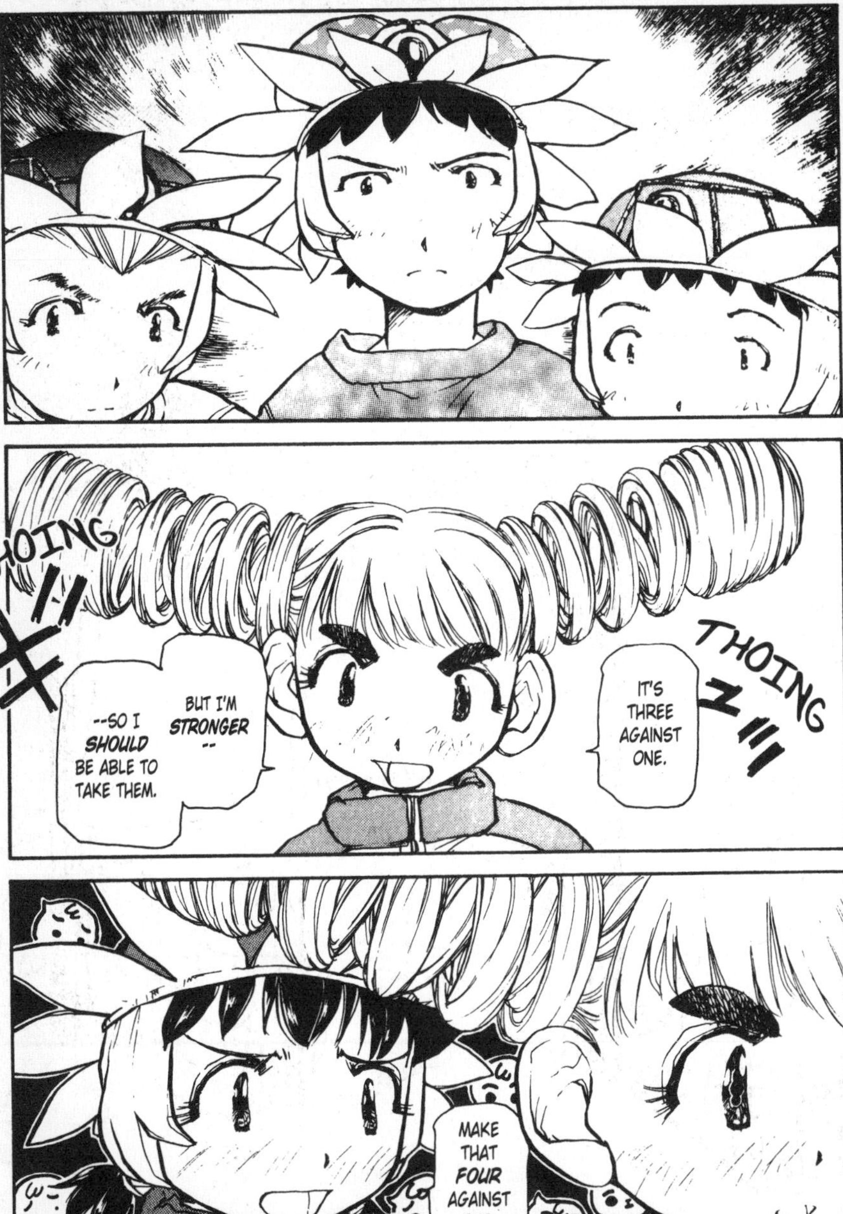
THOING
IT'S THREE AGAINST ONE.
BUT I'M **STRONGER** --
--SO I **SHOULD** BE ABLE TO TAKE THEM.
THOING
MAKE THAT **FOUR** AGAINST ONE.

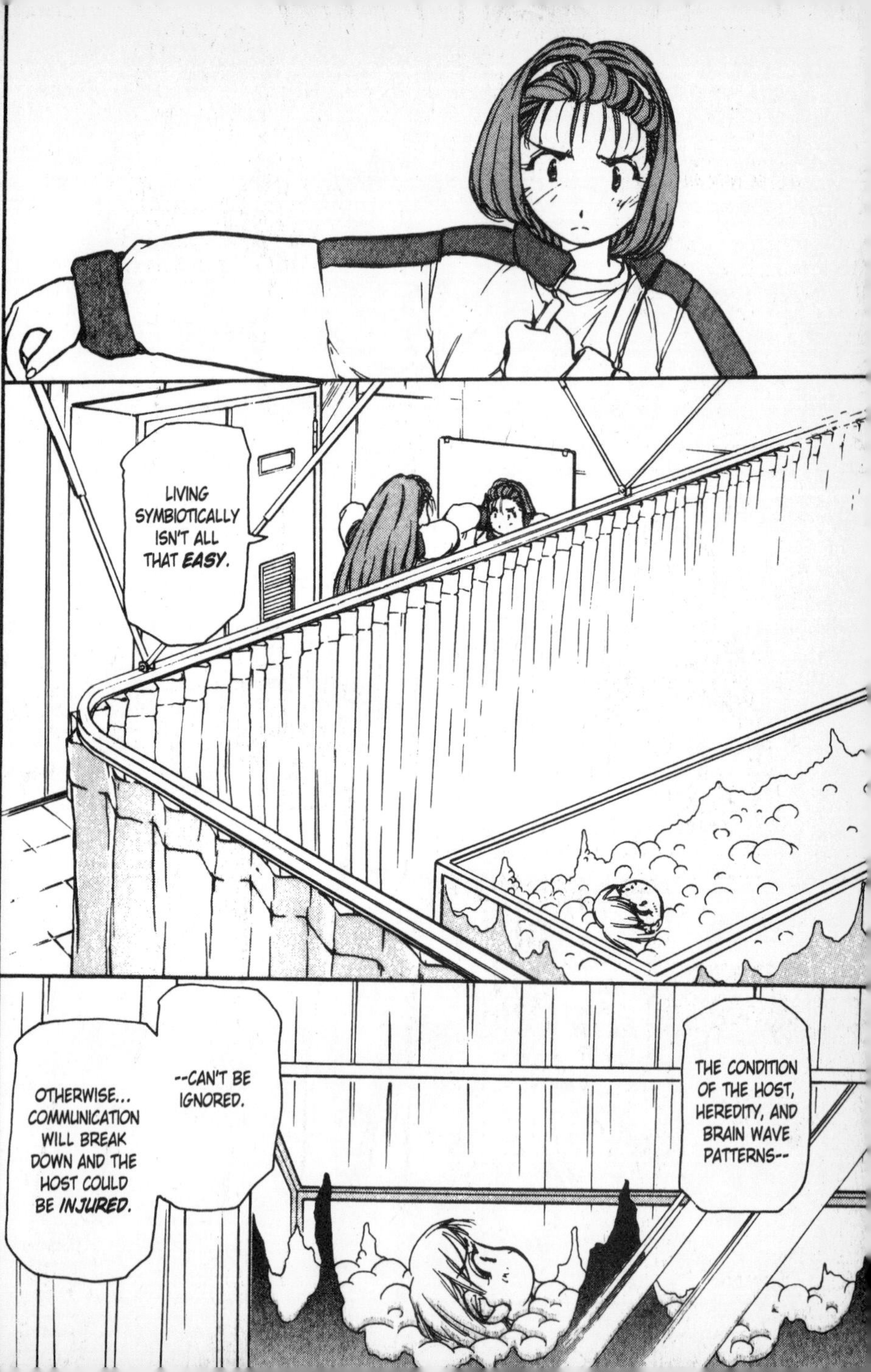
LIVING SYMBIOTICALLY ISN'T ALL THAT *EASY*.
THE CONDITION OF THE HOST, HEREDITY, AND BRAIN WAVE PATTERNS--
--CAN'T BE IGNORED.
OTHERWISE... COMMUNICATION WILL BREAK DOWN AND THE HOST COULD BE *INJURED*.

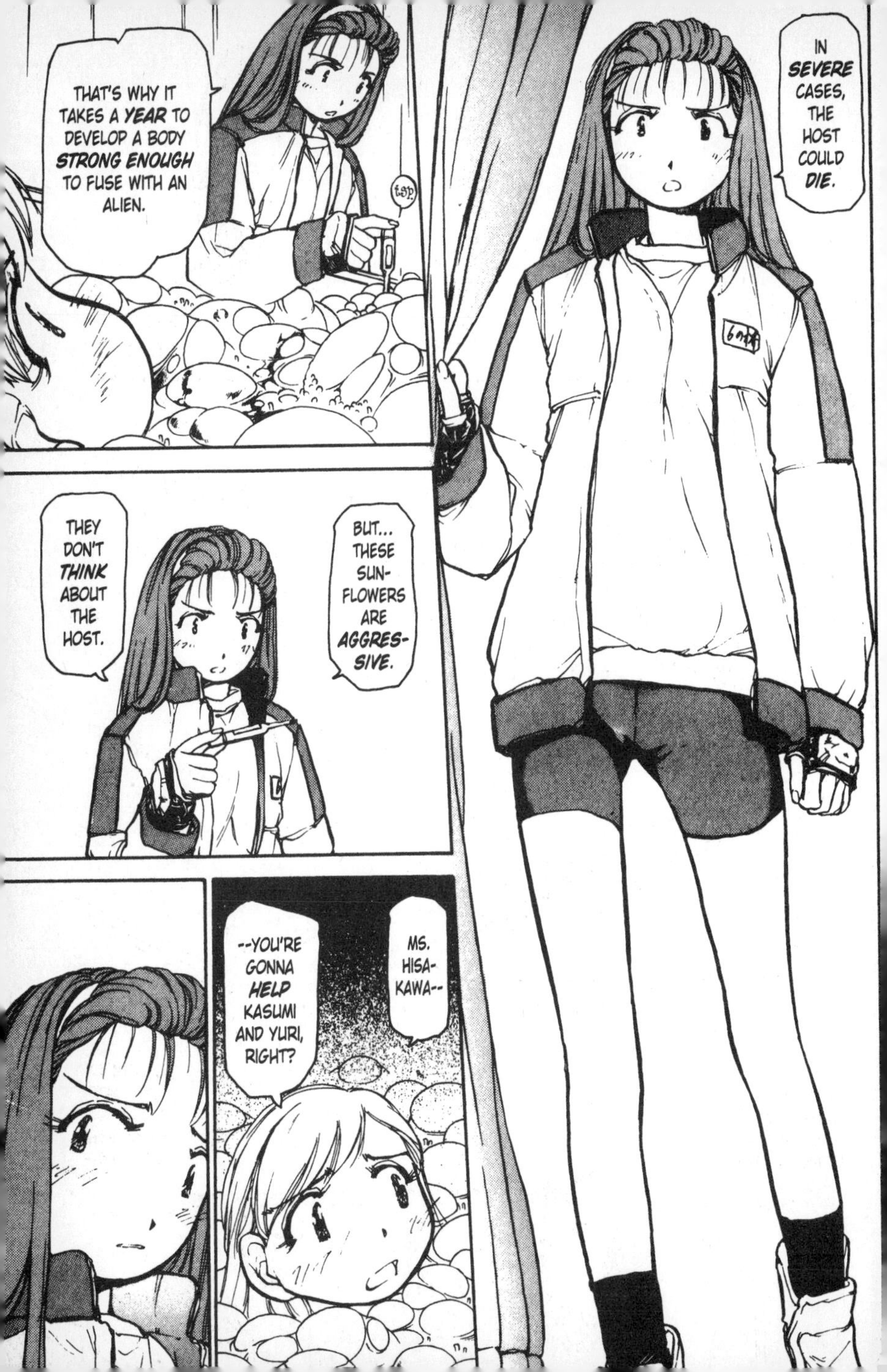
IN SEVERE CASES, THE HOST COULD DIE.
THAT'S WHY IT TAKES A YEAR TO DEVELOP A BODY STRONG ENOUGH TO FUSE WITH AN ALIEN.
tsp
BUT... THESE SUN-FLOWERS ARE AGGRES-SIVE.
THEY DON'T THINK ABOUT THE HOST.
MS. HISA-KAWA--
--YOU'RE GONNA HELP KASUMI AND YURI, RIGHT?

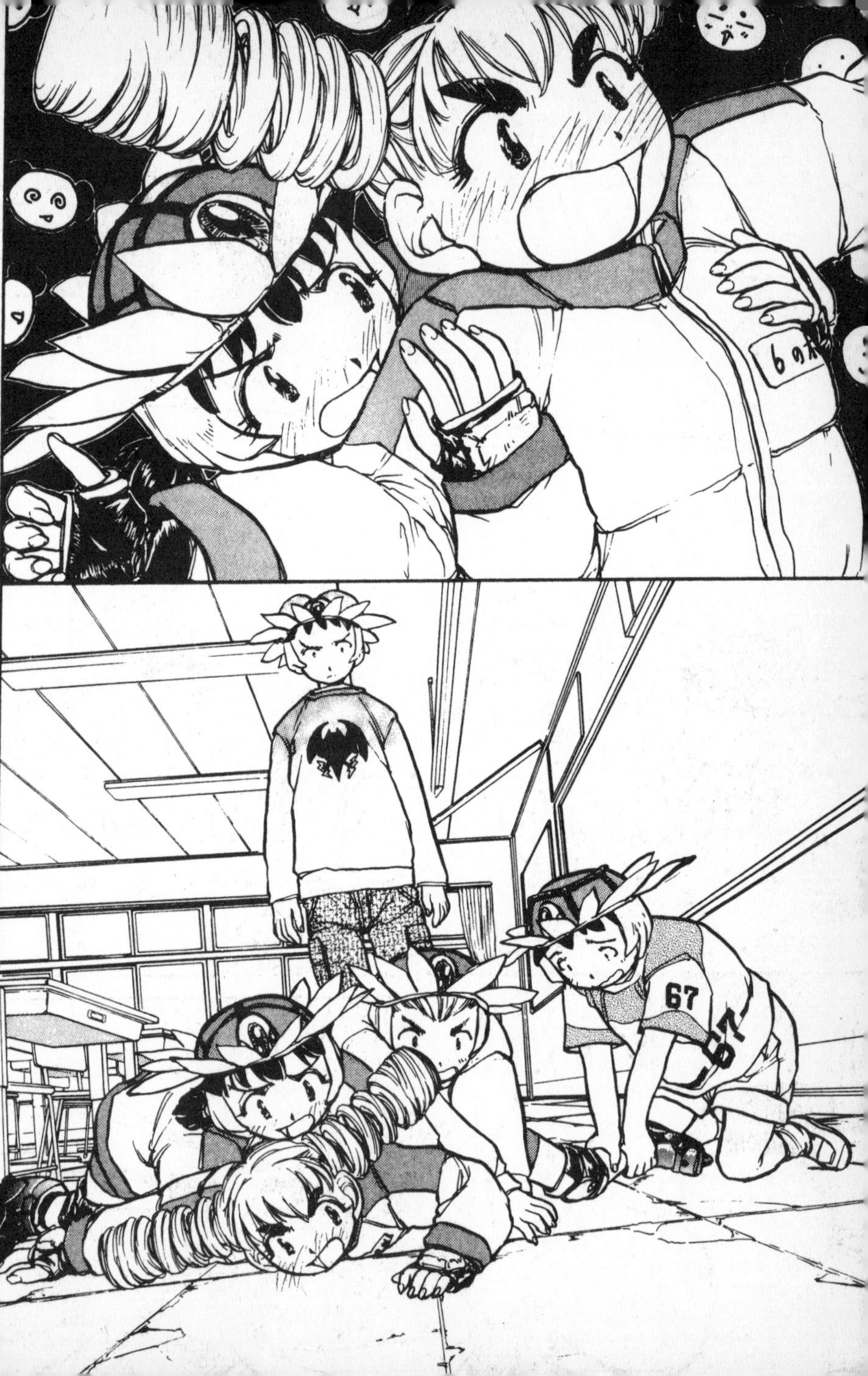
67

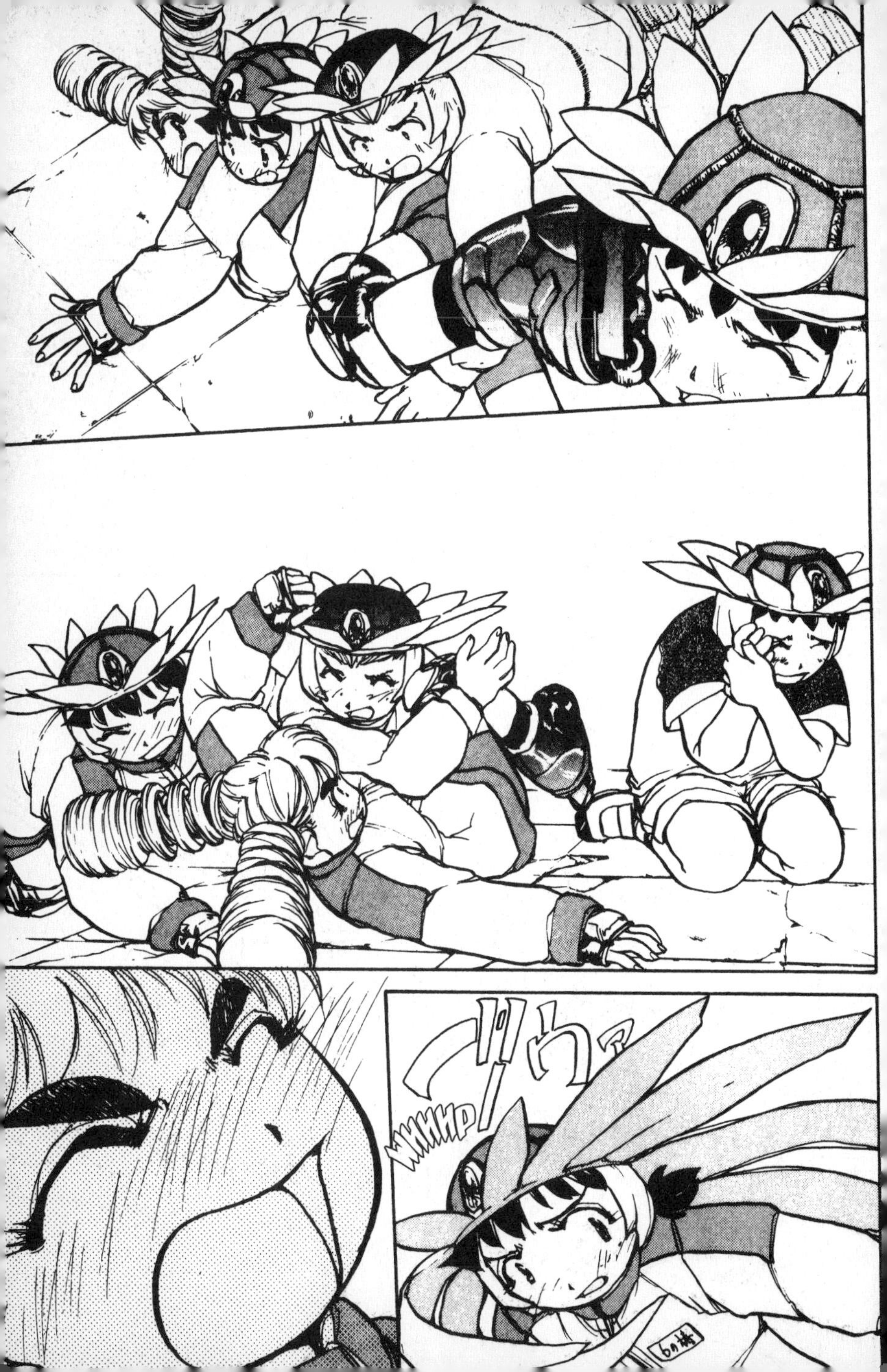
WHHHP!

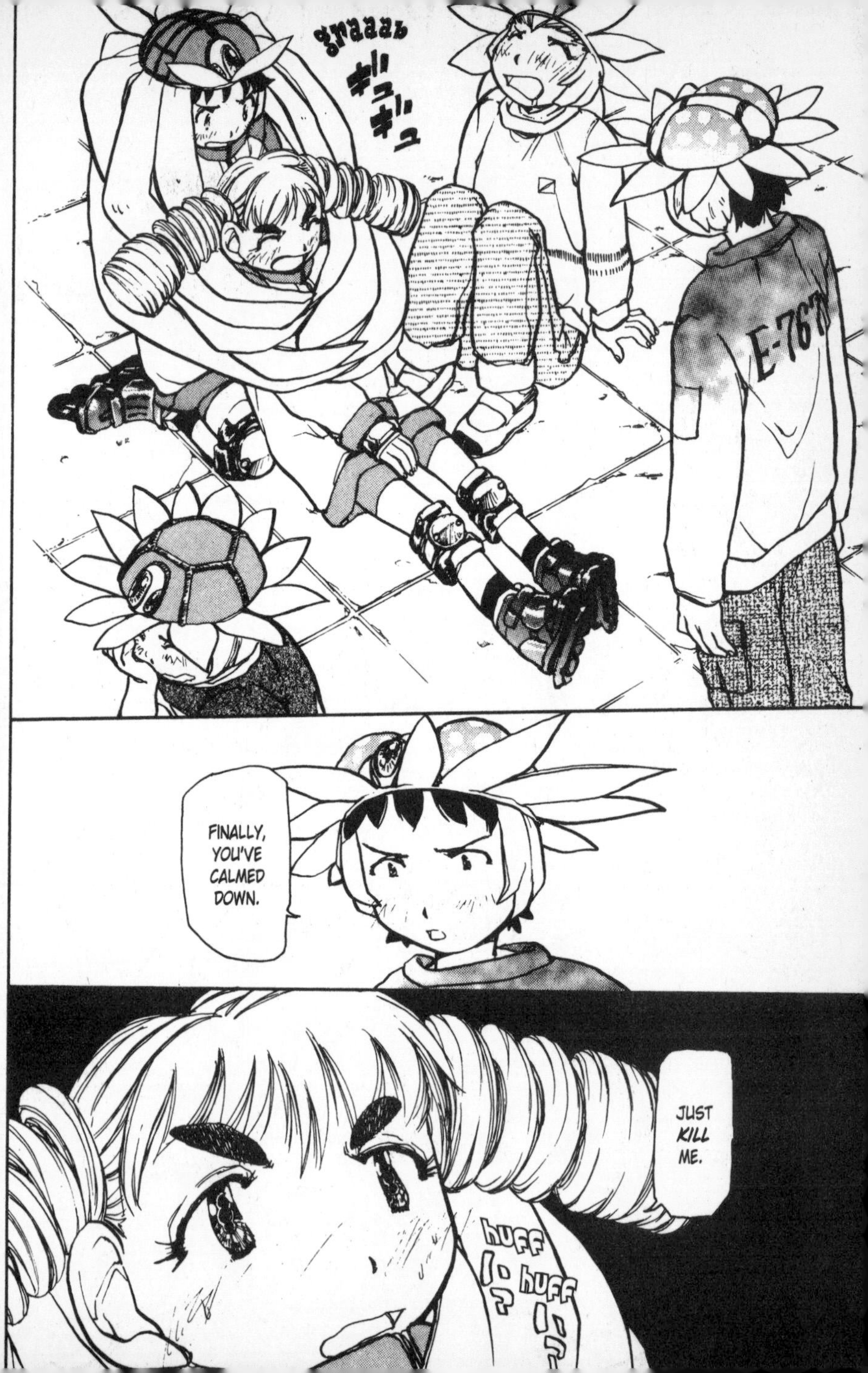
graaab
ギュギュ
FINALLY, YOU'VE CALMED DOWN.
JUST KILL ME.
huff huff

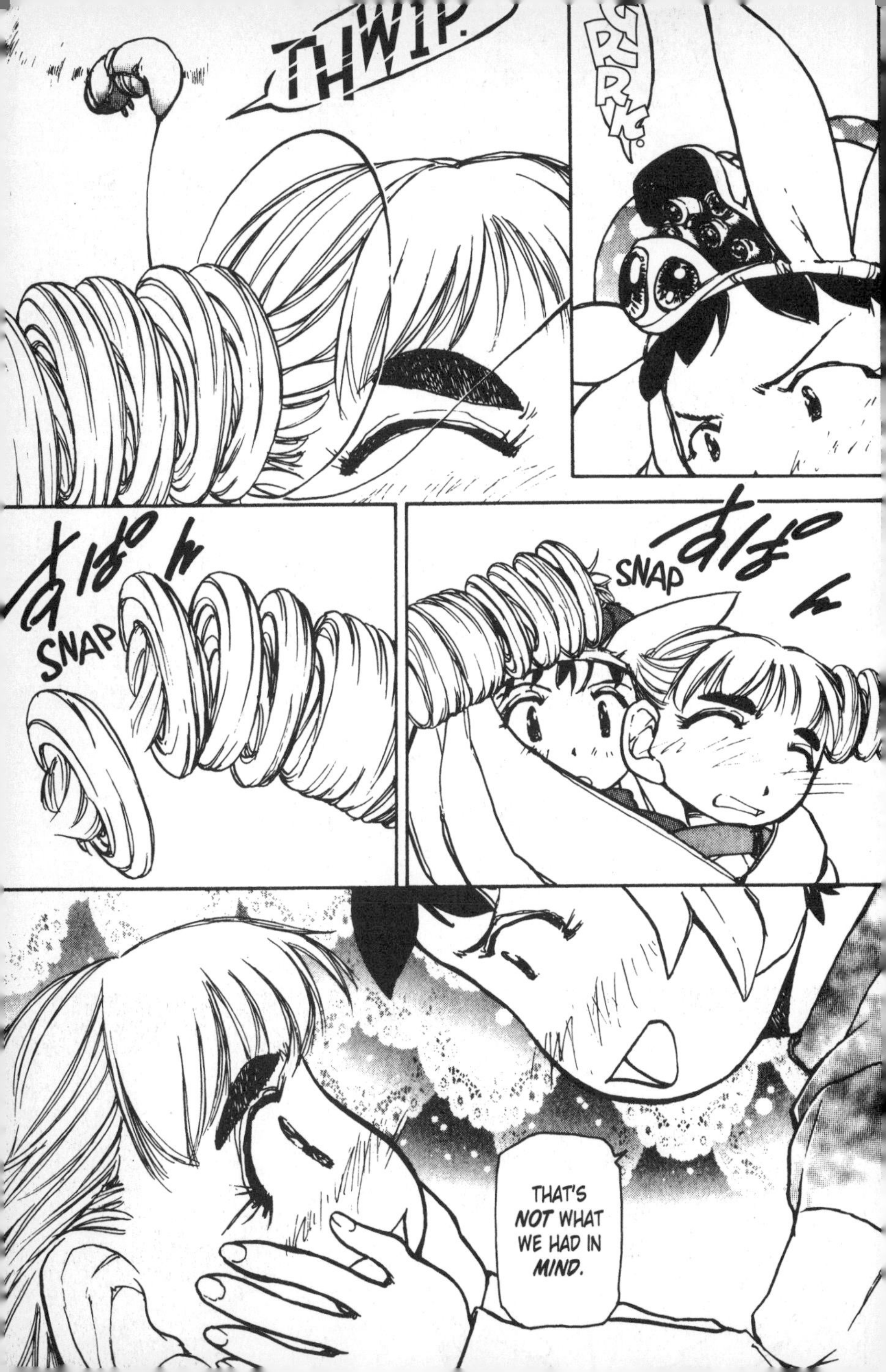

DRK!
THWIP.
すぱん
SNAP
すぱん
SNAP
THAT'S *NOT* WHAT WE HAD IN *MIND.*

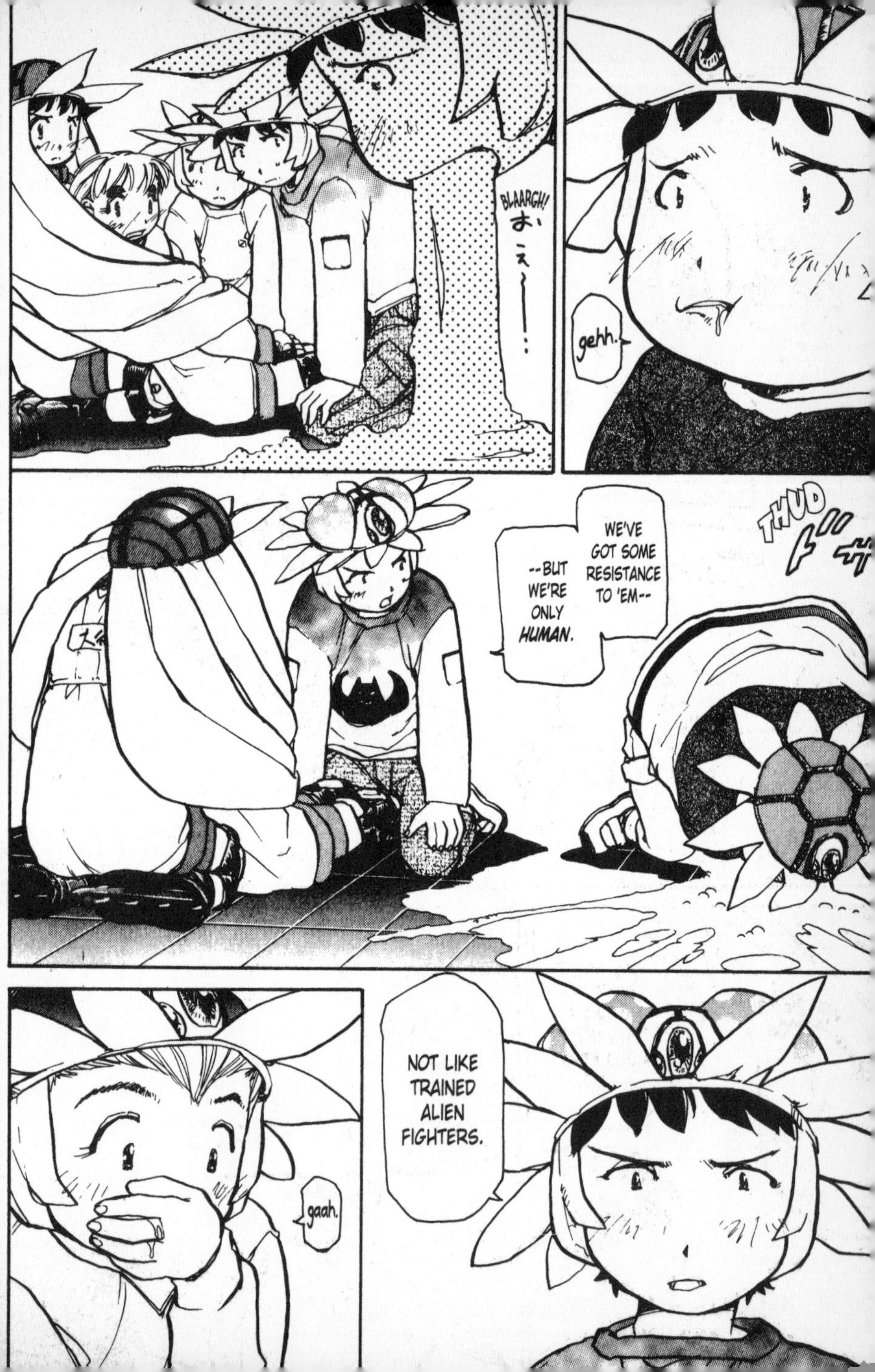
gehh.
BLAARGH!
THUD
WE'VE GOT SOME RESISTANCE TO 'EM--
--BUT WE'RE ONLY *HUMAN*.
NOT LIKE TRAINED ALIEN FIGHTERS.
gaah.

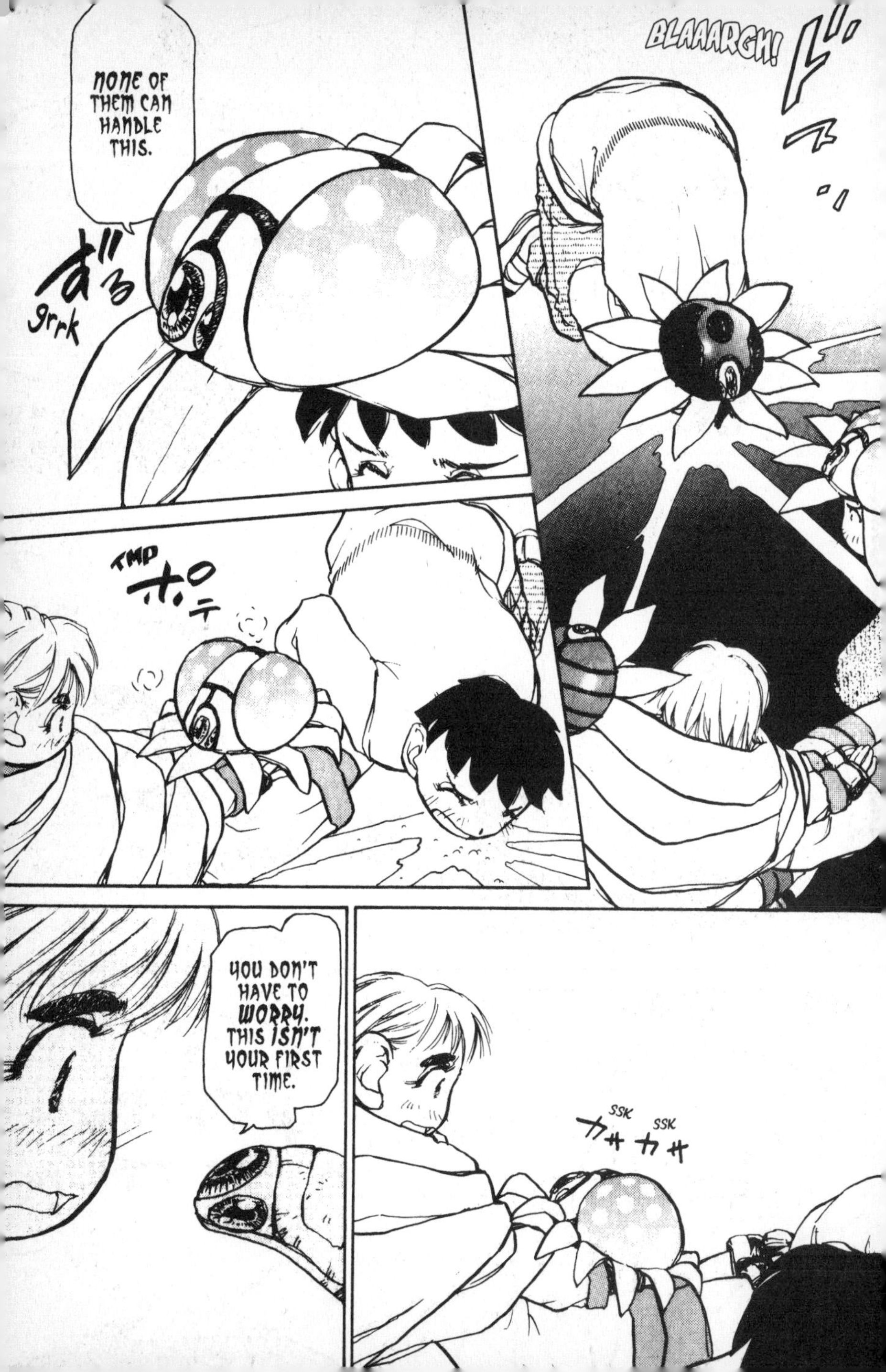
BLAARGH!
NONE OF THEM CAN HANDLE THIS.
ずる
grrk
TMP
ポテ
SSK SSK
カサカサ
YOU DON'T HAVE TO WORRY. THIS ISN'T YOUR FIRST TIME.

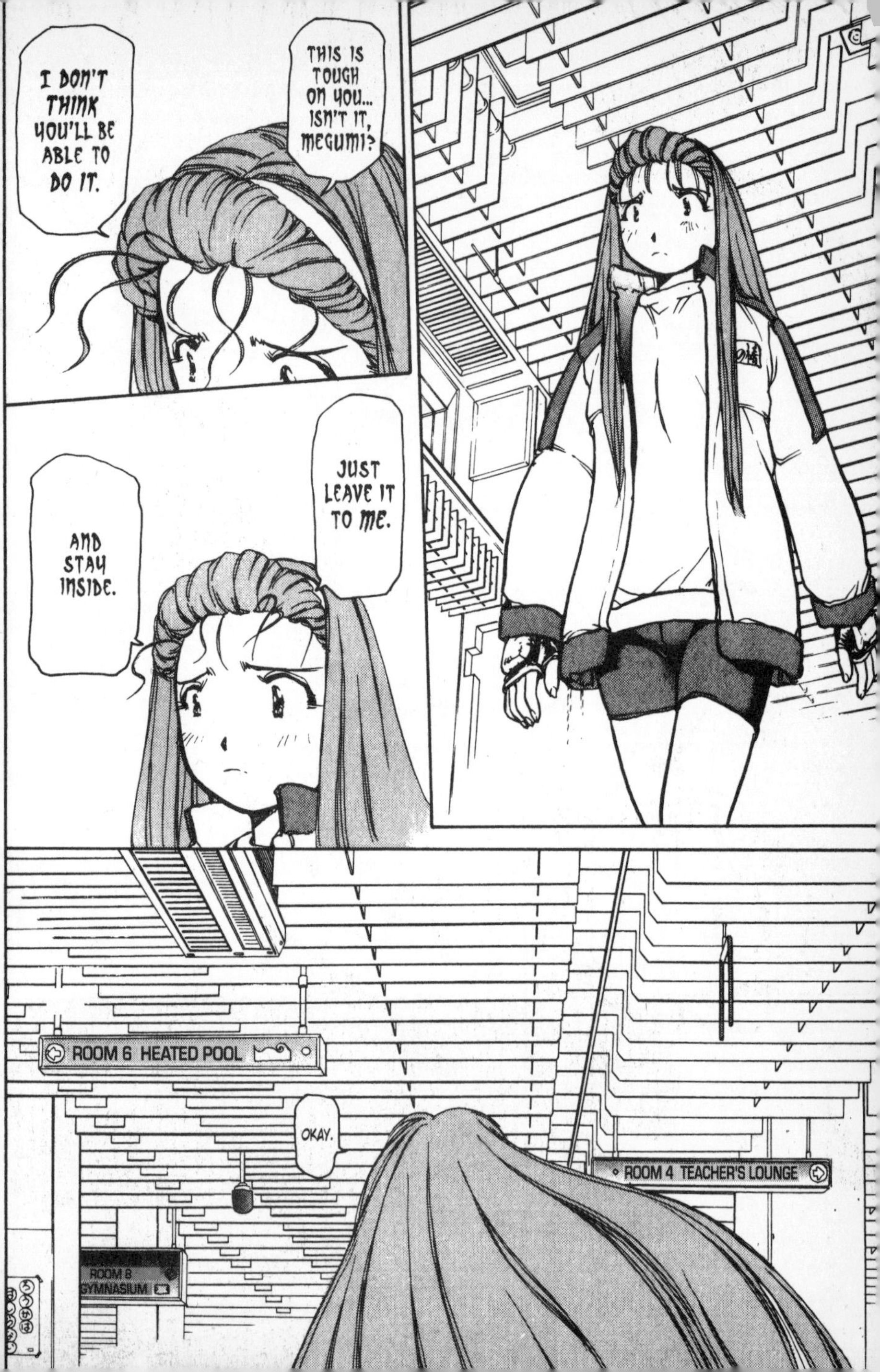
THIS IS TOUGH ON YOU... ISN'T IT, MEGUMI?
I DON'T THINK YOU'LL BE ABLE TO DO IT.
JUST LEAVE IT TO ME.
AND STAY INSIDE.
ROOM 6 HEATED POOL
OKAY.
ROOM 4 TEACHER'S LOUNGE
ROOM 8
GYMNASIUM

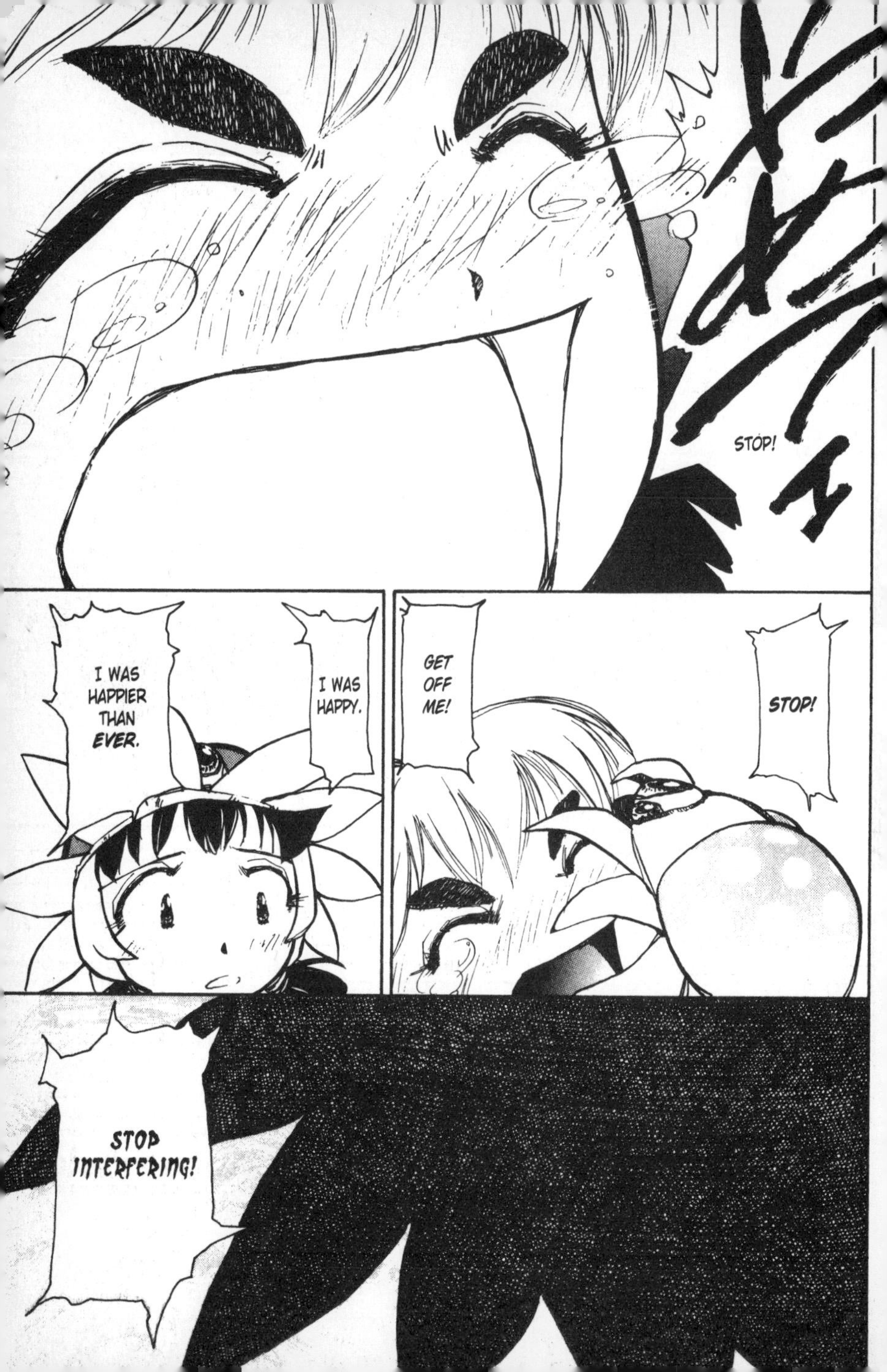
STOP!
STOP!
GET OFF ME!
I WAS HAPPY.
I WAS HAPPIER THAN EVER.
STOP INTERFERING!

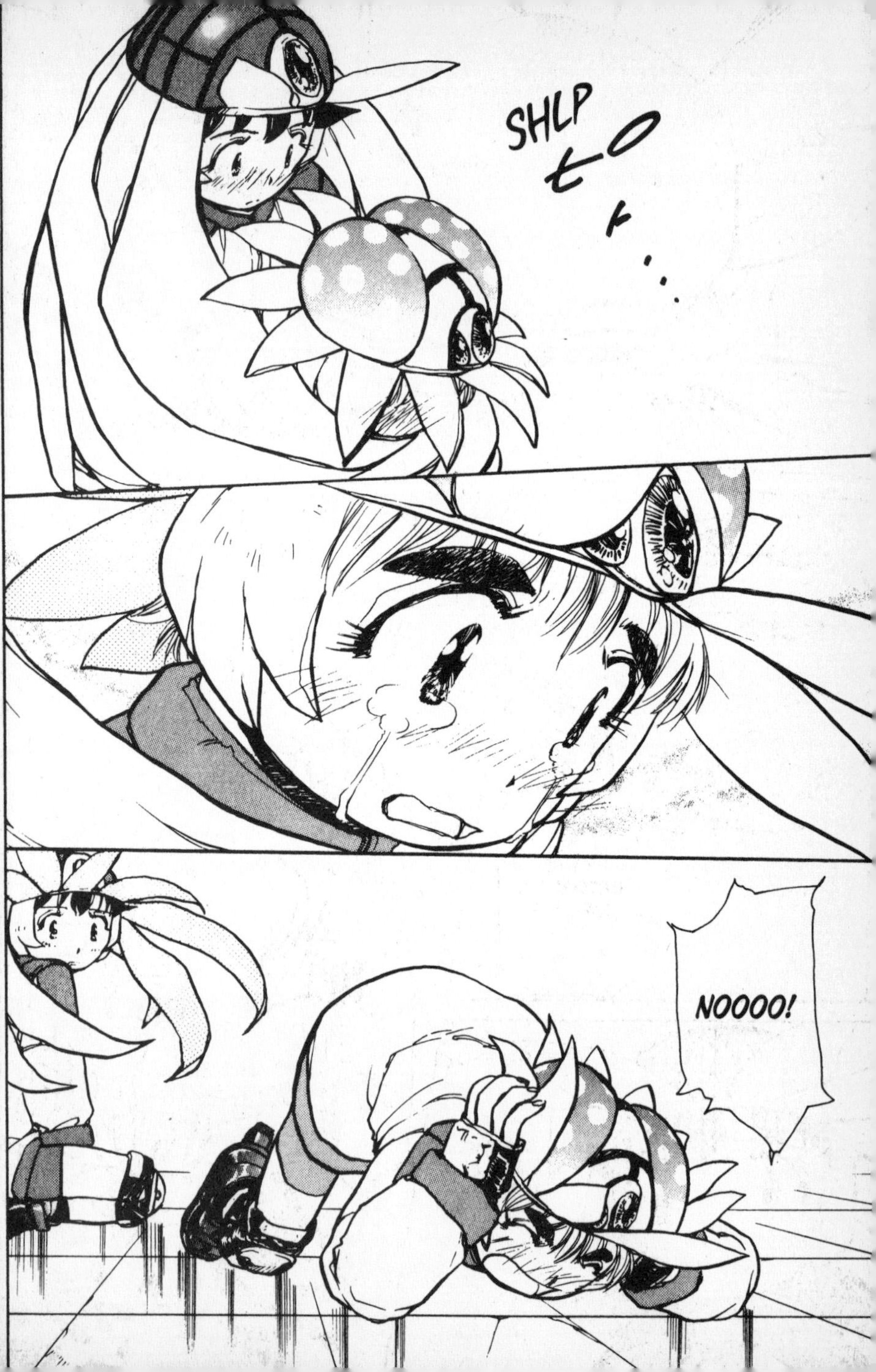
SHLP
NOOOO!

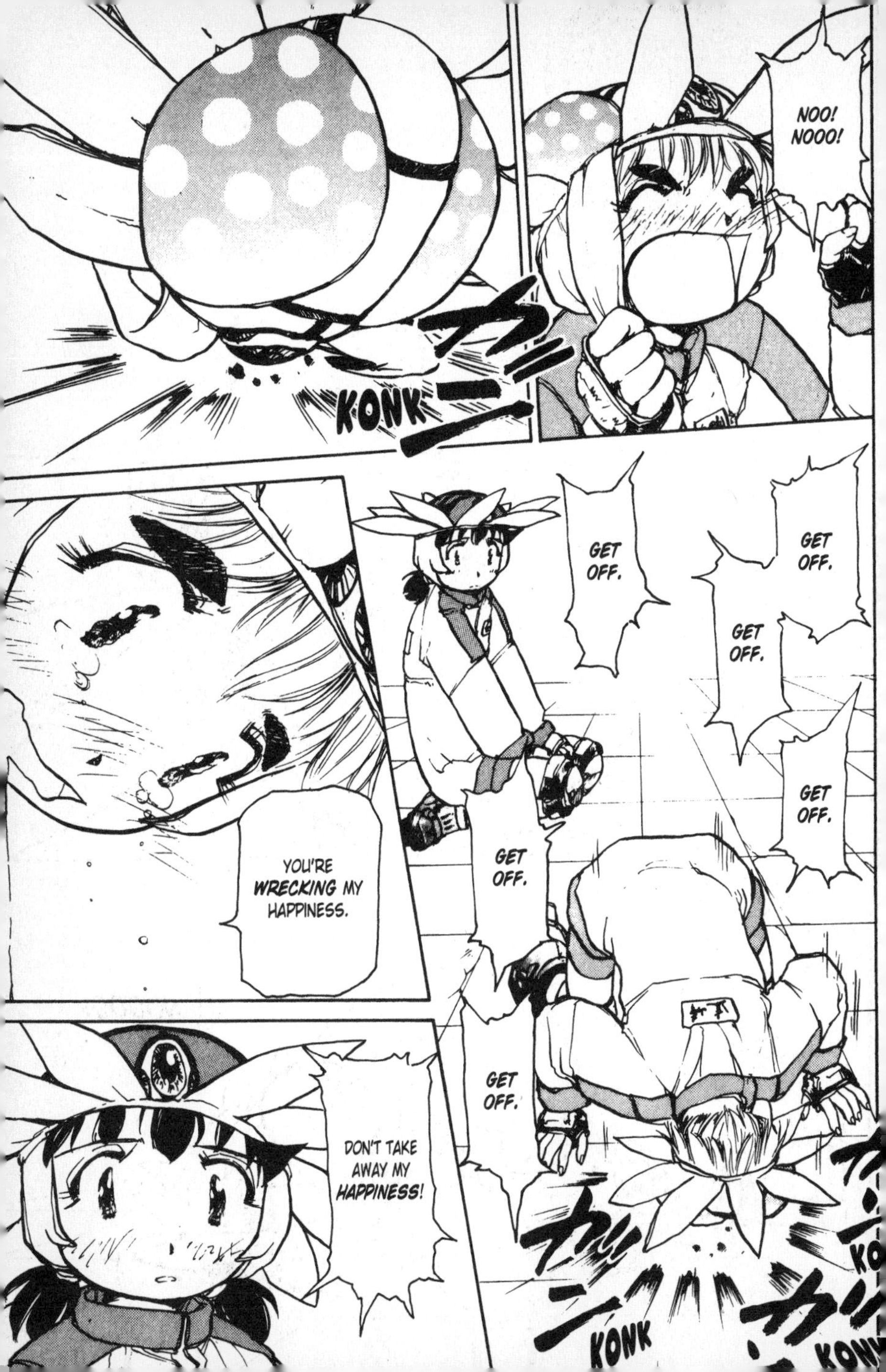
NOO! NOOO!
KONK
GET OFF.
GET OFF.
GET OFF.
GET OFF.
GET OFF.
GET OFF.
KO-
KONK
KONK
YOU'RE *WRECKING* MY HAPPINESS.
DON'T TAKE AWAY MY *HAPPINESS!*

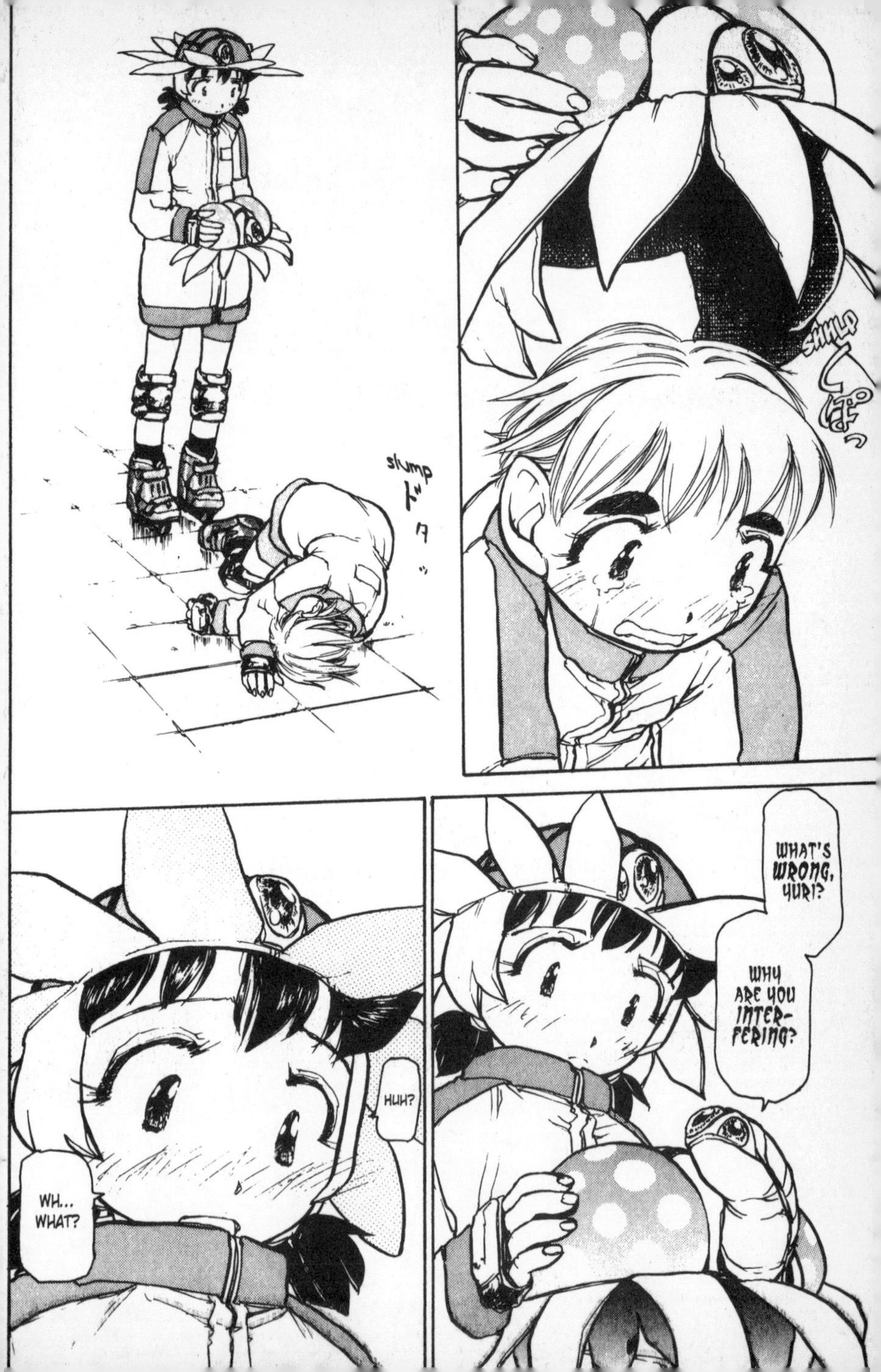
SHHLP
slump
ドタッ
WHAT'S WRONG, YURI?
WHY ARE YOU INTER-FERING?
HUH?
WH... WHAT?

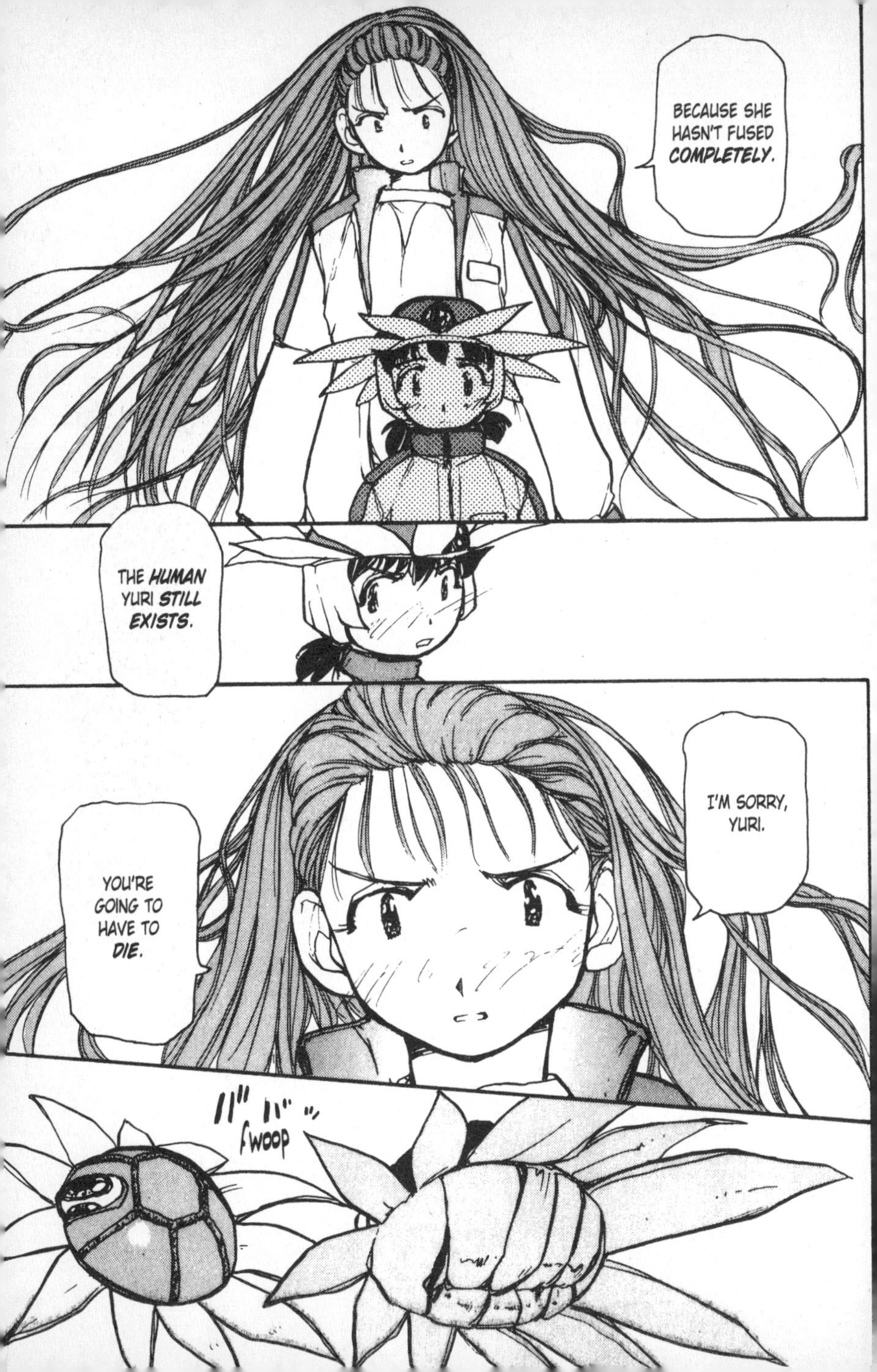
BECAUSE SHE HASN'T FUSED COMPLETELY.
THE HUMAN YURI STILL EXISTS.
I'M SORRY, YURI.
YOU'RE GOING TO HAVE TO DIE.
fwoop

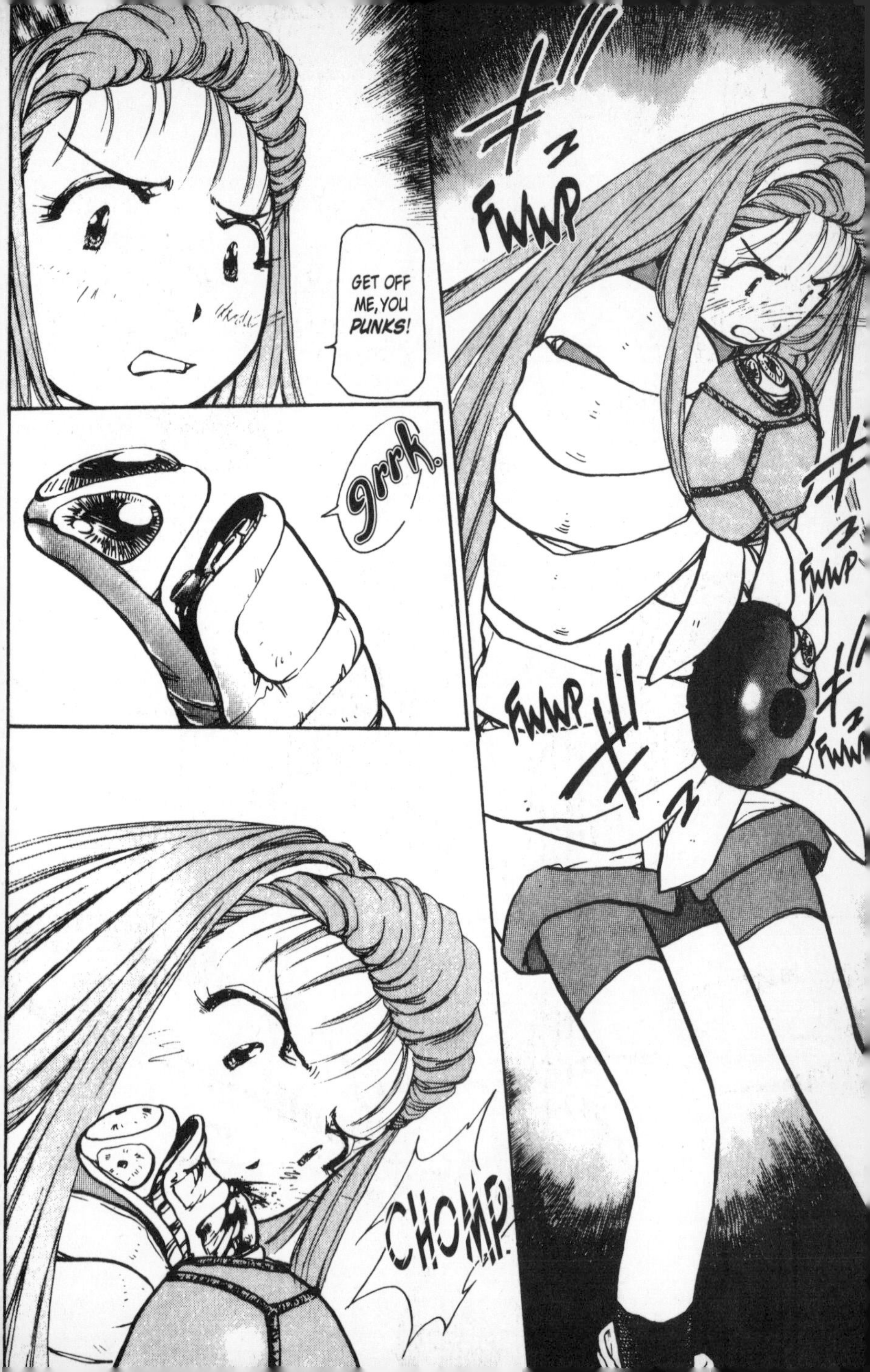
FWMP
FWMP
FWMP
FWMP
GET OFF ME, YOU PUNKS!
grrk.
CHOMP.

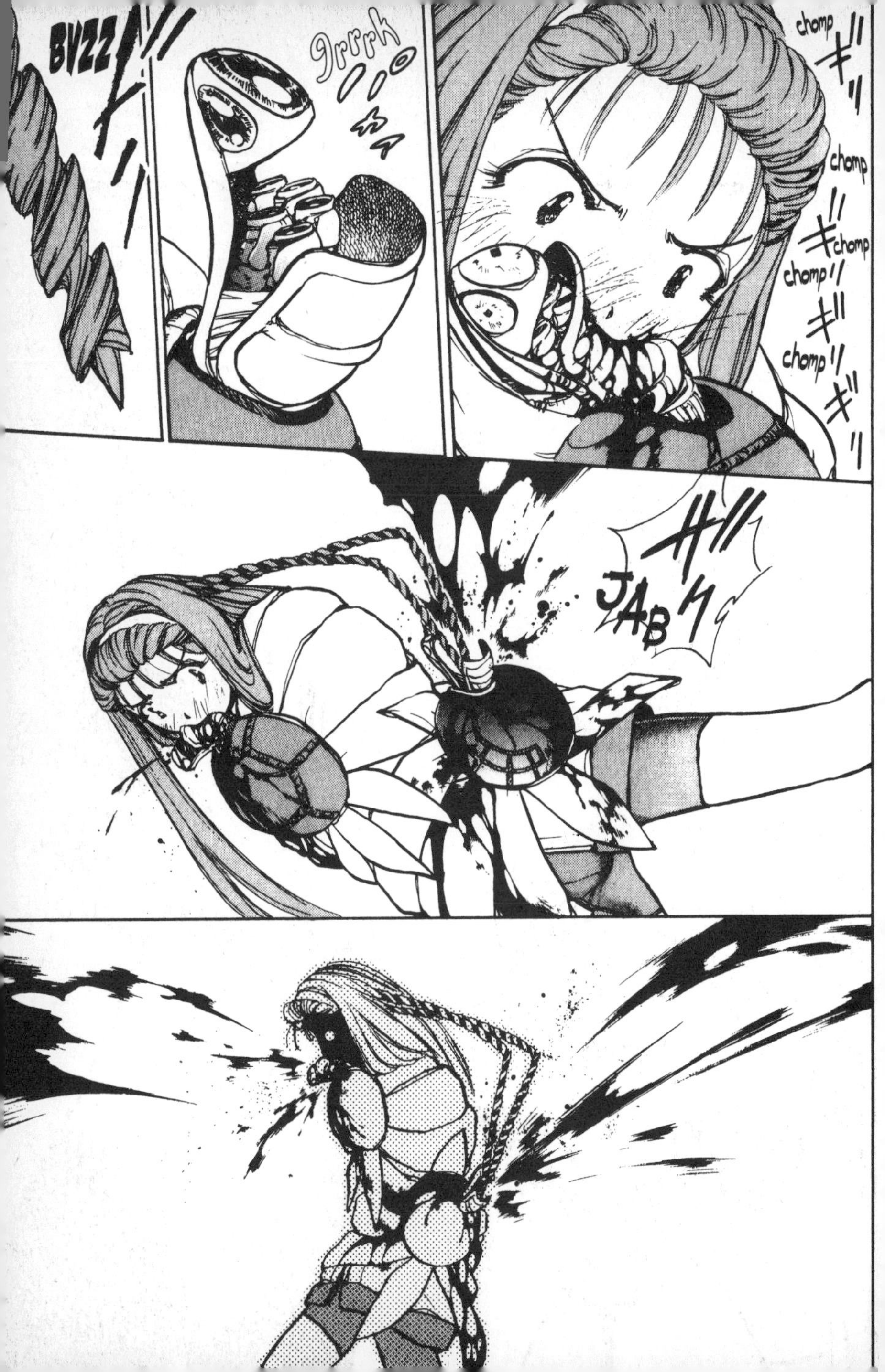
chomp
chomp
chomp
chomp
chomp
grrrk
BUZZ
JAB

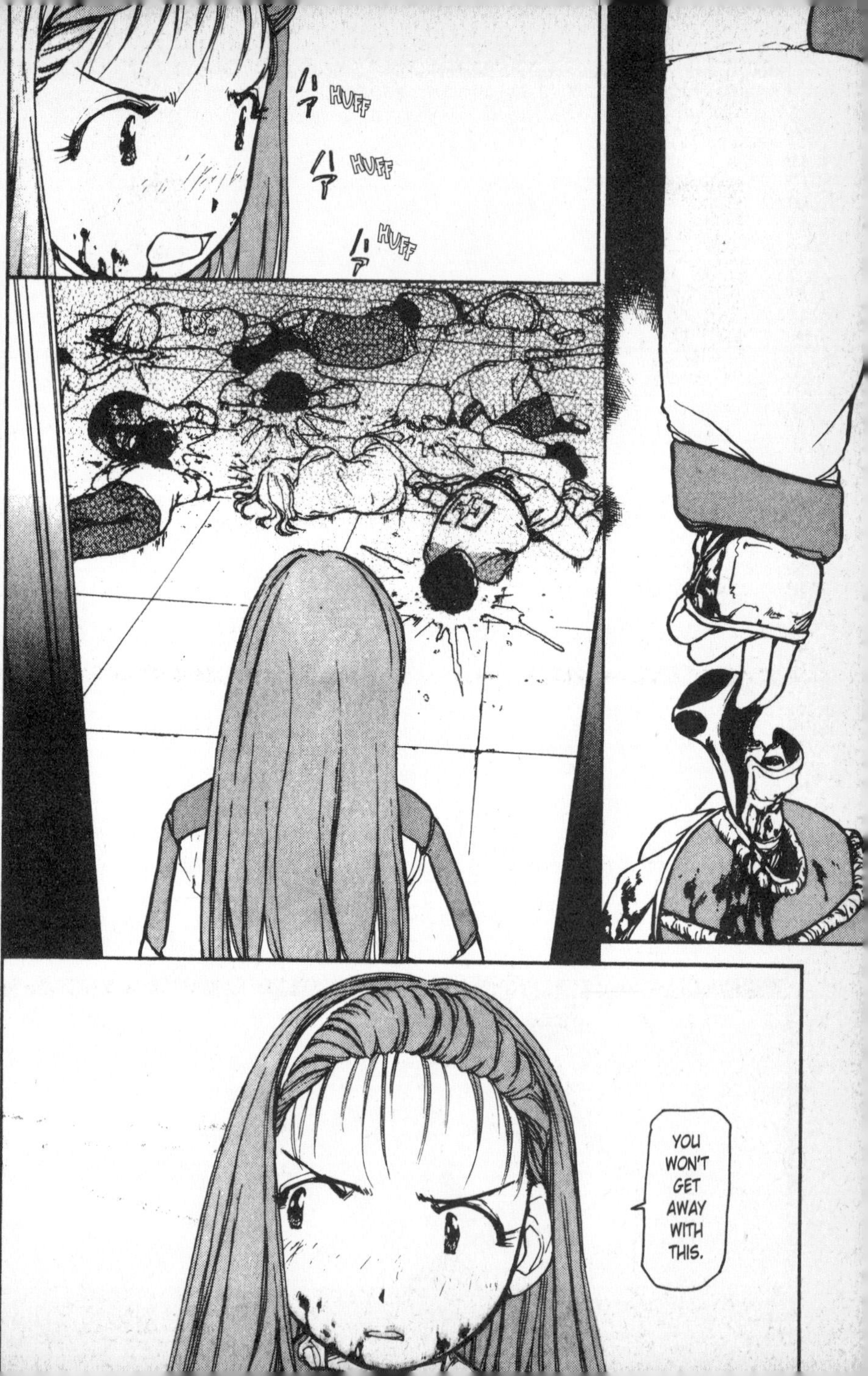
ハァ HUFF
ハァ HUFF
ハァ HUFF
YOU WON'T GET AWAY WITH THIS.

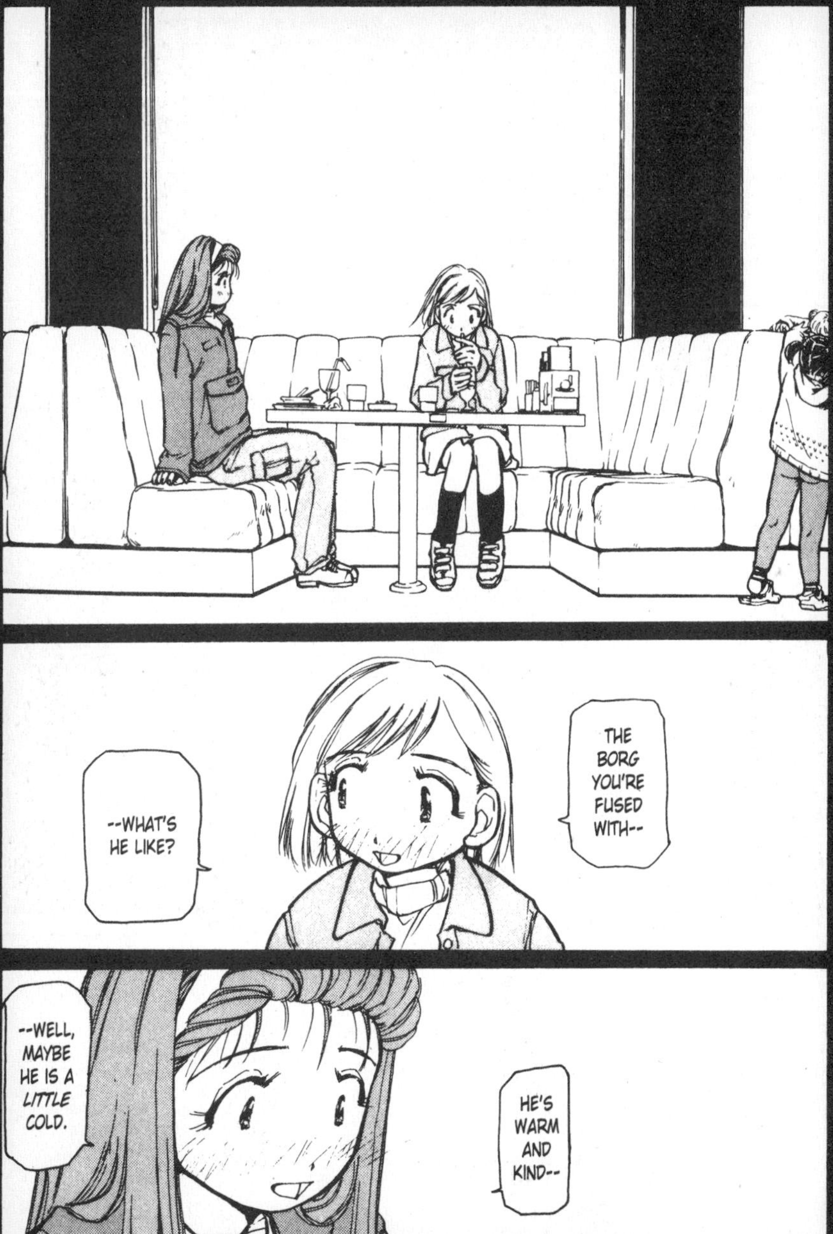
THE BORG YOU'RE FUSED WITH--
--WHAT'S HE LIKE?
HE'S WARM AND KIND--
--WELL, MAYBE HE IS A *LITTLE* COLD.

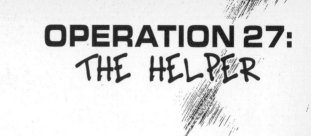
OPERATION 27:
THE HELPER

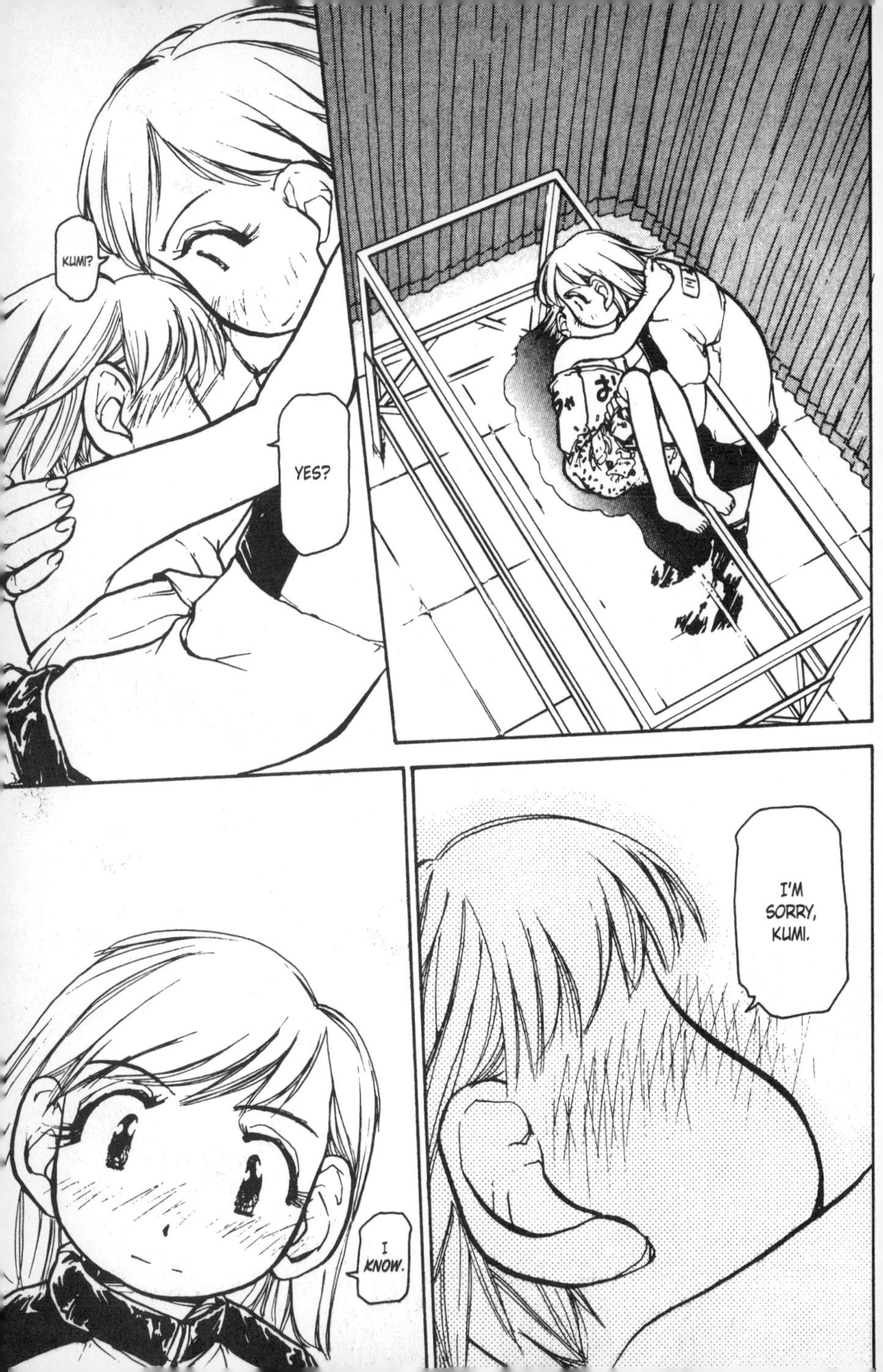
KUMI?
YES?
I'M SORRY, KUMI.
I KNOW.

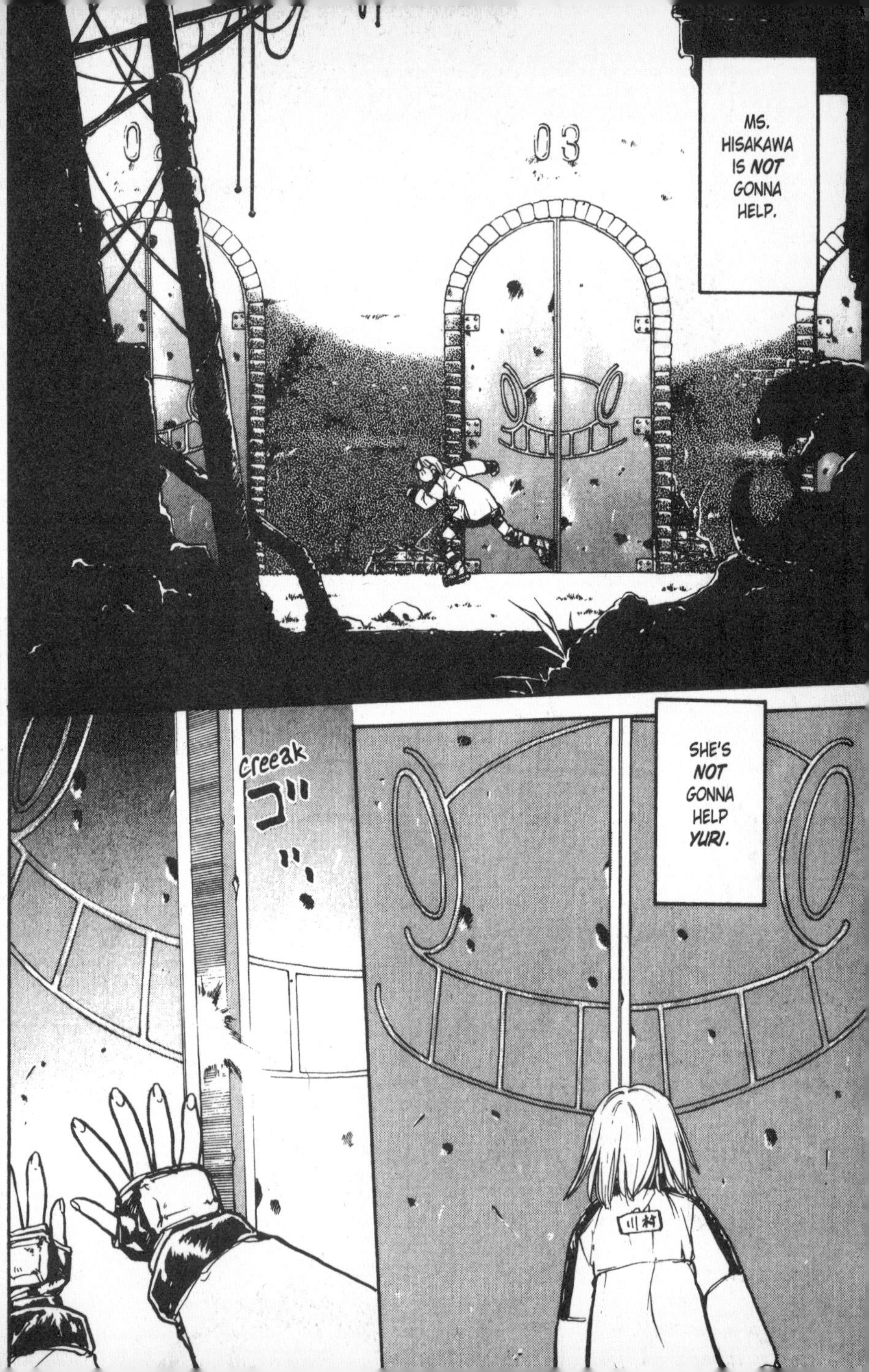
03
MS. HISAKAWA IS *NOT* GONNA HELP.
SHE'S *NOT* GONNA HELP *YURI*.
Creeak
ゴ
川村

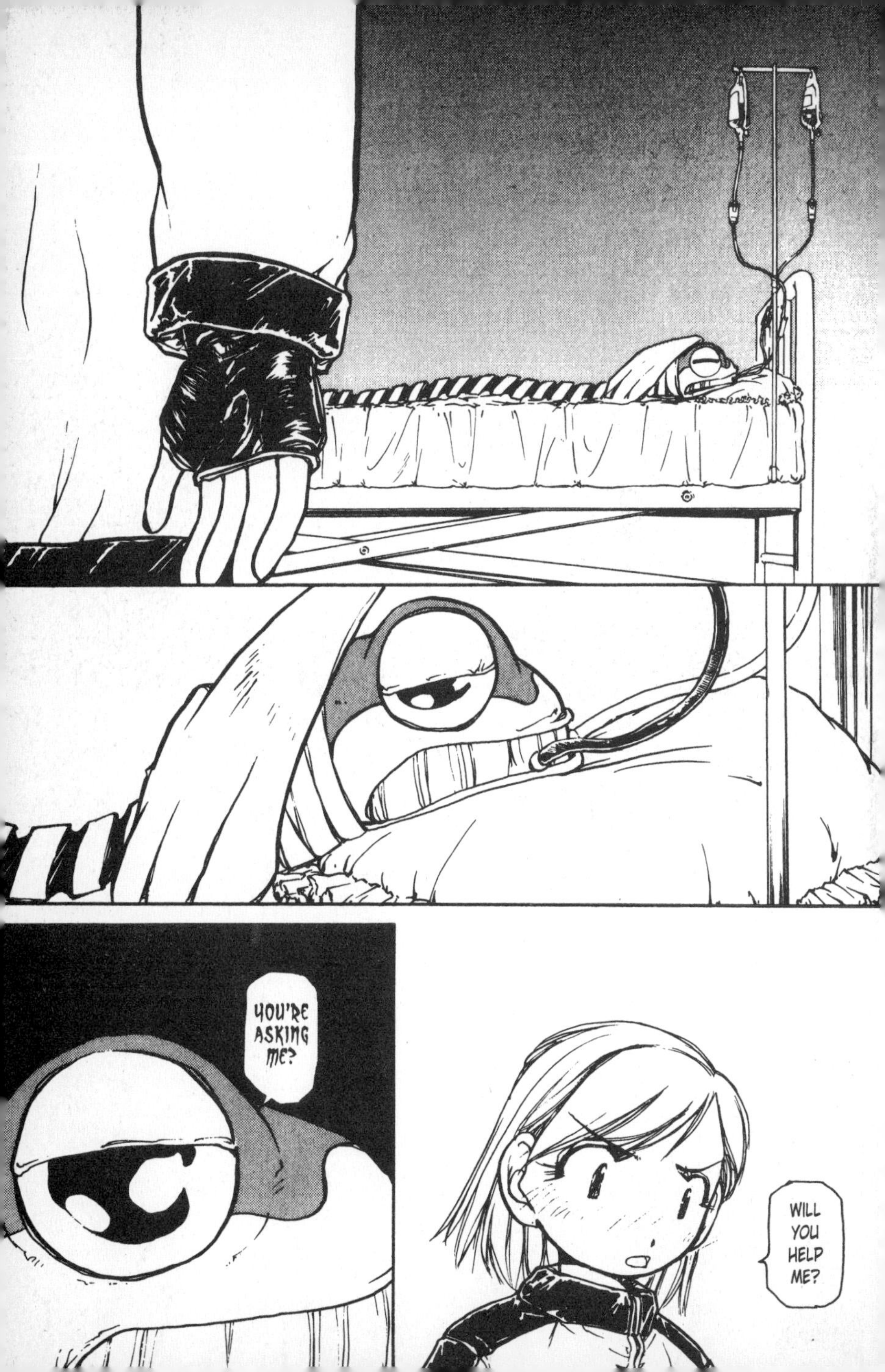
WILL YOU HELP ME?
YOU'RE ASKING ME?

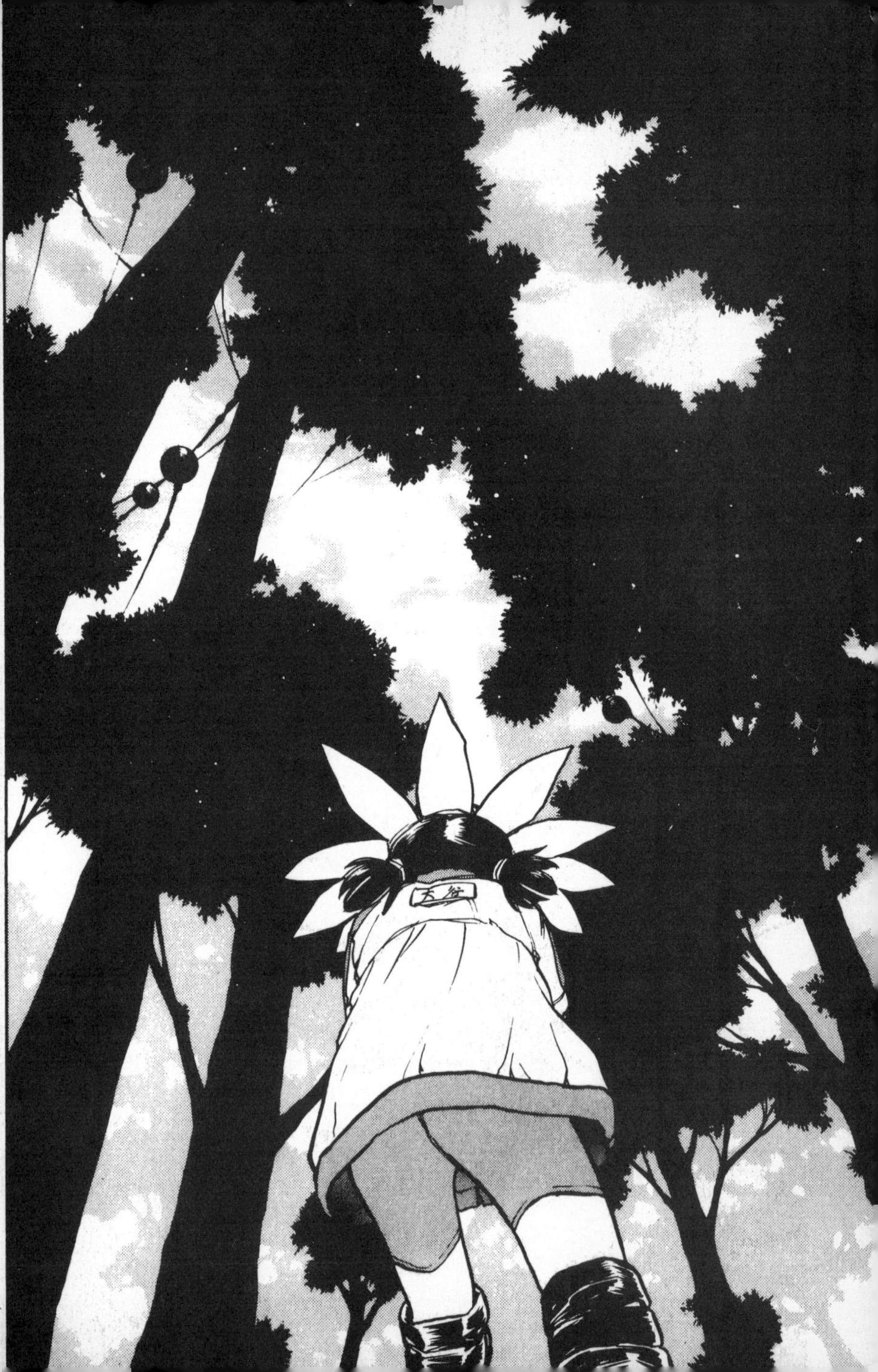

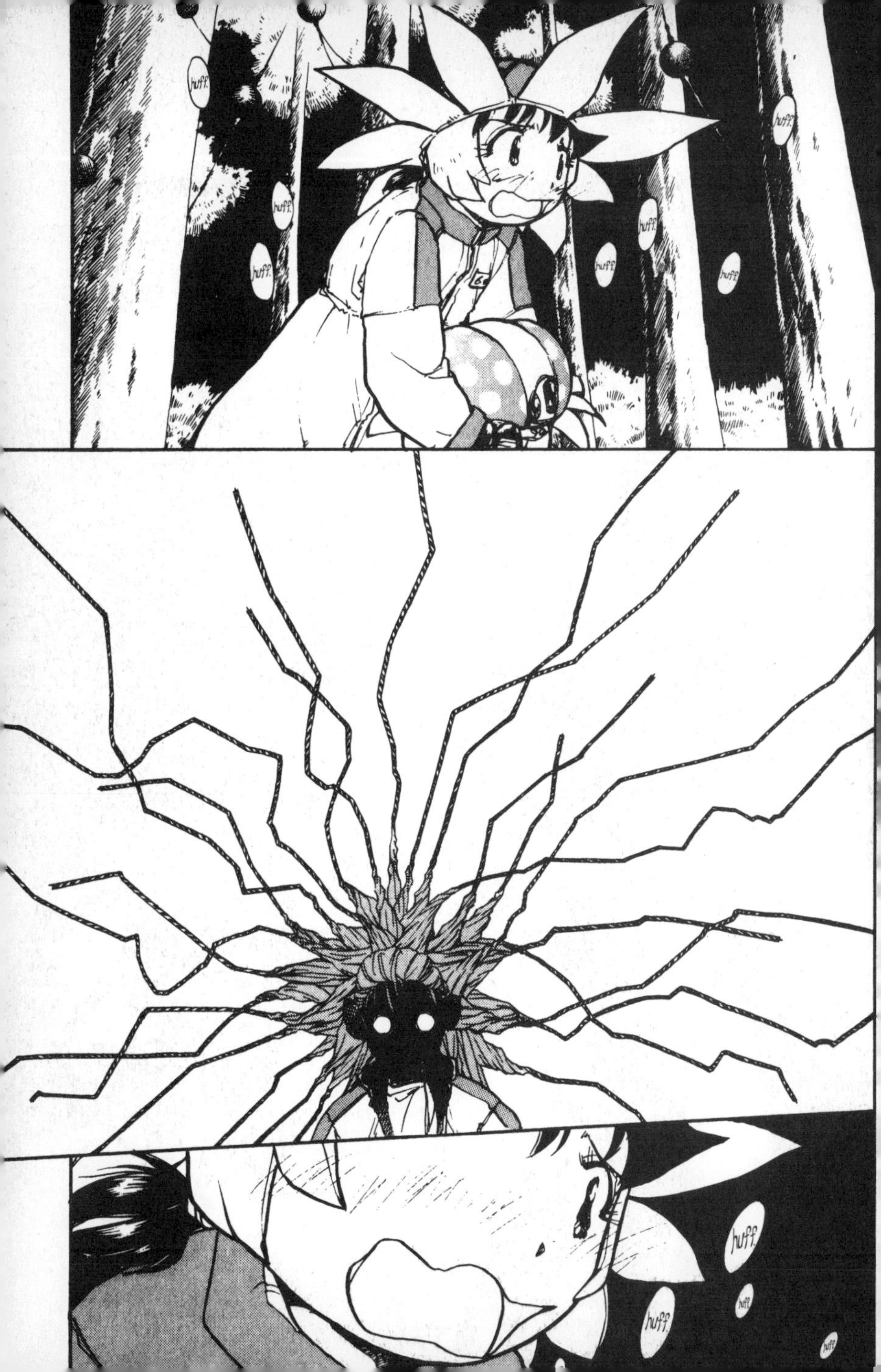
huff.
huff.
huff.
huff.
huff.
huff.
huff.
huff.
huff.
huff.
huff.

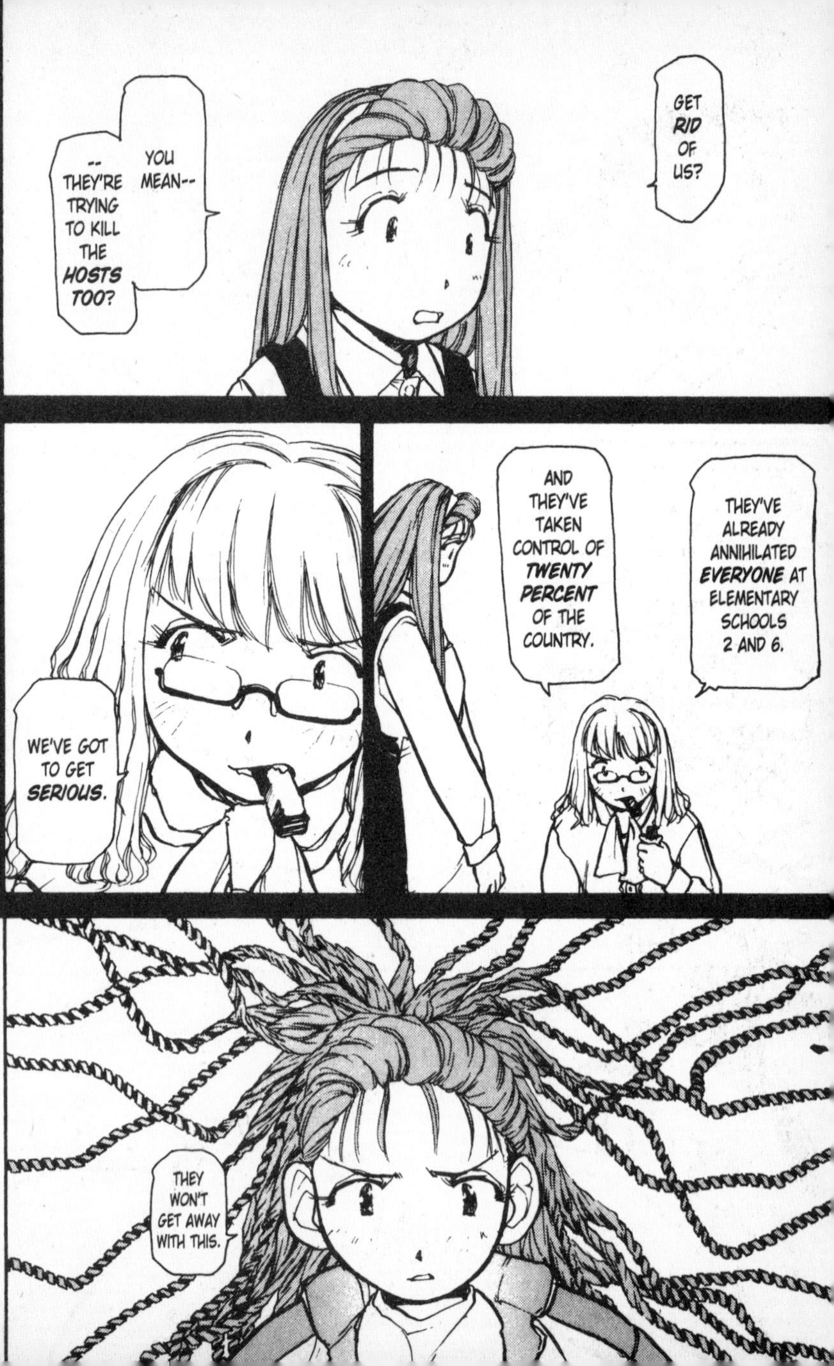
GET RID OF US?
YOU MEAN--
-- THEY'RE TRYING TO KILL THE HOSTS TOO?
THEY'VE ALREADY ANNIHILATED EVERYONE AT ELEMENTARY SCHOOLS 2 AND 6.
AND THEY'VE TAKEN CONTROL OF TWENTY PERCENT OF THE COUNTRY.
WE'VE GOT TO GET SERIOUS.
THEY WON'T GET AWAY WITH THIS.

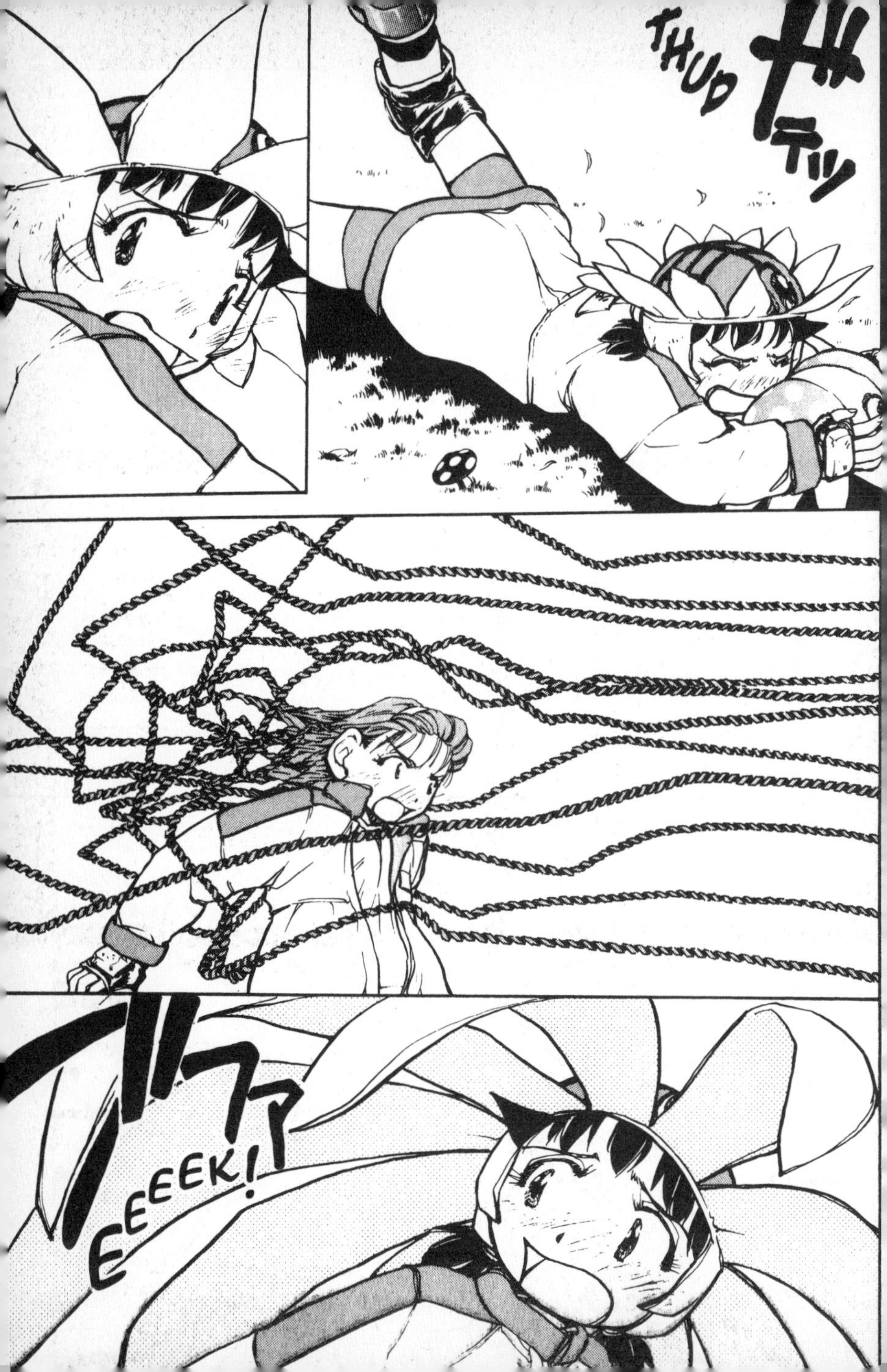
THUD
EEEEEK!

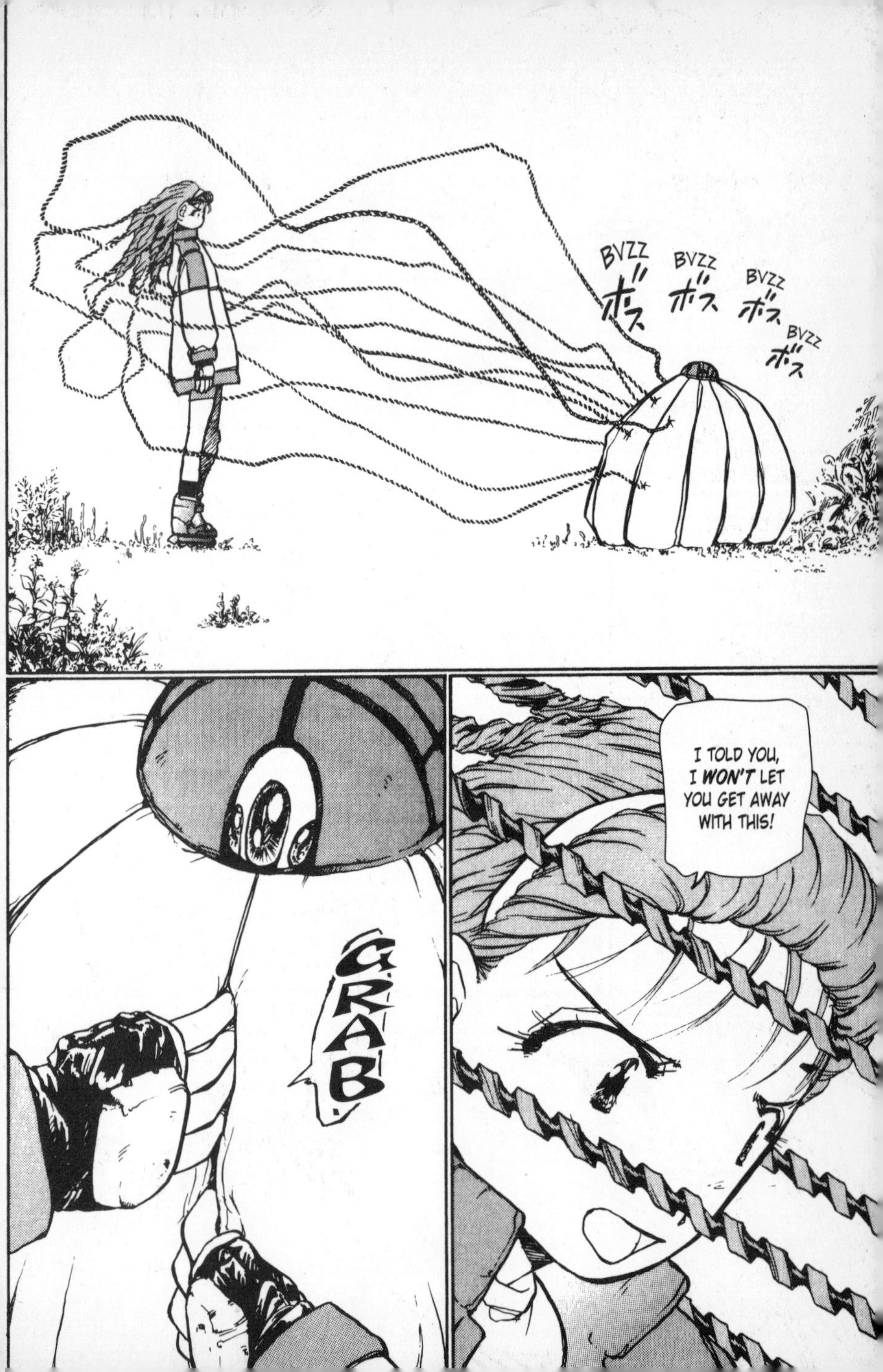
BVZZ
ボス
BVZZ
ボス
BVZZ
ボス
BVZZ
ボス
I TOLD YOU, I ***WON'T*** LET YOU GET AWAY WITH THIS!
GRAB

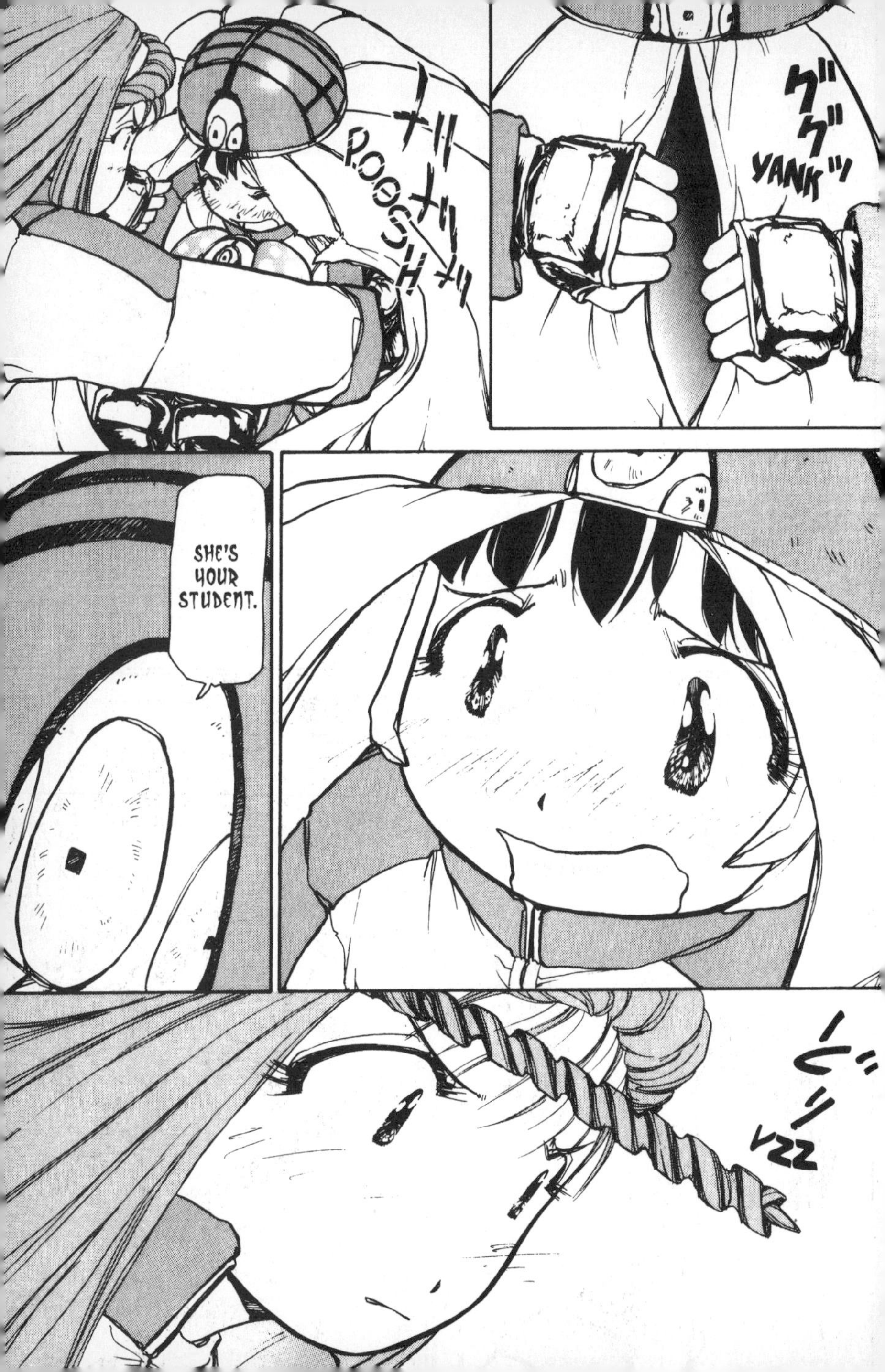
YANK
POOSH
SHE'S YOUR STUDENT.
VZZ

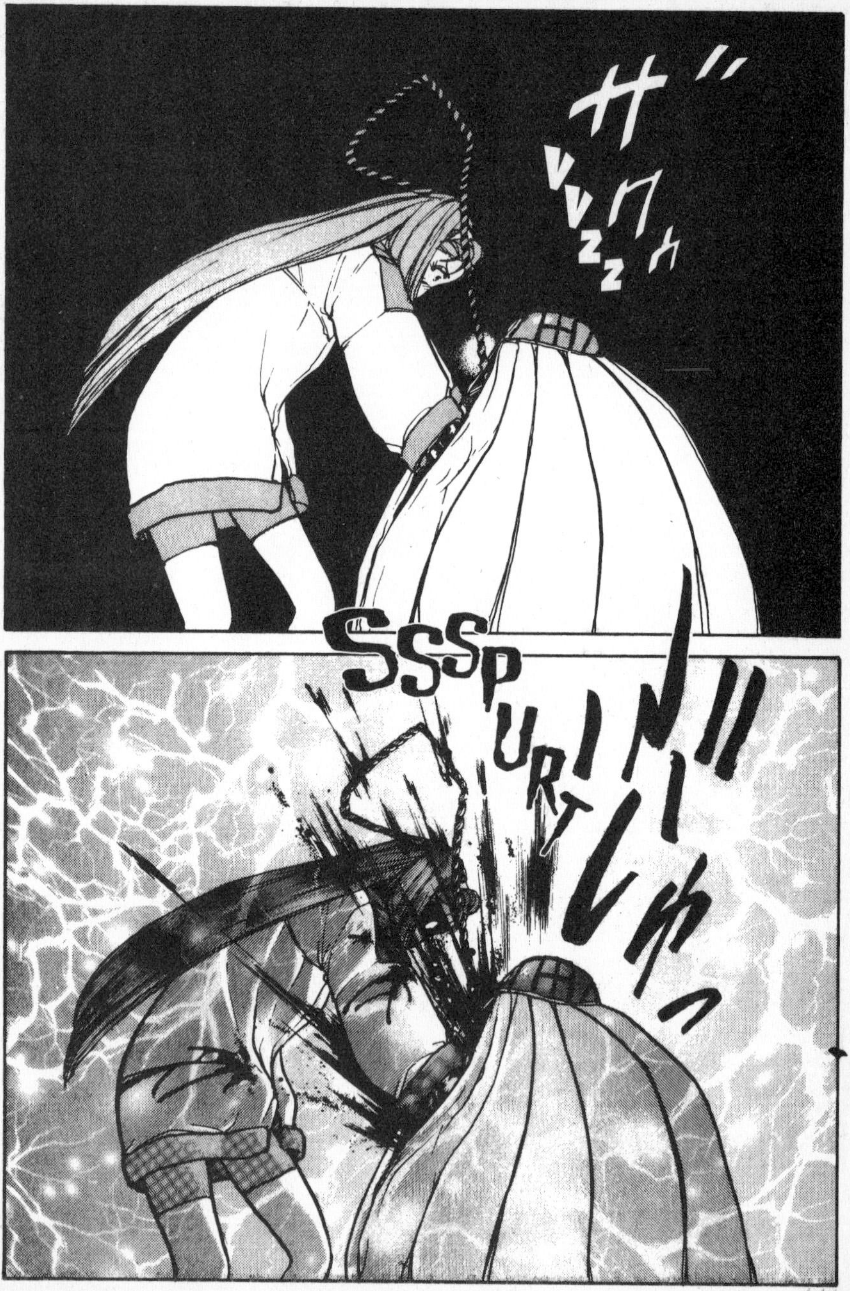
ザワッ
VVVZZ
SSSPURT

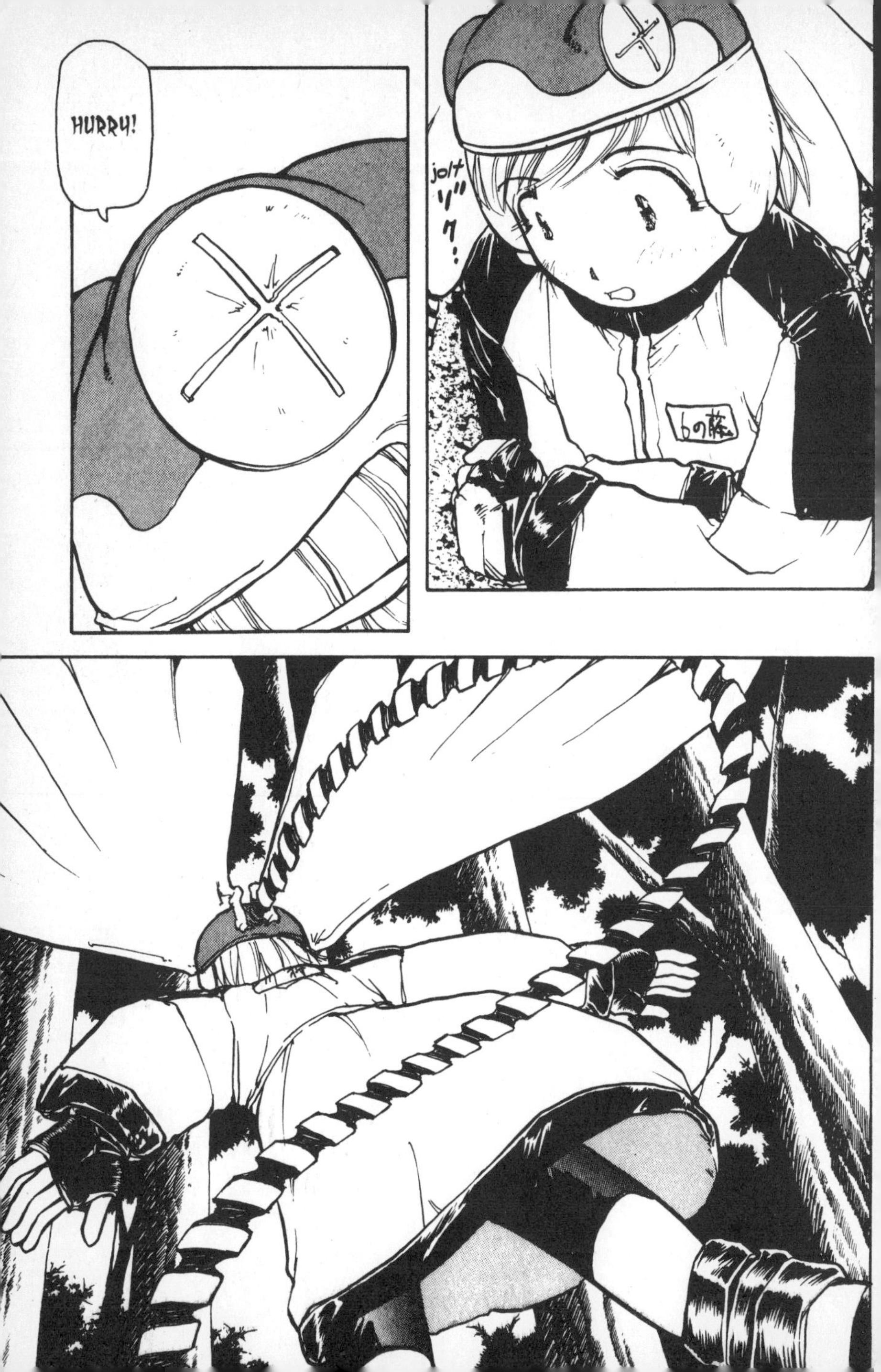
jolt
ゾク!
HURRY!

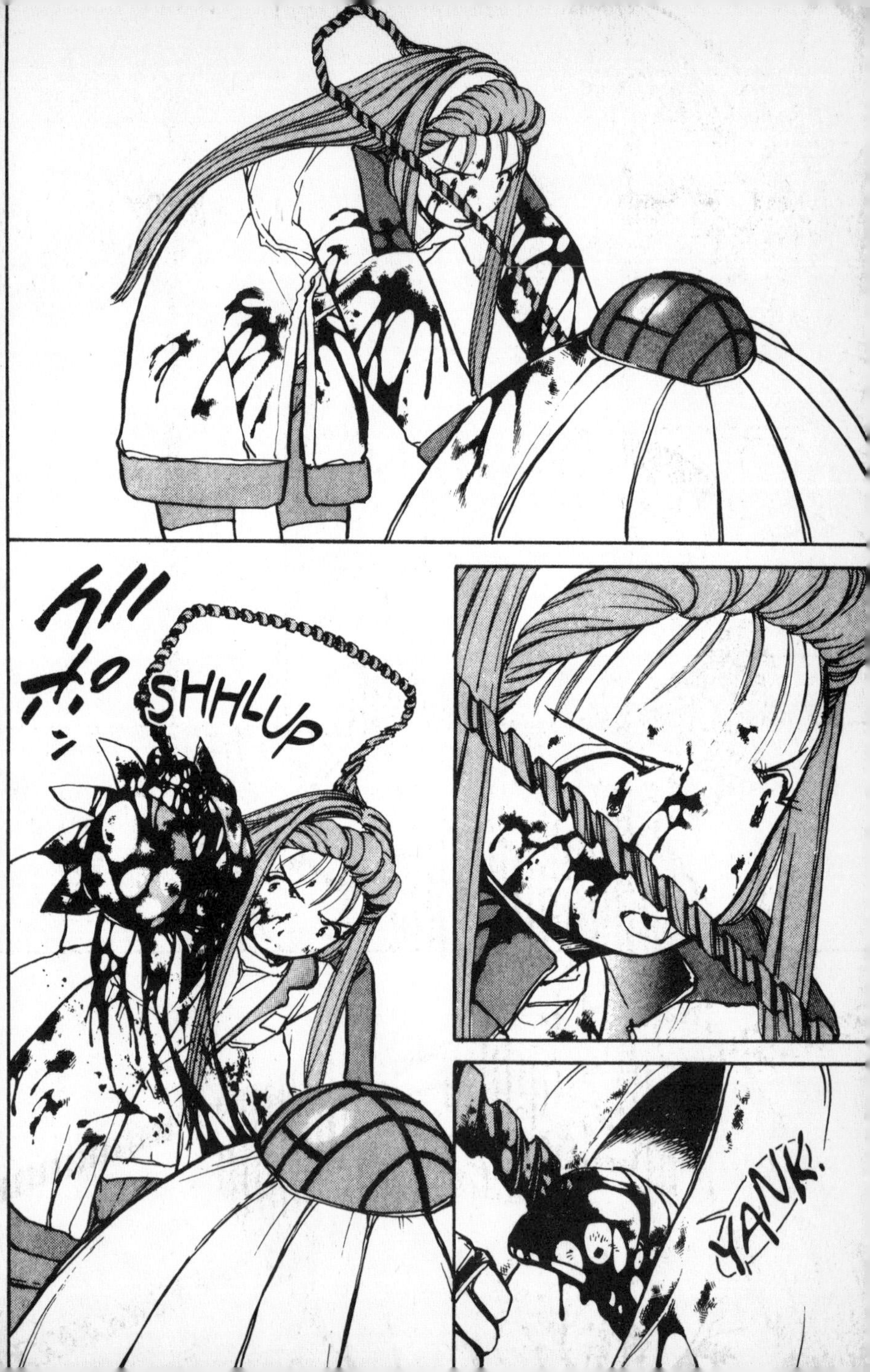
YANK!
SHHLUP

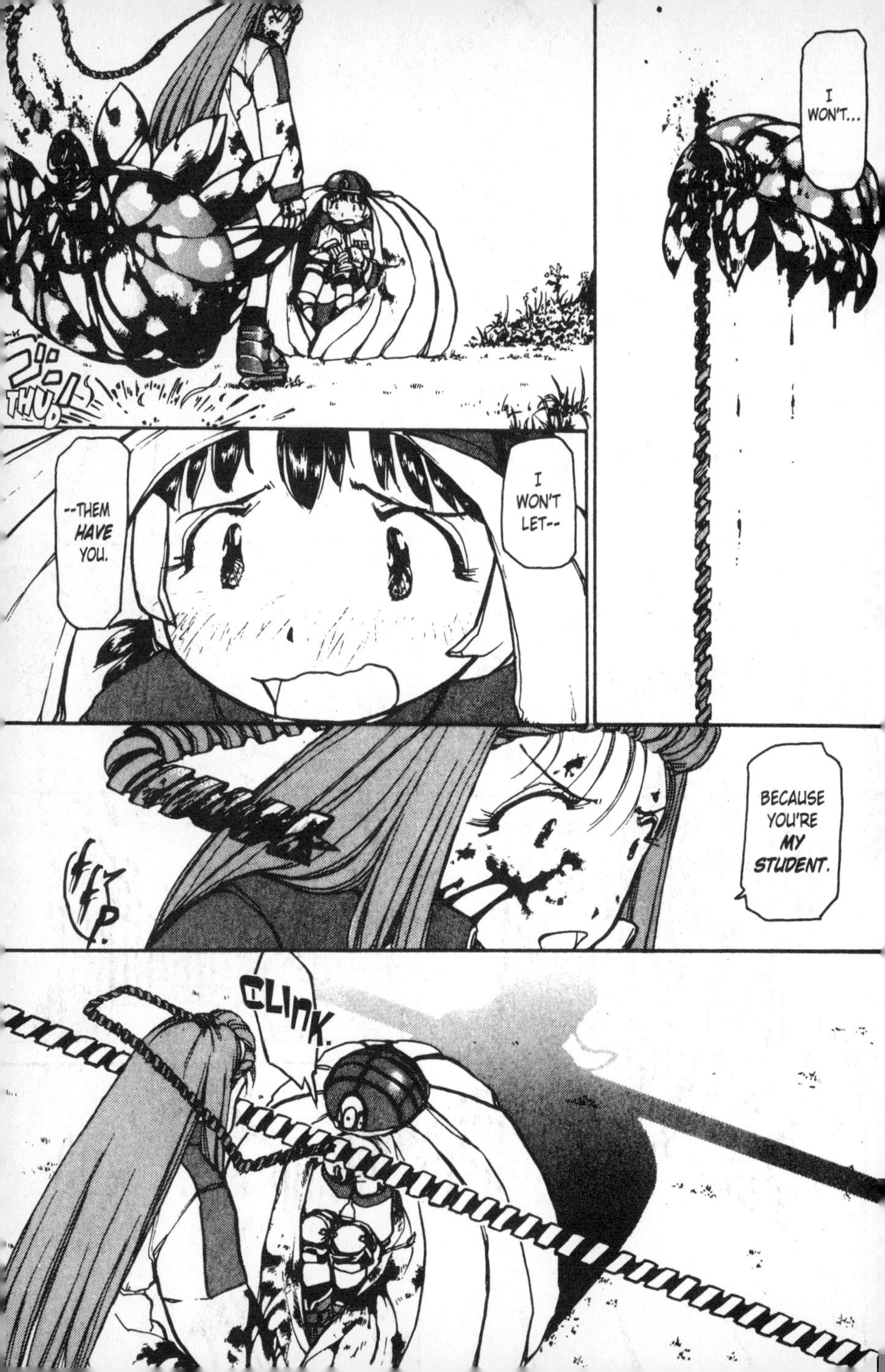
I WON'T...
THUD
I WON'T LET--
--THEM HAVE YOU.
BECAUSE YOU'RE MY STUDENT.
FFP.
CLINK.

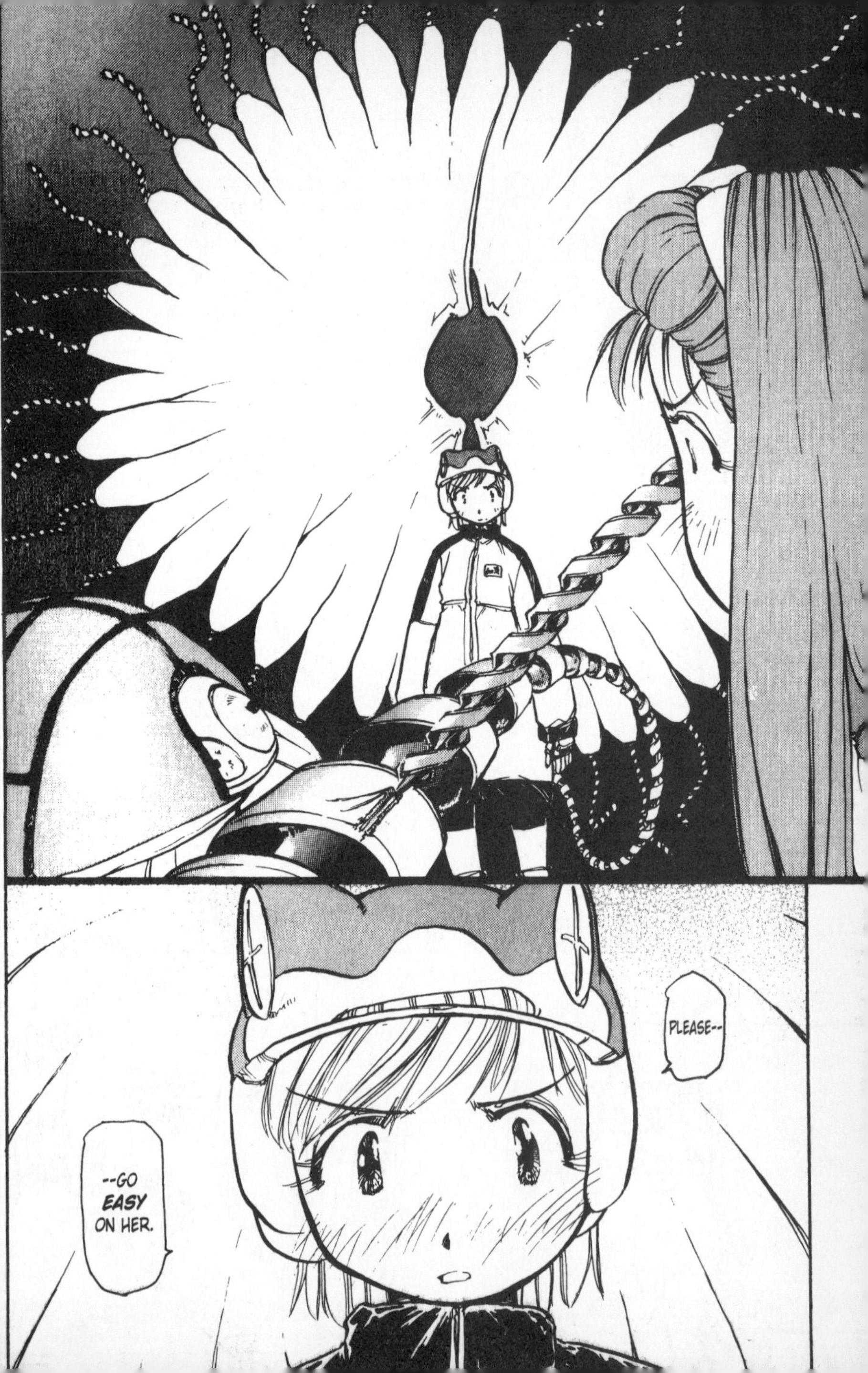
PLEASE--
--GO **EASY** ON HER.

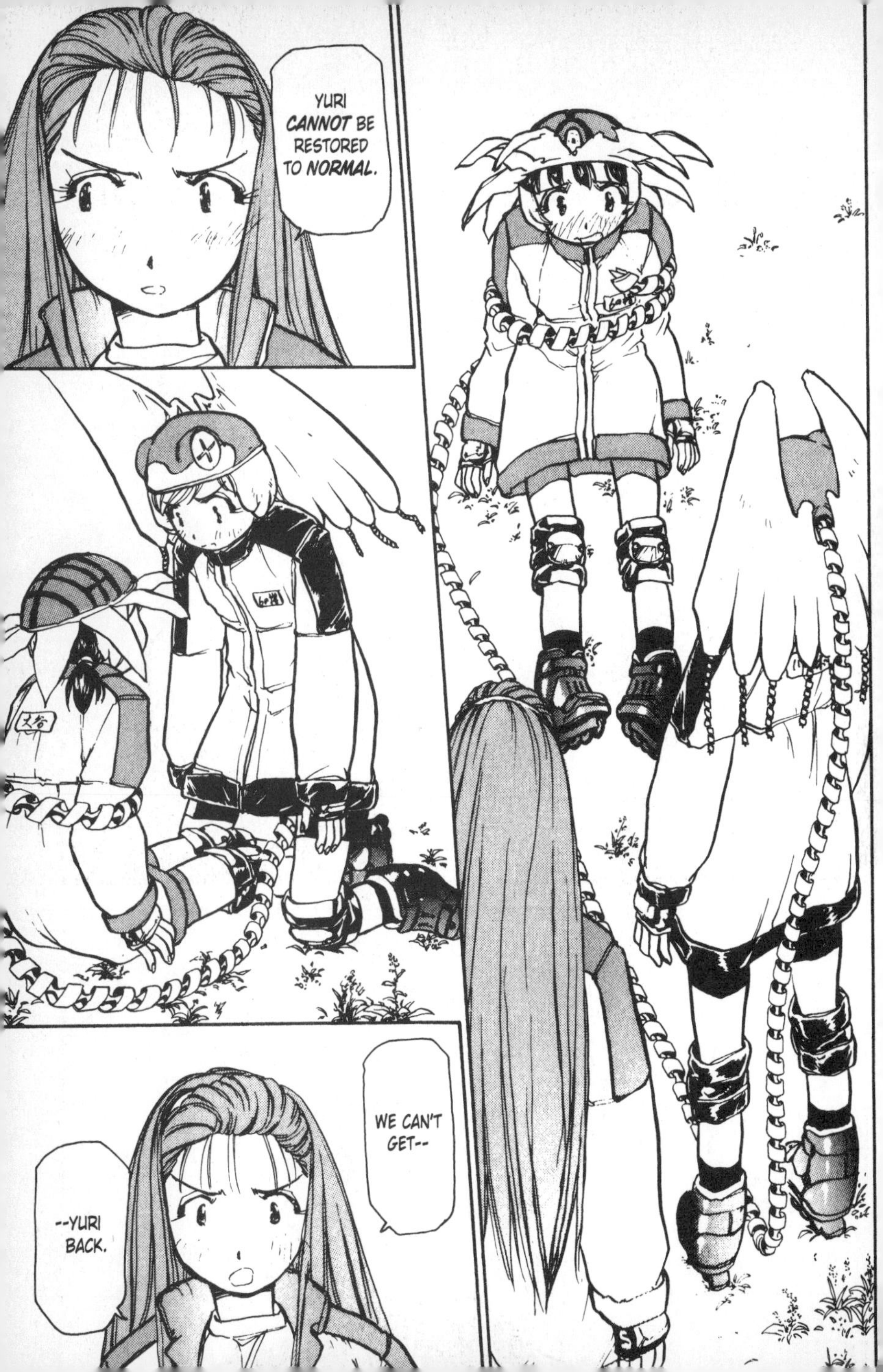
YURI CANNOT BE RESTORED TO NORMAL.
WE CAN'T GET--
--YURI BACK.

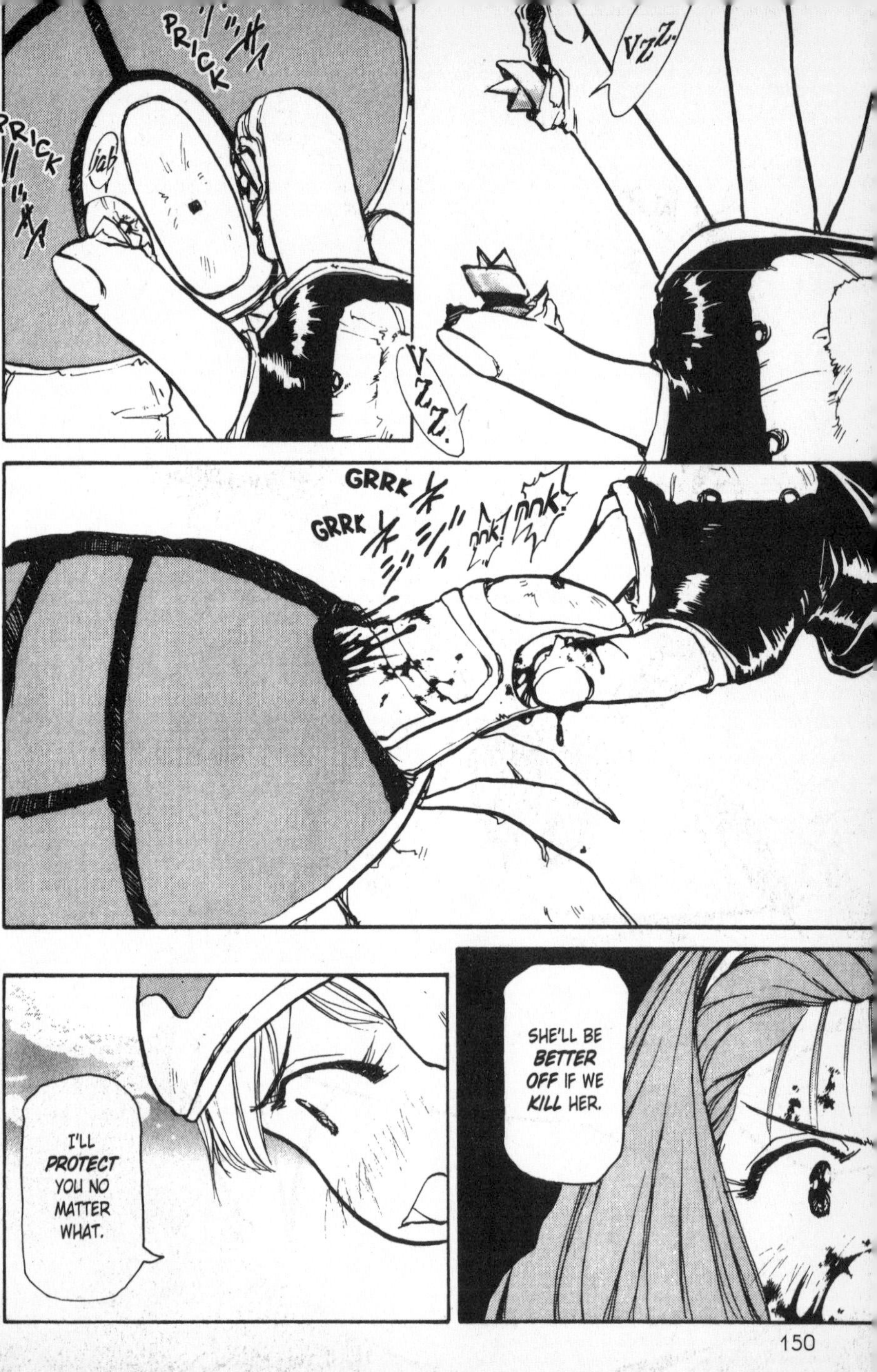

VZZ.
PRICK
jab
PRICK
VZZ.
GRRK
GRRK
nnk!
nnk!
SHE'LL BE *BETTER OFF* IF WE *KILL* HER.
I'LL *PROTECT* YOU NO MATTER WHAT.

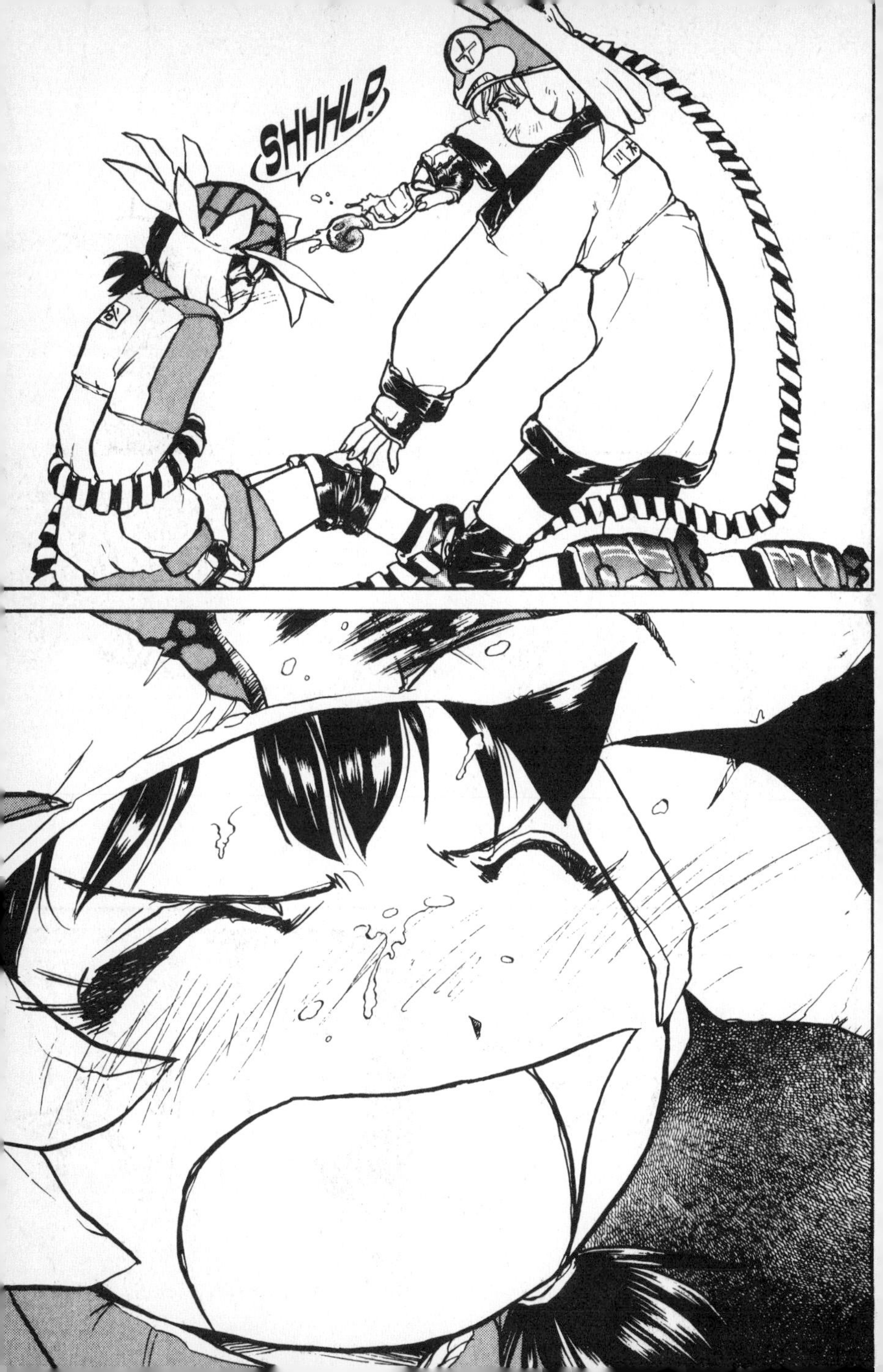
SHHHLP.

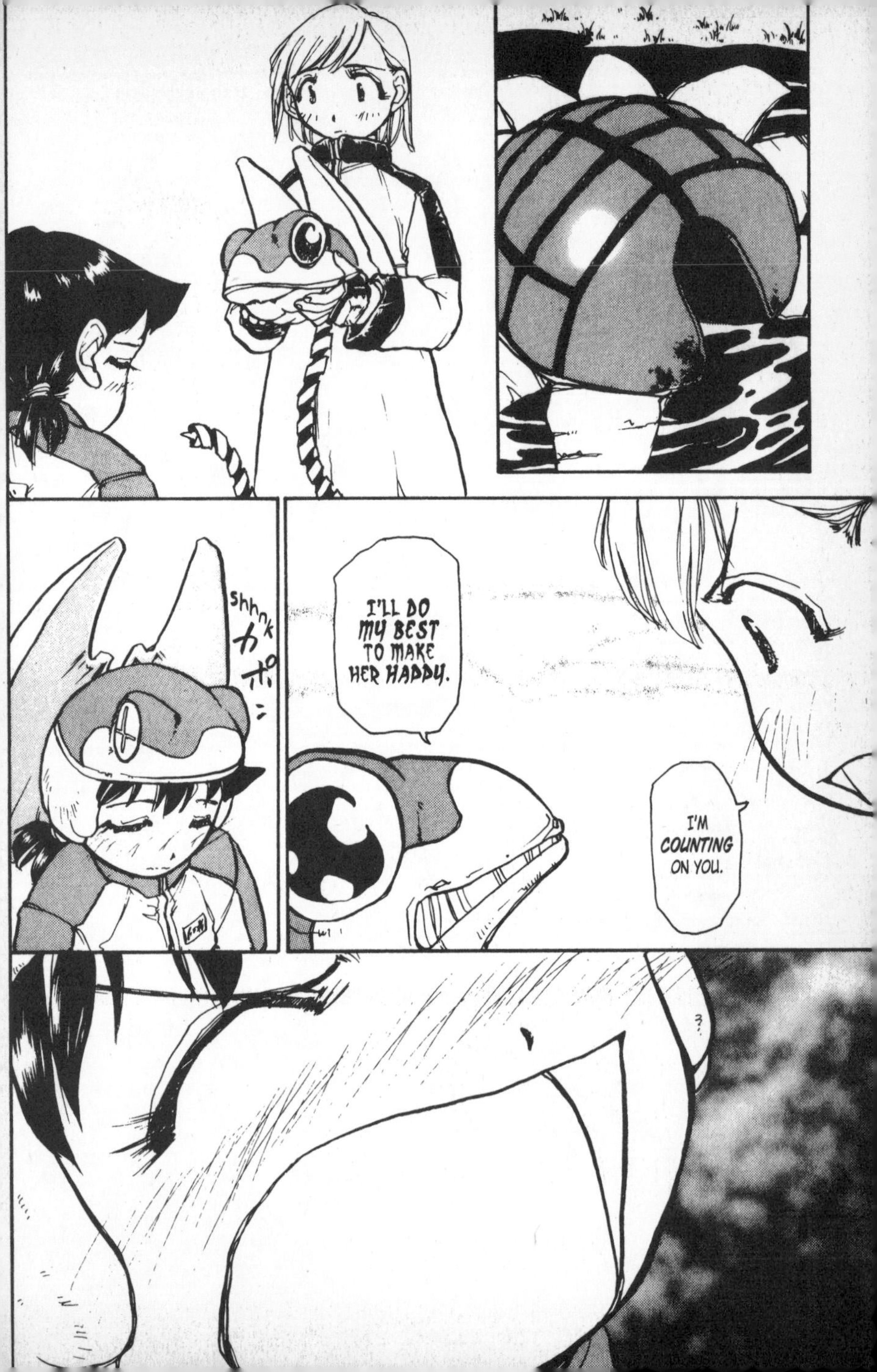
I'LL DO MY BEST TO MAKE HER HAPPY.
I'M COUNTING ON YOU.
shhnk
カポ

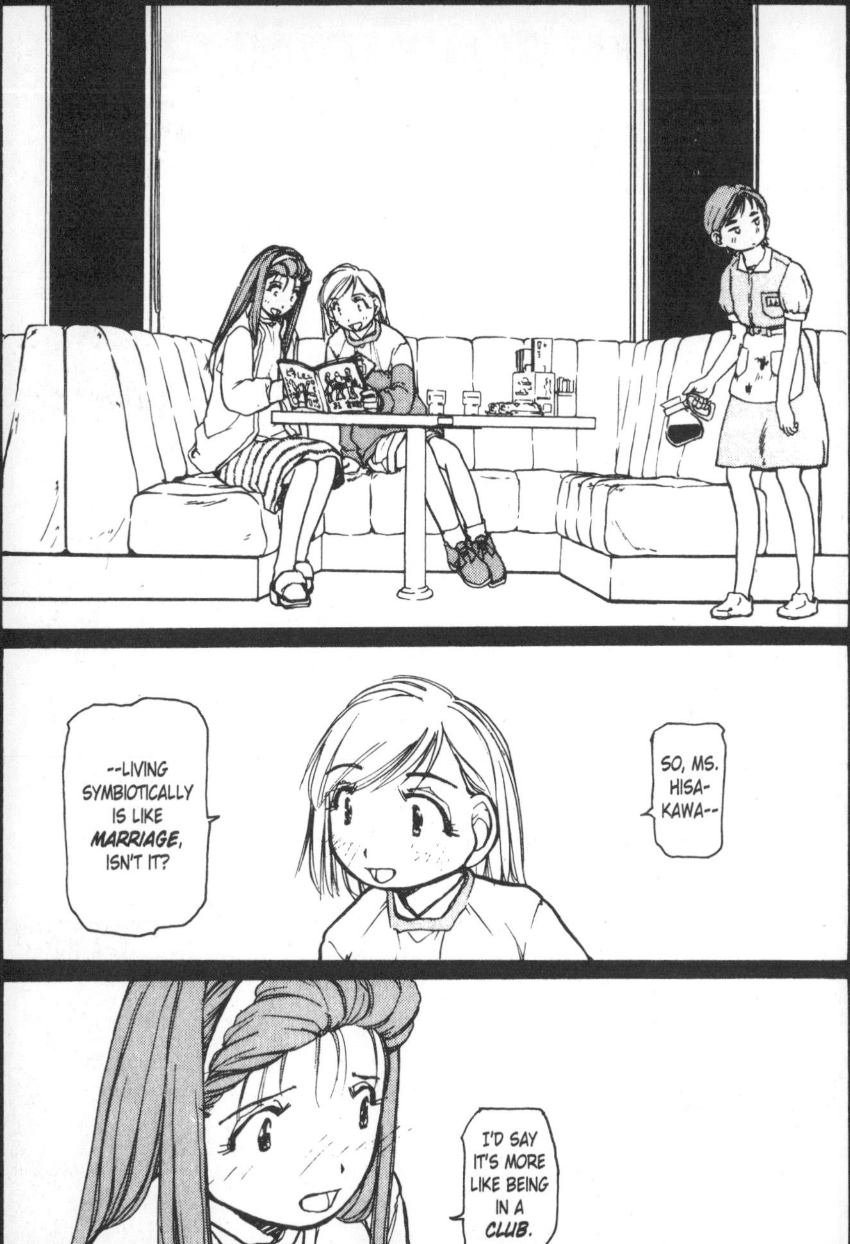
SO, MS. HISA-KAWA--
--LIVING SYMBIOTICALLY IS LIKE MARRIAGE, ISN'T IT?
I'D SAY IT'S MORE LIKE BEING IN A CLUB.

OPERATION 28: THE ALIEN PARTY

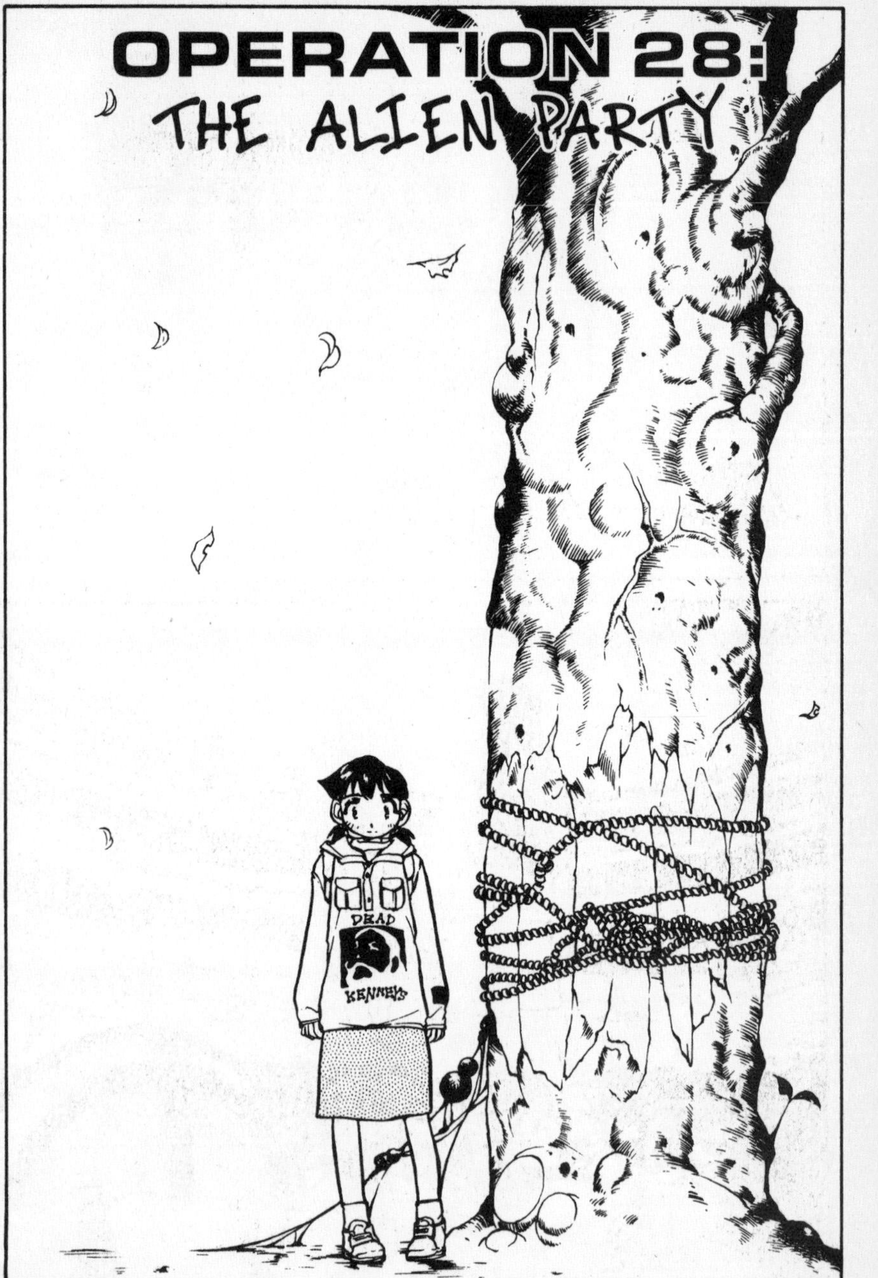
DEAD
KENNEDYS

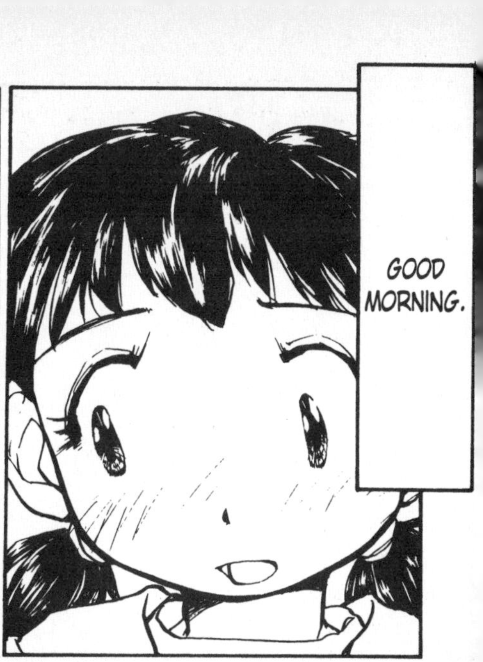
GOOD MORNING.

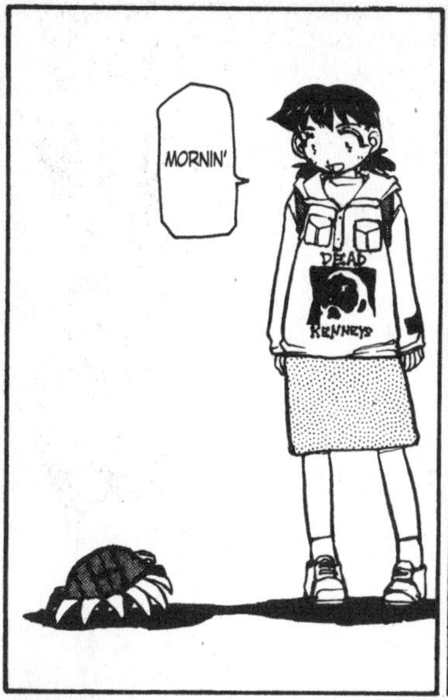
MORNIN'
DEAD

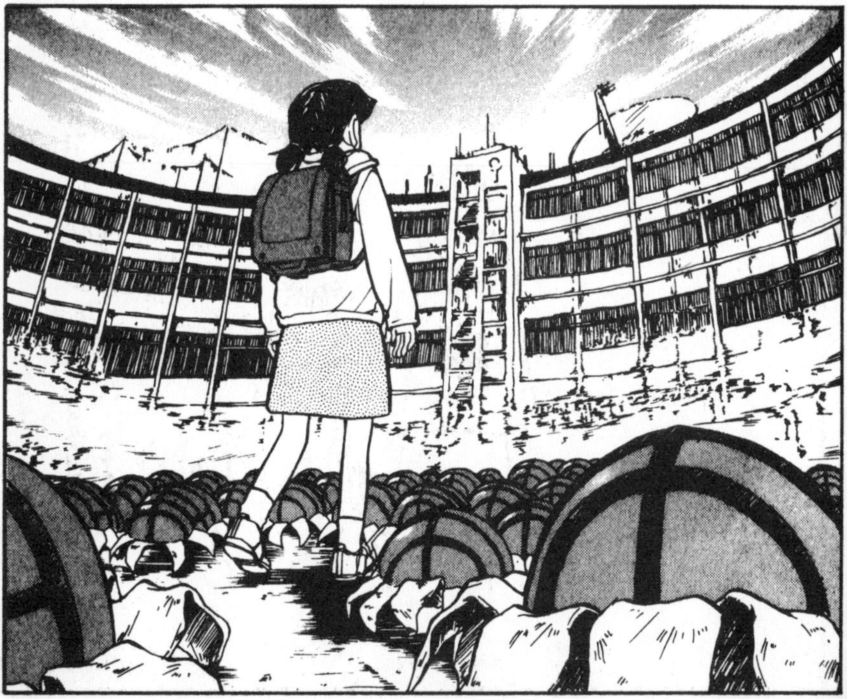

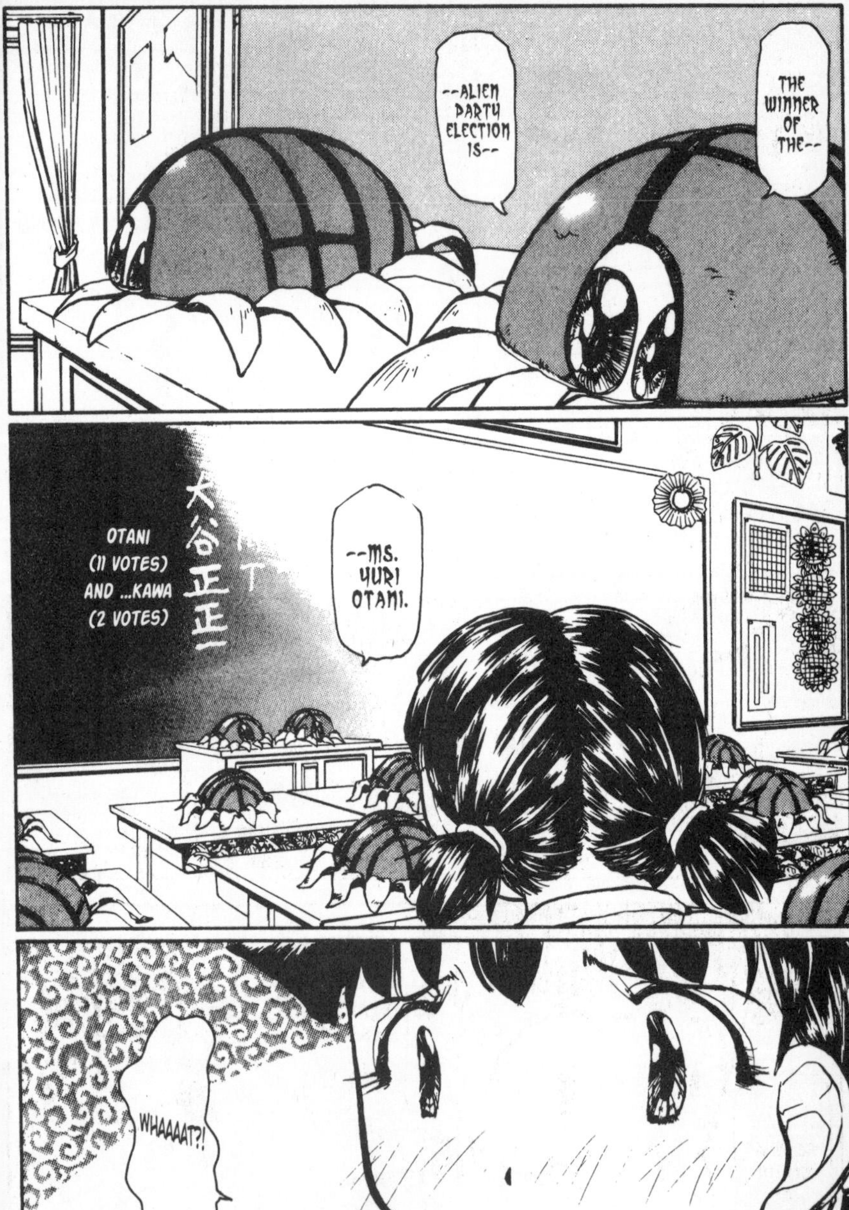
THE WINNER OF THE--
--ALIEN PARTY ELECTION IS--
--MS. YURI OTANI.
大谷正正一
OTANI (11 VOTES) AND ...KAWA (2 VOTES)
WHAAAAT?!

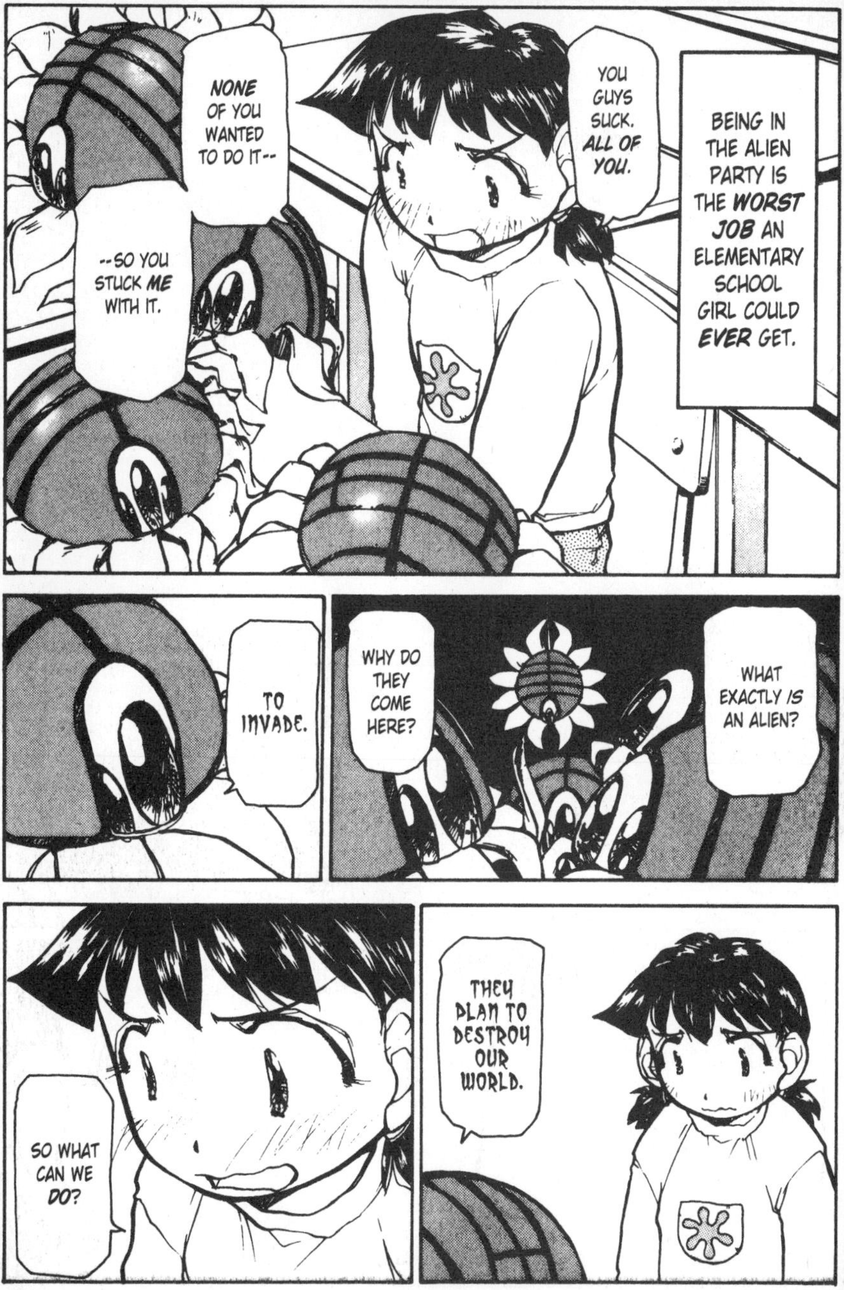
BEING IN THE ALIEN PARTY IS THE WORST JOB AN ELEMENTARY SCHOOL GIRL COULD EVER GET.
YOU GUYS SUCK. ALL OF YOU.
NONE OF YOU WANTED TO DO IT--
--SO YOU STUCK ME WITH IT.
WHAT EXACTLY IS AN ALIEN?
WHY DO THEY COME HERE?
TO INVADE.
THEY PLAN TO DESTROY OUR WORLD.
SO WHAT CAN WE DO?

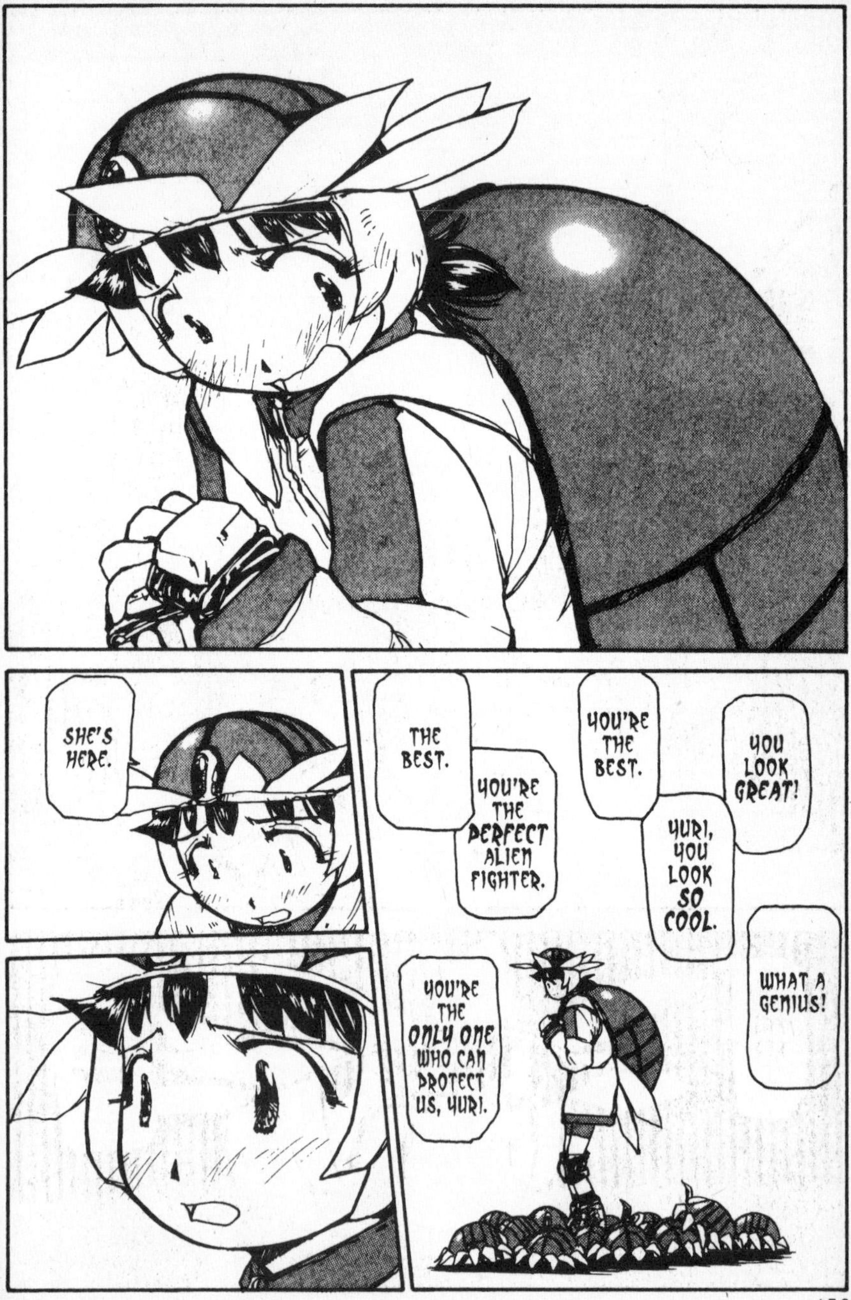
YOU LOOK GREAT!
YOU'RE THE BEST.
YURI, YOU LOOK SO COOL.
THE BEST.
YOU'RE THE PERFECT ALIEN FIGHTER.
WHAT A GENIUS!
YOU'RE THE ONLY ONE WHO CAN PROTECT US, YURI.
SHE'S HERE.

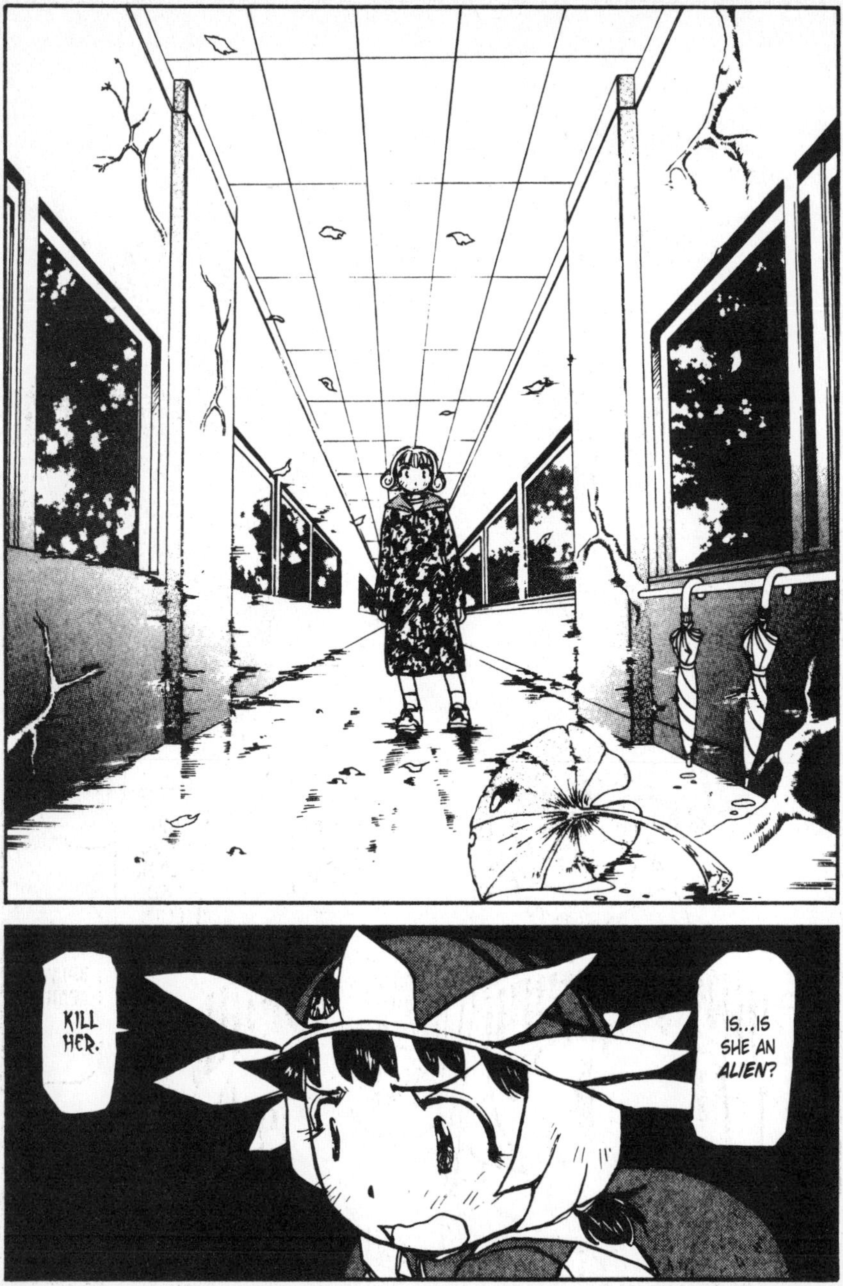
IS...IS SHE AN ALIEN?
KILL HER.

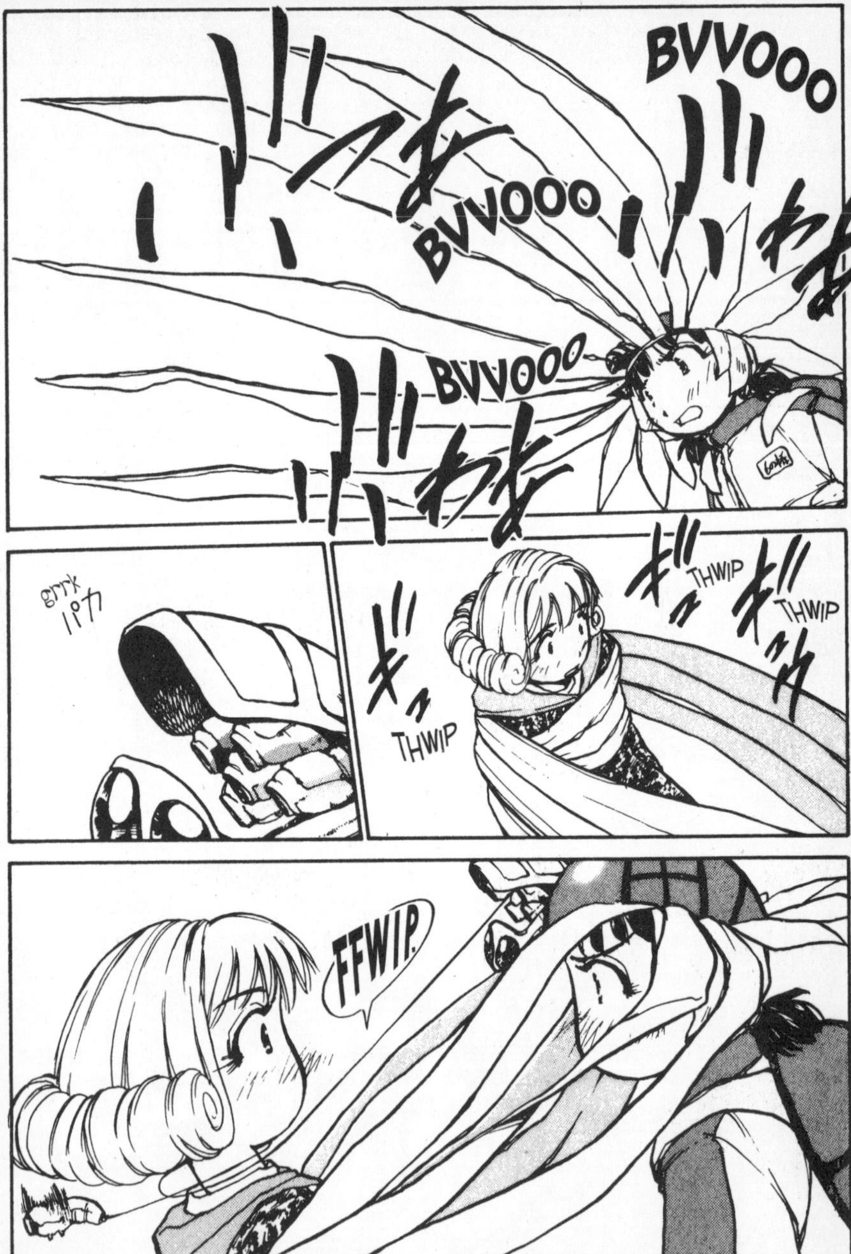
BVVOOO
BVVOOO
BVVOOO
THWIP
THWIP
THWIP
grrk
パカ
FFWIP.

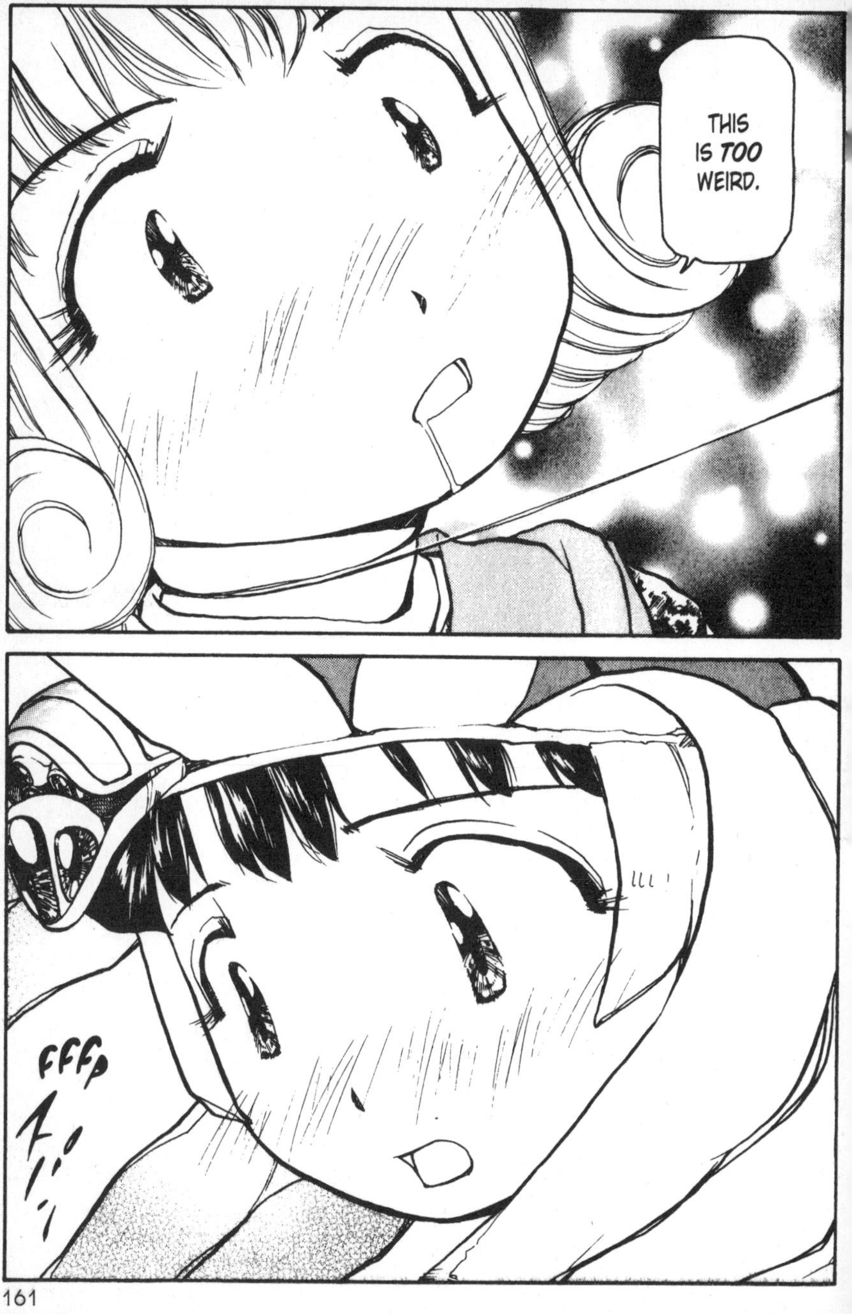
THIS IS *TOO* WEIRD.
FFFP

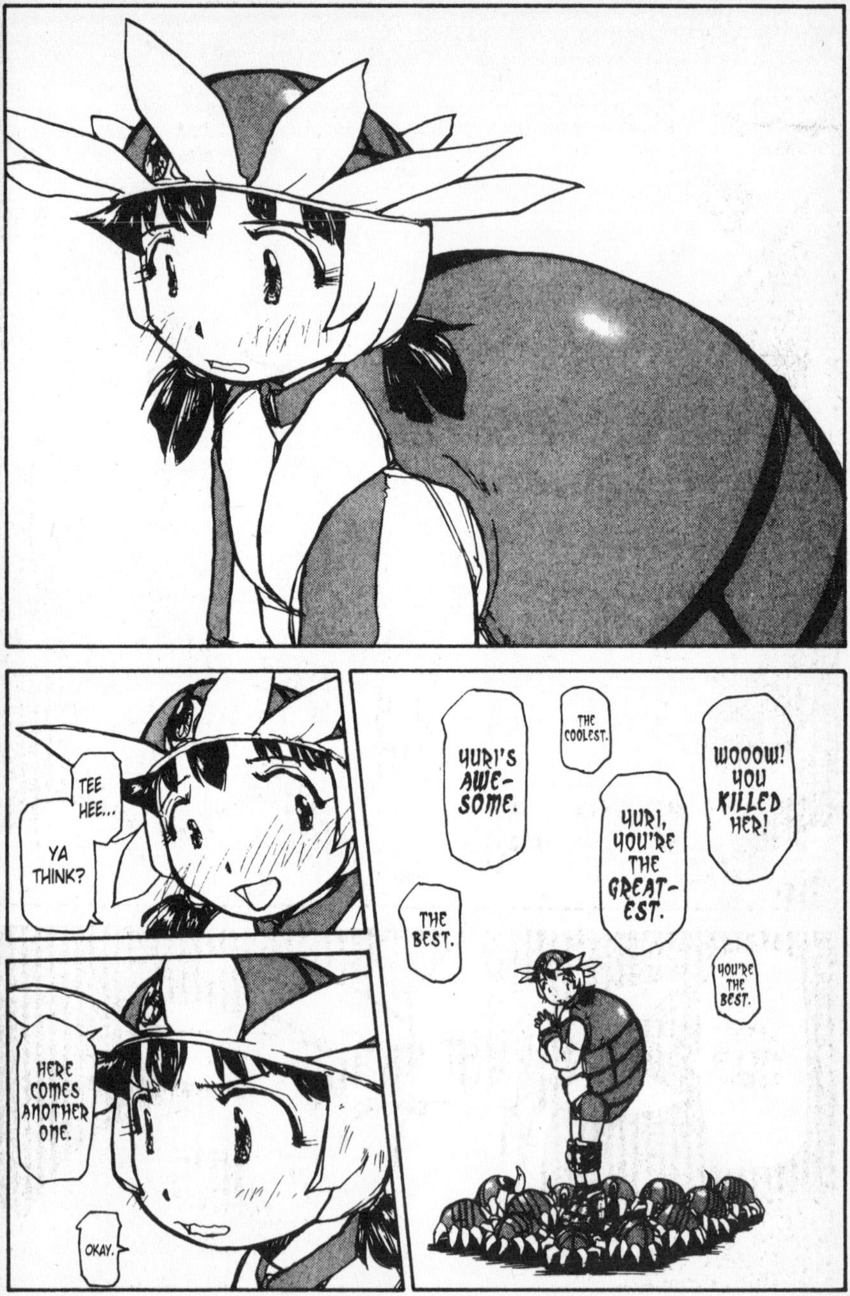
WOOOW! YOU KILLED HER!
THE COOLEST.
YURI'S AWE-SOME.
YURI, YOU'RE THE GREAT-EST.
YOU'RE THE BEST.
THE BEST.
TEE HEE...
YA THINK?
HERE COMES ANOTHER ONE.
OKAY.

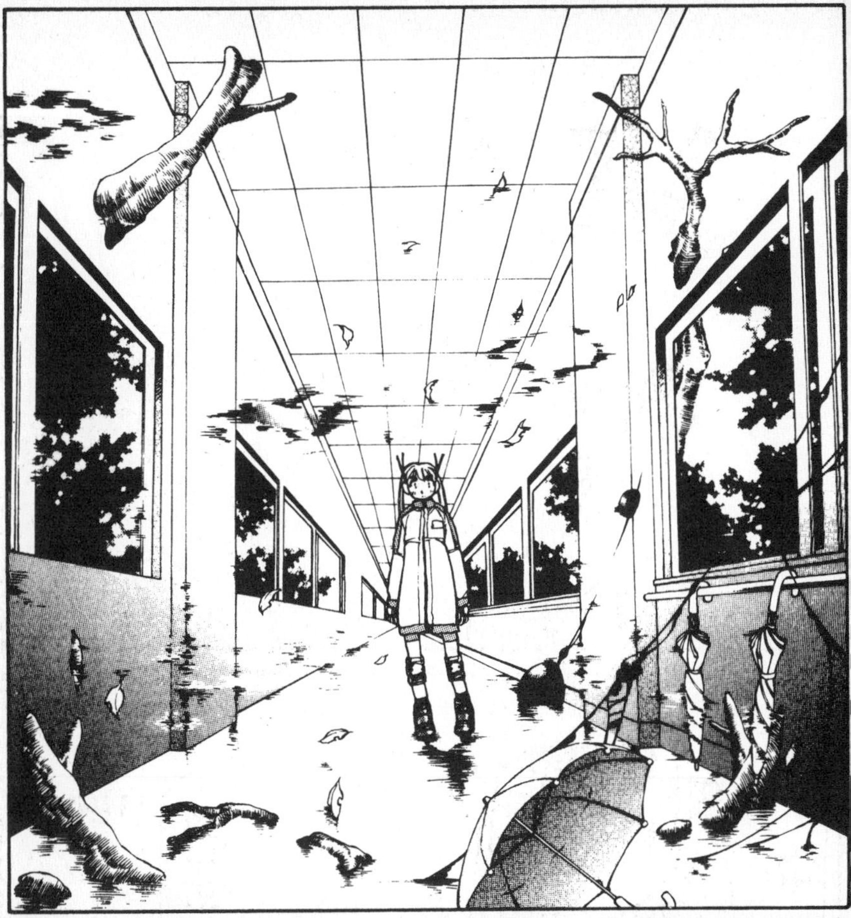

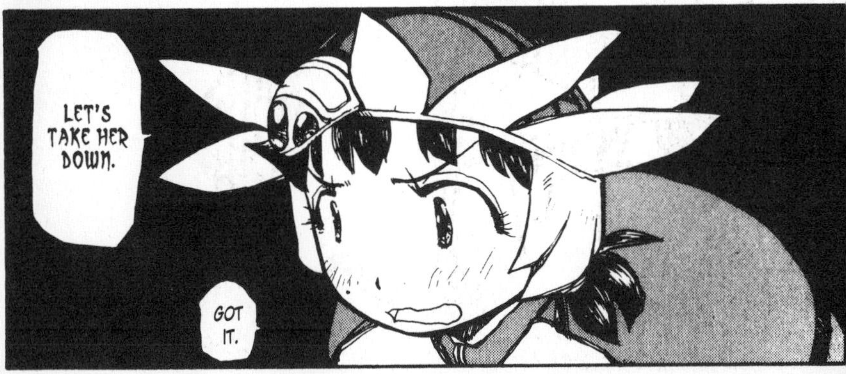
LET'S TAKE HER DOWN.
GOT IT.

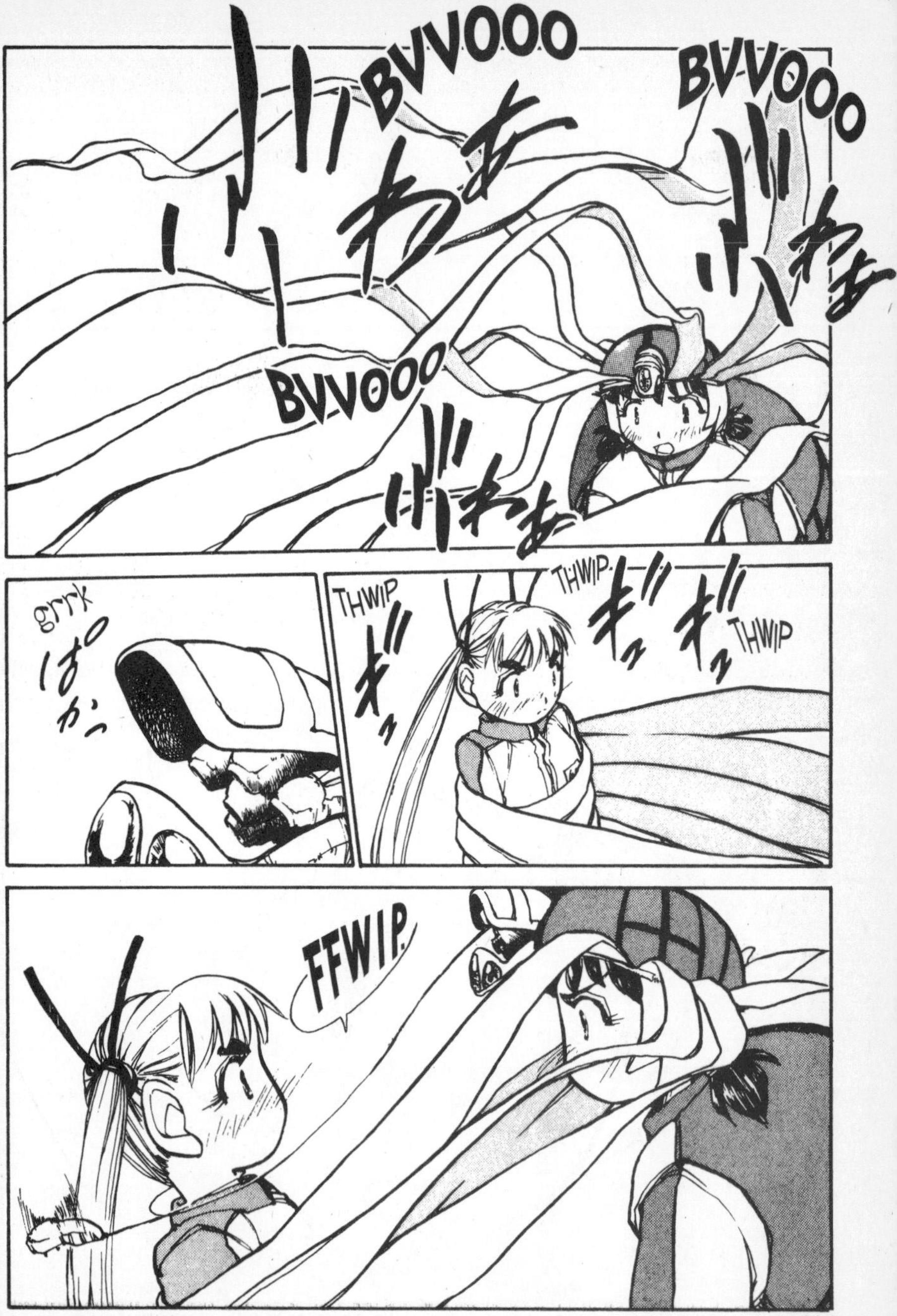
BVVOOO
BVVOOO
BVVOOO
THWIP
THWIP
THWIP
grrk
FFWIP.

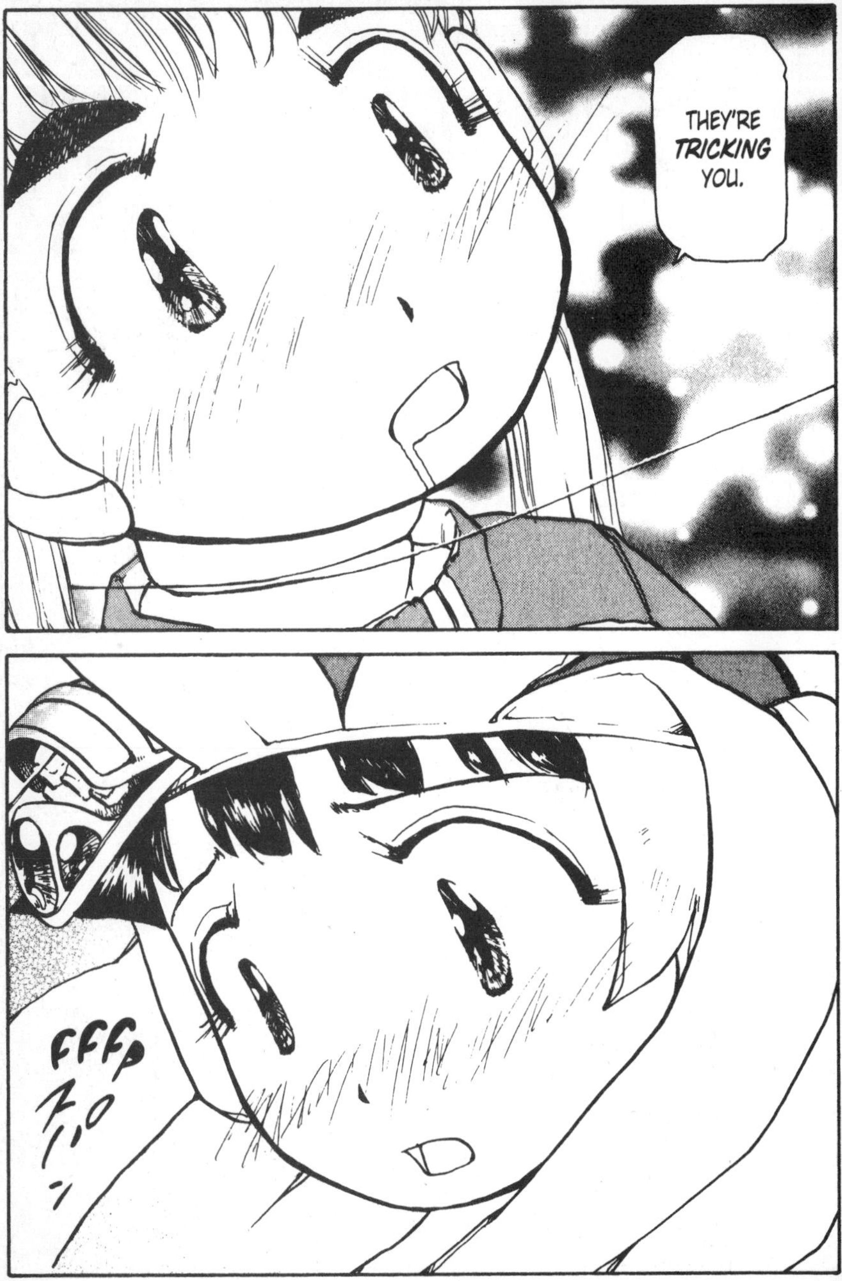
THEY'RE TRICKING YOU.
FFFP

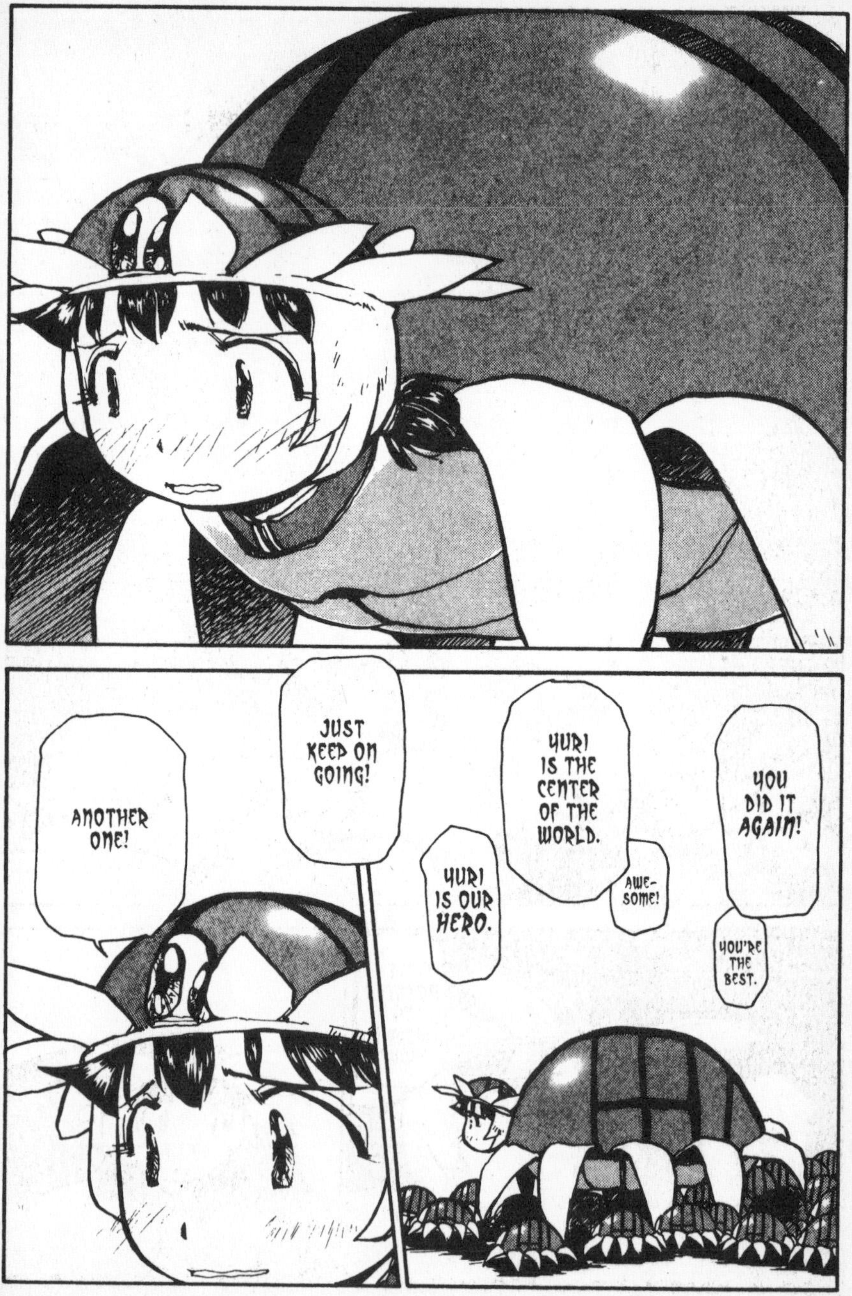
YOU DID IT AGAIN!
YOU'RE THE BEST.
YURI IS THE CENTER OF THE WORLD.
AWE-SOME!
YURI IS OUR HERO.
JUST KEEP ON GOING!
ANOTHER ONE!

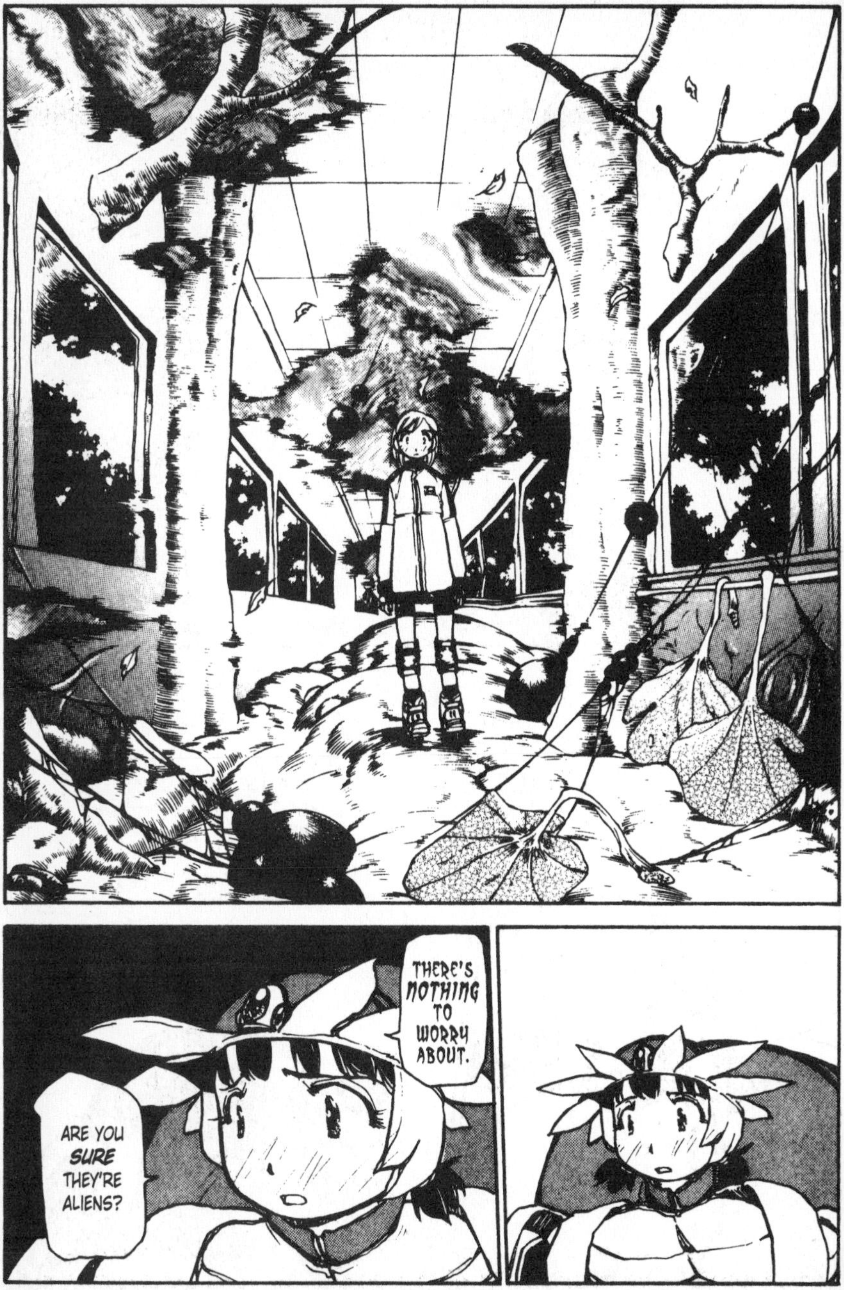
THERE'S *NOTHING* TO WORRY ABOUT.
ARE YOU *SURE* THEY'RE ALIENS?

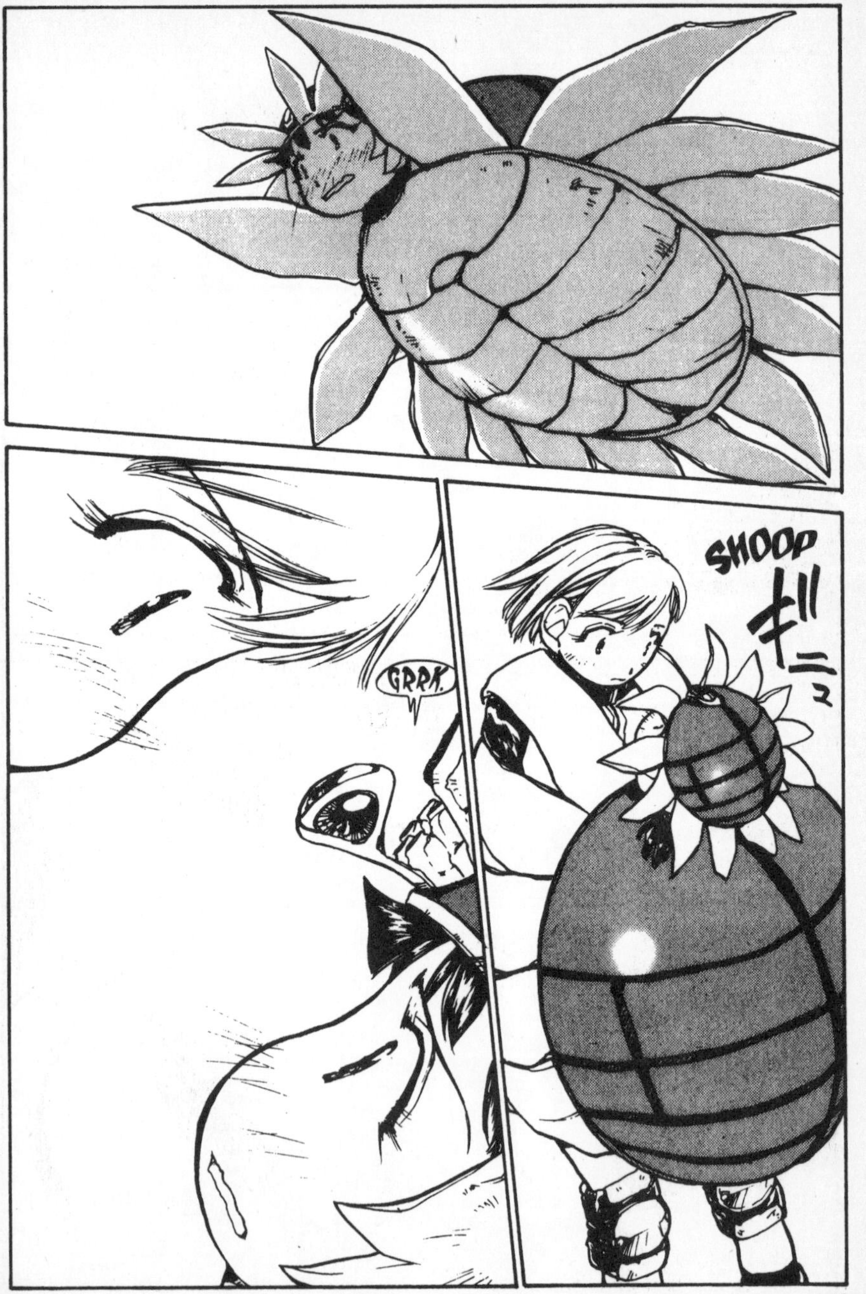
SHOOP
GRRK.

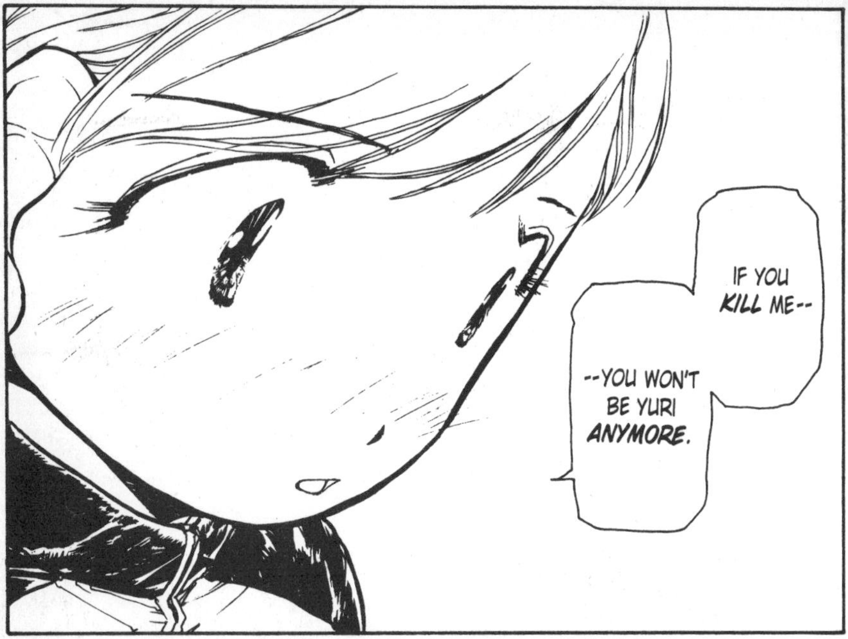
IF YOU KILL ME--
--YOU WON'T BE YURI ANYMORE.
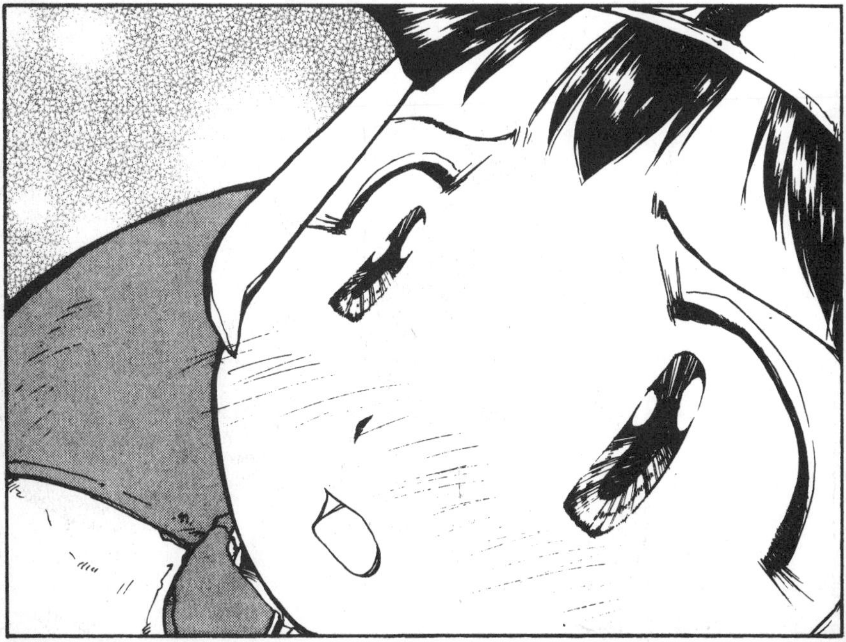

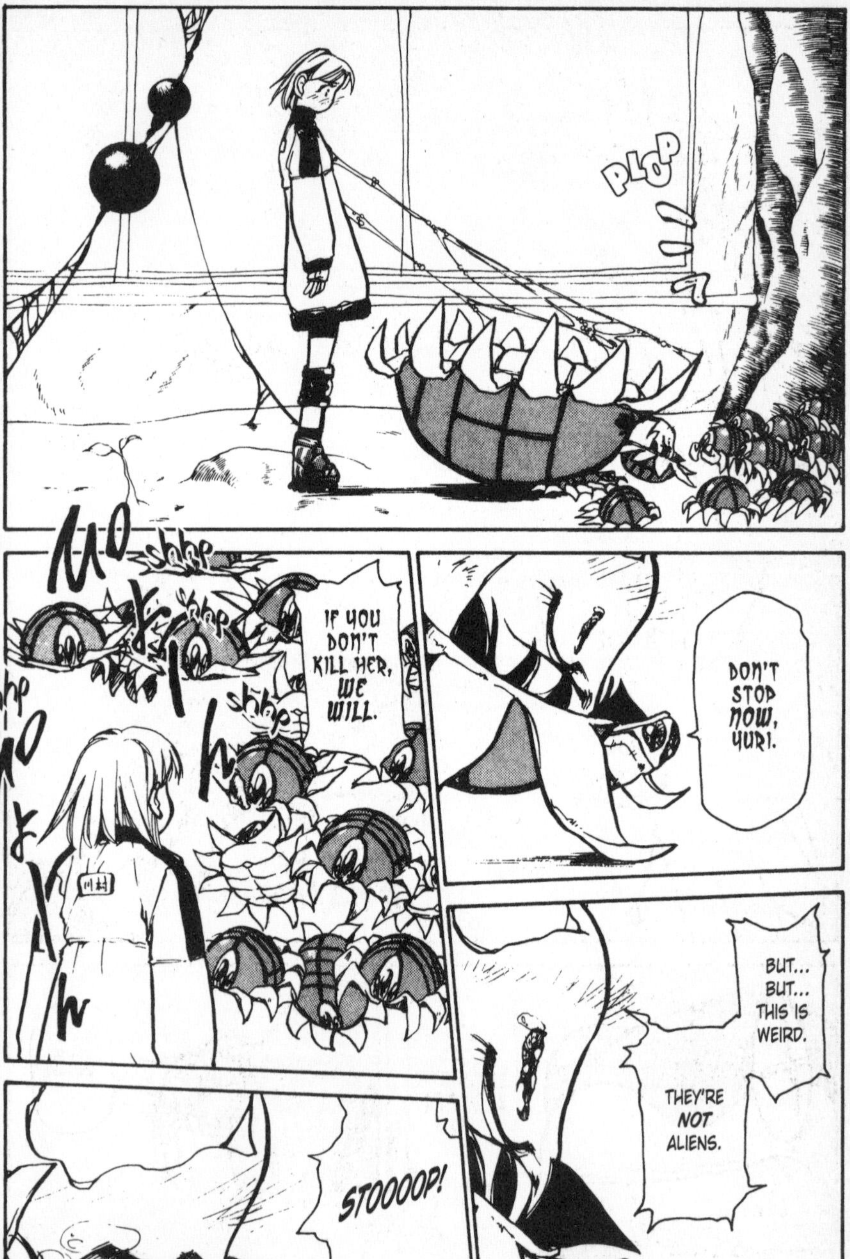
PLOP
DON'T STOP NOW, YURI.
shhp
shhp
shhp
IF YOU DON'T KILL HER, WE WILL.
BUT... BUT... THIS IS WEIRD.
THEY'RE NOT ALIENS.
STOOOOP!

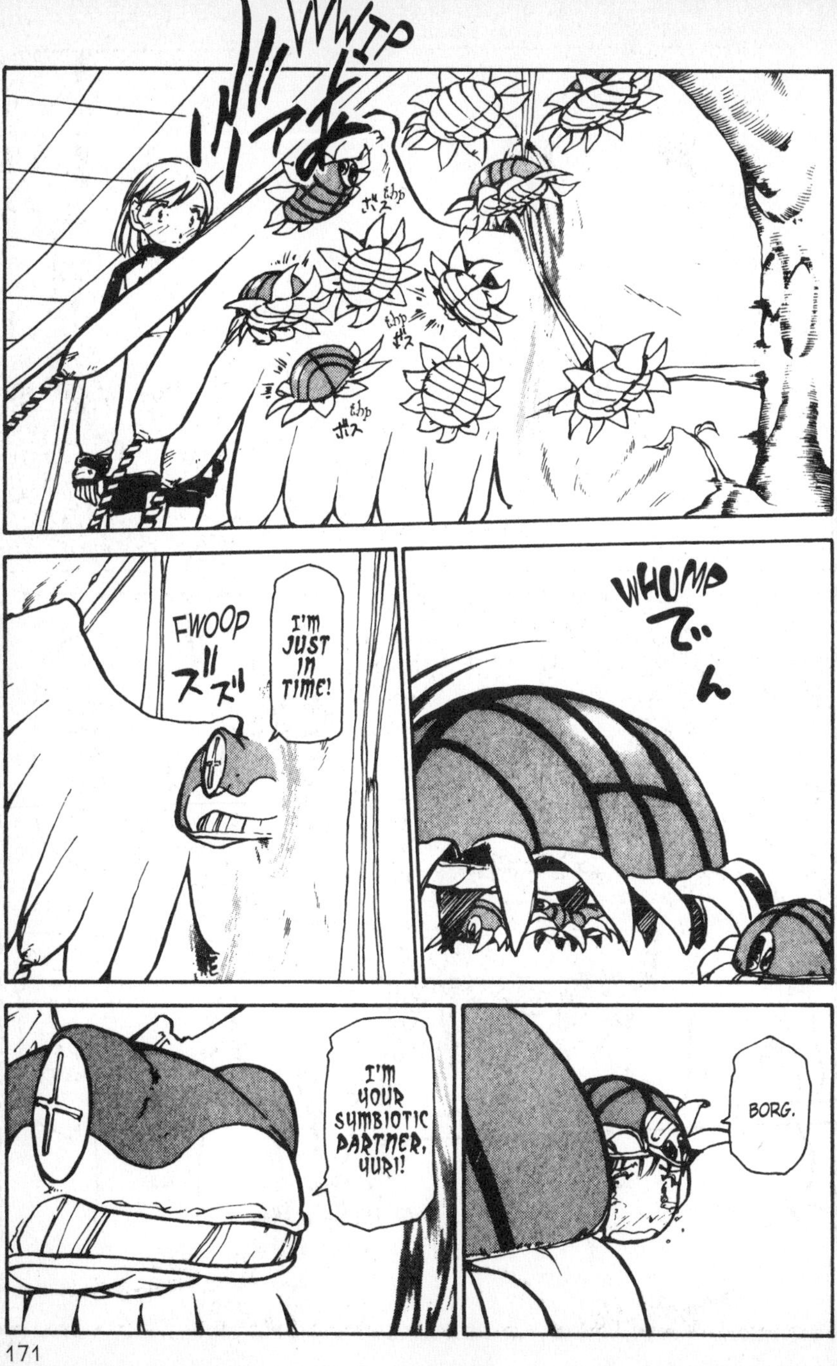
VVWIP
thhp
ボス
thhp
ボス
thhp
ボス
WHUMP
でん
FWOOP
ズズ
I'M JUST IN TIME!
BORG.
I'M YOUR SYMBIOTIC PARTNER, YURI!

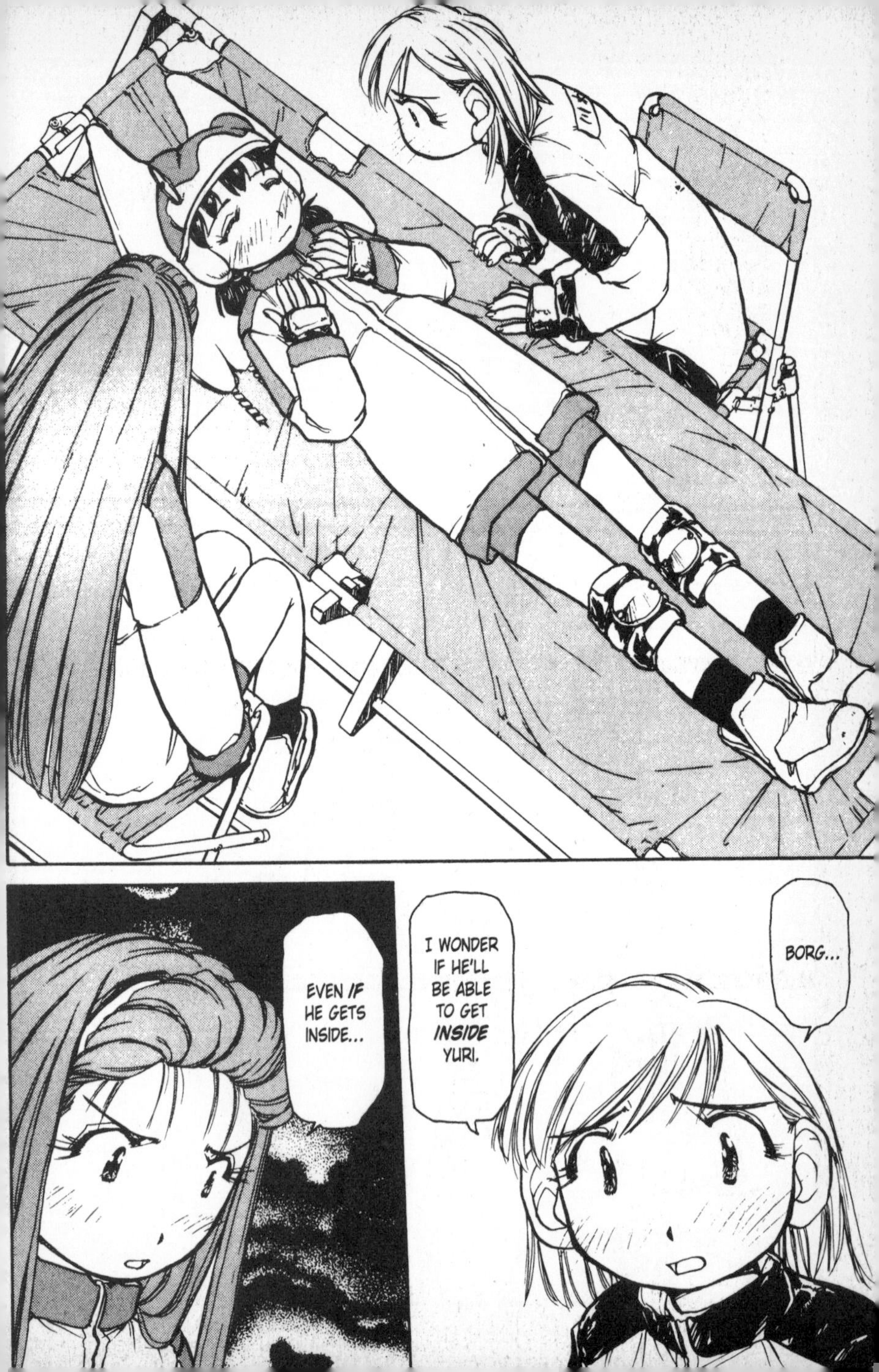
BORG...
I WONDER IF HE'LL BE ABLE TO GET *INSIDE* YURI.
EVEN *IF* HE GETS INSIDE...

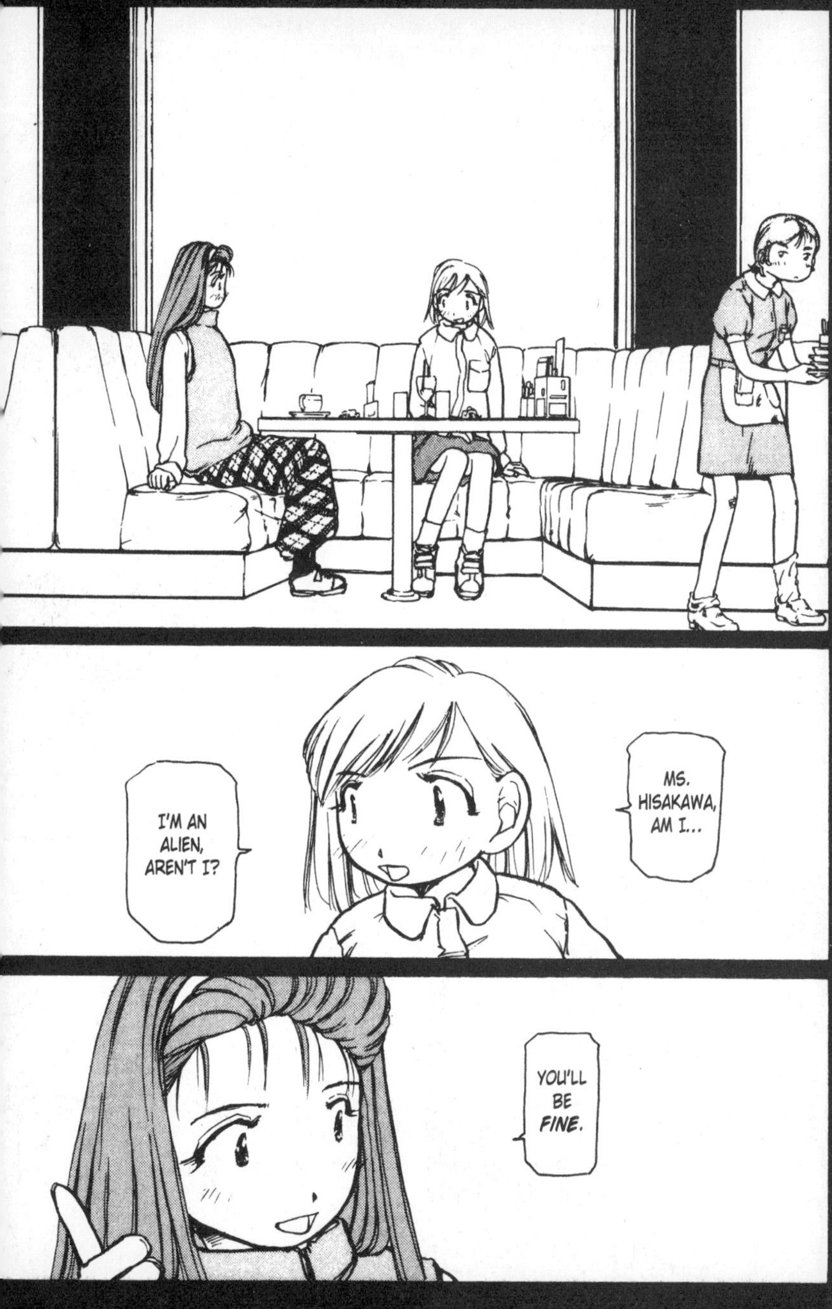
MS. HISAKAWA, AM I...
I'M AN ALIEN, AREN'T I?
YOU'LL BE *FINE.*

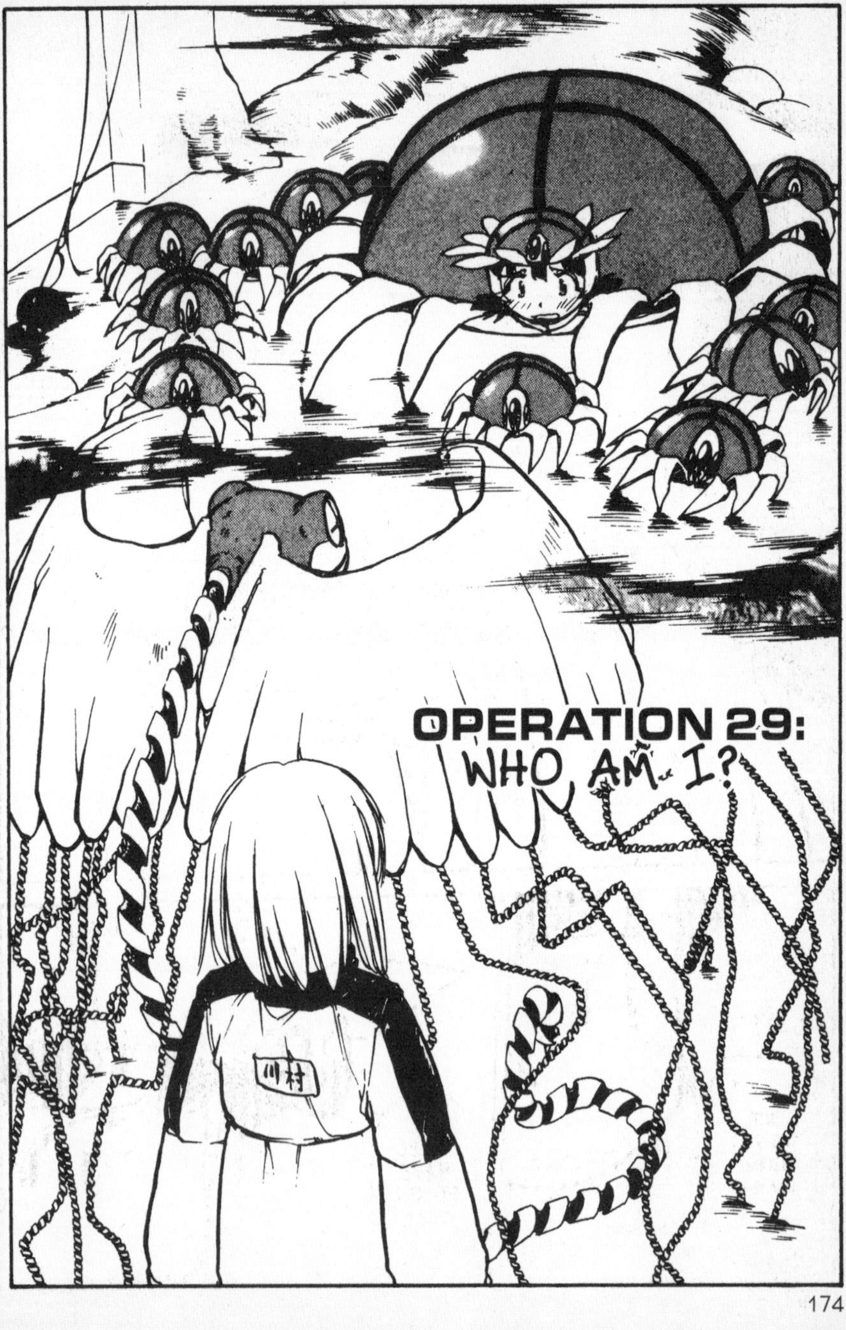
OPERATION 29:
WHO AM I?
川村

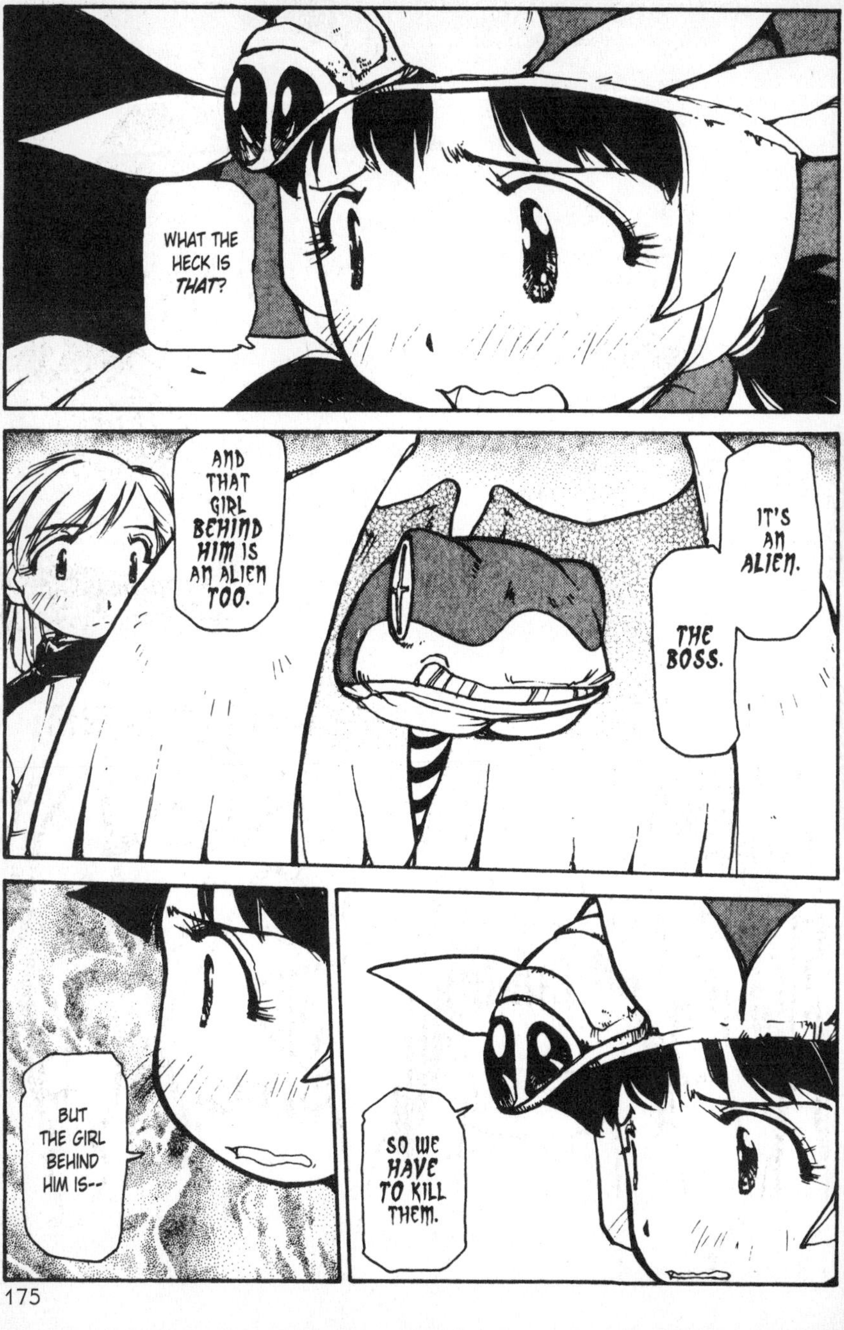
WHAT THE HECK IS THAT?
IT'S AN ALIEN.
THE BOSS.
AND THAT GIRL BEHIND HIM IS AN ALIEN TOO.
SO WE HAVE TO KILL THEM.
BUT THE GIRL BEHIND HIM IS--

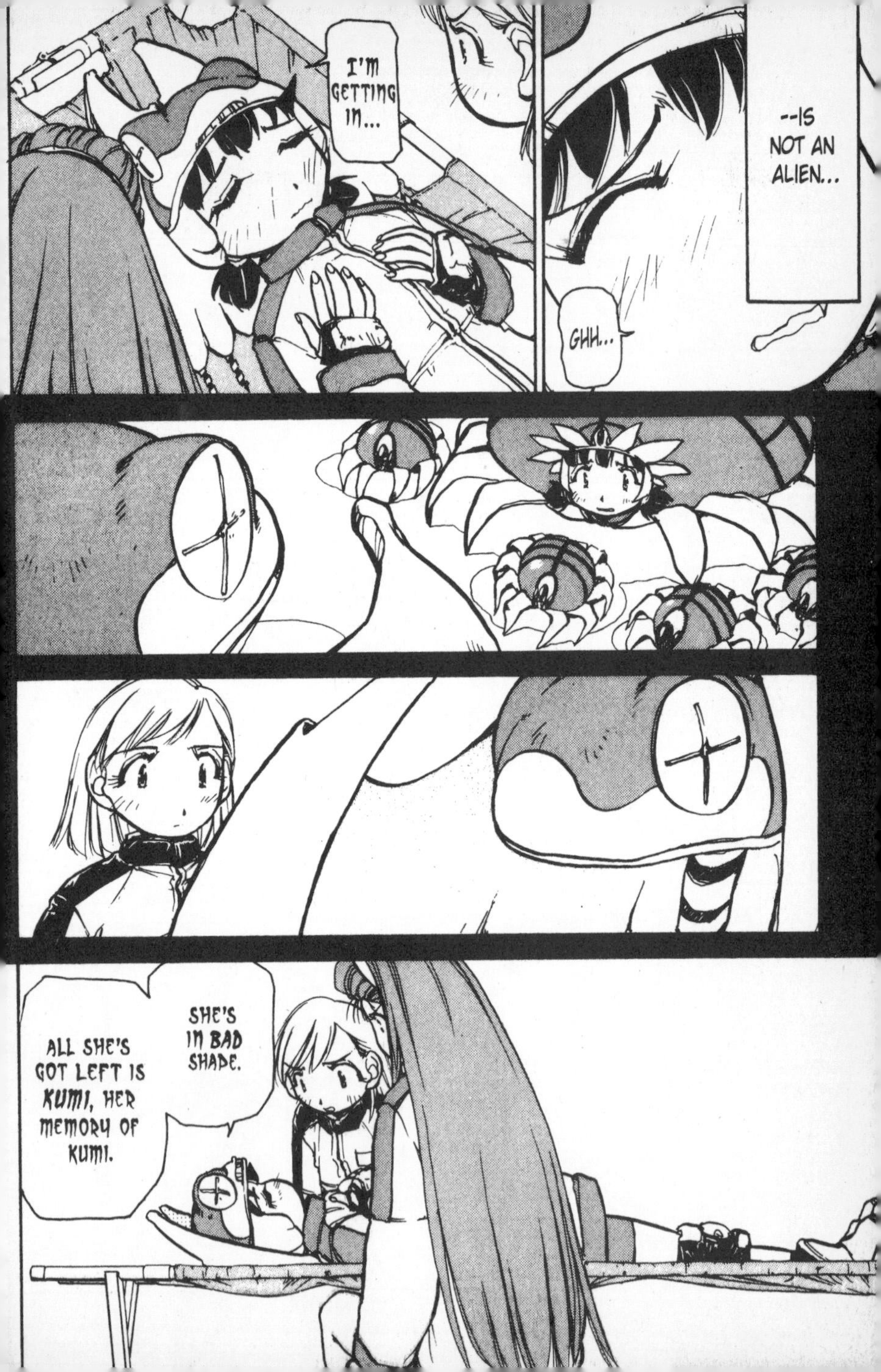
--IS NOT AN ALIEN...
GHH...
I'M GETTING IN...
SHE'S IN BAD SHAPE.
ALL SHE'S GOT LEFT IS KUMI, HER MEMORY OF KUMI.

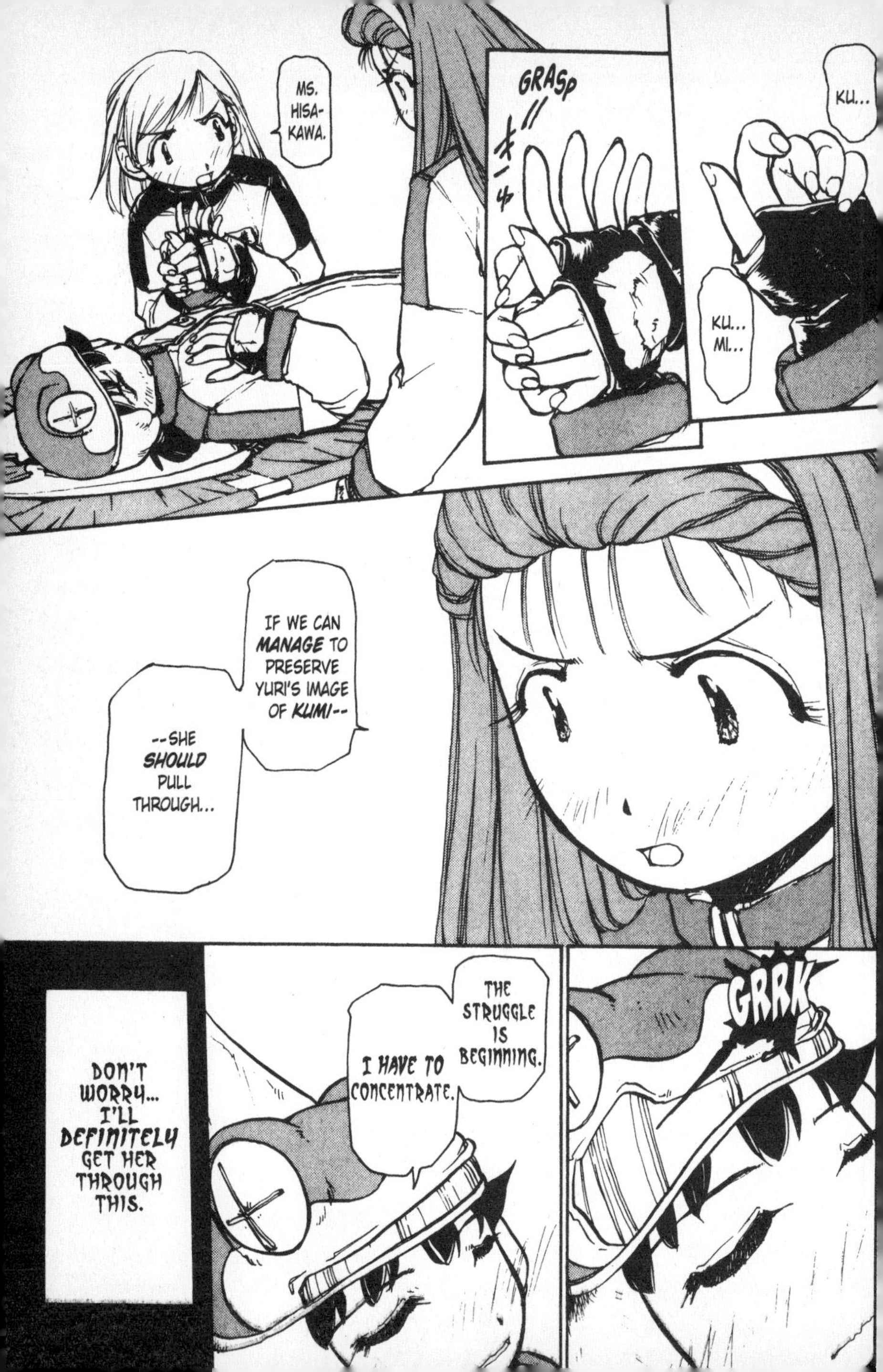
KU...
KU... MI...
GRASP
MS. HISA-KAWA.
IF WE CAN MANAGE TO PRESERVE YURI'S IMAGE OF KUMI--
--SHE SHOULD PULL THROUGH...
GRRK
THE STRUGGLE IS BEGINNING.
I HAVE TO CONCENTRATE.
DON'T WORRY... I'LL DEFINITELY GET HER THROUGH THIS.

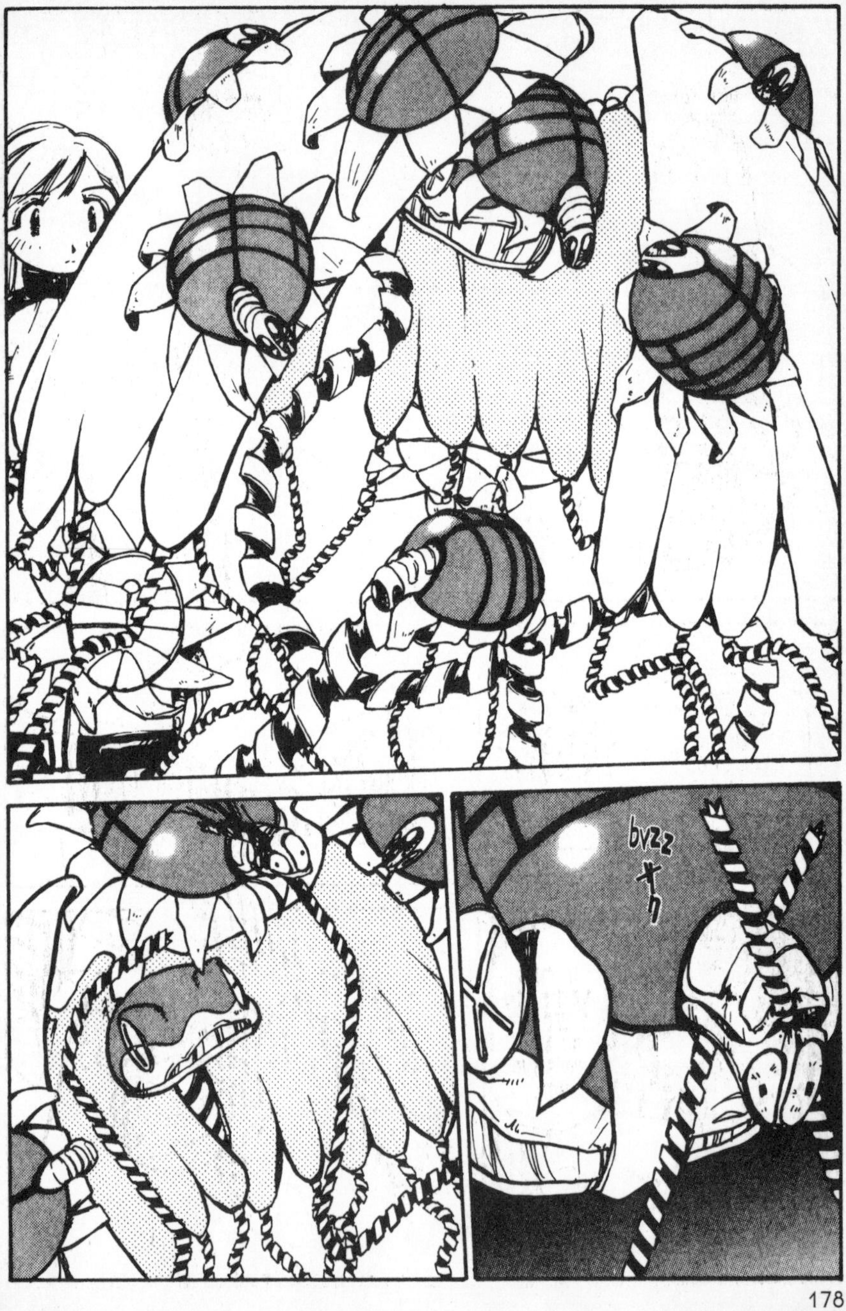
bvzz
ギク

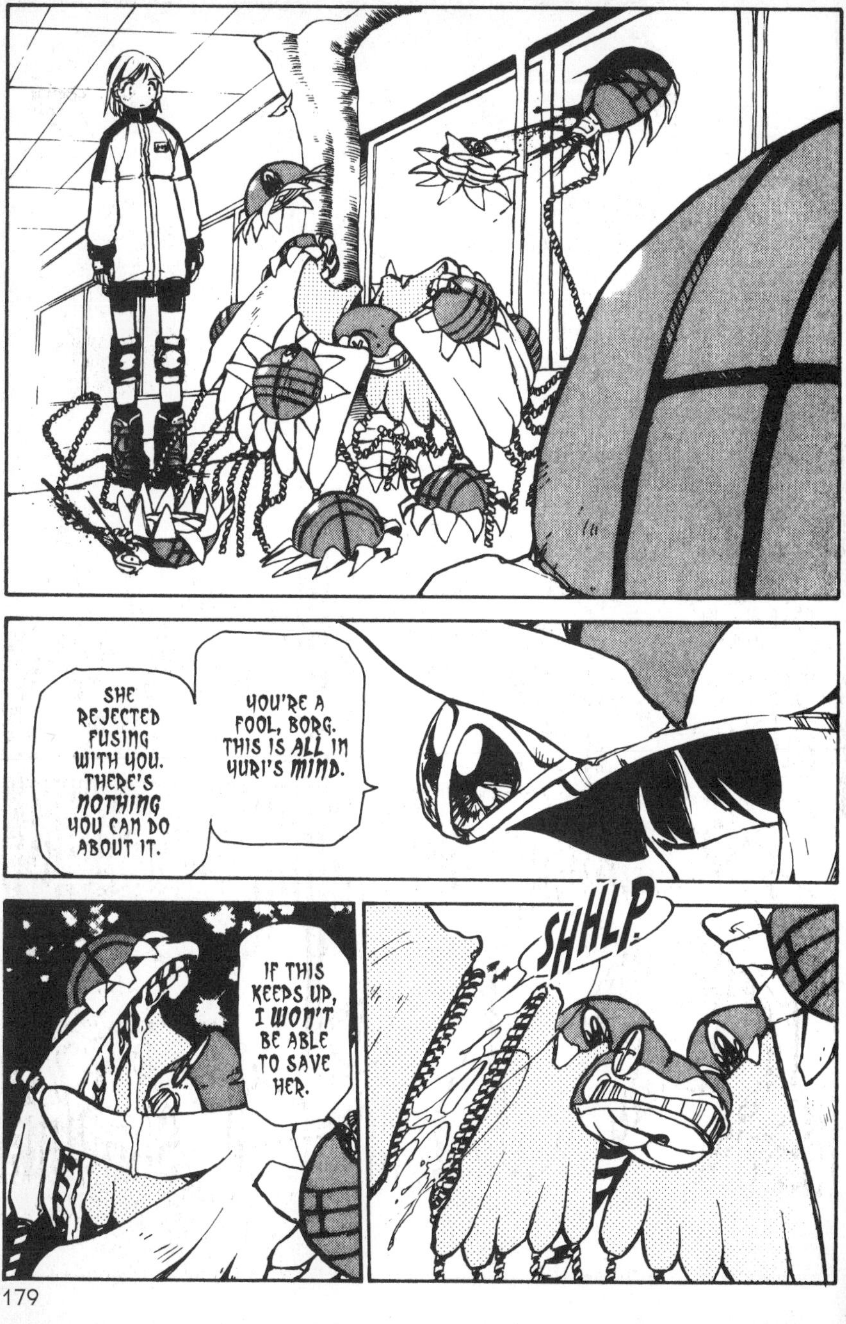
YOU'RE A FOOL, BORG. THIS IS ALL IN YURI'S MIND.
SHE REJECTED FUSING WITH YOU. THERE'S NOTHING YOU CAN DO ABOUT IT.
SHHLP.
IF THIS KEEPS UP, I WON'T BE ABLE TO SAVE HER.

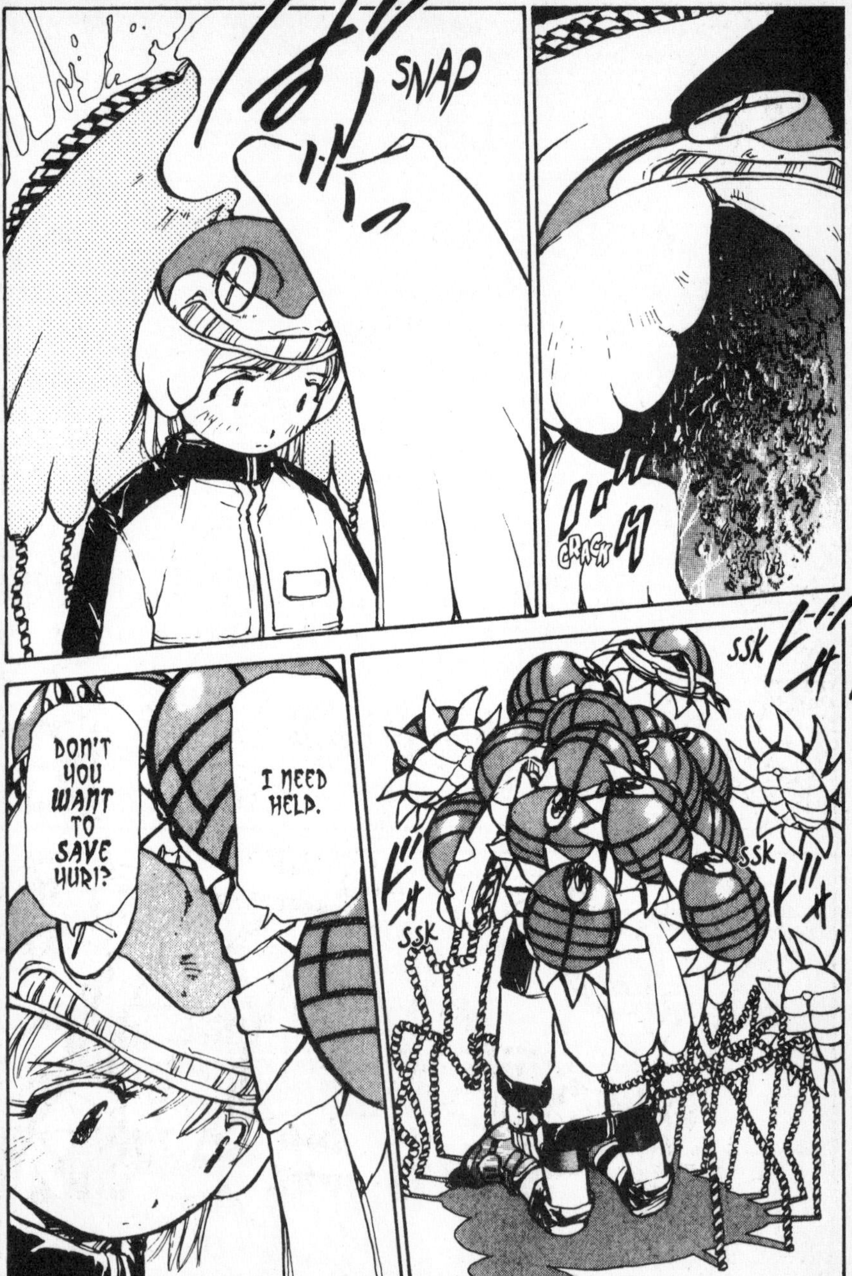
CRACK
SNAP
SSK
SSK
SSK
I NEED HELP.
DON'T YOU WANT TO SAVE YURI?

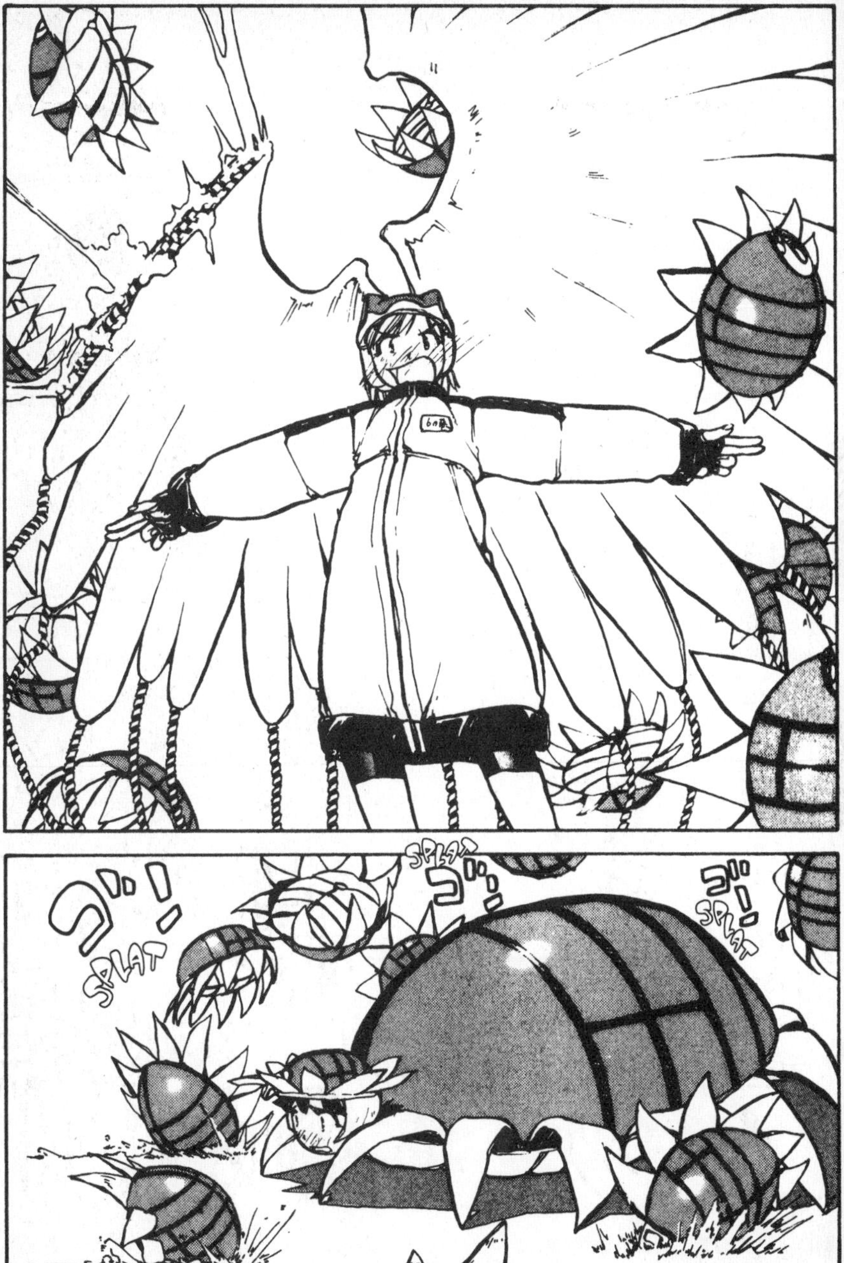
SPLAT
SPLAT
SPLAT

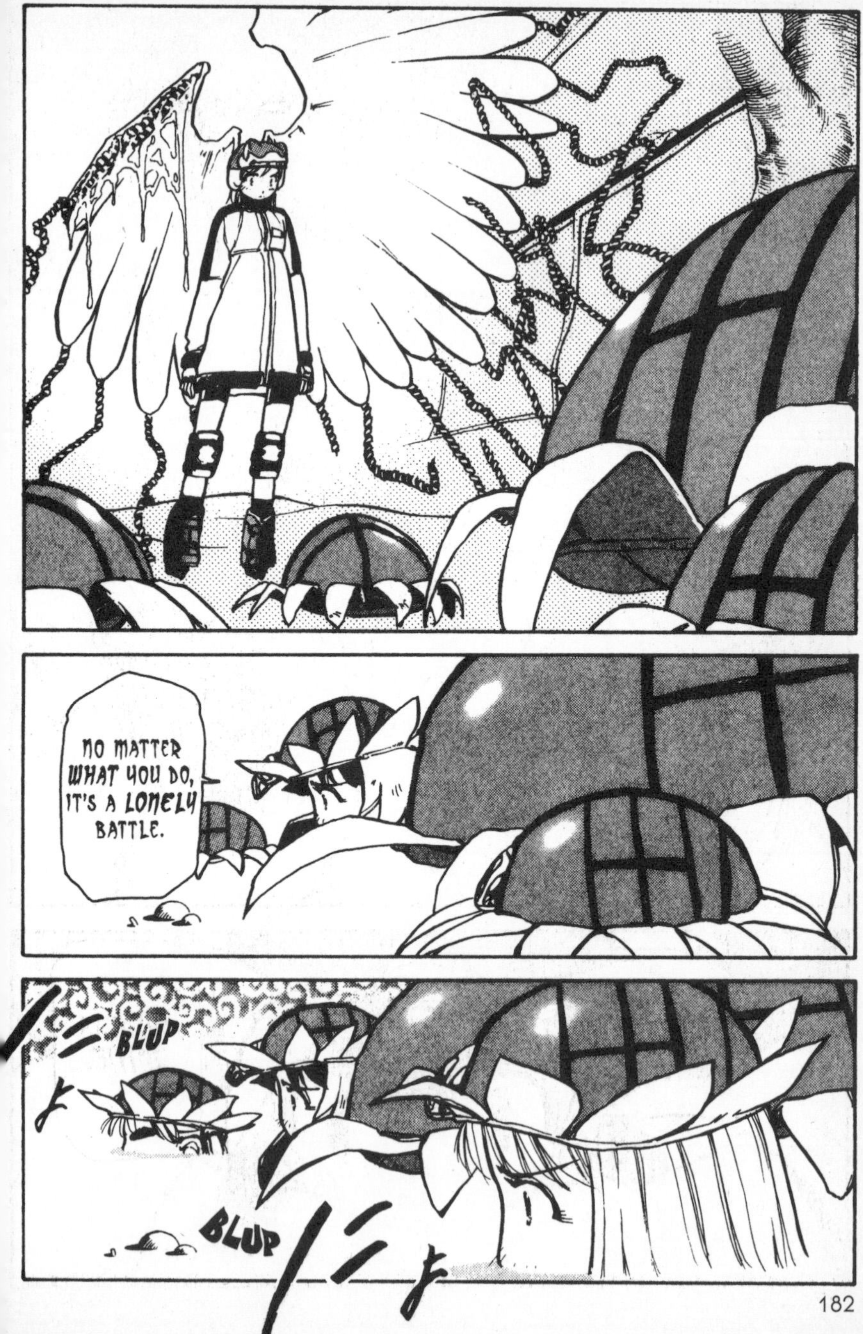
NO MATTER WHAT YOU DO, IT'S A LONELY BATTLE.
BLUP
BLUP

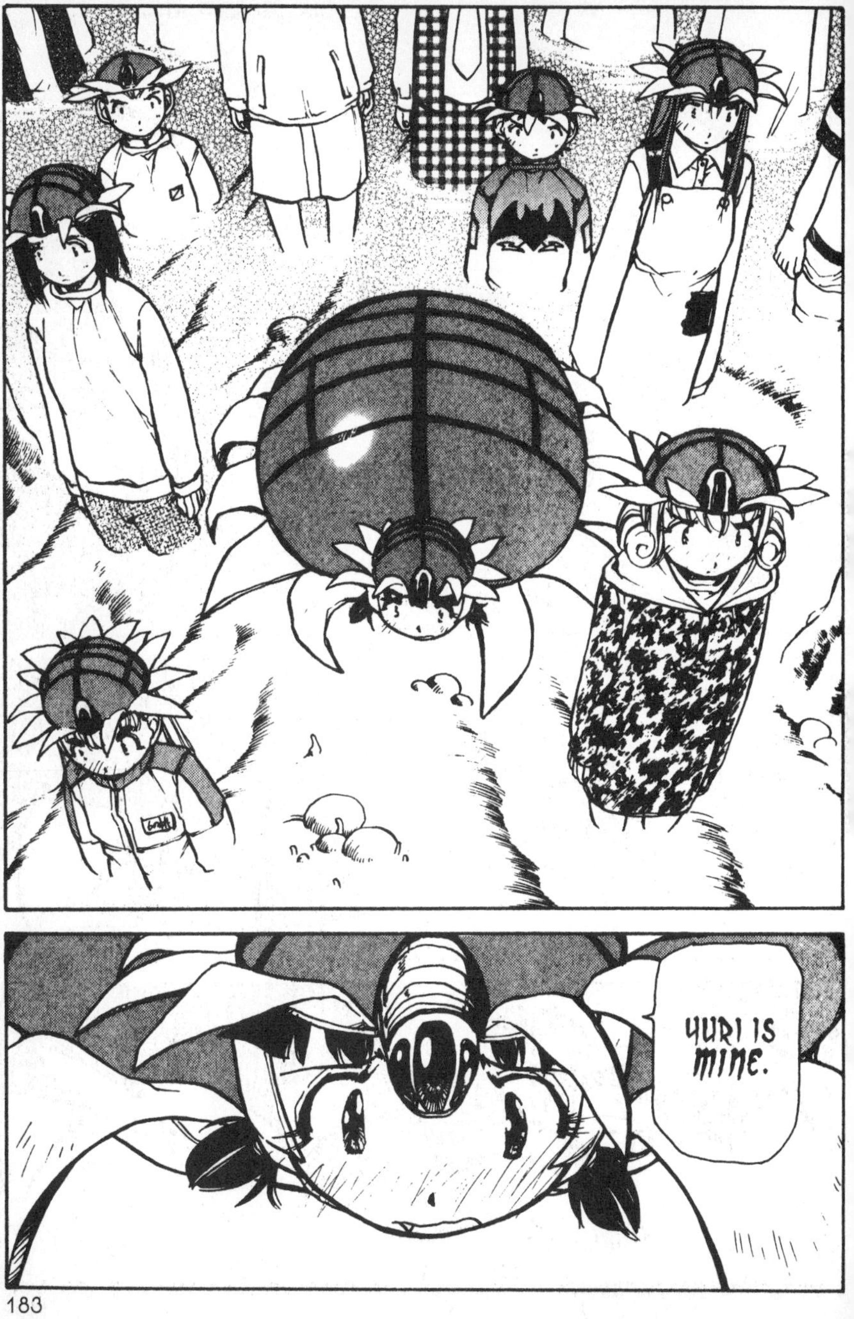
YURI IS MINE.

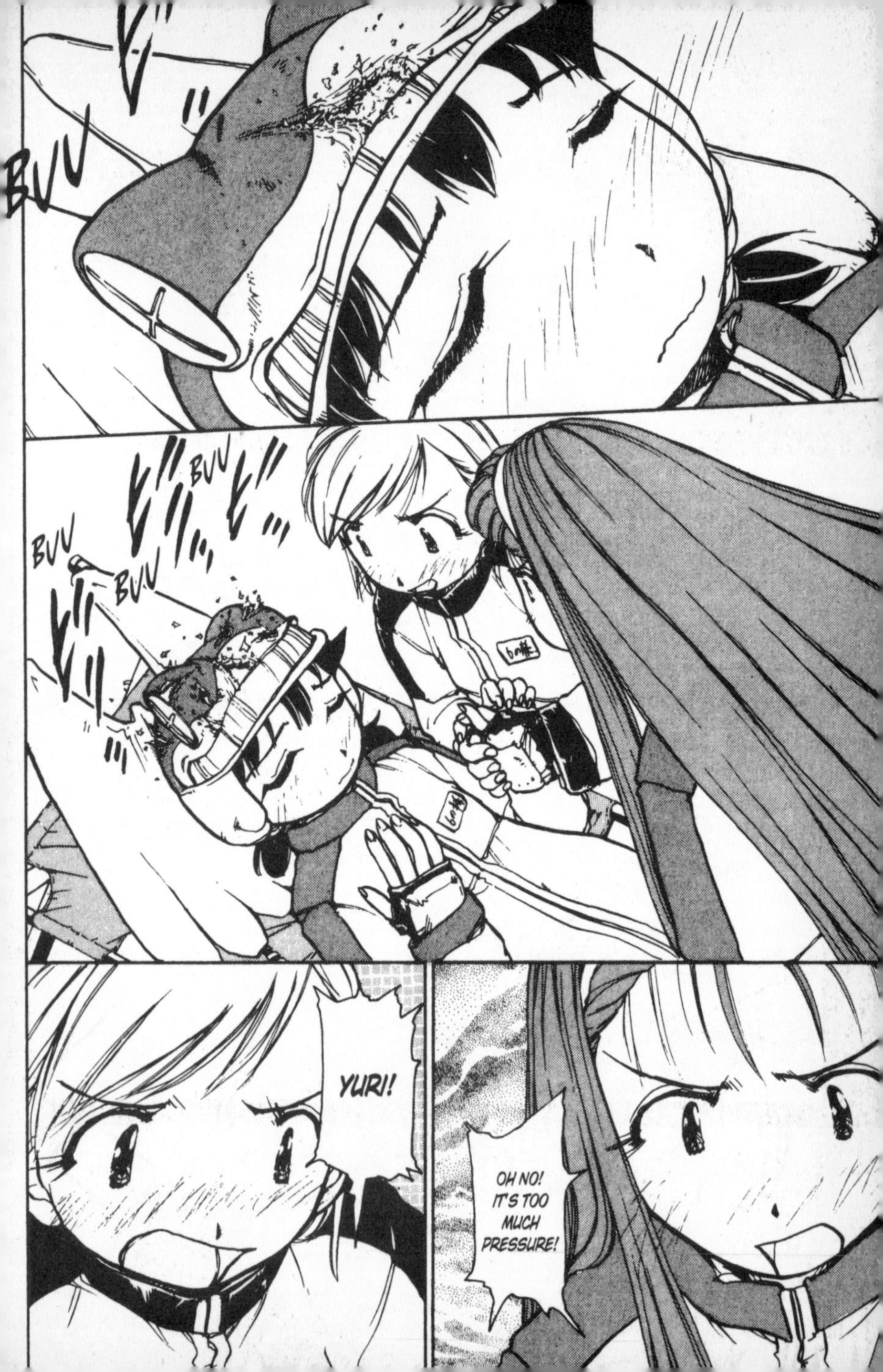
BUU
BUU
BUU
BUU
OH NO! IT'S TOO MUCH PRESSURE!
YURI!

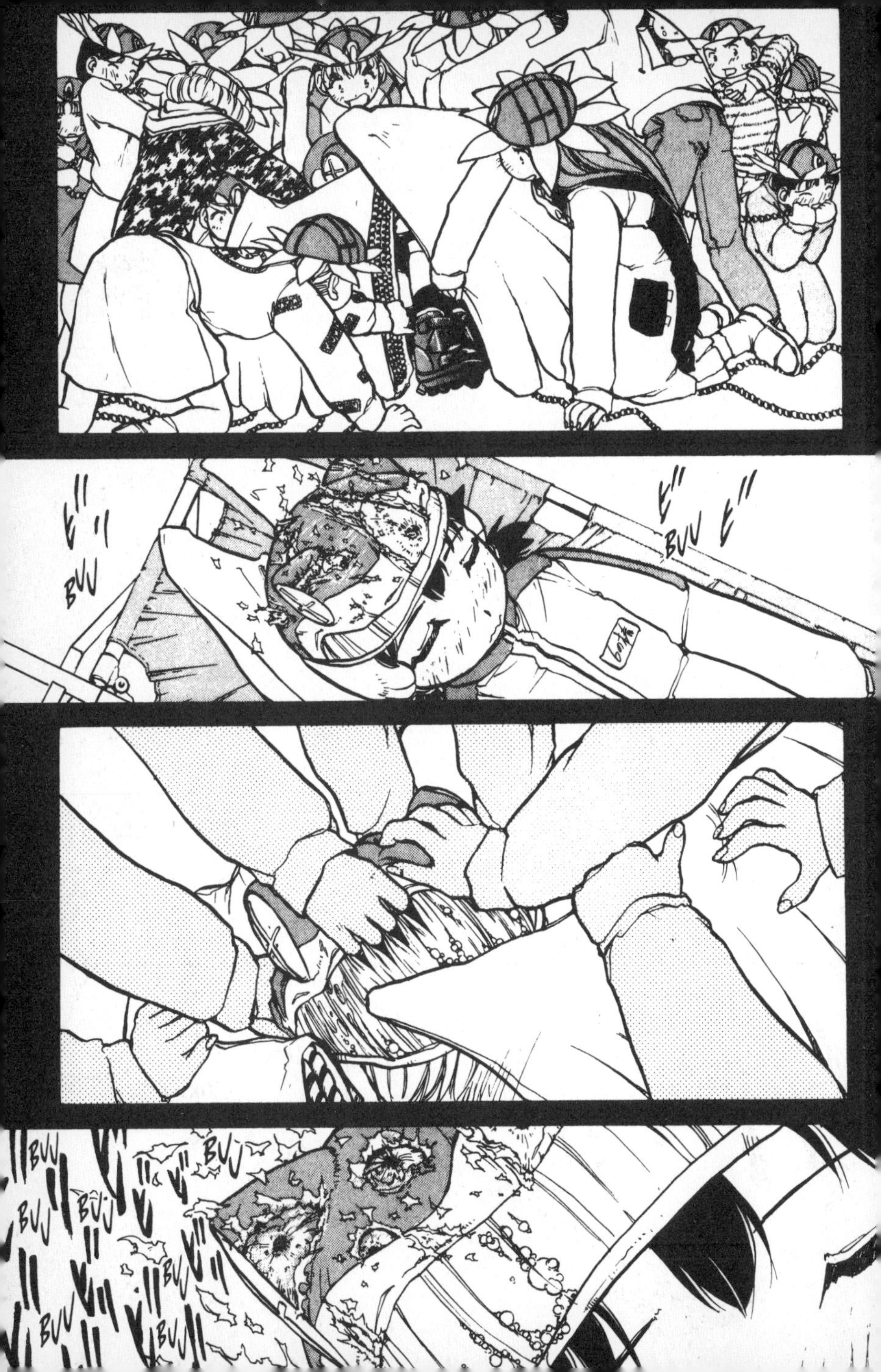

ビ BVV ビ
ビ BVV
BVV
BVV
BVV
BVV
BVV
BVV
BVV
BVV

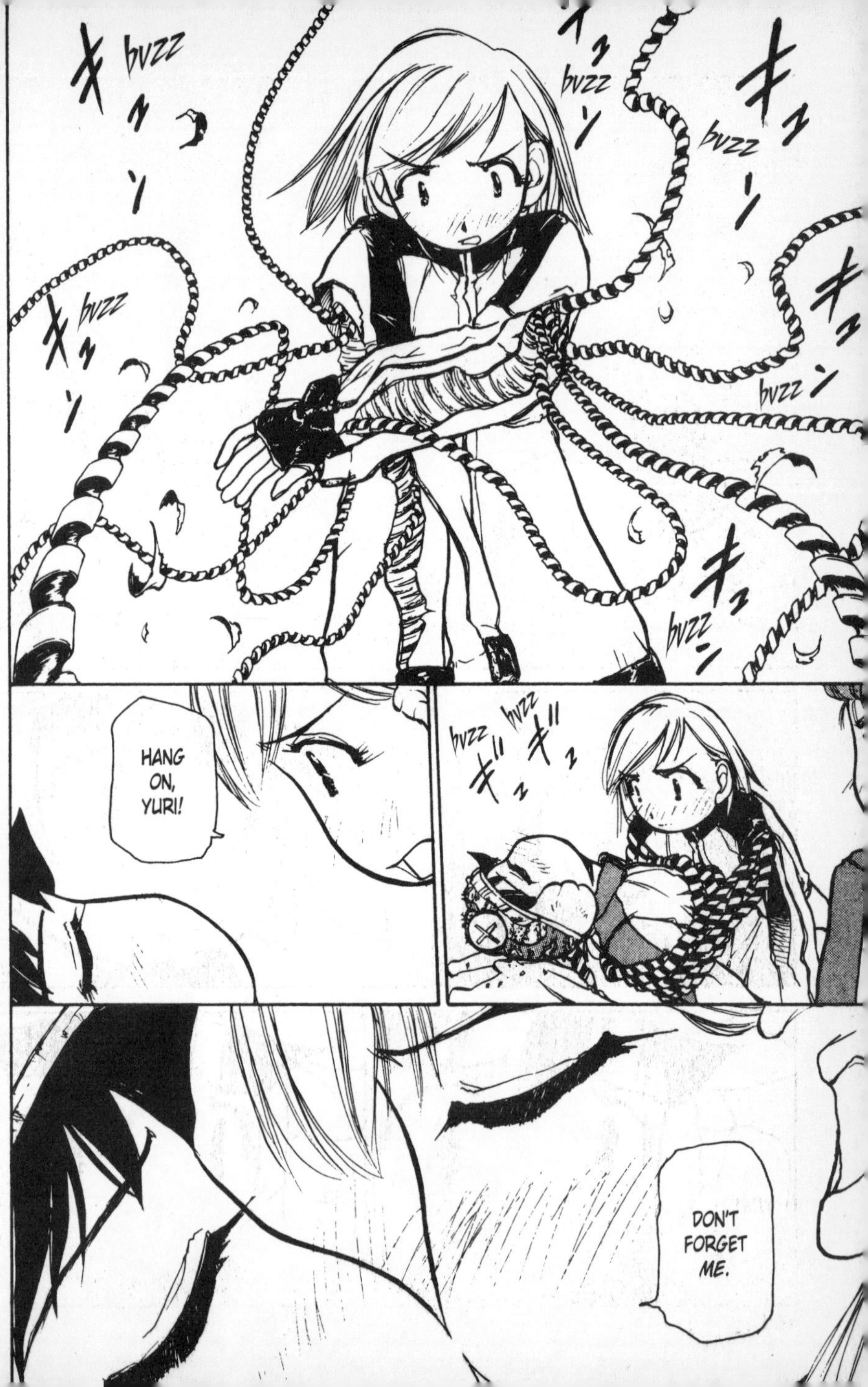

buzz
キュン
buzz
キュン
buzz
キュン
buzz
キュン
buzz
キュン
buzz
キュン
buzz
ギュ
buzz
ギュ
HANG ON, YURI!
DON'T FORGET ME.

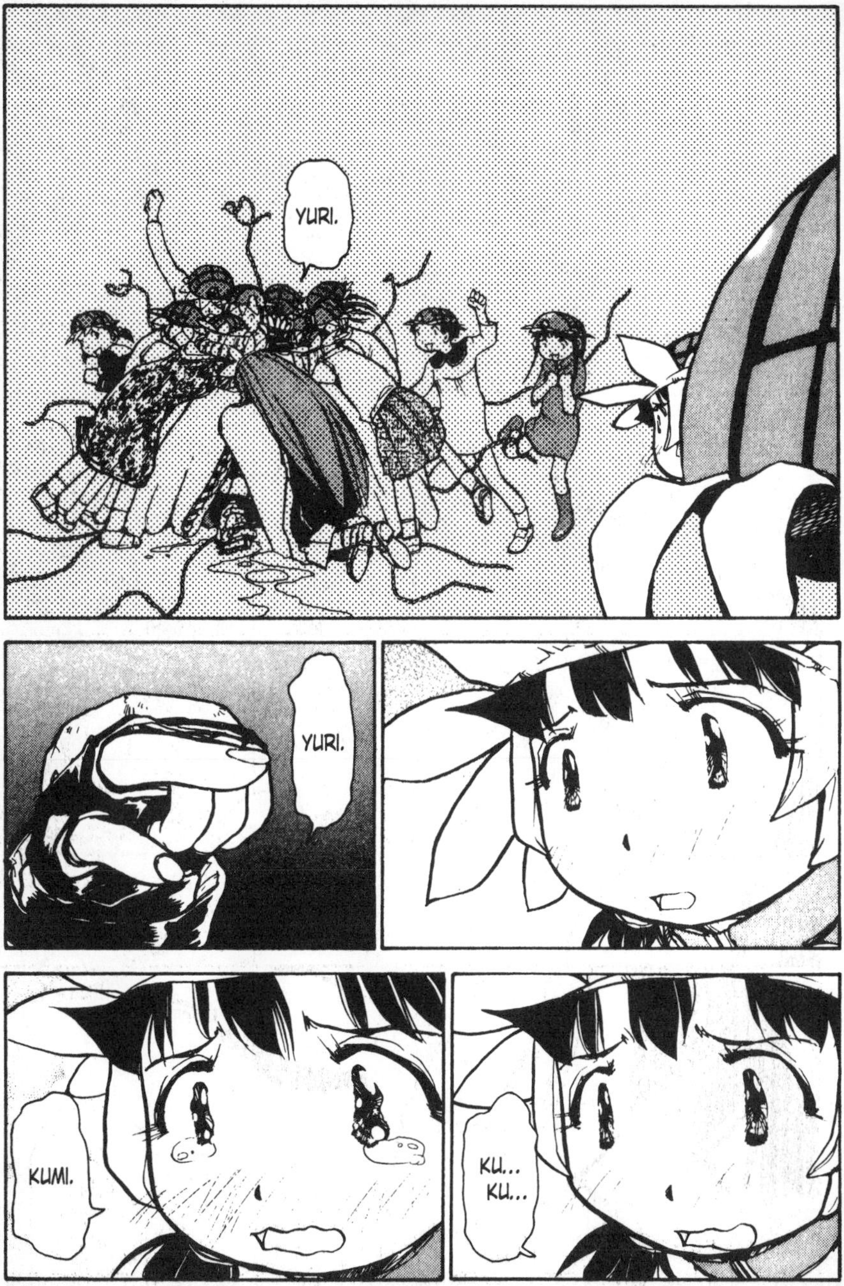
YURI.
YURI.
KU... KU...
KUMI.

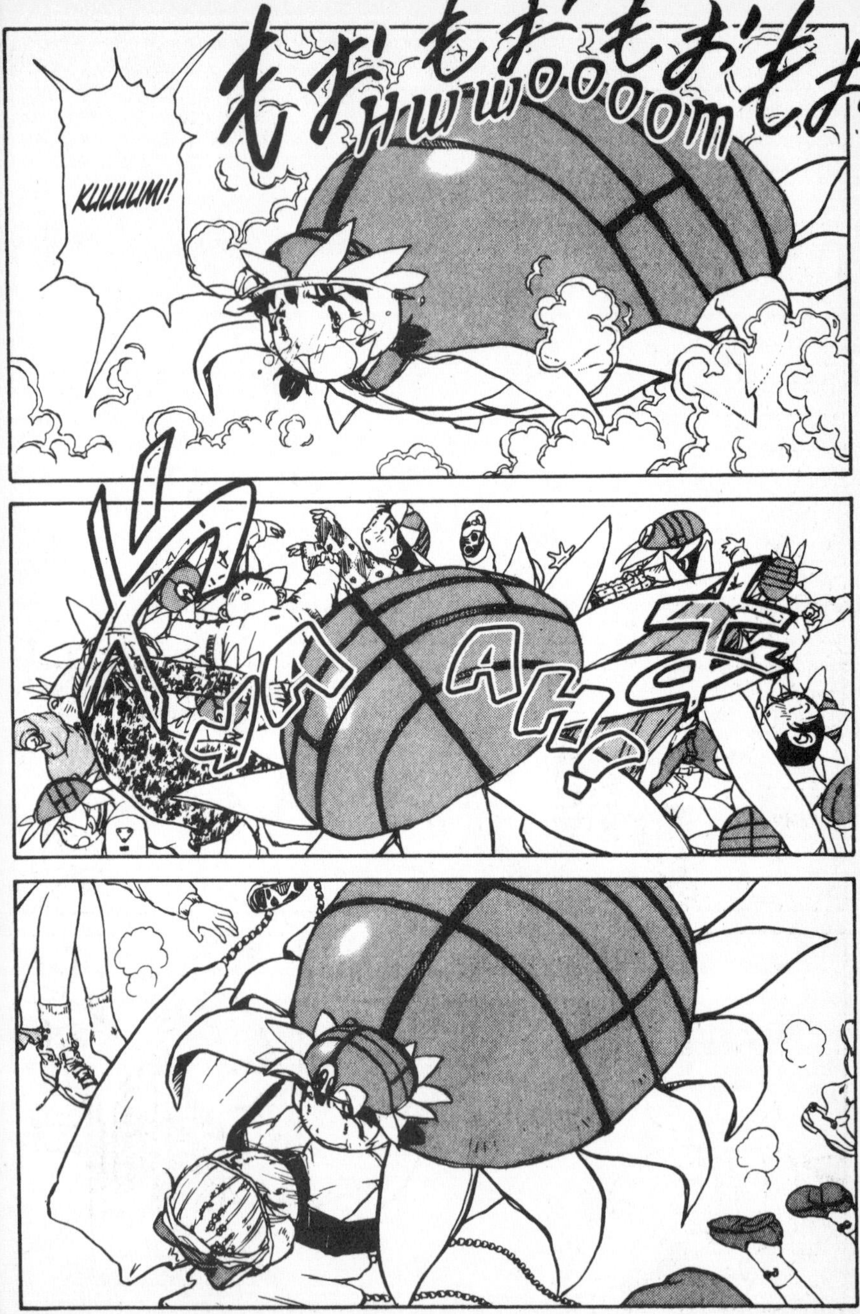
もおもおもおもお
HWWOOOOOM
KUUUUMI!
AH!?

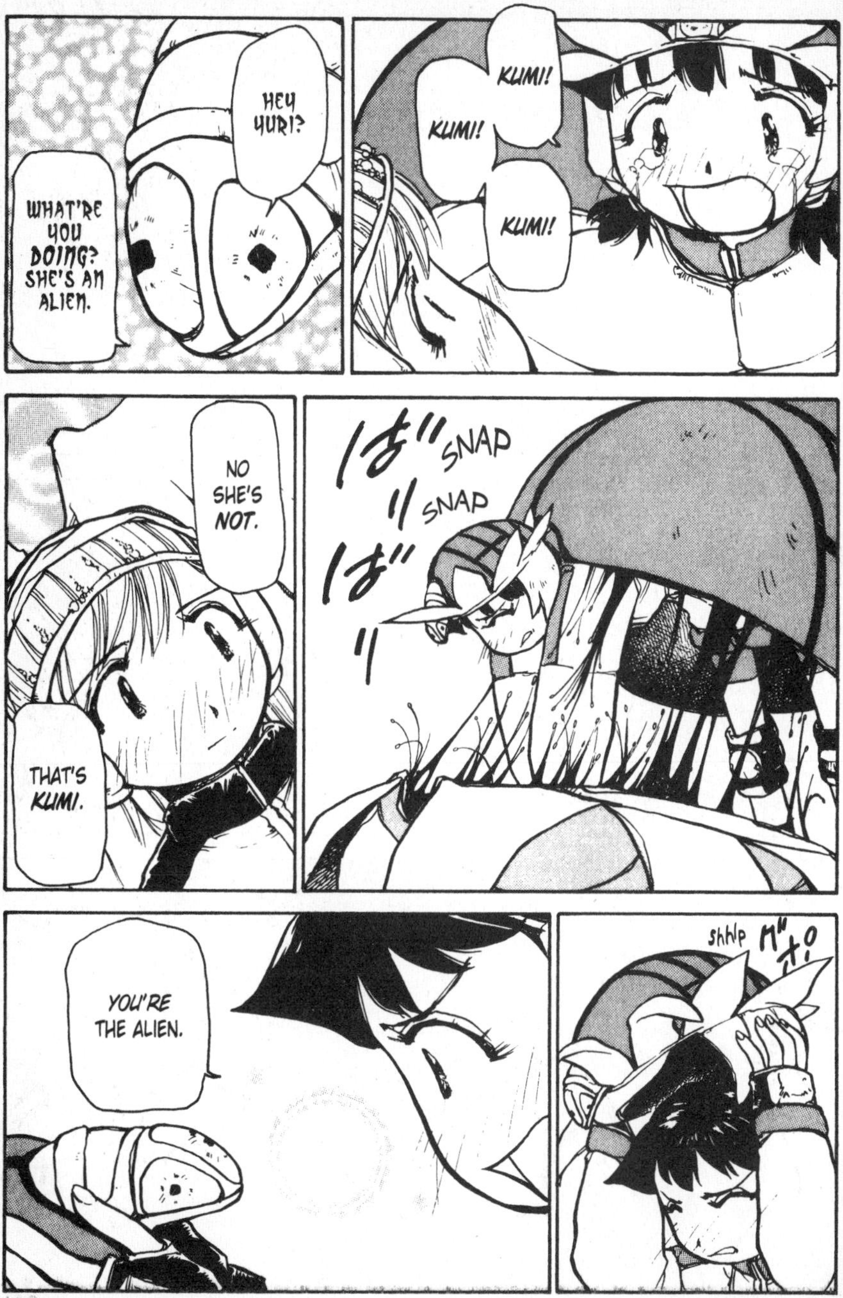
KUMI!
KUMI!
KUMI!
HEY YURI!?
WHAT'RE YOU DOING? SHE'S AN ALIEN.
SNAP
SNAP
NO SHE'S NOT.
THAT'S KUMI.
shhp
YOU'RE THE ALIEN.

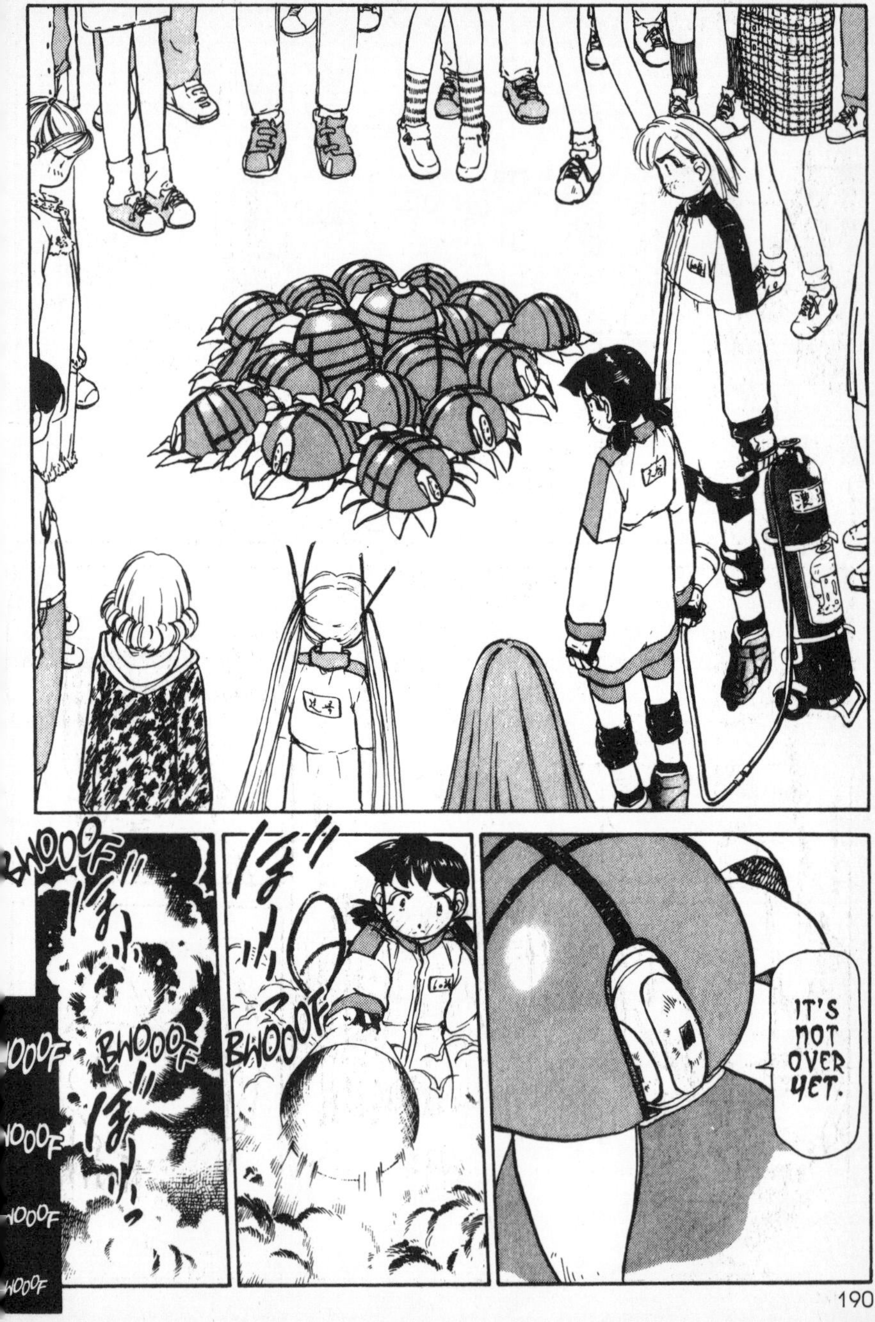
IT'S NOT OVER YET.
BWOOOF
BWOOOF
BWOOOF
WOOOF
WOOOF
WOOOF
WOOOF

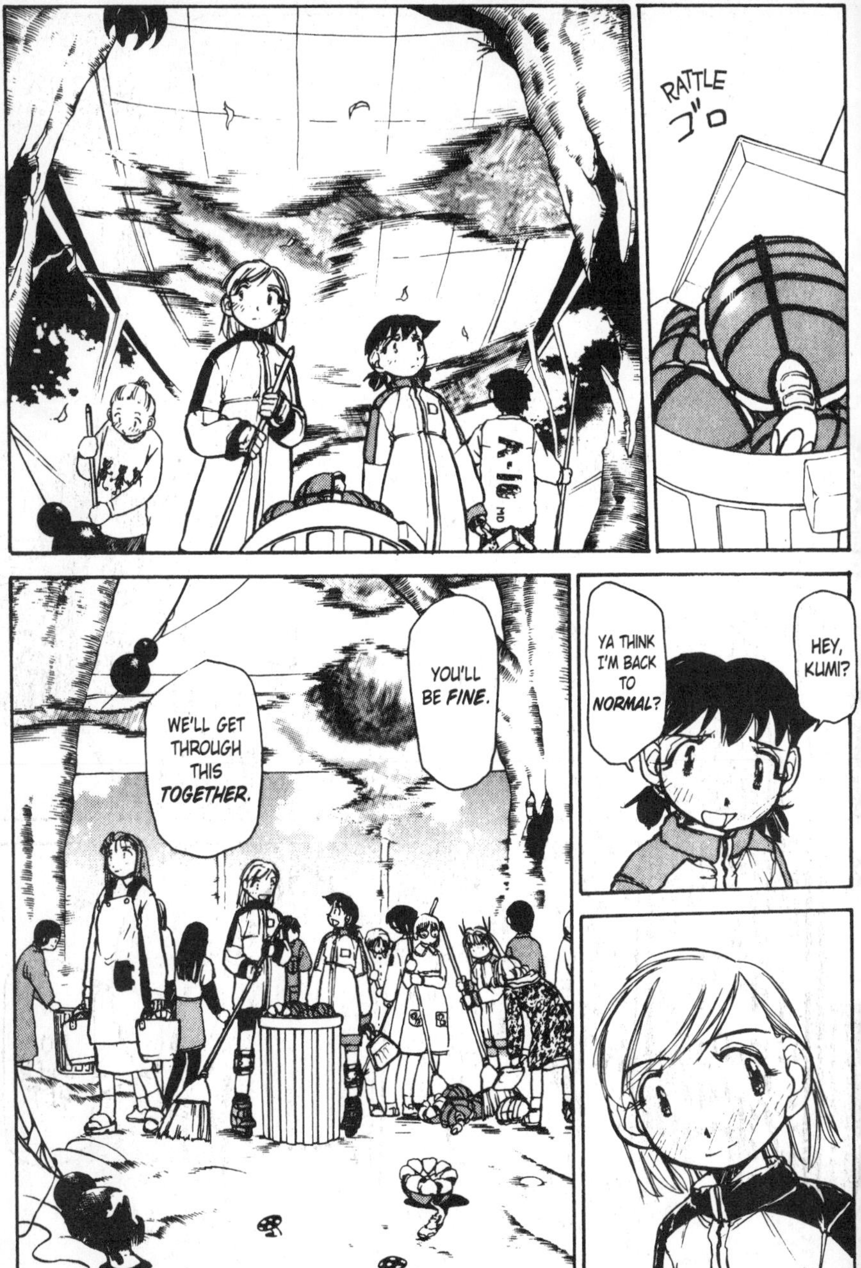
RATTLE
ゴロ
HEY, KUMI?
YA THINK I'M BACK TO NORMAL?
YOU'LL BE FINE.
WE'LL GET THROUGH THIS TOGETHER.

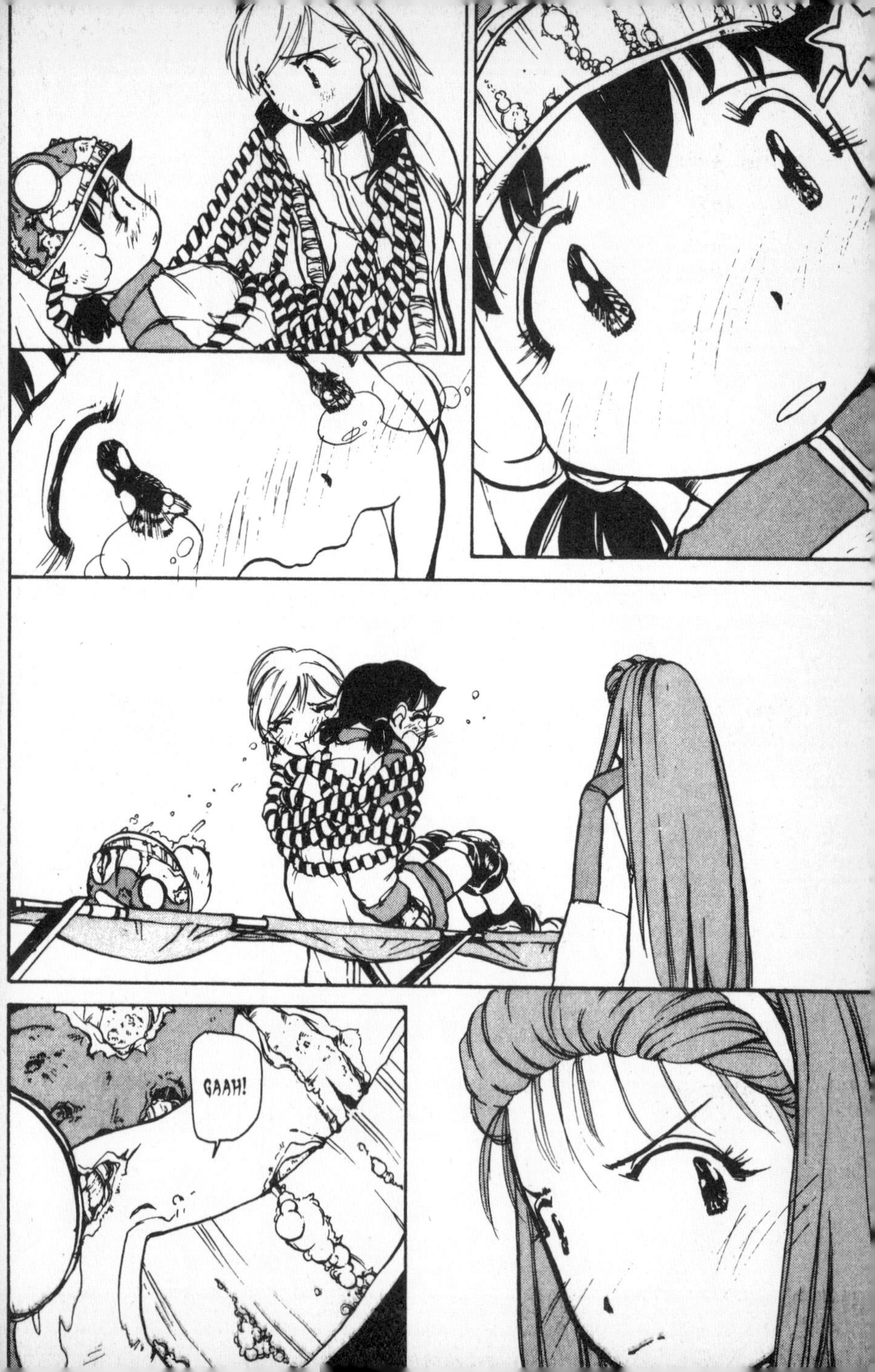
GAAH!

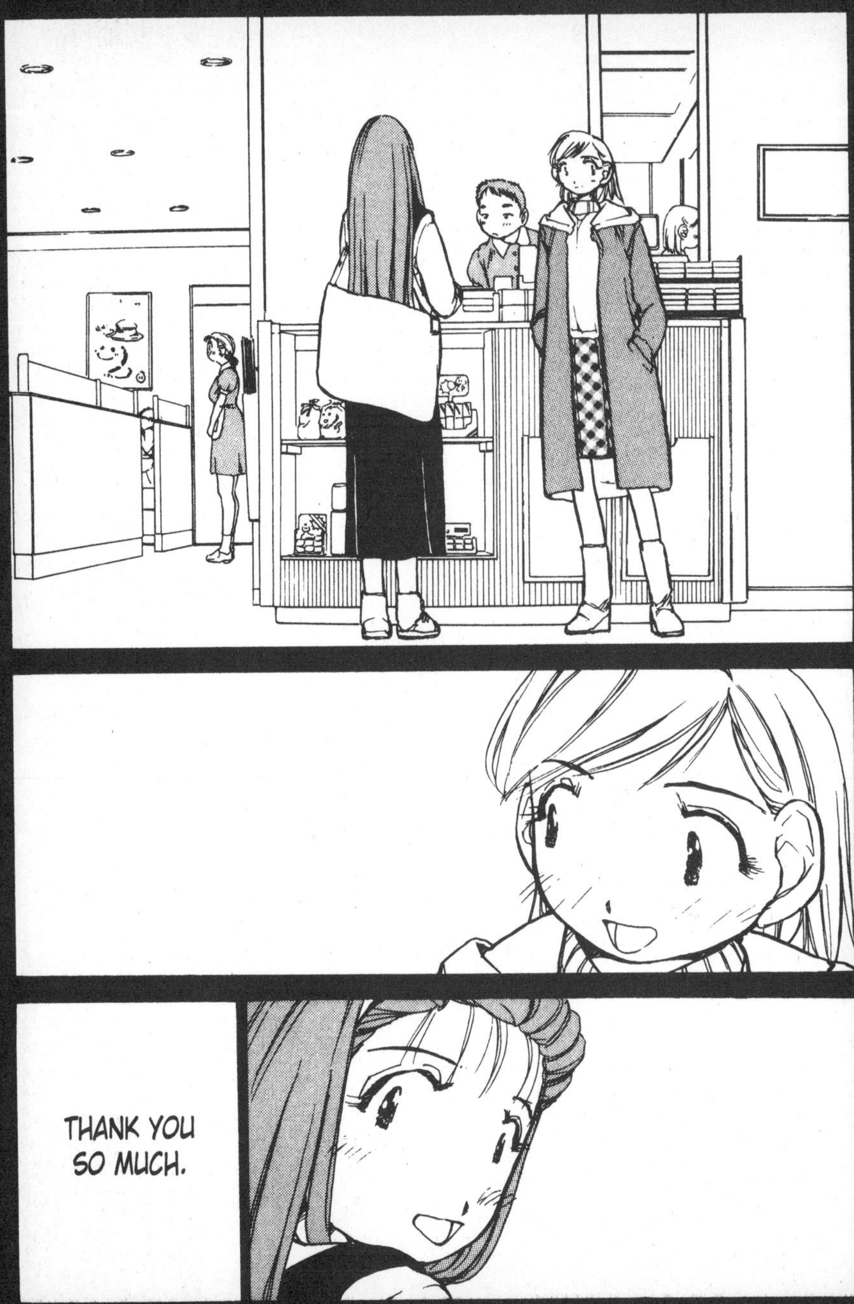
THANK YOU SO MUCH.

OPERATION 30: BACK TO NORMAL

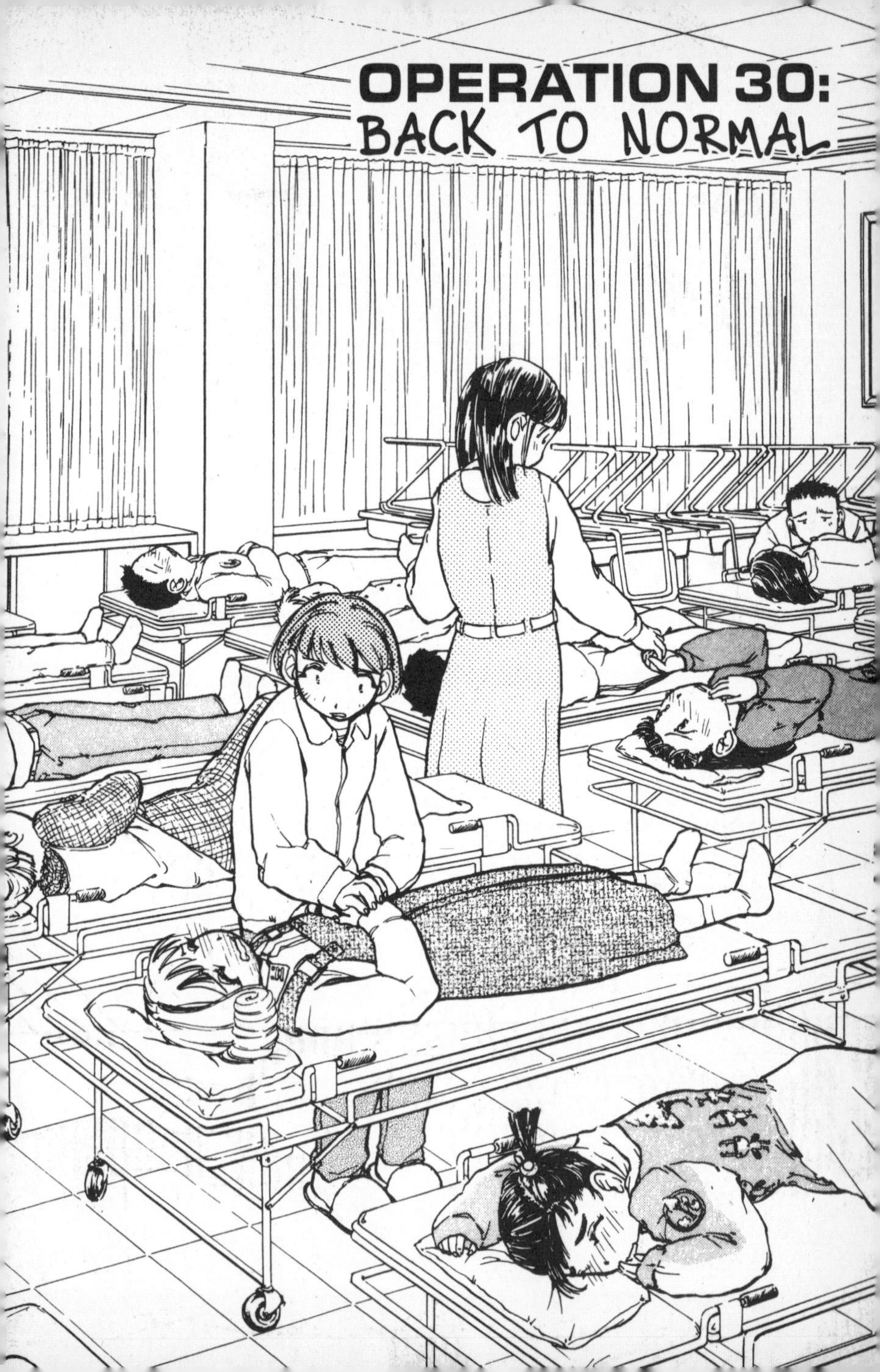

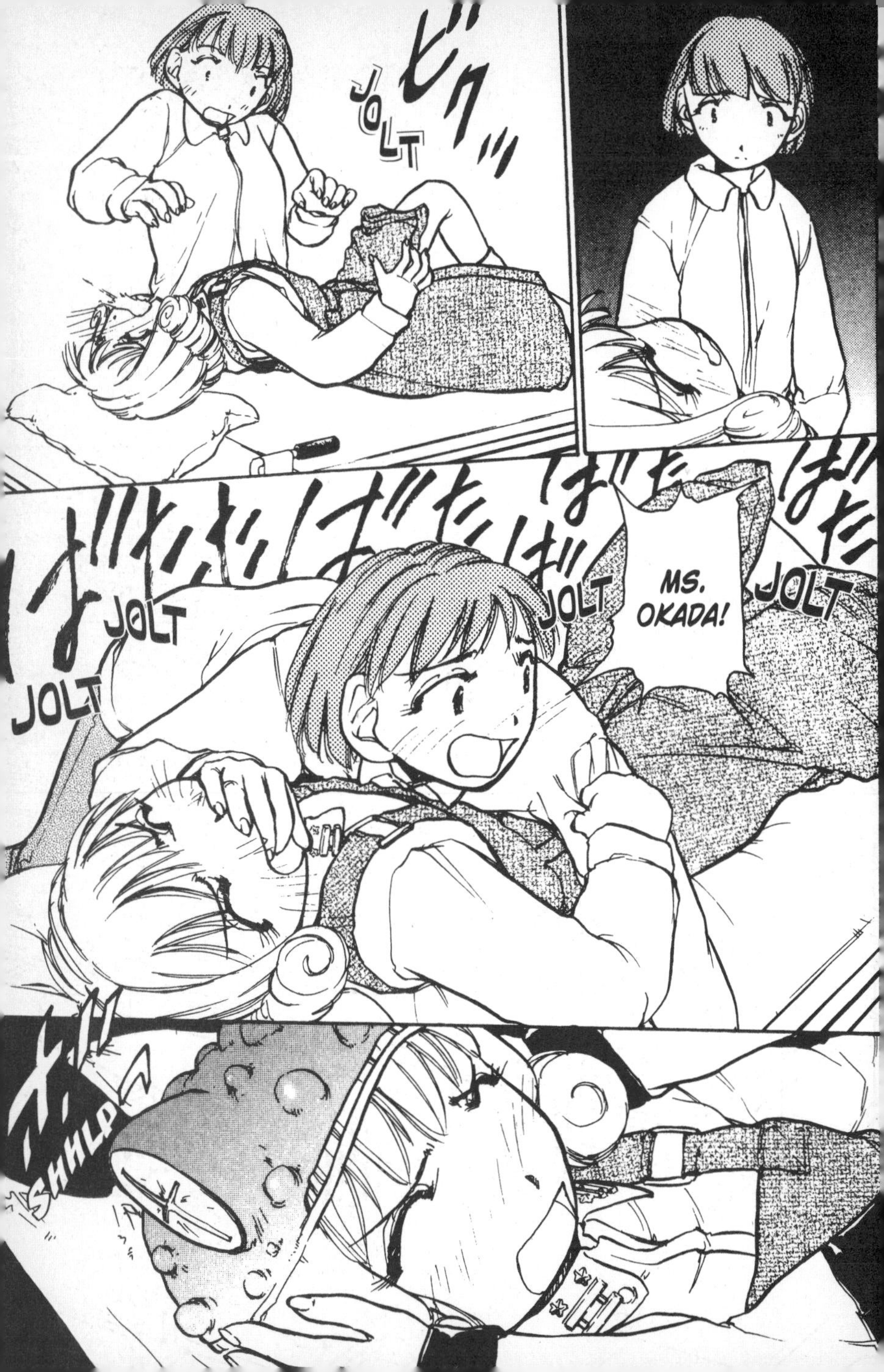

ビクッ
JOLT
JOLT
MS. OKADA!
JOLT
JOLT
JOLT
SHHLP

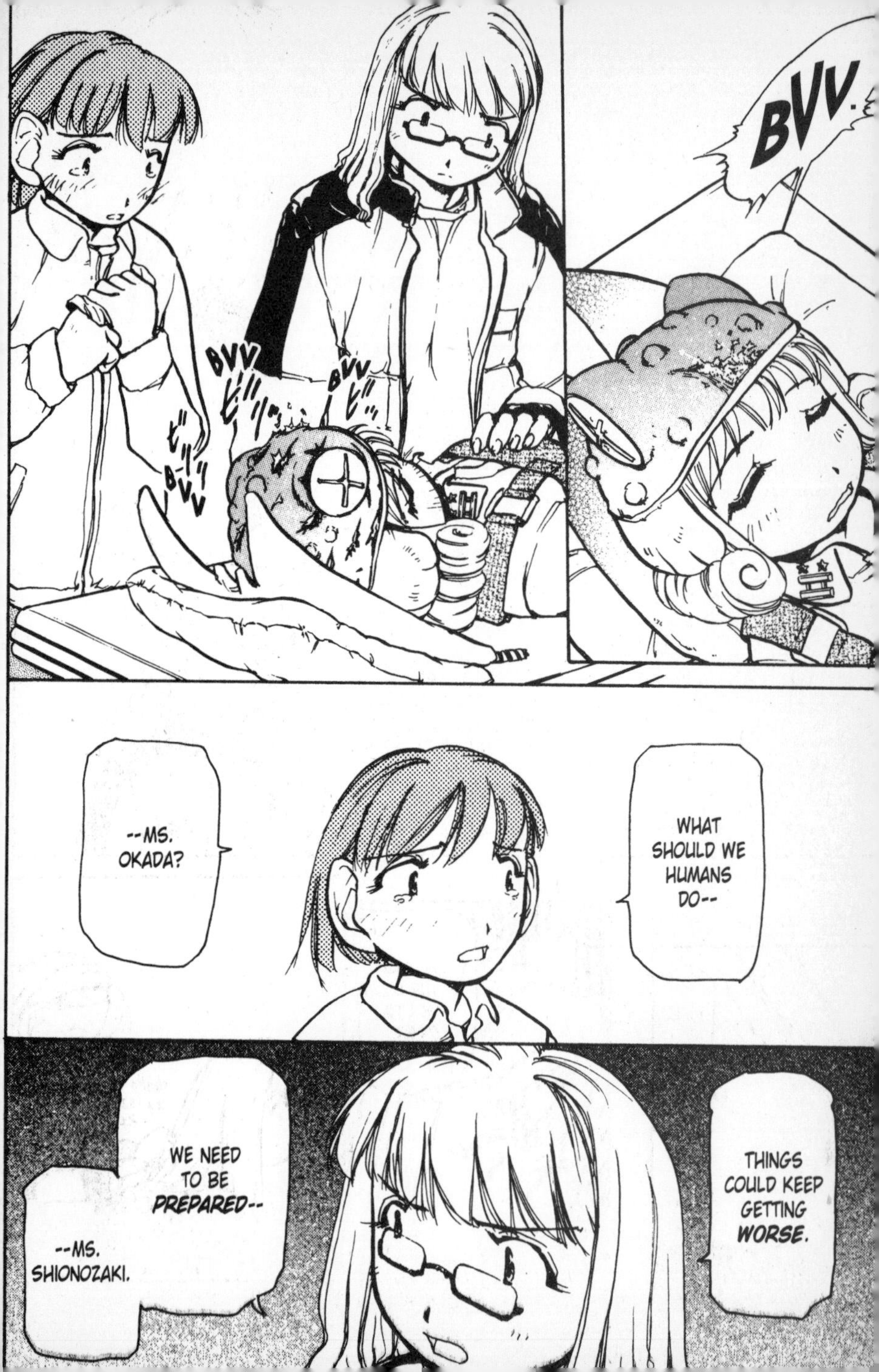
BVV.
BVV
BVV
BVV
WHAT SHOULD WE HUMANS DO--
--MS. OKADA?
THINGS COULD KEEP GETTING **WORSE**.
WE NEED TO BE **PREPARED**--
--MS. SHIONOZAKI.

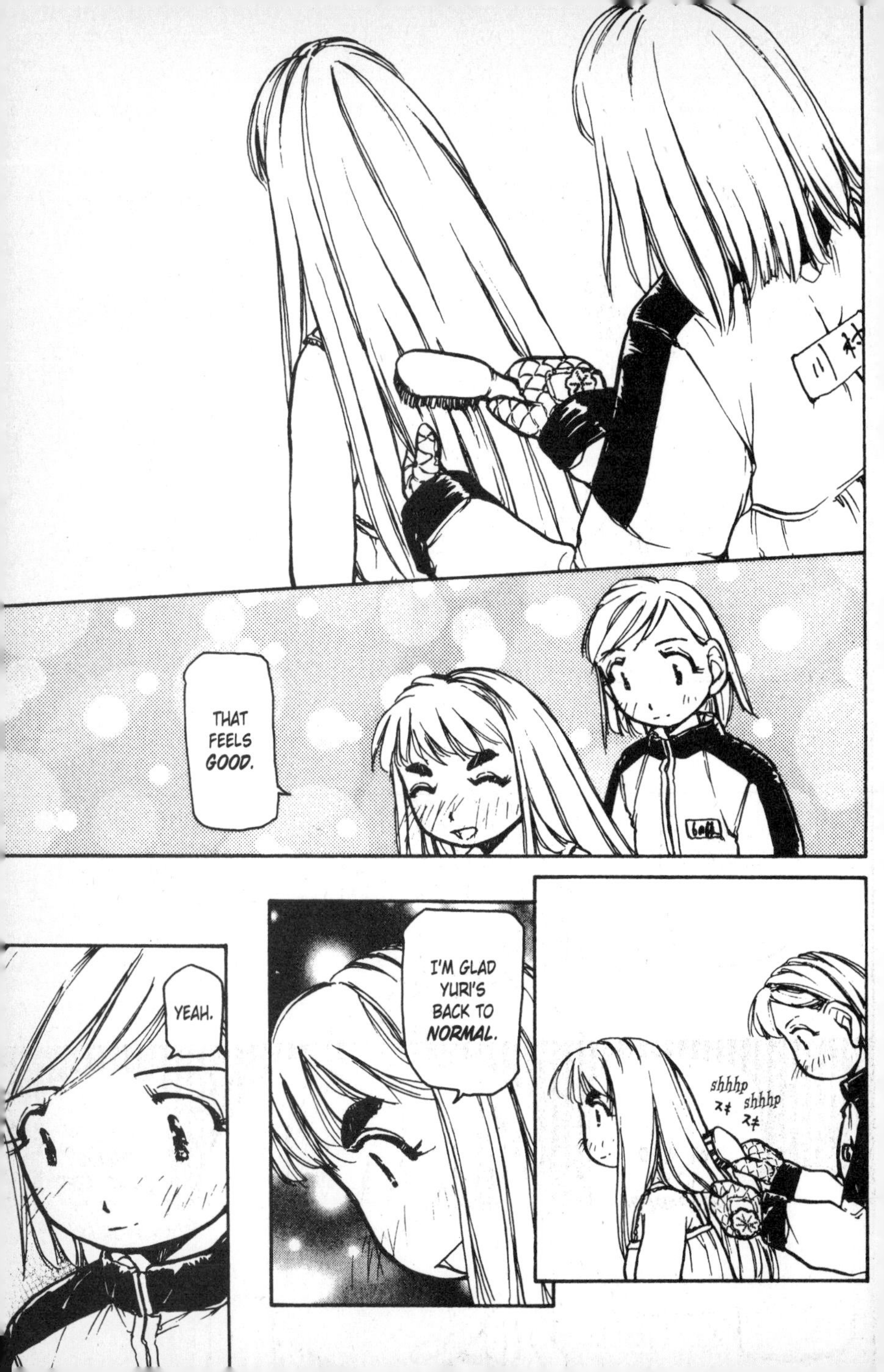
THAT FEELS GOOD.
shhhp
スキ
shhhp
スキ
I'M GLAD YURI'S BACK TO NORMAL.
YEAH.

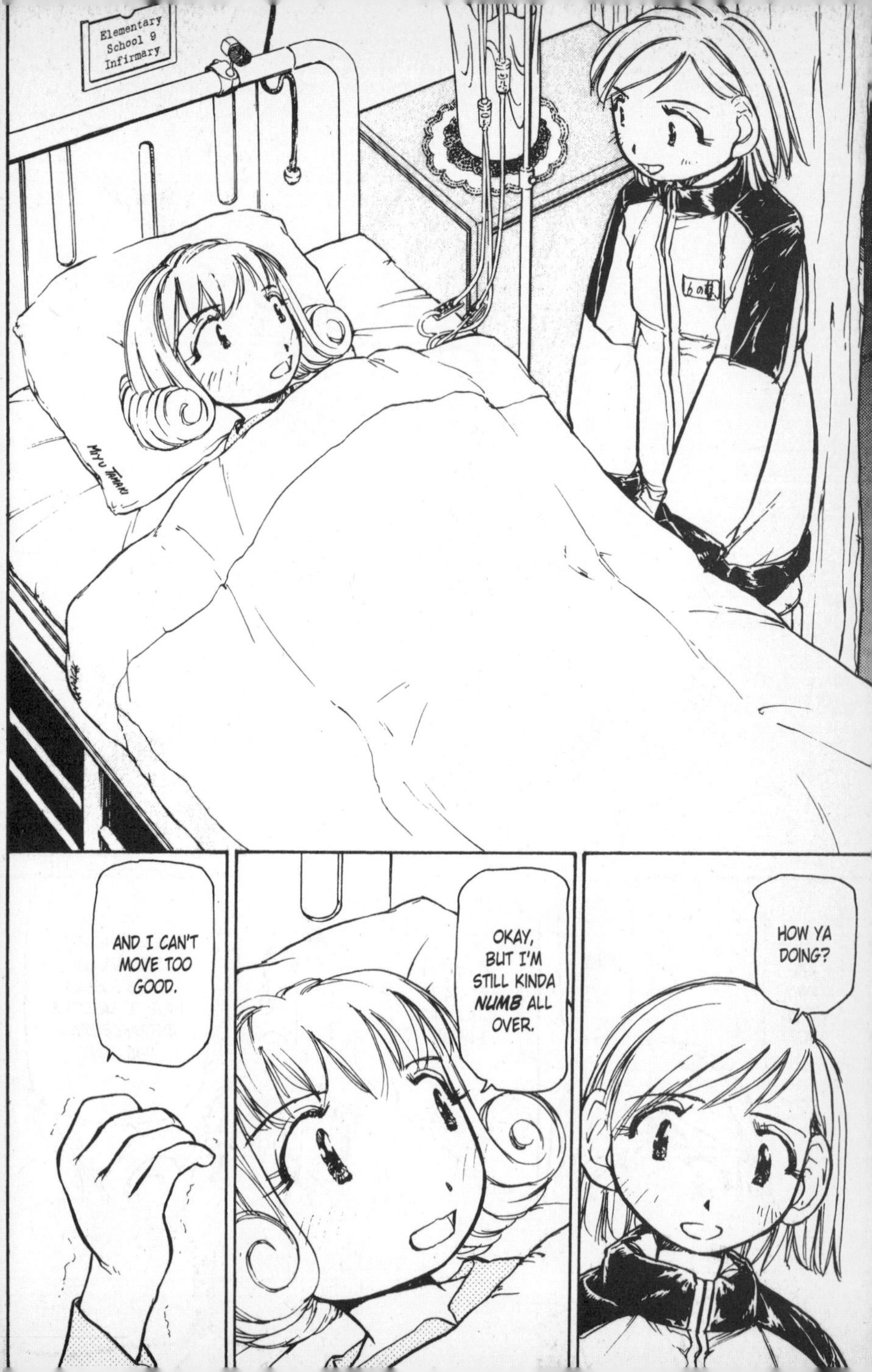
Elementary School 9 Infirmary
MIYU TAMAKI
HOW YA DOING?
OKAY, BUT I'M STILL KINDA NUMB ALL OVER.
AND I CAN'T MOVE TOO GOOD.

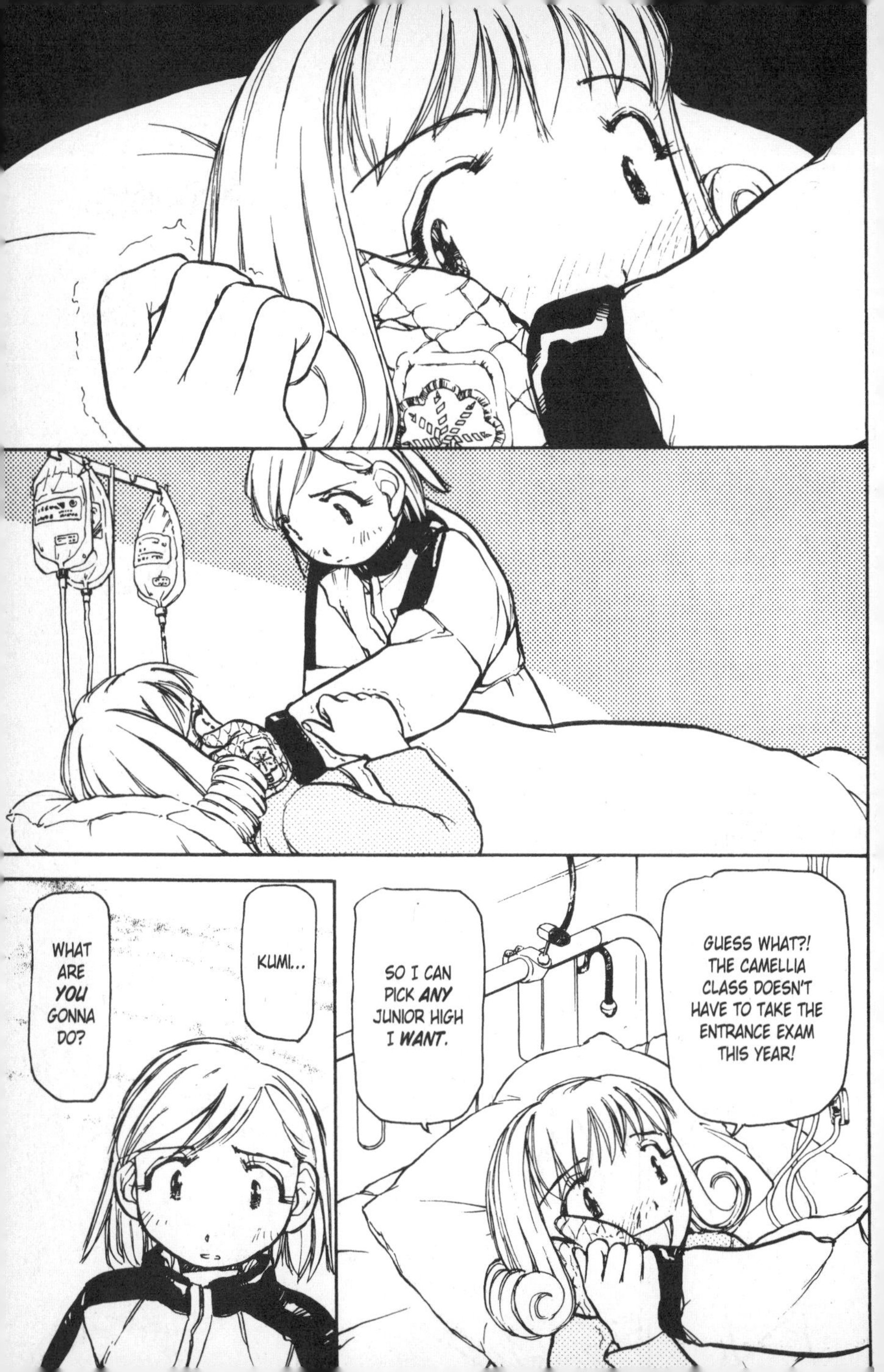
GUESS WHAT?! THE CAMELLIA CLASS DOESN'T HAVE TO TAKE THE ENTRANCE EXAM THIS YEAR!
SO I CAN PICK *ANY* JUNIOR HIGH I *WANT*.
KUMI...
WHAT ARE *YOU* GONNA DO?

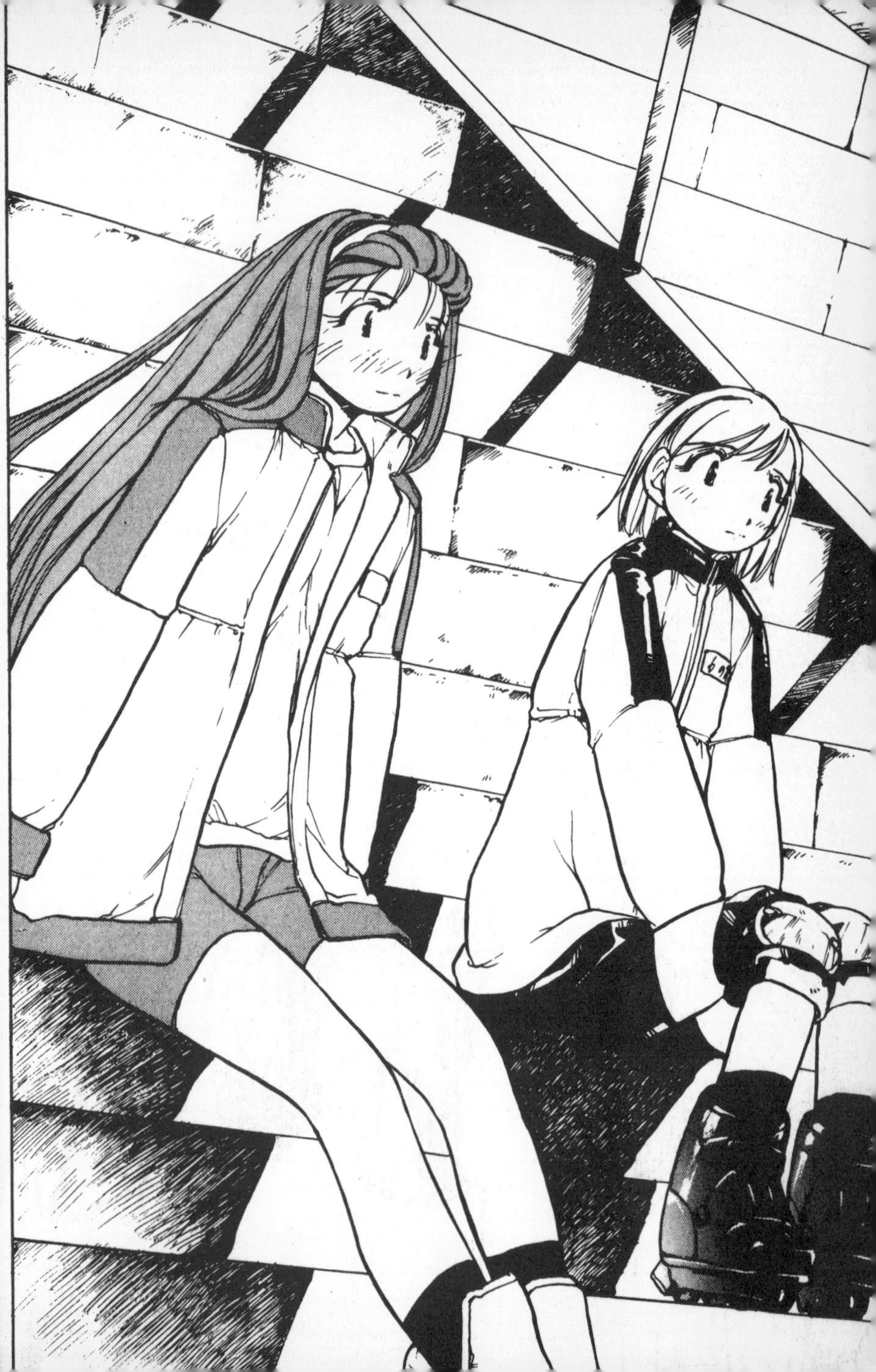

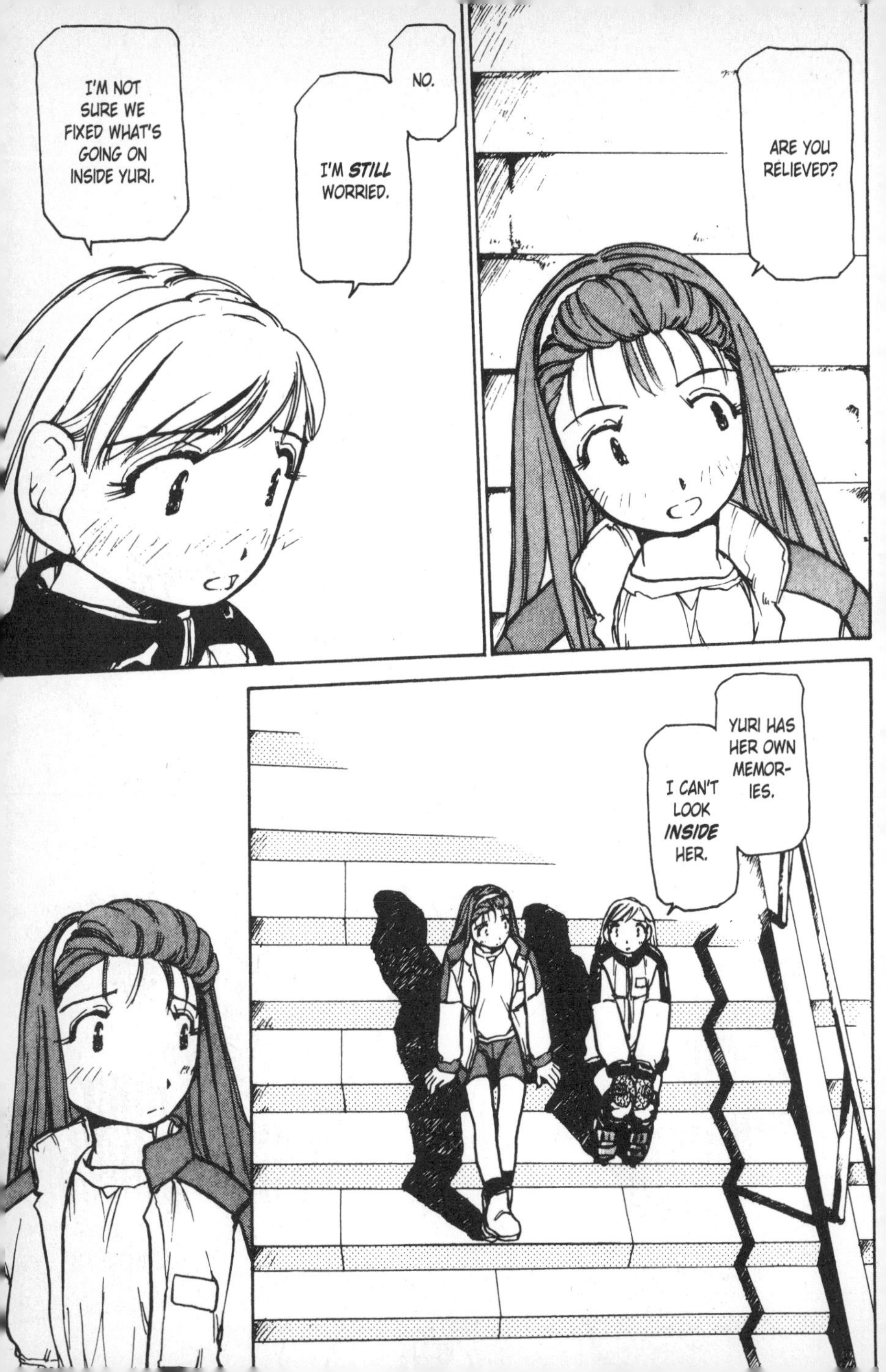
ARE YOU RELIEVED?
NO.
I'M STILL WORRIED.
I'M NOT SURE WE FIXED WHAT'S GOING ON INSIDE YURI.
YURI HAS HER OWN MEMOR-IES.
I CAN'T LOOK INSIDE HER.

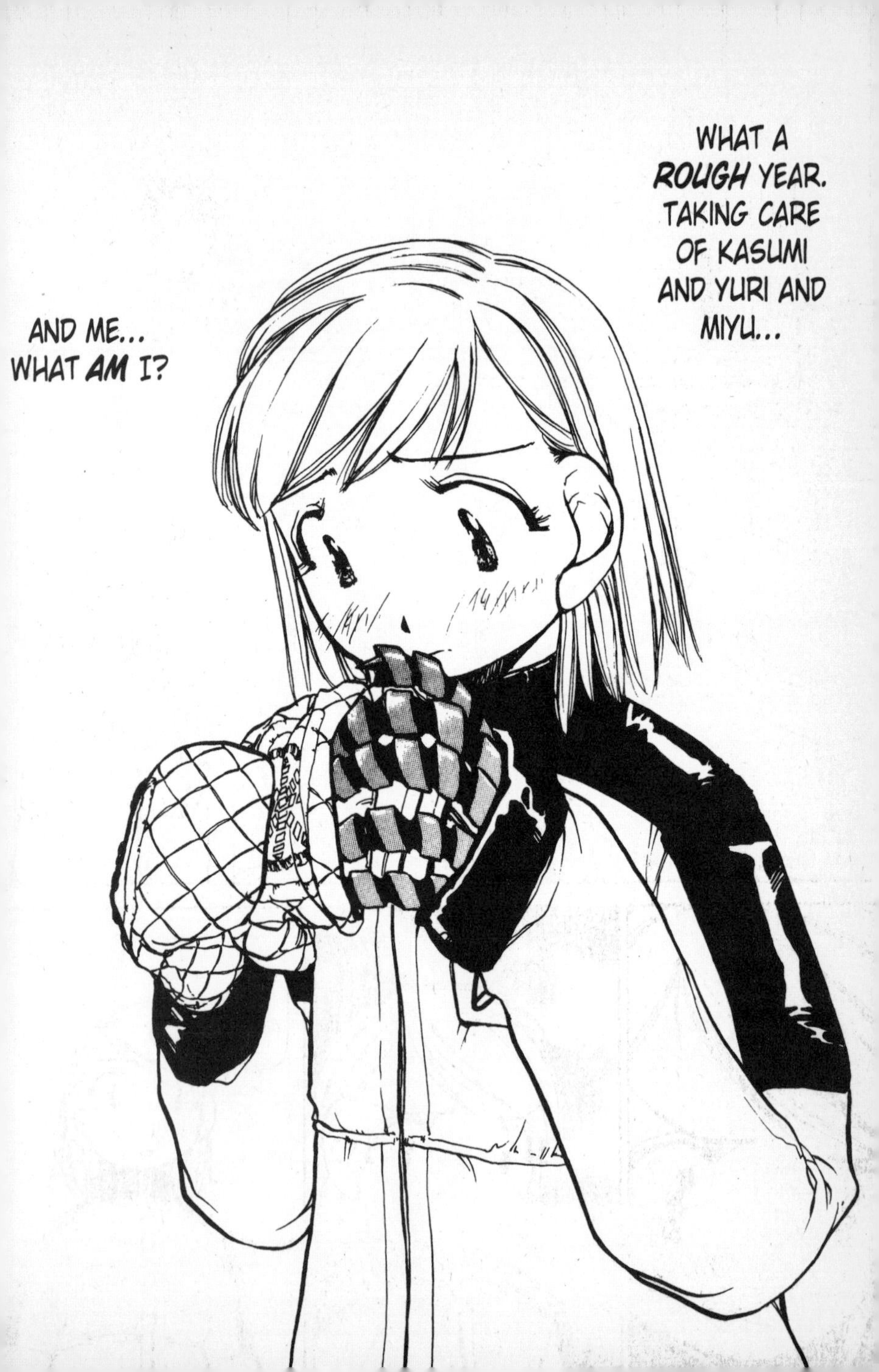
WHAT A *ROUGH* YEAR. TAKING CARE OF KASUMI AND YURI AND MIYU...
AND ME... WHAT *AM* I?

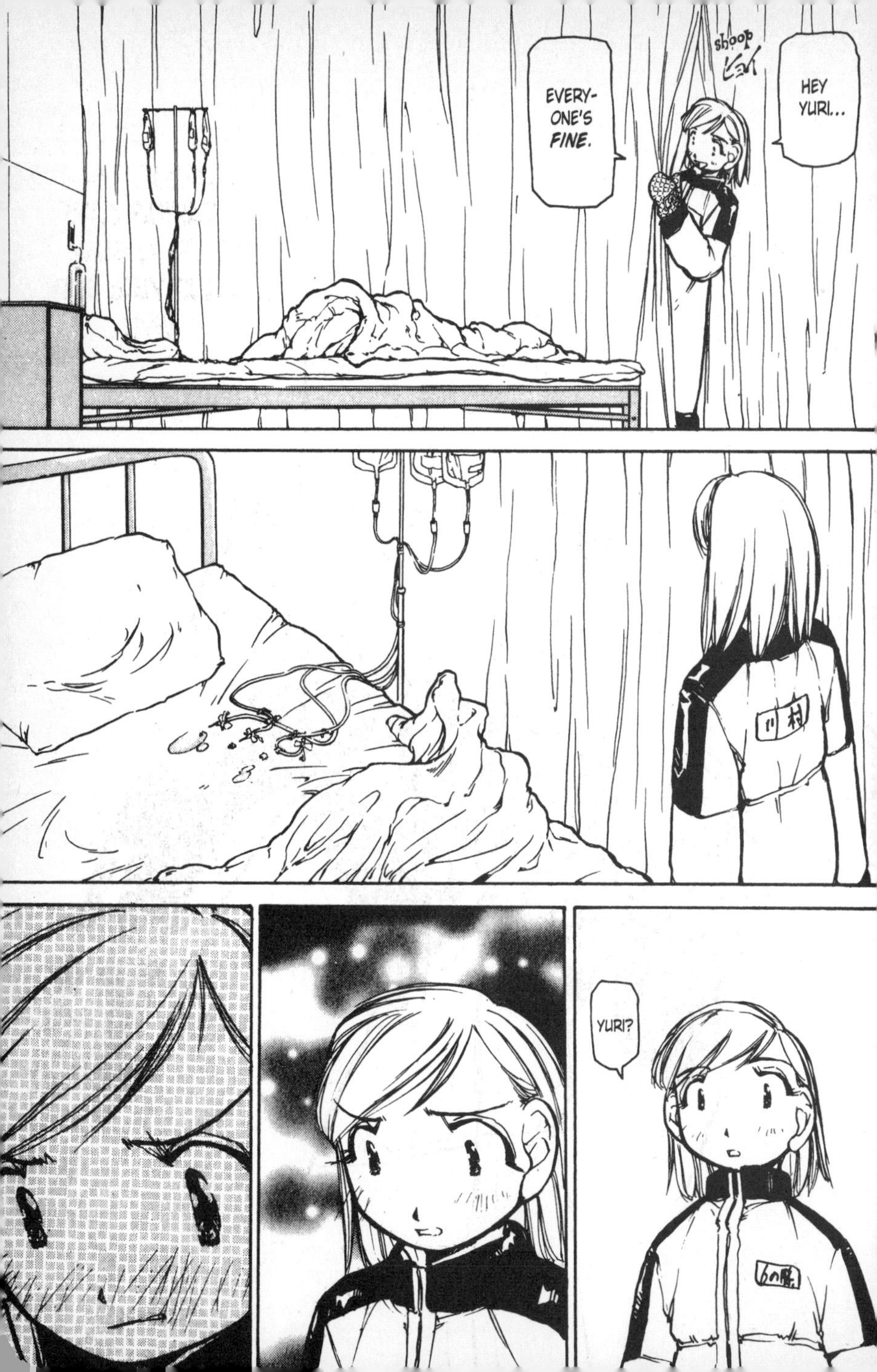
HEY YURI...
shoop
EVERY-ONE'S FINE.
YURI?

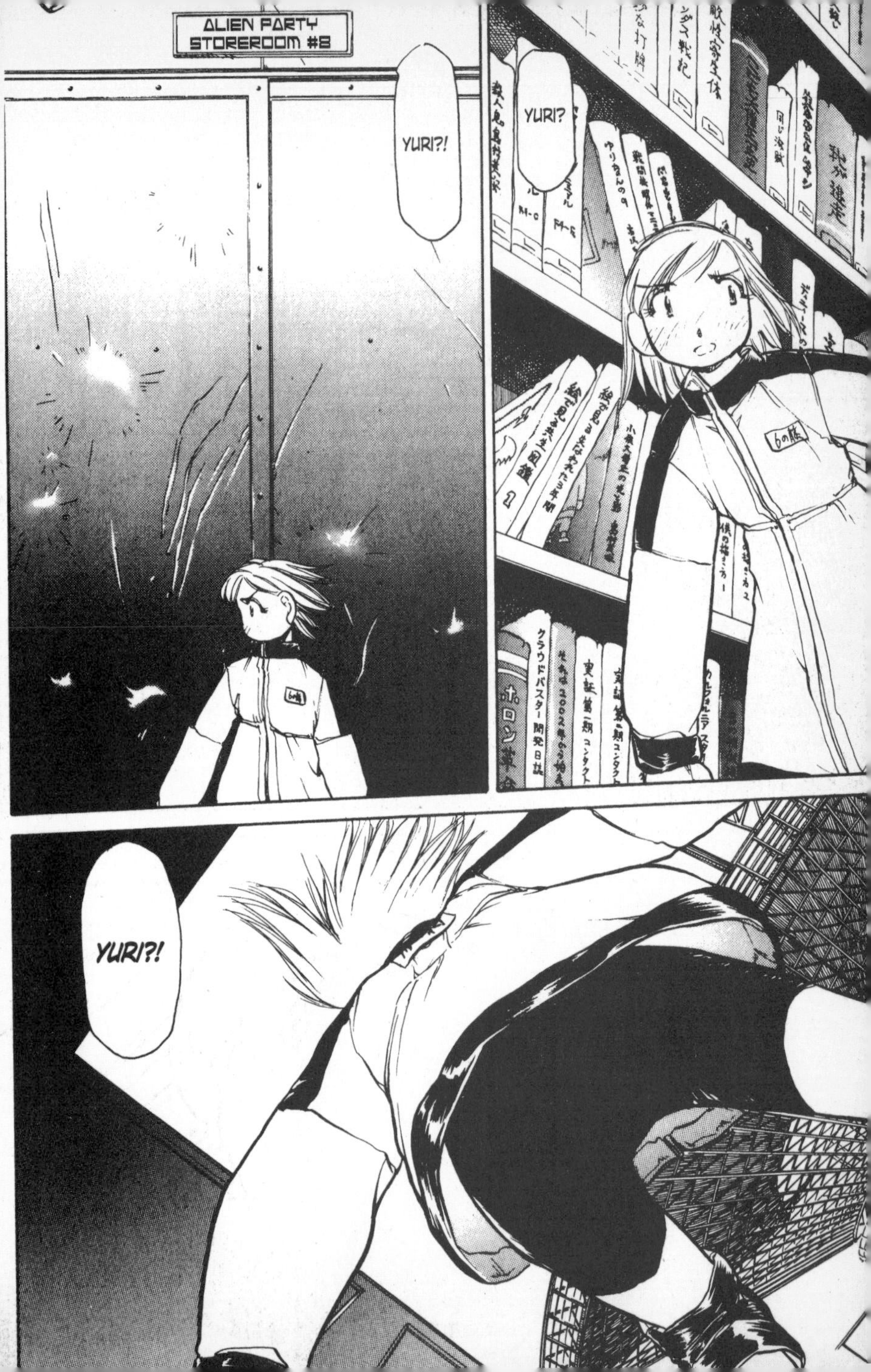
YURI?
ALIEN PARTY STOREROOM #8
YURI?!
YURI?!

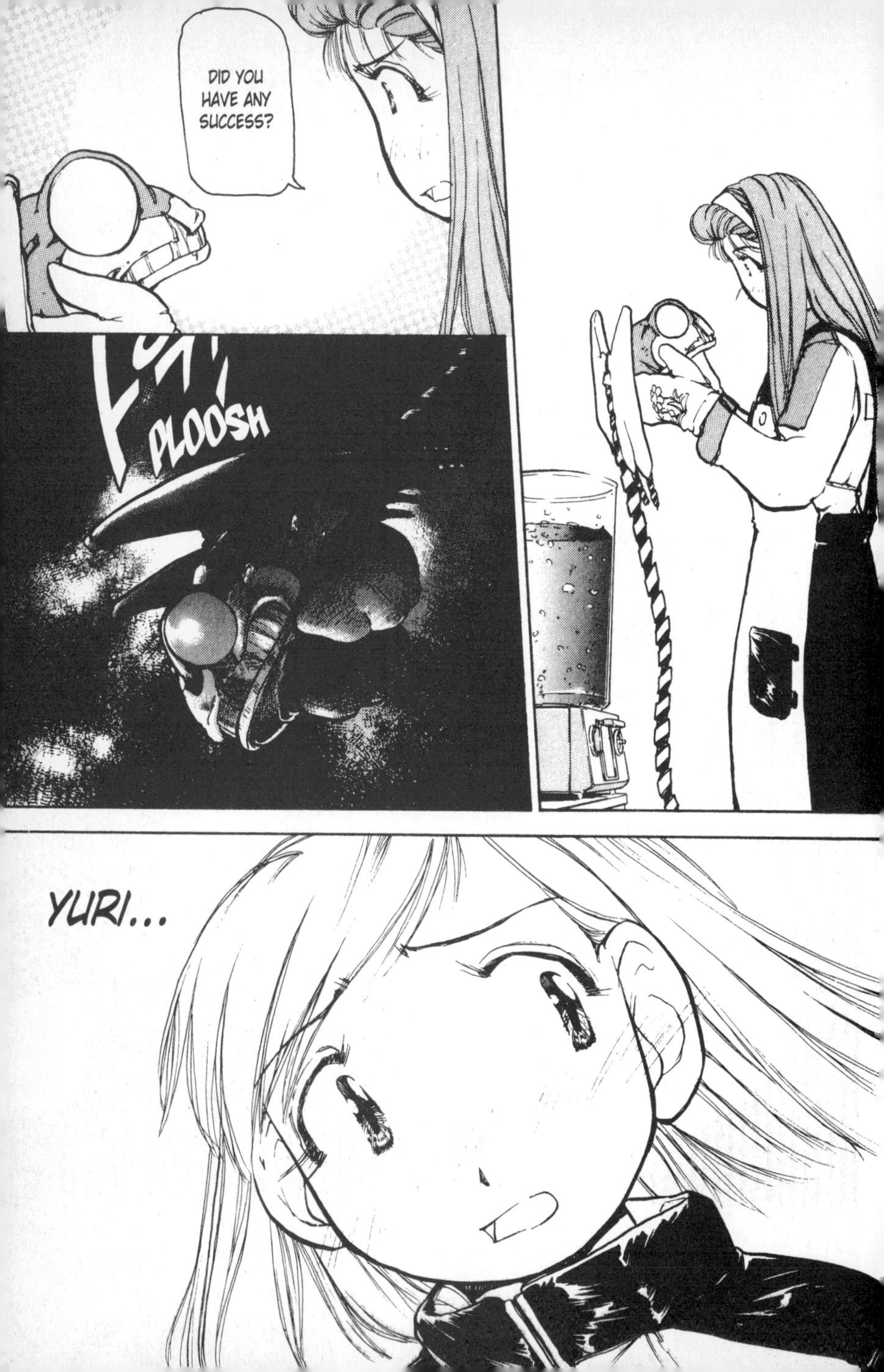
DID YOU HAVE ANY SUCCESS?
PLOOSH
YURI...

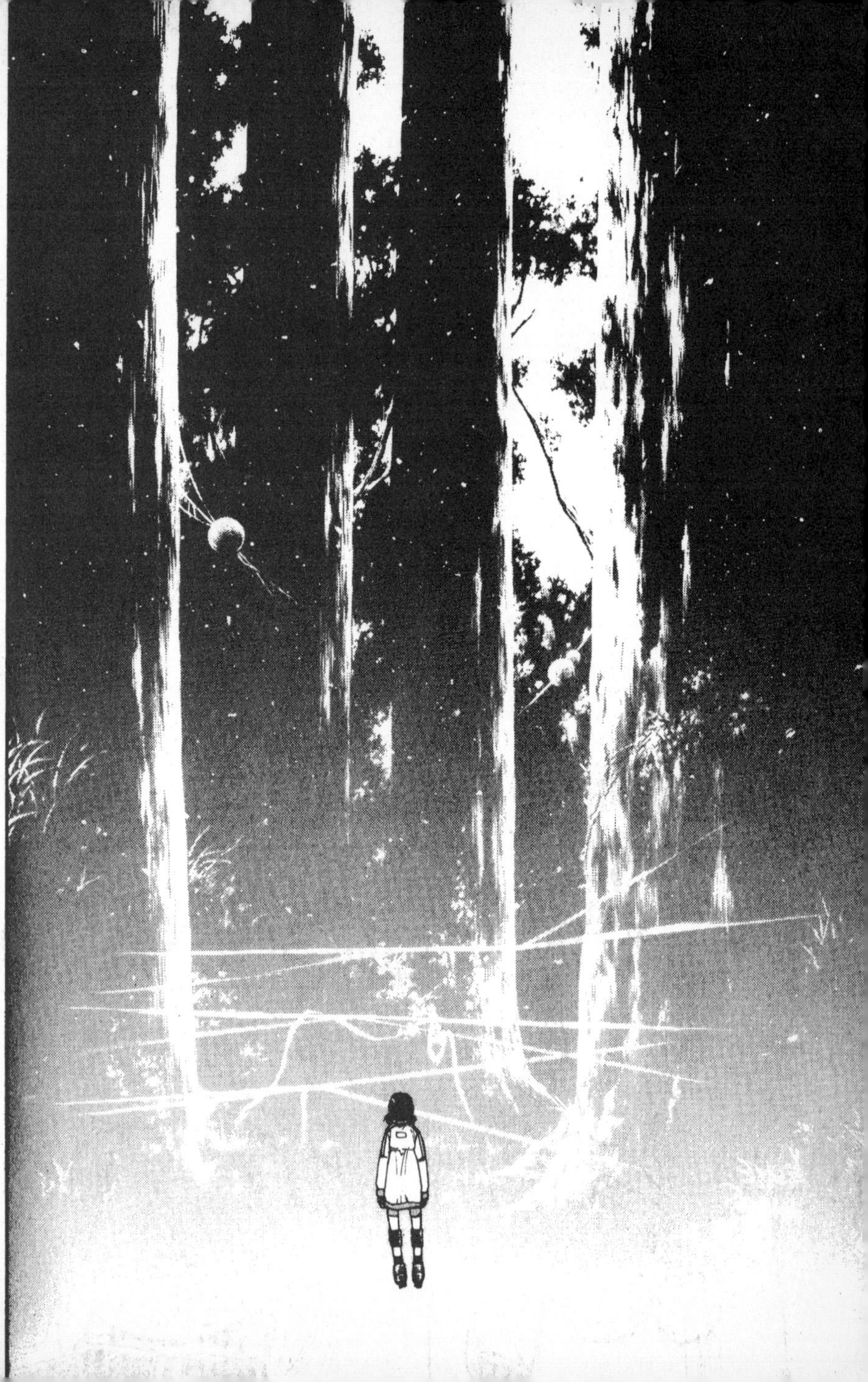

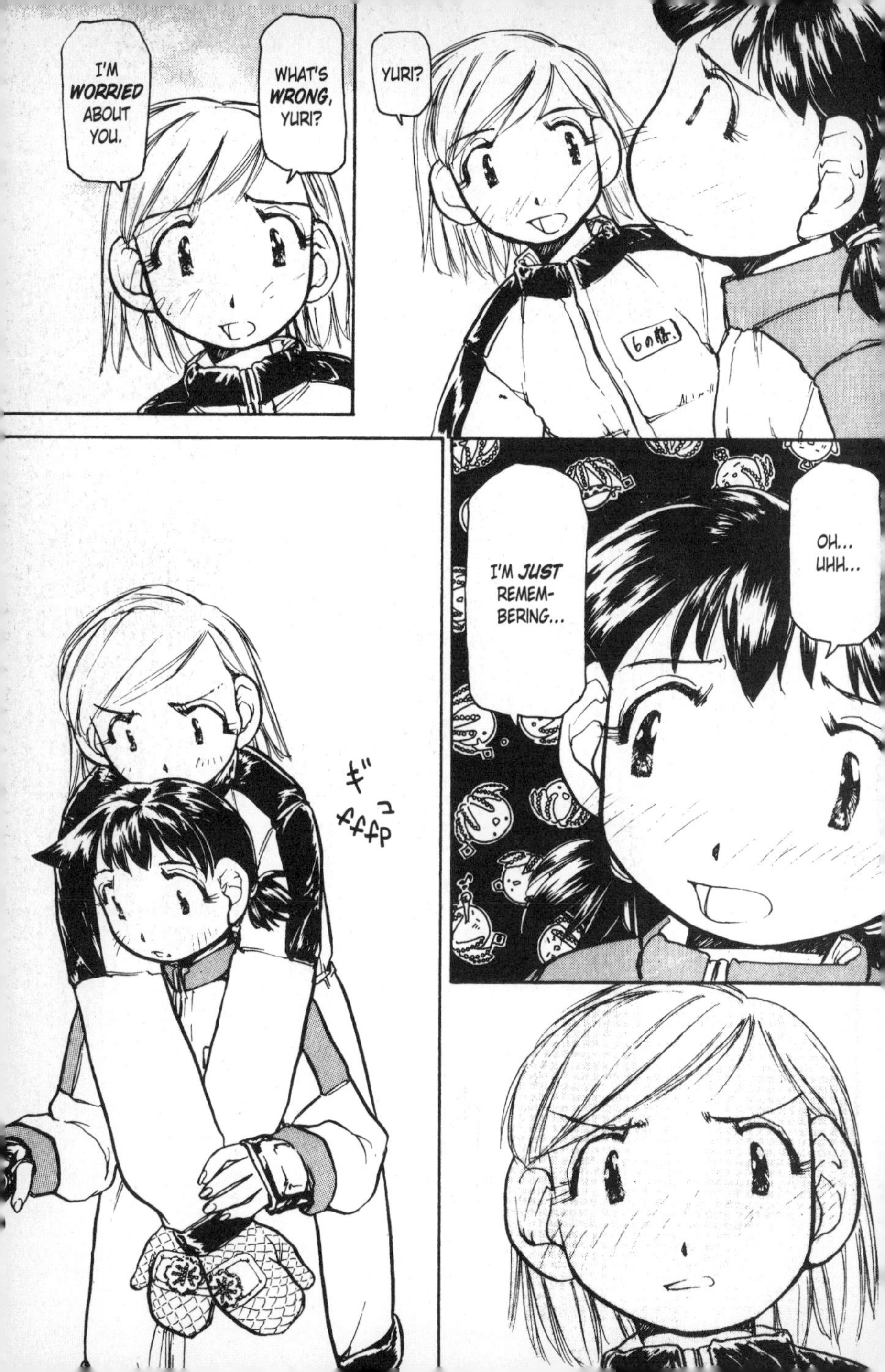
YURI?
WHAT'S WRONG, YURI?
I'M WORRIED ABOUT YOU.
OH... UHH...
I'M JUST REMEMBERING...
ギュ
fffp

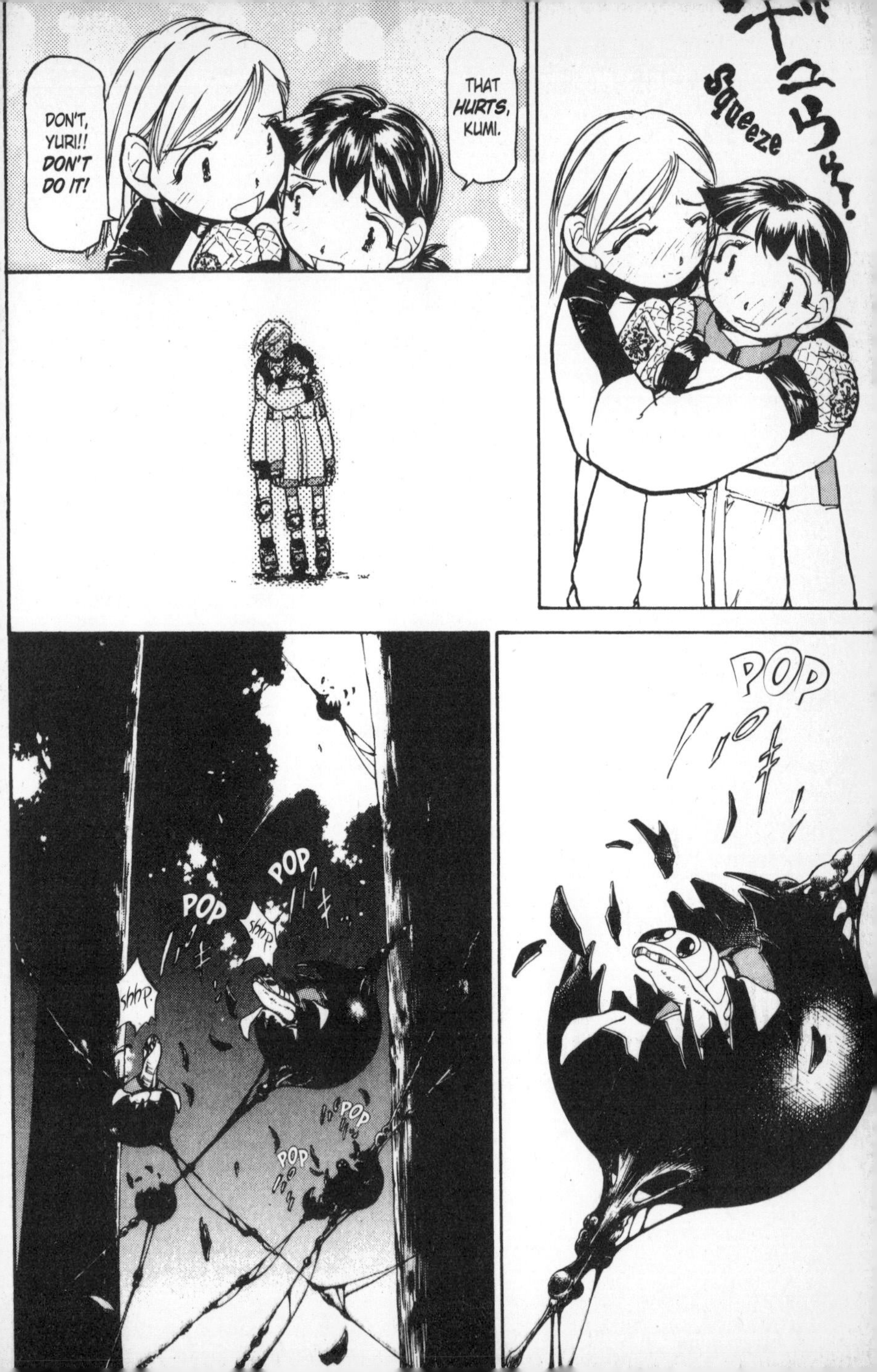
squeeze
THAT HURTS, KUMI.
DON'T, YURI!! DON'T DO IT!
POP
POP
shhp.
POP
shhp.
POP
POP

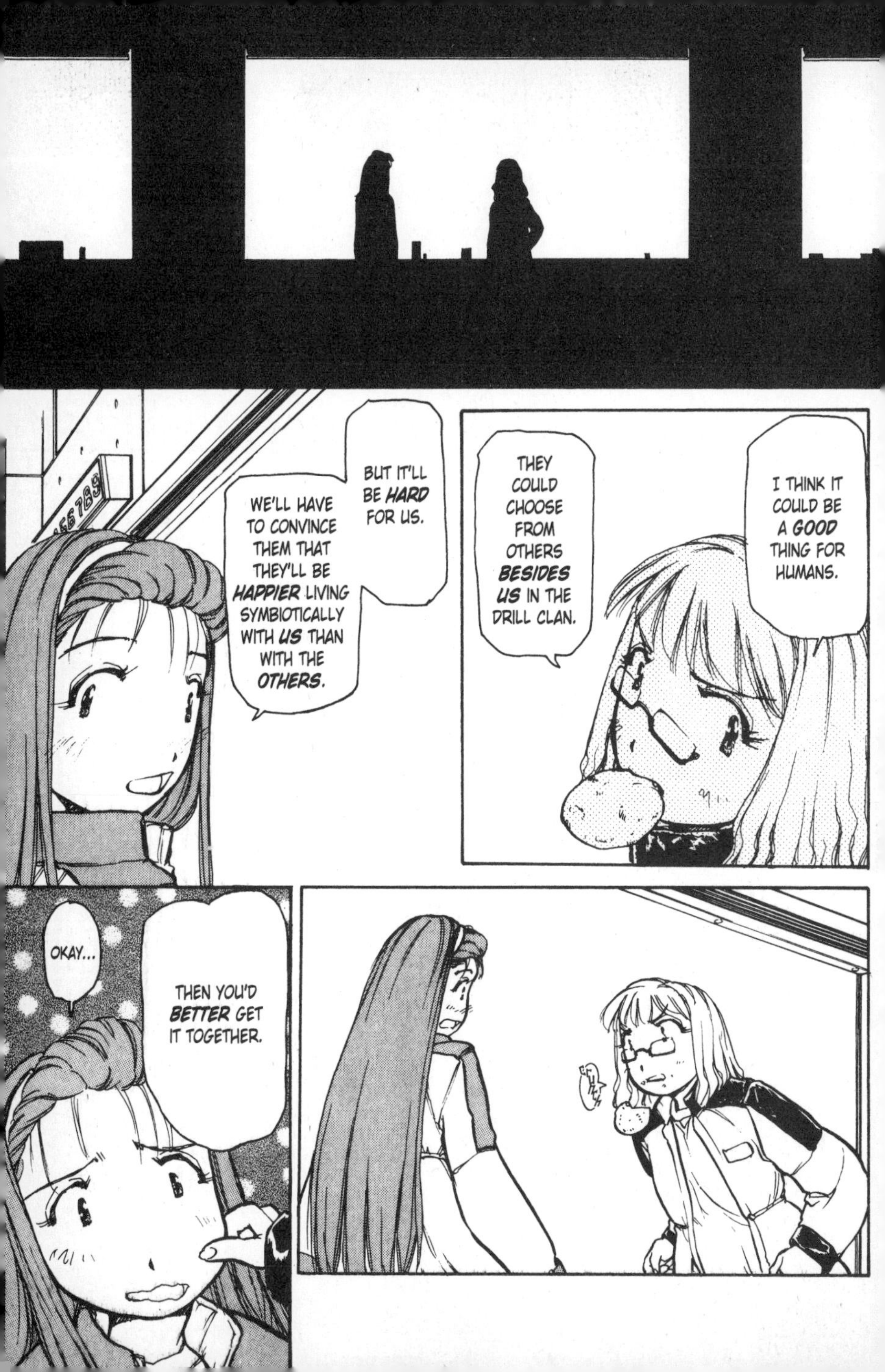
I THINK IT COULD BE A GOOD THING FOR HUMANS.
THEY COULD CHOOSE FROM OTHERS BESIDES US IN THE DRILL CLAN.
BUT IT'LL BE HARD FOR US.
WE'LL HAVE TO CONVINCE THEM THAT THEY'LL BE HAPPIER LIVING SYMBIOTICALLY WITH US THAN WITH THE OTHERS.
THEN YOU'D BETTER GET IT TOGETHER.
OKAY...

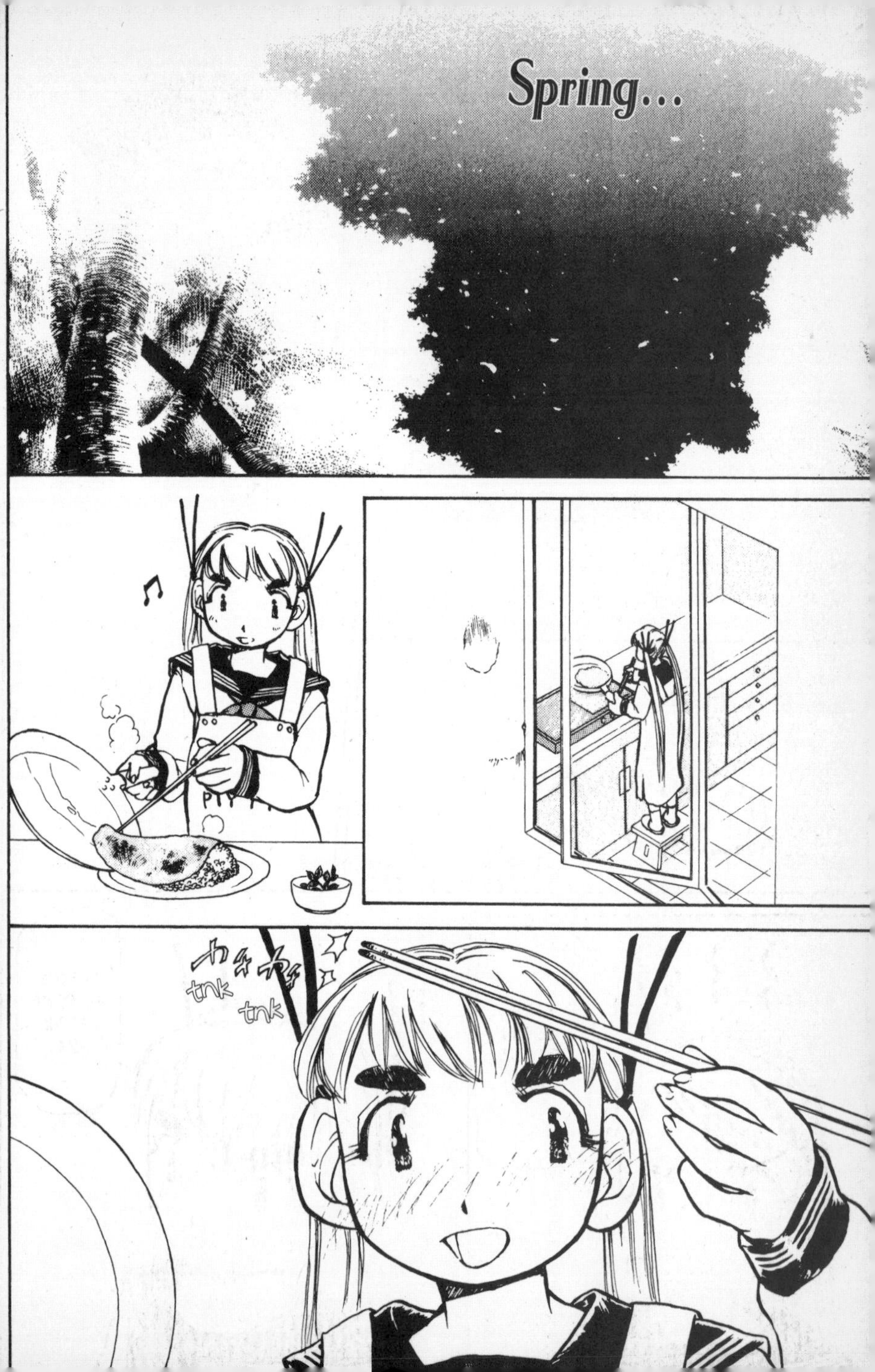
Spring...
tnk
tnk

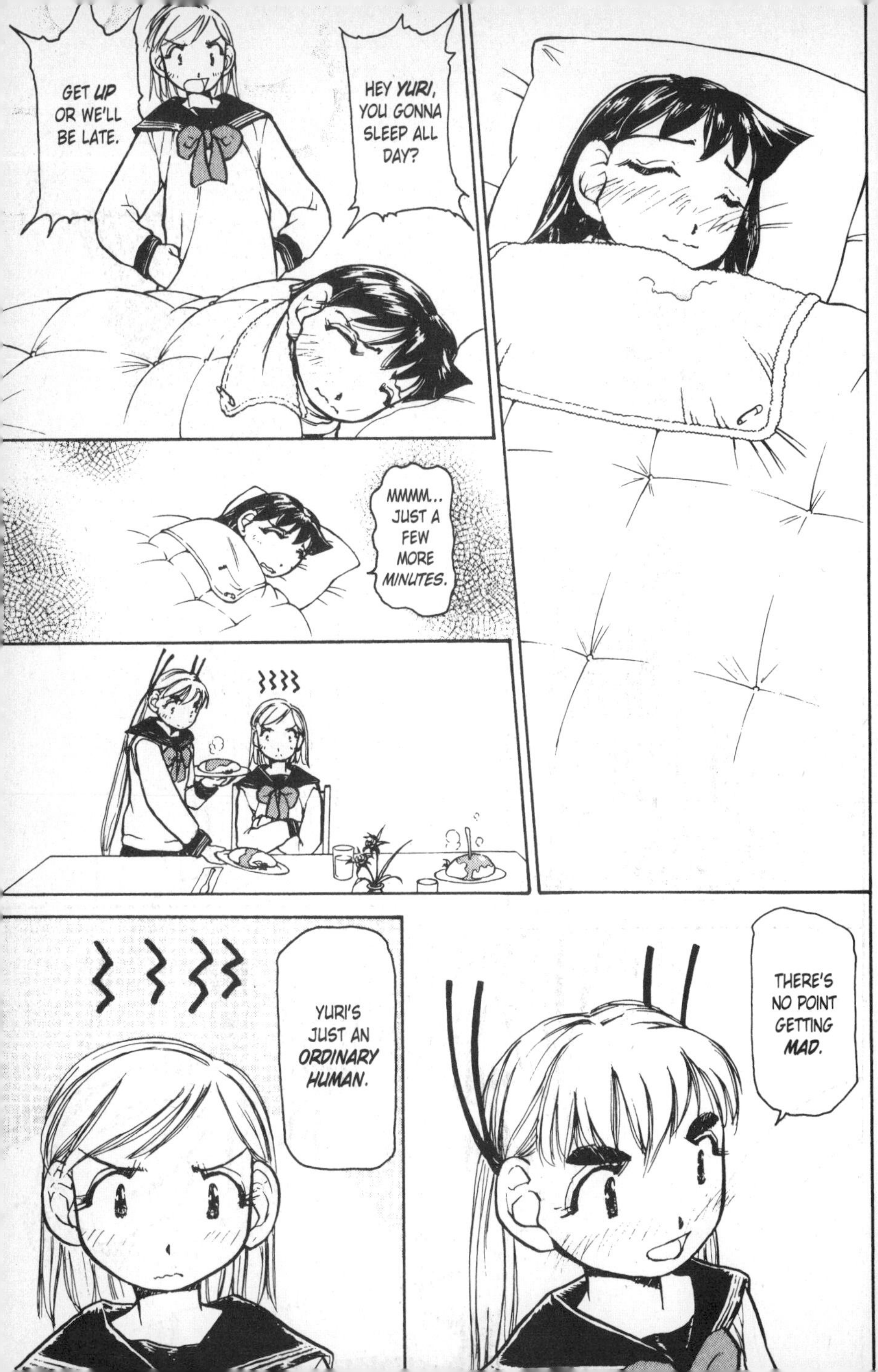
HEY YURI, YOU GONNA SLEEP ALL DAY?
GET UP OR WE'LL BE LATE.
MMMM... JUST A FEW MORE MINUTES.
THERE'S NO POINT GETTING MAD.
YURI'S JUST AN ORDINARY HUMAN.

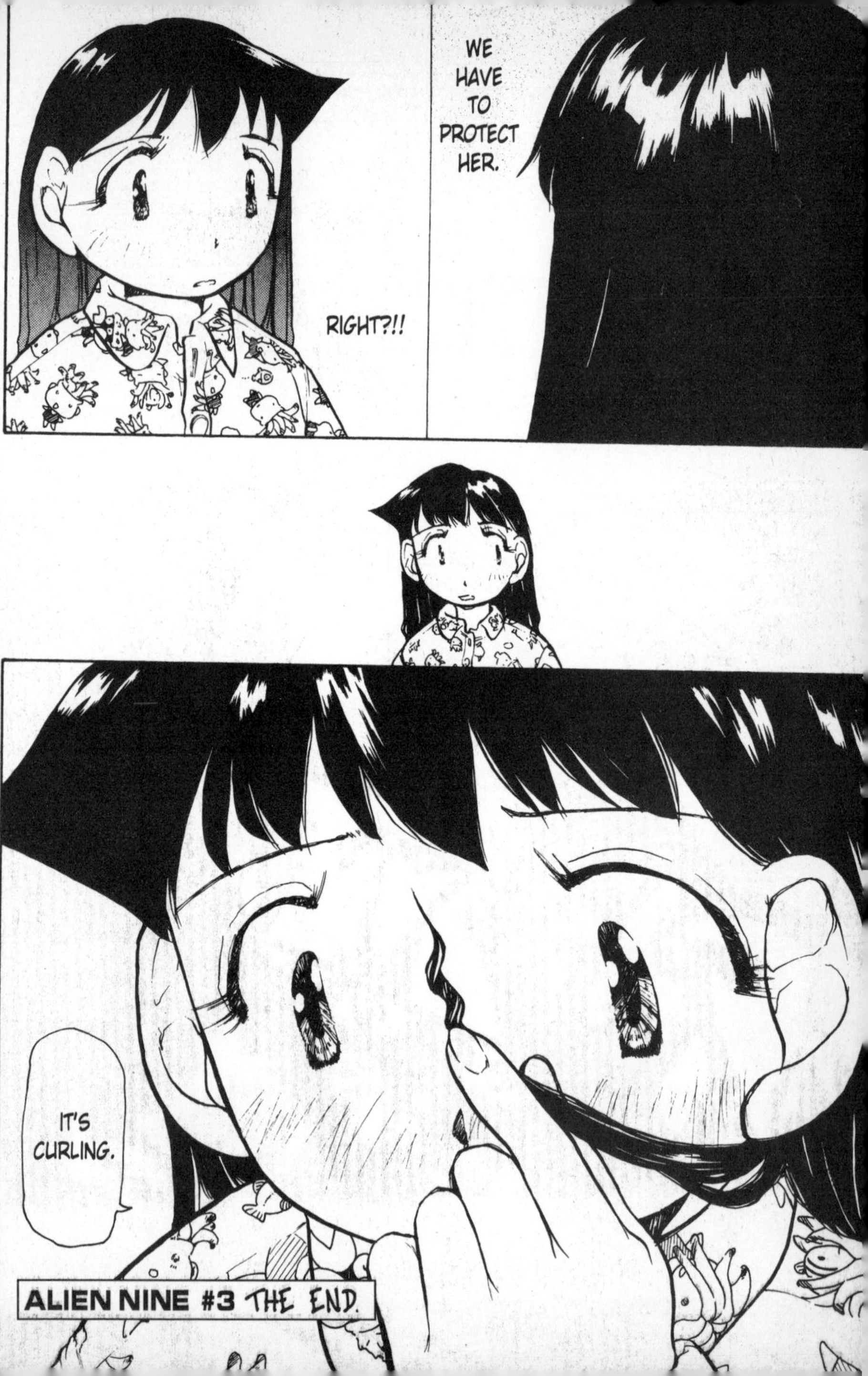
WE HAVE TO PROTECT HER.
RIGHT?!!
IT'S CURLING.
ALIEN NINE #3 THE END.

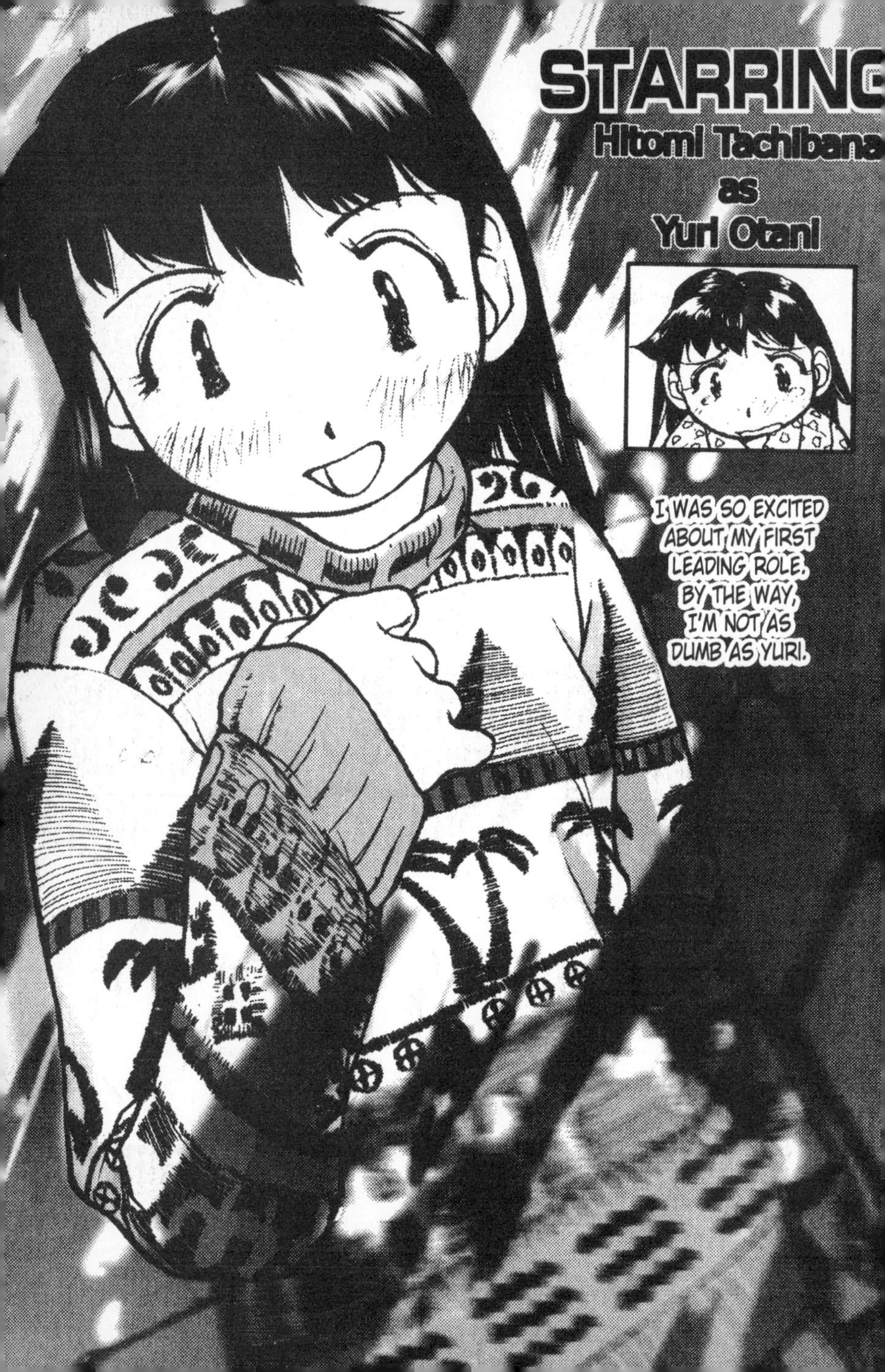
STARRING
Hitomi Tachibana
as
Yuri Otani
I WAS SO EXCITED ABOUT MY FIRST LEADING ROLE. BY THE WAY, I'M NOT AS DUMB AS YURI.

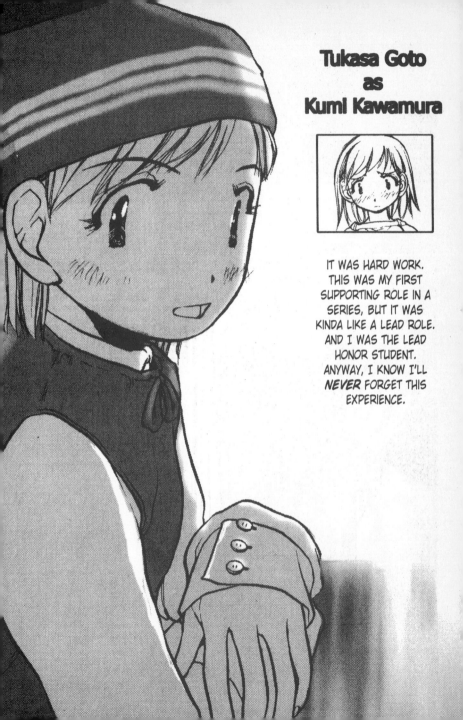

Tukasa Goto as Kumi Kawamura

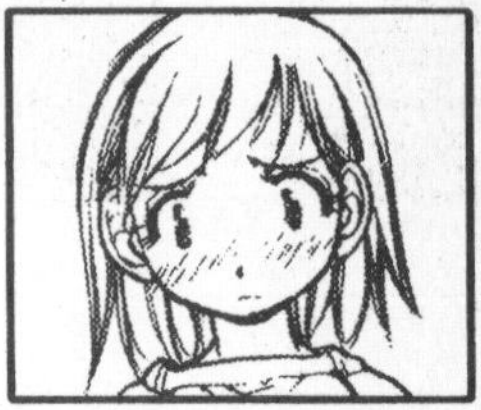

IT WAS HARD WORK. THIS WAS MY FIRST SUPPORTING ROLE IN A SERIES, BUT IT WAS KINDA LIKE A LEAD ROLE. AND I WAS THE LEAD HONOR STUDENT. ANYWAY, I KNOW I'LL ***NEVER*** FORGET THIS EXPERIENCE.

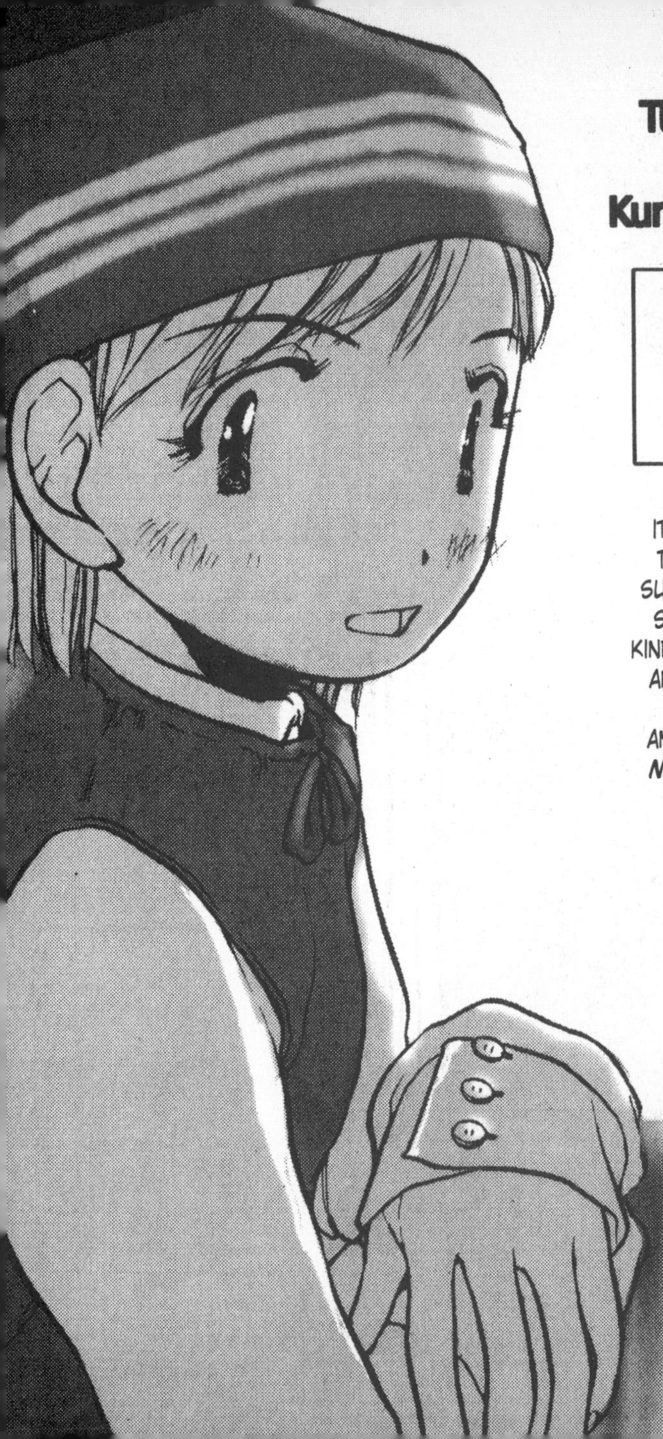

Satiko Oda
as
Kasumi Tomine

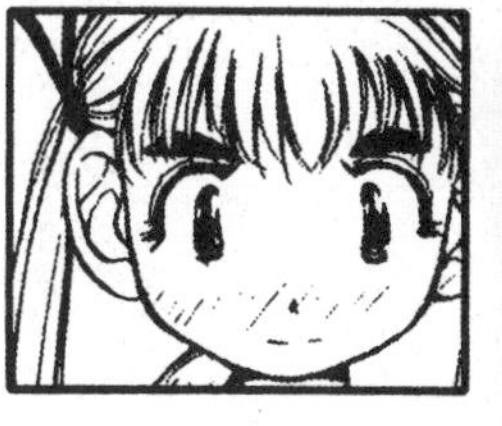

ACTUALLY, I'M A LOT LIKE THE YURI CHARACTER. AT FIRST IT WAS A DRAG 'CAUSE I HAD TO SHAVE MY EYEBROWS, BUT I ENDED UP ENJOYING IT ALL.

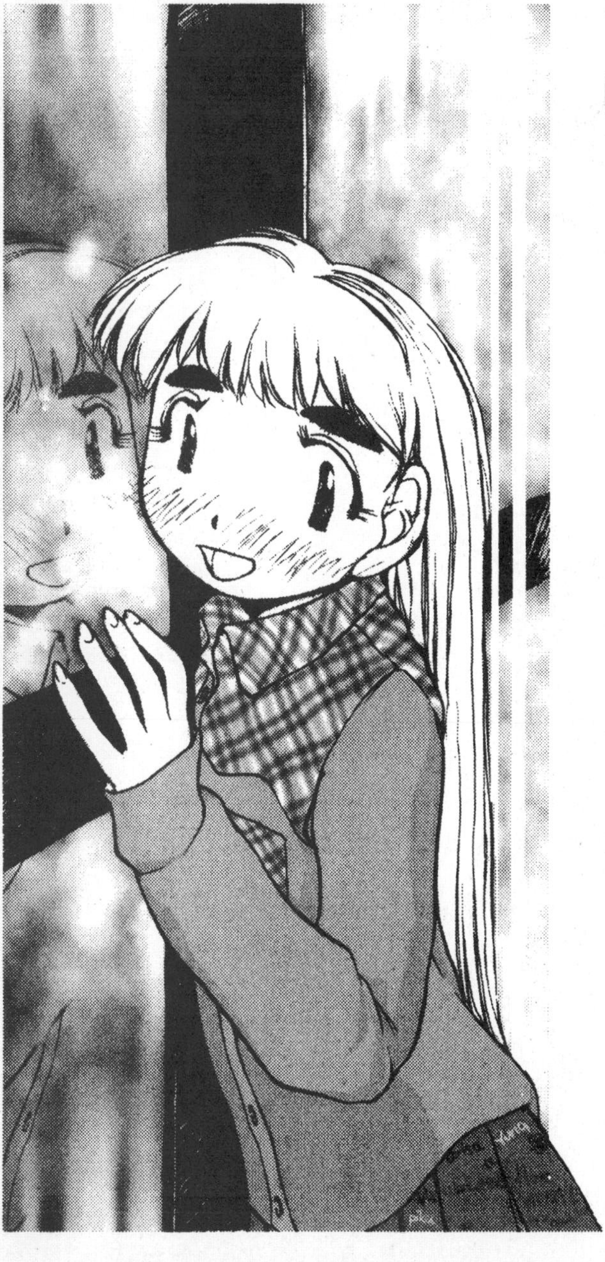

Sizuka Sakamoto
as
Miyu Tamaki

Mika Abe
as
Megumi Hisakawa

and
Harumi Tanaka
as
Chisa Okada
(headmistress)

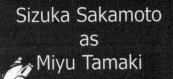

ALIEN9

mission objectives complete

ALIEN NINE SKETCHBOOK

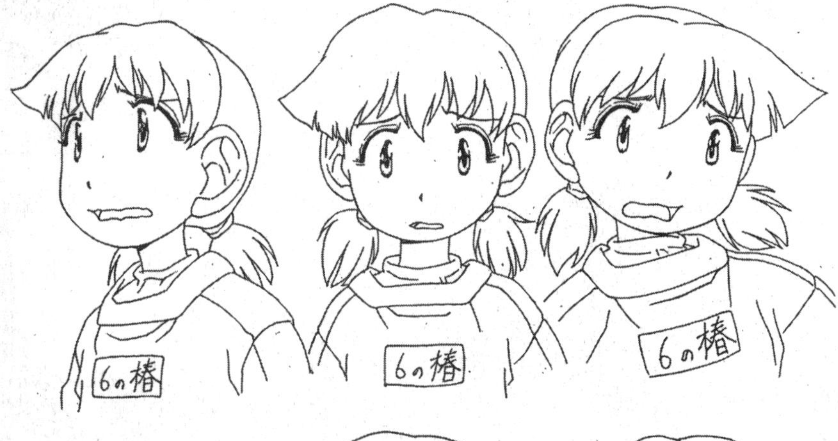
6の椿
6の椿
6の椿
6の椿
6の椿
6の椿

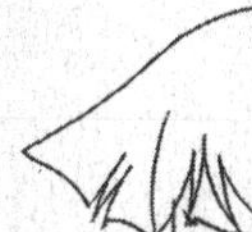
大谷ゆり

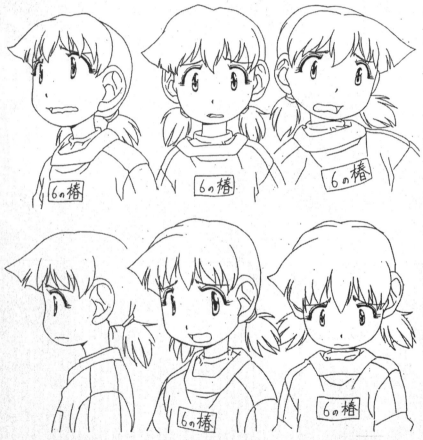

The sketches on the following pages are concepts and references used to create the *ALIEN NINE* video available on DVD through Central Park Media.

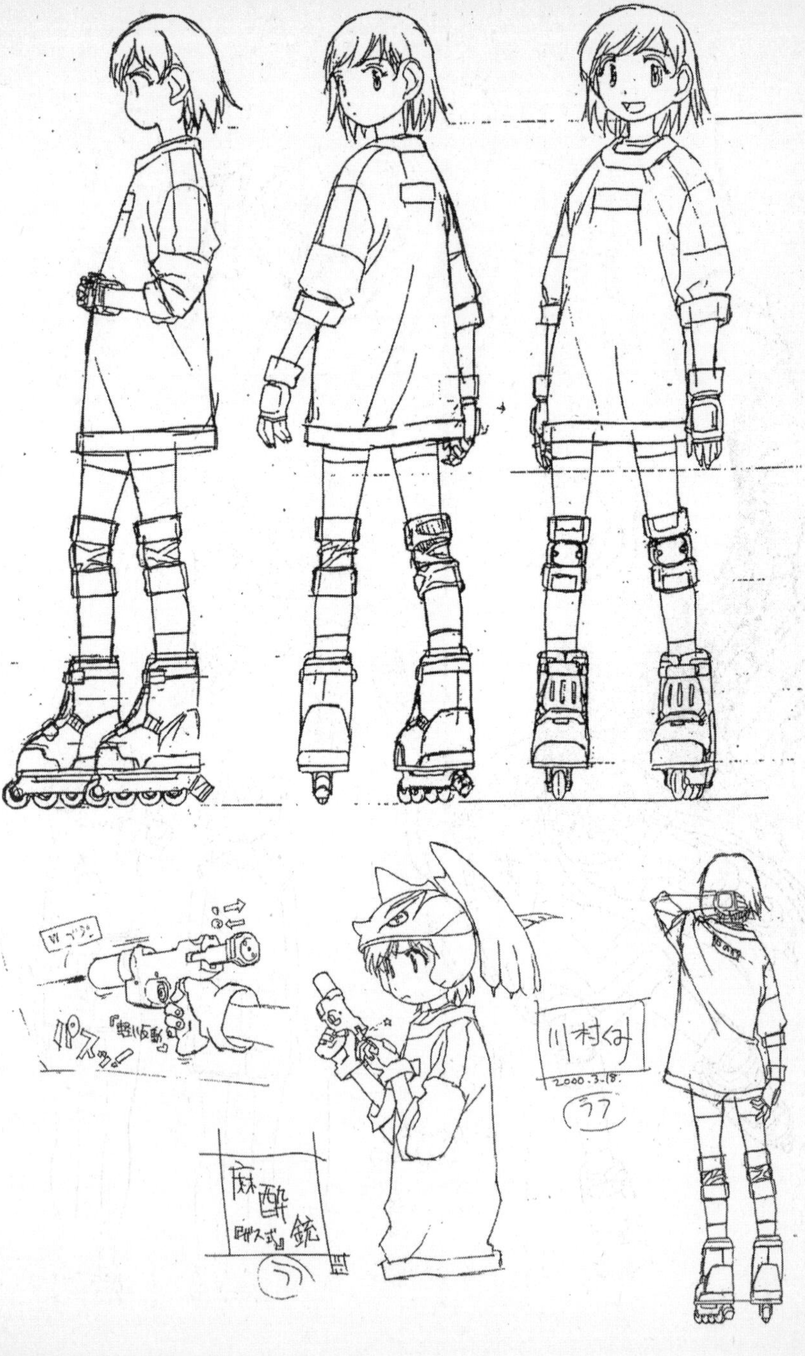
川村くみ
2000.3.18.
ラフ
麻酔銃
『ガス式』
パスッ!
『軽い反動』

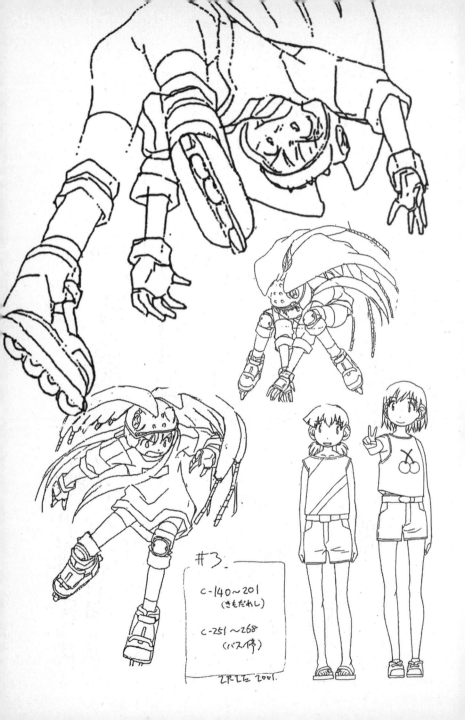

#3.

C-140～201
(きもだめし)

C-251～268
(バス停)

えんどう 2001.

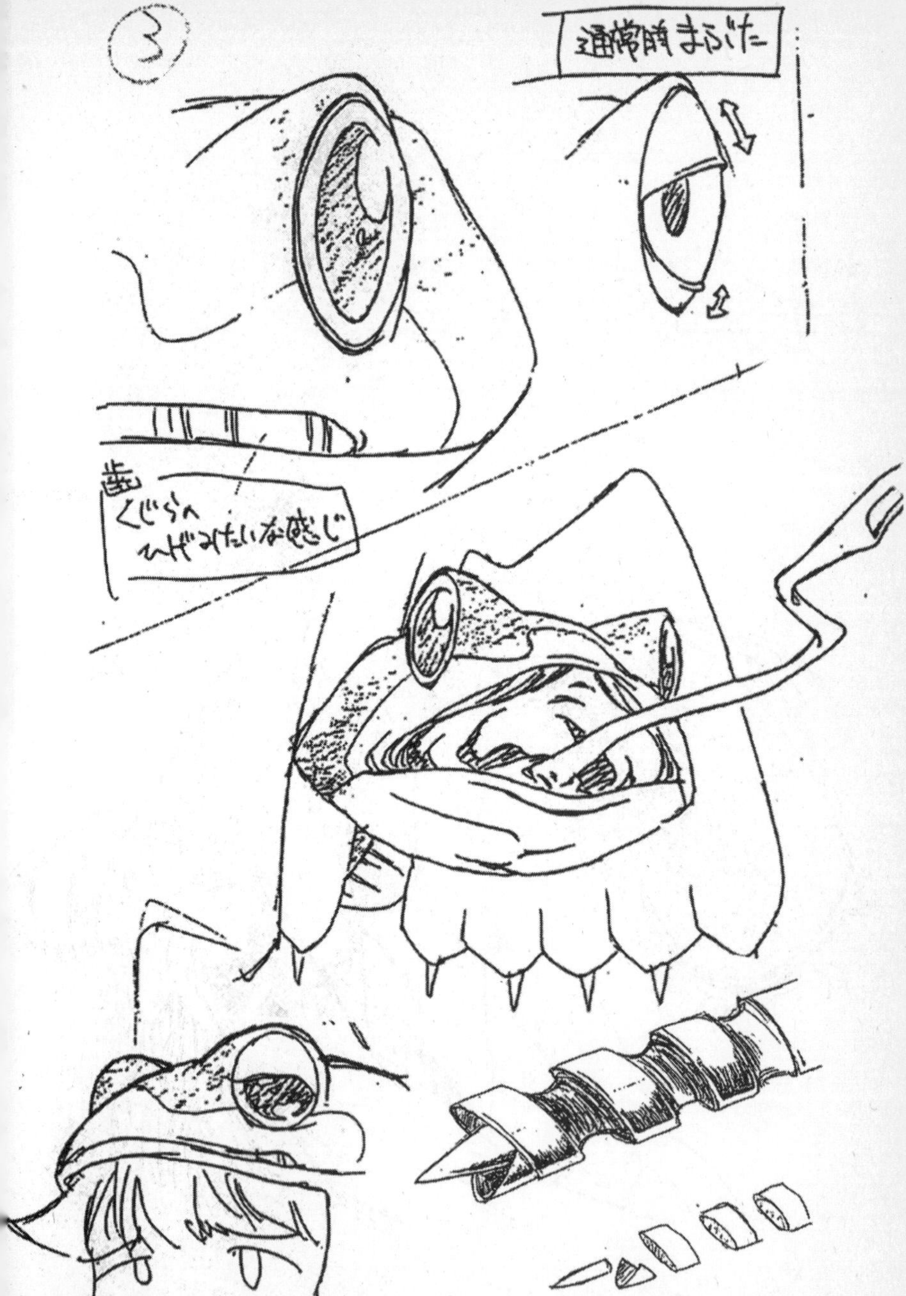
3
通常時まぶた
歯
くじらへ
ひげみたいな感じ

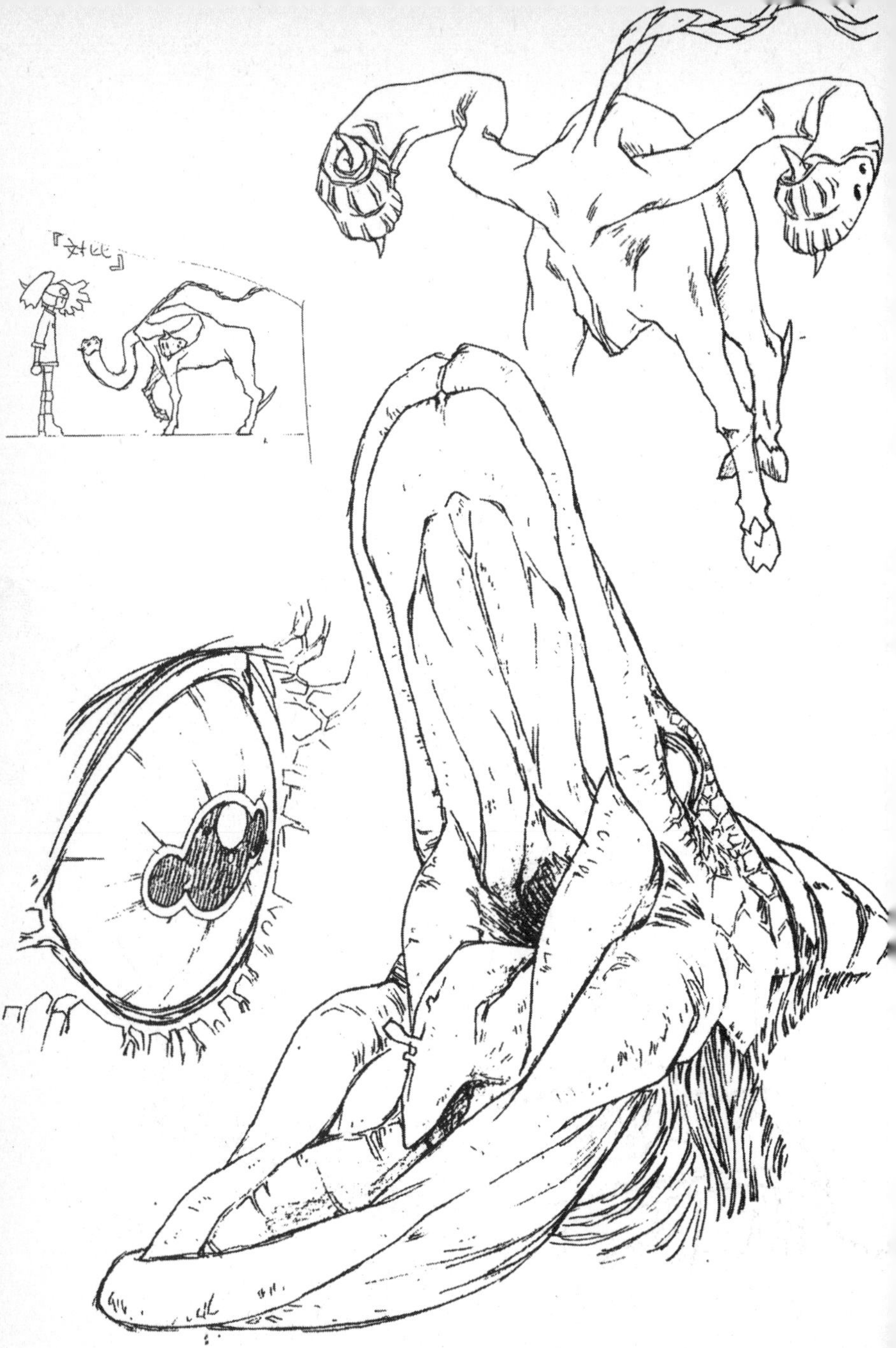
『対比』

This sign reads "Tomare" and it means:

STOP!

THIS IS THE LAST PAGE
OF THE BOOK! DON'T
RUIN THE ENDING
FOR YOURSELF.
This book is printed in the
original Japanese format,
which means that it reads
from right to left
(example on right).

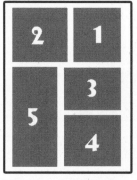

You'll find that all CPM Manga books that are part of our Original
Manga line are published in this format. The original artwork
and sound effects are presented just like they were in Japan
with minimal sound-effect translation so that you can see and
enjoy the comic like the creators intended.

The format we have decided to use to present the books was
chosen by YOU, the fans. We conducted a survey online and
found that the overwhelming majority of fans prefer their
manga sound effects translated in just the format we are using.

The symbol in our Original Manga logo
is "shin". It means "real" or "true".